FORBIDDEN CITY

IMPERIAL TREASURES FROM THE PALACE MUSEUM, BEIJING

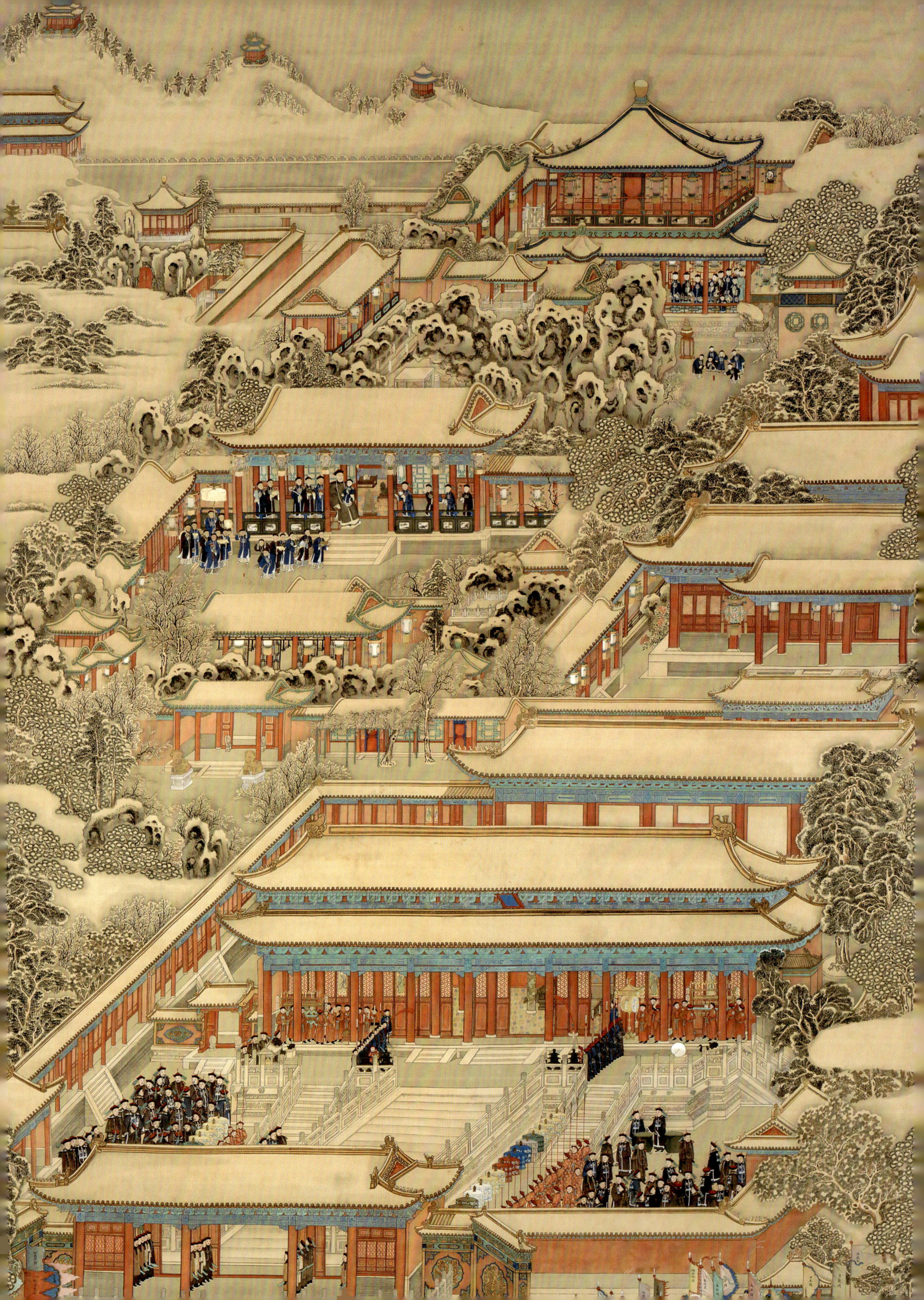

FORBIDDEN CITY

IMPERIAL TREASURES FROM THE PALACE MUSEUM, BEIJING

LI JIAN
WITH HE LI, HOU-MEI SUNG, AND MA SHENGNAN

VMFA
VIRGINIA MUSEUM OF FINE ARTS

Presented by

Altria

E. RHODES AND LEONA B. CARPENTER FOUNDATION

ART WORKS. National Endowment for the Arts arts.gov

This catalogue accompanies the exhibition *Forbidden City: Imperial Treasures from the Palace Museum, Beijing,* organized by the Palace Museum and the Virginia Museum of Fine Arts, presented from October 18, 2014 to January 11, 2015, in Richmond, Virginia.

Cataloging information is available from the Library of Congress.

ISBN 978-1-934351-06-2 (softbound); 978-1-934351-07-9 (hardbound)
Printed in the United States of America

Produced by the Office of Publications, Virginia Museum of Fine Arts, 200 N. Boulevard, Richmond, Virginia 23220, USA

Distributed by
University of Washington Press
Seattle
www.washington.edu/uwpress

Copy Editor: Lucy Keshishian Grey
Graphic Designer: John Hoar
Photographers: Li Fan, Feng Hui, and Liu Zhigang
Indexer: Frances Bowles
Composed and typeset in Minion Pro by the designer
Separations by David Ridderhof, Richmond, Virginia
Printed on 100# Camelot Silk Text by Worth Higgins & Associates, Inc., Richmond, Virginia

Front cover and p. xvi: *Emperor Qianlong in Ceremonial Robe*, detail (cat. no. 3)
Back: *Wine Set of Cup and Saucer* (cat. no. 67)
Frontispiece: *Arrival of Envoys from Thousands of Regions*, detail (cat. no. 24)
Dividers: p.x, *Portrait of Emperor Tianqi*, detail (cat. no.2)
p. 64, *Emperor Qianlong Writing in His Studio*, detail (cat. no. 48)
p. 136, *Emperor Qianlong Celebrating the New Year*, detail (cat. no. 106)

Contents

致辞 FOREWORD

文化是人们相互沟通与交流的纽带和桥梁。不同国家、不同民族的文化背景、价值取向或许不尽相同，但对美好事物的追求和欣赏是共通的。当一件件或大气磅礴或巧夺天工的艺术品呈现在您眼前时，相信每个人都会为之折服与赞叹。在美国弗吉尼亚美术馆举办的《紫禁城—故宫博物院皇家珍品展》将会让您享受一次中国传统文化艺术的饕餮大餐。

故宫是明清两代的皇宫，占地72万平方米，高大巍峨的宫殿鳞次栉比、错落有致，留下了明清24位皇帝的足迹。在这些金碧辉煌的殿宇之中演绎了一幕幕惊天动地的历史事件，令人唏嘘不已。

故宫庋藏的数以百万计的珍贵文物，是中国传统文化艺术宝库中的瑰宝，是中华民族智慧的结晶。这些历久弥新的珍贵文物折射出了明清两代政治、经济、文化的轨迹，集中反映了明清帝后的物质和精神文化生活，他们的喜怒哀乐、情趣雅好彰显其间。随着中外文化交流的日益深入，这些精美的艺术珍品正在扮演着越来越重要的文化使者的角色。

《紫禁城—故宫博物院皇家珍品展》近200件展品,是从故宫博物院180余万件文物中精心选取的，包括绘画、金银器、玉器、漆器、陶瓷、织绣等多个门类。展品丰富多彩、美轮美奂，且不少为孤品或首次展出。

作为一个综合性展览，《紫禁城—故宫博物院皇家珍品展》多角度、多方位地反映了明清皇家的政务典礼、宗教信仰、文化生活等内容。这些题材广泛的展品带着我们穿越时空的隧道，走近明清帝后们的生活，近距离地体验博大精深的中国传统文化，更深入地了解中国传统文化的内涵和精髓。

中美两国同为世界大国，地处亚、美两洲，远隔千山万水，但在世界进入全球化的今天，距离已不能成为阻隔两国文化交流的障碍，希望《紫禁城—故宫博物院皇家珍品展》在中美两国之间架起一座友谊的桥梁，使得两国人民相互了解、相互交流、相互学习。这也正是本次展览的初衷，诚能如此，我们将感到莫大的欣慰。

故宫博物院院長

Foreword

Cultural exchange can serve as a bridge that connects people from different backgrounds through a common appreciation of art. *Forbidden City: Imperial Treasures from the Palace Museum, Beijing* at the Virginia Museum of Fine Arts offers a great opportunity for the people of Virginia to enjoy Chinese culture as represented by magnificent visual arts of the Ming and Qing dynasties.

Twenty-four Ming and Qing emperors left their footprints on the Forbidden City's 180 acres, where many historical events and important activities took place. The Forbidden City is now the site of the Palace Museum, home to an encyclopedic collection of more than 1.8 million objects that represent a large part of traditional Chinese artistic culture. These works of art and artifacts reveal the political, economic, and cultural aspects of the Ming and Qing dynasties, and they reflect the social and spiritual lives of emperors, empresses, and their families. Today, these masterpieces play an increasingly important role as envoys in cross-cultural exchanges between China and other countries.

Forbidden City: Imperial Treasures from the Palace Museum, Beijing features nearly two hundred works, including paintings, gold and silver objects, jade pieces, lacquerware, ceramics, and textiles. Many of the featured works are the only surviving ones of their kind, while others are presented to the general public for the first time ever. By exploring the rich and profound aspects of traditional Chinese culture, *Forbidden City: Imperial Treasures from the Palace Museum, Beijing* traverses time and space, enhancing cultural understanding through a comprehensive selection of works and diverse subject matter.

As two of the largest countries in the world, China and the United States, located on different continents with an ocean between them, are brought together by globalization. I hope that *Forbidden City: Imperial Treasures from the Palace Museum, Beijing* will build a cultural bridge between China and the United States that enhances mutual understanding, exchange, and learning. In fact, this is our motivation and wish, and it is with great pleasure that we share these Palace Museum treasures with you.

Shan Jixiang
Director of Palace Museum

Preface

China, an ancient and storied country, has always held a prominent place on the world stage. Its artistic traditions, which combine majesty, beauty, and drama, are embodied in the special exhibition *Forbidden City: Imperial Treasures from the Palace Museum, Beijing* and this accompanying catalogue. Both exhibition and catalogue are the result of a multiyear, multifaceted collaboration between the Palace Museum and the Virginia Museum of Fine Arts. The partnership was formally inaugurated in 2011 when the Honorable Robert F. McDonnell, then governor of Virginia, met in Beijing with Zheng Xinmiao, director of the Palace Museum, to sign a Memorandum of Understanding that encompassed an exchange of exhibitions and museum staff.

Envisaged as part of a greater cultural and commercial relationship between the Commonwealth of Virginia and the People's Republic of China—and warmly endorsed as such by our new Virginia governor, the Honorable Terry McAuliffe, and the new director of the Palace Museum, Shan Jixiang—this historic agreement was made possible by the vision and efforts of Li Ji, former executive deputy director of the Palace Museum who supported this endeavor from its inception during a 2010 planning visit. The benefits of the exchange have been significant, especially for the staff of the two museums—curators, conservators, exhibition designers, and educators—who have had the opportunity to share information with their counterparts. Following the 2014 landmark exhibition in Virginia, the collaboration culminates in Beijing in 2016, when the Palace Museum presents an exhibition of the Virginia Museum's world-renowned collection of Fabergé objects, marking the first time an American museum's collection is exhibited in the Palace Museum.

Curated by Li Jian, the Virginia Museum's talented E. Rhodes and Leona B. Carpenter Curator of East Asian Art, *Forbidden City* has enjoyed exceptional support at every level. We would particularly like to thank Ambassador Cui Tiankai of the People's Republic of China and the embassy staff in Washington, D.C., especially Lu Kang, the minister and deputy chief of mission, and Li Hong, the minister counselor from the embassy's Office of Cultural Affairs. Friends of the Virginia Museum of Fine Arts have been incredibly generous, recognizing the critical importance of developing major cultural ties between the United States and China. Thanks go to the presenting sponsors that made *Forbidden City* possible: Altria Group is an ongoing contributor to VMFA and its special exhibitions program, and the E. Rhodes and Leona B. Carpenter Foundation funded both traditional and innovative aspects of the exhibition, including the incorporation of new technology in the exhibition itself and associated educational programming. Without the support of these and other corporate and individual donors this majestic group of Chinese treasures could never have come to Virginia.

At the Virginia Museum of Fine Arts, the greatest credit for this exhibition goes to its curator, Li Jian, who has worked tirelessly on this exhibition for many years and is, of course, the primary author of this catalogue. She has been ably supported by our professional staff, including Robin Nicholson, former deputy director for art and education, who provided general oversight of the project; Sylvia Yount, chief curator, who provided curatorial guidance; and Courtney Burkhardt, exhibitions coordinator, who managed the myriad complexities of the exhibition. The innovative educational components were developed by Lulan Yu, adult programs coordinator, with the help of Celeste Fetta, chief educator, and J. Barry Matthews, adult programs assistant. Stephen Bonadies, deputy director for facilities and collections management, supervised the team that was responsible for the presentation and logistical aspects of the exhibition, including Doug Fisher, director of exhibition design and production; conservators Kathy Gillis, Carol Sawyer, Bruce Suffield, and Sheila Payaqui; and registrars Karen Daly and Susan Turbeville. Financial management was handled by Mark Johnson, interim chief financial officer, and Fern Spencer, former chief financial officer, and the project has come to fruition under the direction of Lee Anne Hurt Chesterfield, interim deputy director for art and education. For successful fundraising and exhibition marketing, we are grateful to Claudia Keenan, executive director of the VMFA Foundation and deputy director for resources and visitor experience, and to her team, including Jayne Shaw, director of development; Mary Scott Swanson, manager of institutional giving; Naomi Crown, corporate relations manager; and Bob Tarren, director of marketing.

Finally, thank you to all of the staff and supporters of the Virginia Museum and the Palace Museum for their exceptional work on this catalogue. On behalf of everyone who has had a hand in this collaborative project and historic exchange, I hope you enjoy this beautiful publication that commemorates one of the most important exhibitions in the museum's seventy-eight year history. My hope is that through these extraordinary efforts, we will be able to better appreciate and understand the rich art and history of China and its wonderful people so that our two countries will prosper together in the twenty-first century.

Alex Nyerges
Director, Virginia Museum of Fine Arts

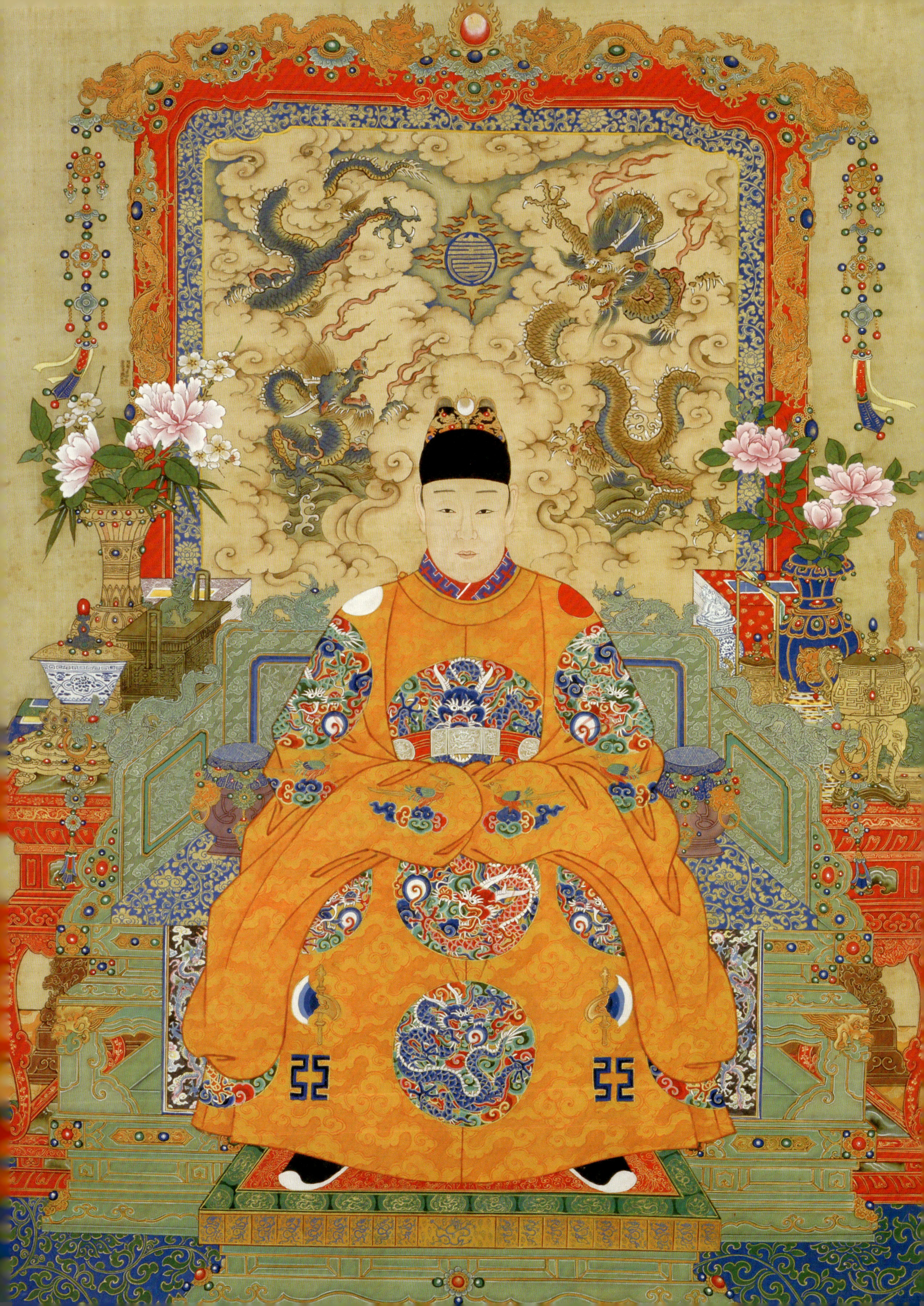

ACKNOWLEDGMENTS

This publication is a collaborative endeavor involving curators and scholars from the United States and China. I extend my appreciation to He Li from the Asian Art Museum of San Francisco and Hou-mei Sung from the Cincinnati Art Museum for their essays and entries and to Ma Shengnan from the Palace Museum for her essay. Our research is largely based on primary sources in Chinese, including imperial regulations, palace property inventories, and daily activities as documented by the Ming and Qing courts and made accessible in printed and electronic publications. We have also integrated recent research and publications by scholars from China, the United States, and beyond.

The curator and authors would like to express our gratitude to the following individuals for their invaluable assistance during the realization of this catalogue: from the Palace Museum's Department of Painting and Calligraphy, Lang Wei, Li Shi, Li Tianyin, Nie Hui, Tian Yimin, Wang Hu, Wang Zhongxu, Yuan Jie, Zhao Bingwen, and Zhang Zhen; from the Department of Decorative Arts, Fu Chao, Guan Xueling, Huang Ying, Wang He, Xu Lin, Xu Wei, Yun Limei, Zhao Guiling, Zhao Lihong, and Zhang Linjie; from the Department of Furniture, Huang Jian and Rui Qian; from the Department of Palace Culture, Liu Zhenghong, Mao Xianmin, and Sun Shaohua; from the Department of Religion, Li Jun, Luo Wenhua, Ma Shengnan, Ma Yunhua, and Wen Ming; from the Department of Costume and Textiles, Fang Hongjun, Jing Wen, Ruan Weiping, Wang Hebei, and Yang Zitong; from the Library, Li Shijuan and Zhu Zhu; from the Department of Architecture, Li Yue and Liu Hongwu. Special thanks to Wang Lei from the Department of the Foreign Affairs and Cao Lianming from the Department of Palace Culture for their continued collaboration in the project.

Many colleagues at the Virginia Museum of Fine Arts made this catalogue possible. I am grateful to Alex Nyerges, Robin Nicholson, and Sylvia Yount for their encouragement and support and to Tucker Harris for her curatorial assistance. Thanks also go to Rosalie West, Sarah Lavicka, and Suzanne Freeman for their expertise and experience. Special thanks to Lucy Grey, dedicated editor, and John Hoar, graphic designer, for their invaluable contributions to the catalogue.

Li Jian
E. Rhodes and Leona B. Carpenter Curator of East Asian Art
Virginia Museum of Fine Arts

Plan of the Forbidden City

Key Sites

1. Meridian Gate (Wumen) 午門
2. Gate of the Hall of Supreme Harmony (Taihemen) 太和門
3. Hall of Supreme Harmony (Taihedian) 太和殿
4. Hall of Central Harmony (Zhonghedian) 中和殿
5. Hall of Preserving Harmony (Baohedian) 保和殿
6. Palace of Heavenly Purity (Qianqinggong) 乾清宮
7. Hall of Union (Jiaotaidian) 交泰殿
8. Palace of Earthly Tranquility (Kunninggong) 坤寧宮
9. Hall of the Intellectual Cultivation (Yangxindian) 養心殿
10. Six Eastern Chambers (Dongliugong) 東六宮
11. Six Western Chambers (Xiliugong) 西六宮
12. Palace of the Double Splendor (Chonghuagong) 重華宮
13. Palace of Eternal Longevity (Yongshougong) 永壽宮
14. Palace of Benevolent Tranquility (Cininggong) 慈寧宮
15. Palace of Longevity and Health (Shoukanggong) 壽康宮
16. Garden of Benevolent Tranquility (Cininghuayuan) 慈寧花園
17. Garden of Building Happiness (Jianfugonghuayuan) 建福宮花園
18. Hall of Rectitude (Zhongzhengdian) 中正殿
19. Imperial Garden (Yuhuayuan) 御花園
20. Hall of Imperial Peace (Qin'andian) 欽安殿
21. Hall of Ancestral Worship (Fengxiandian) 奉先殿
22. Hall of Heavenly Sky (Tianqiongbaodian) 天穹寶殿
23. Palace of Tranquil Longevity (Ningshougong) 寧壽宮
24. Hall of Imperial Supremacy (Huangjidian) 皇極殿
25. Hall of Spiritual Cultivation (Yangxingdian) 養性殿
26. Hall of Joyful Longevity (Leshoutang) 樂壽堂
27. Pavilion of Auspicious View (Jingqige) 景祺閣
28. Pavilion of Buddhist Glory (Fanhualou) 梵華樓
29. Pavilion of Buddha's Sun (Forilou) 佛日樓
30. Qianlong Garden (Qianlonghuayuan) 乾隆花園
31. Hall of Following Instincts (Suichutang) 遂初堂
32. Pavilion of Lasting Amusement (Yanqulou) 延趣樓
33. Pavilion of Illuminating Clouds (Yunguanglou) 雲光樓
34. Pavilion of Viewing Destiny (Fuwangge) 符望閣
35. Studio for Retirement from Diligent Service (Juanqinzhai) 倦勤齋
36. Imperial Cabinet Offices (Neigedatang) 內閣大堂
37. Hall of Literary Glory (Wenhuadian) 文華殿
38. Pavilion of Literary Profundity (Wenyuange) 文淵閣
39. South Three Lodges (Nansansuo) 南三所
40. Imperial Kitchen (Yushanfang) 御膳房
41. Hospital and Pharmacy (Taiyiyuan) 太醫院
42. Archery Pavilion (Jianting) 箭亭
43. Imperial Stable (Yumajiu) 御馬廄
44. Hall of Southern Fragrance (Nanxundian) 南薰殿
45. Hall of Military Eminence (Wuyingdian) 武英殿
46. Imperial Household Department (Neiwufu) 內務府
47. Zaobanchu imperial workshop 造辦処

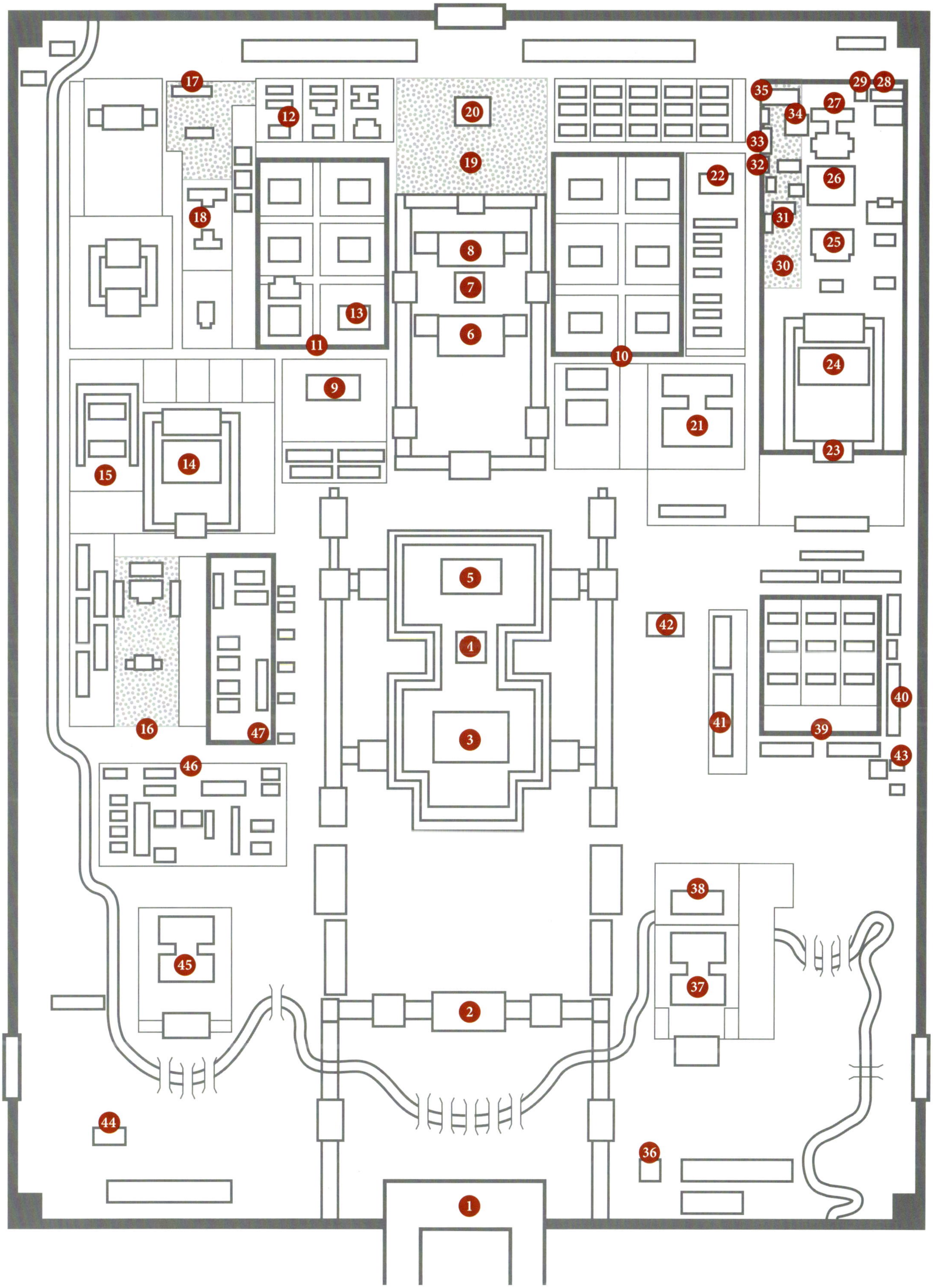
1
2
3
4
5
6
7
8
9
10
11
12
13
14
15
16
17
18
19
20
21
22
23
24
25
26
27
28
29
30
31
32
33
34
35
36
37
38
39
40
41
42
43
44
45
46
47

Introduction

Serving as the center of Chinese dynastic government for nearly five hundred years, the Forbidden City was the residence for twenty-four emperors beginning in 1420 and continuing through the Ming dynasty (1368–1644) and the Qing dynasty (1644–1911). The walled compound encompassed 180 acres in Beijing. Emperor Yongle (r. 1403–24), the third Ming emperor, relocated the capital from Nanjing to his former princely fief, Beijing, shortly after his enthronement. Fourteen Ming emperors lived in the palace consecutively until 1644, when Manchu forces crossed the Great Wall from the northeast and established the Qing dynasty. For the next three centuries, ten consecutive Qing emperors resided in the Forbidden City. The last emperor, Xuantong (Puyi, 1906–1967), was expelled from the palace in 1924, thirteen years after the 1911 revolution.

Built on the ruins of the palace of the Yuan dynasty (1279–1368), the new imperial palace was laid out on a central axis, facing south. Surrounded by a defensive moat and a thirty-foot-high wall with a watchtower at each corner, the Forbidden City contained more than a thousand structures, including ceremonial buildings, private complexes, gardens, and temples. Leading architect Cai Xin (act. 1400–20), a native of Changzhou, Jiangsu Province, designed the palace, and Kuai Xiang (1398–1481), from Suzhou, also in the Jiangsu Province, supervised its construction, which was completed in 1420. Notwithstanding several reconstructions and expansions, the primary layout of the Forbidden City remains the same, even after nearly six hundred years. With cross-cultural elements of Han, Manchu, Mongol, and Tibetan influences, the Forbidden City stands today as the largest complex of wooden structures and the best preserved of any such architecture in the world.

The Forbidden City was originally called Zijincheng, a name derived from *zihui,* the supreme star or North Star, which in Chinese legend was the home of the Heavenly Lord (Tiandi), making Zijincheng its earthly counterpart. In the name Zi-jin-cheng, *jin* means "inaccessible" to the public, and *cheng* means "city." As a palace for the emperor, who believed he was the Son of Heaven, the Forbidden City was constructed based on this constellation and the yin-yang theory. Accordingly, its rectangular design rests on a south-north central axis with a gate on each side.[1]

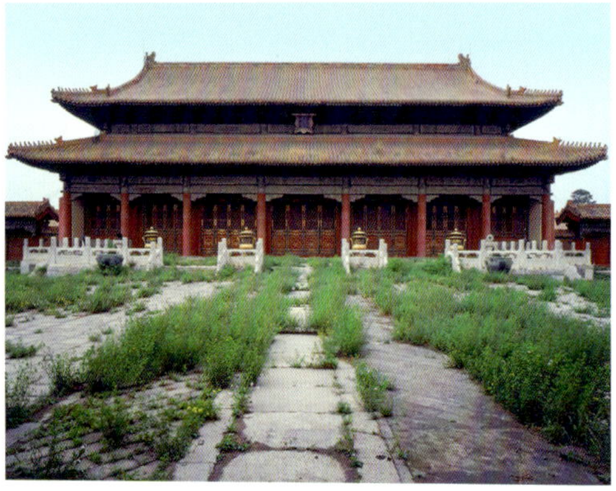

Fig. 1 Cining Palace, 1982, © The Palace Museum

Divided into an outer court and inner court, the Forbidden City's layout allowed for separation of public and private activities. Located at the front, or south end, of the palace, the outer court represents imperial prerogative. With its three major halls constructed on a marble platform, the outer court was the setting for the most important state events, including the emperors' inaugurations and birthdays, New Year's celebrations, receptions for foreign ambassadors and honorary guests, and imperial state examinations.

The inner court houses three primary buildings for the emperor and empress on the central axis: Qianqinggong, Jiaotaidian, and Kunninggong. The first syllables of these building names (*qian, jiao,* and *kun*) mean "heaven," "unite," and "earth," respectively. These buildings are flanked by two gates on

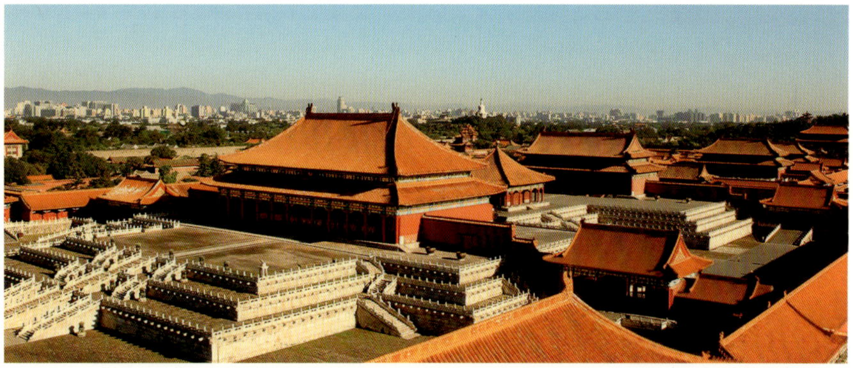

Fig. 2 Hall of Supreme Harmony, 2008, © The Palace Museum

the east and west (named after the Sun and the Moon) and by twelve chambers that symbolize the twelve constellations. The chambers serve as private living quarters for the empress and consorts, and each chamber features a throne room for the emperor. The Qianqinggong, the central palace where daily administrative affairs were conducted, was the political center and home for emperors Shunzhi (r. 1644–61) and Kangxi (r. 1662–1722). The Yangxindian complex on the western side of the inner court was used as the business and residential area for emperors Yongzheng (r. 1723–35) and Qianlong (r. 1736–95). However, Emperor Qianlong's retirement complex was located on the eastern side of the inner court. Widowed empresses occupied the western side.

In keeping with ancient Chinese architectural design, the palace's inner court contained numerous landscaped gardens, including the Yuhuayuan for the imperial family, the Qianlonghuayuan for Emperor Qianlong, and the Jianfugonghuayuan for widowed empresses. Temples and shrines were constructed within the residential complexes and gardens of the inner court. Thirty-five Tibetan Buddhist temples and structures constructed from the late seventeenth to the eighteenth centuries spread across the inner court in six areas: the Zhongzhengdian Buddhist complex; Jianfugong garden; Cining Palace; Cininggong garden; Yuhuayuan garden; and Ningshougong, Emperor Qianlong's retirement compound. In addition to Tibetan temples, Daoist shrines are represented by the Qin'andian and Tianqiongbaodian, also built in the inner court. Private chambers belonging to the emperor or members of his family contain private chapels, indicating religion's important role in their lives.

Unlike other studies that explore the broad scope of imperial activities beyond the residential compound, this catalogue and accompanying exhibition focus on the history and culture of the Forbidden City, its residents, and the works of art and their functions and themes. While imperial activity extended to villas such as Yuanmingyuan in Beijing or Bishushanzhuang in Chengde, this publication explores imperial life within the Forbidden City. Nearly two hundred works drawn from the collection of the Palace Museum, which was established in 1925 on the site of the Forbidden City, are presented here, as well as several works from the collection of the Virginia Museum of Fine Arts (VMFA). The catalogue is divided into four sections: Qing imperial rituals, court arts in the living quarters, Qing court paintings, and religious life in the palace. The essays and entries address how the Qing Manchu empire inherited its nomadic tradition; how it adopted Han, Mongolian, and Tibetan cultural elements; and how it created a diverse government and societal harmonic. The book examines works of art and artifacts and interprets how they were shaped by imperial patronage, cultural influences, and European styles. Lastly, in presenting religious works, the catalogue reveals the essential role of religion and its impact on the lives of emperors and their families. LJ

NOTE

1. Yu 1992, 19–21.

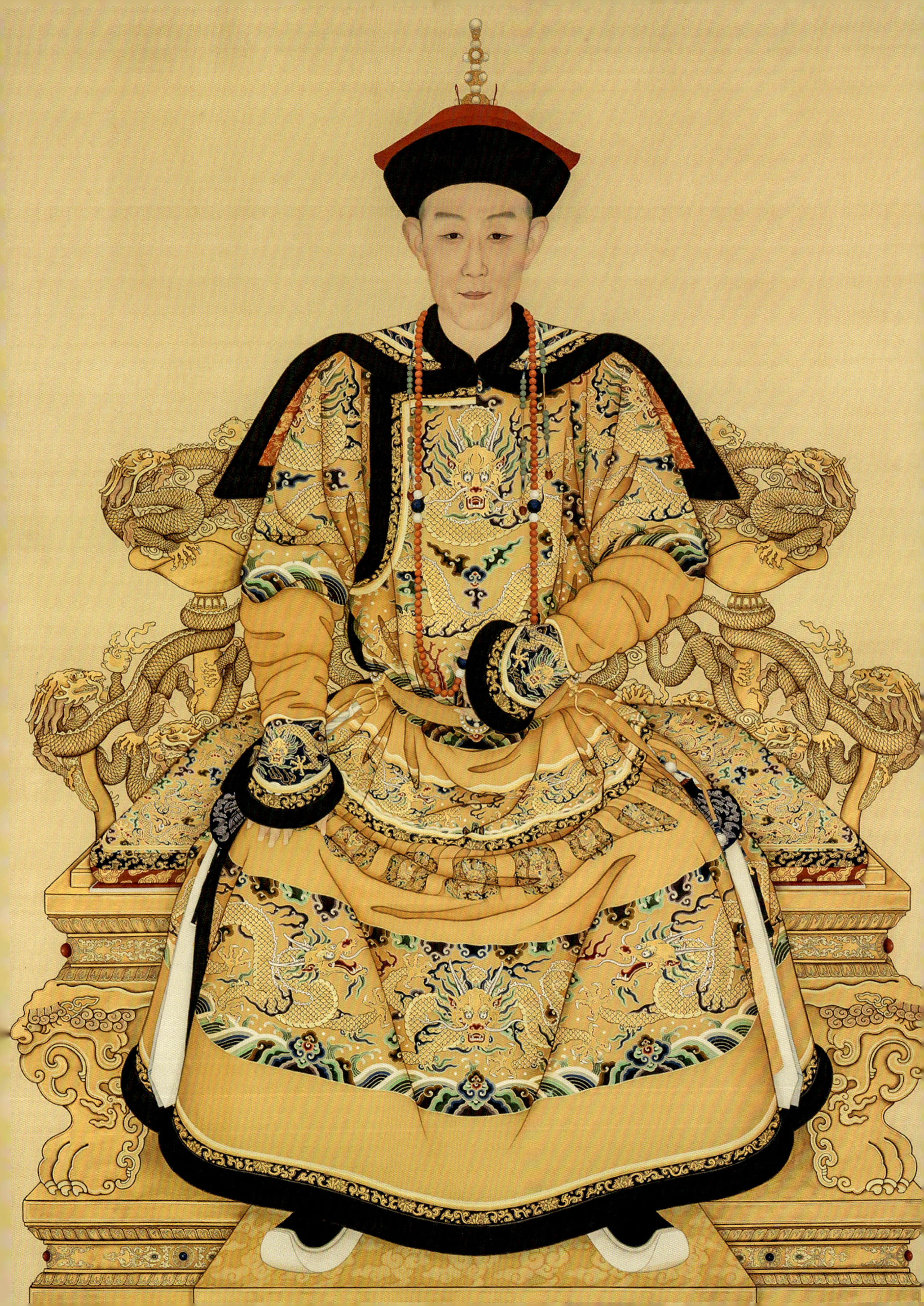

敬天勤民 Rituals in the Qing Court

Li Jian

Rituals in ancient China were considered dialogues between humans and gods in which humans made supplications for bountiful harvests, good fortune, and societal peace. After the Manchus took over the Forbidden City from the last Ming-dynasty emperor, the Qing rulers adopted previous dynastic rituals and etiquette to maintain cultural consistency. By doing so, they hoped to secure the trust of the people and transfer power peacefully. This essay outlines the five rites (*wuli*), codified in *Collected Rituals of the Qing Dynasty* (*Da Qing Tongli*), a manual issued in the mid-eighteenth century, and examines how paintings and objects featured in this catalogue bring rituals of the Forbidden City to life.

As early as the Warring States period (476–221 BC), the Zhou kingdom inscribed the Rites of Zhou (*zhouli*) into bronze vessels. For centuries, the Zhou rituals served as the guide for interpreting and carrying out court rites. Shortly after Emperor Qianlong (r. 1736–95) ascended the throne in 1736, he ordered court officials to compile the rites in a manual following Ming protocols. *Collected Rituals of the Qing Dynasty* was issued in 1756 and became one of the most comprehensive ritual documents in Chinese feudal history. Containing thirty-six volumes and fifty chapters, the manual recorded 256 imperial functions,[1] including sacrifices, weddings, inaugurations, and funerals, and encompassed every phase of court life. The publication identifies five categories of rites: auspicious rites for sacrifices and worship, joyful rites for celebratory events, martial rites for strengthening skills and forces, guest rites for cultivating relationships, and misfortune rites for honoring the deceased.

The auspicious rites (*jili*) involved sacrifices to honor heavenly deities or to worship ancestors and nature. The first-priority sacrifices included the winter-solstice rite at the Altar of Heaven, a few miles south of the Forbidden City, and the summer-solstice rite at the Altar of Earth, a few miles north of the Forbidden City. Other ritual sites were the Temple of Imperial Ancestors (Taimiao) and the Altar of Land and Grain, both located just inside the Tian'anmen Gate; the Hall of Ancestral Worship (Fengxiandian) in the inner court; and imperial mausoleums outside Beijing. The second-priority rites were performed at the Altar of the Sun and the Altar of the Moon, the Altar of Agriculture, the Temple of Previous Dynastic Emperors, Confucius's Temple in Beijing, and Confucius's Temple and Cemetery in Qufu, Shandong Province. Other rituals to worship heavenly and earthly deities were performed at sacred mountain landmarks like Taishan and the Daoist temples in the palace dedicated to Zhenwu (cat. no. 134) and Heavenly Lords (cat. no. 131).[2] The top-ranking rites were often conducted by the emperors themselves, and the second-level acts of homage were administered either by the emperor or by appointed officials. Strict costume codes were applied to all participants. The hierarchy of rites indicated that north was superior to south, and east to west.

The Qing rulers adopted the Ming's *zhonghe shaoyue* court orchestra, which contained two hundred or more performers for grand sacrifices and more than eighteen types of instruments made of eight materials: metal, stone, string, bamboo, clay, wood, gourd, and leather. Zhonghe shaoyue, which means "harmonious and beautiful music," was derived from the Zhou dynasty's style of classical music known as Elegant Music (*yayue*). The orchestra performed

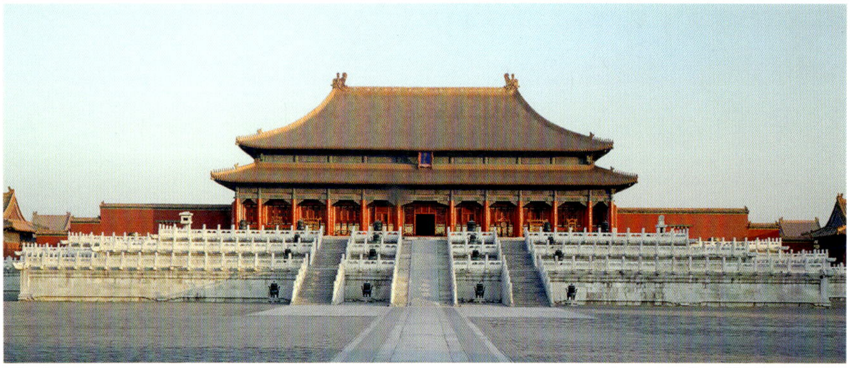

Fig. 1 Hall of Supreme Harmony, 1982, © The Palace Museum

classical court music at sacrifices, court assemblies, and state banquets. Through prayers, animal sacrifices, ritual music, and incense burning, Ming and Qing rulers sought cosmic harmony, good harvest, peace, and prosperity.

The joyful rites (*jiali*) dealt with celebratory functions at the court, including the three grand annual assemblies at the Hall of Supreme Harmony (Taihedian), on New Year's Day, the winter solstice, and the emperor's birthday. The joyful rites observed the empress dowager's birthday; the emperor's administrative assembly on the fifth, fifteenth, and twenty-fifth of each month; his inauguration; the honoring of the empress dowager; and the emperor's wedding. Also categorized as joyful rites were activities that involved the emperor plowing and the empress tending mulberry leaves for silk weaving (cat. nos. 21.1–2), as well as the court hosting state banquets.

Notable for its rich display of ritual objects and regalia formation, the series of paintings known as *Wedding of Emperor Guangxu* (cat. nos. 25.1–5) narrates one of the most celebrated rites by showing the empress's bridal procession into the palace, the wedding announcement at the Gate of Heavenly Peace, and the banquet with performers from Manchu, Mongol, Uighur, Korea, and Burma at the Hall of Supreme Harmony. Four Qing emperors had weddings at the Forbidden City—Shunzhi (r. 1644–61), Kangxi (r. 1662–1722), Tongzhi (r. 1862–74), and Guangxu (r. 1875–1908)—but only Emperor Guangxu's was documented in paintings. This rare series not only offers a glimpse of the wedding rites as conducted in 1889 but also sheds light on the diversity of the Qing court and the rituals that ensured cultural continuity.

Banquet at Cining Palace (cat. no. 23) illustrates a display of ritual implements and seating assignments for attendees at a state birthday banquet for Empress Dowager Chongqing (1693–1777). As described in *Collected Rituals of the Qing Dynasty,* the empress and consorts were dressed in court robes (*lifu*) and were inside the hall with princesses and noblewomen. The zhonghe shaoyue orchestra performed six compositions during the banquet, beginning with the playing of gold bells (cat. no. 28) under the eaves in the northeast of the courtyard when the empress dowager arrived. Across the courtyard in the southwest, the *danbi qingyue* orchestra, containing string, wind, and percussion instruments, played twice, first during tea service and again when wine was poured. The *zhonghe qingyue* orchestra on the northwest began to play the jade chimes (cat. no. 27) when the meal was offered. Following performances in the southeast by the *danbi dayue* troupe, the zhonghe shaoyue orchestra performed a second time at the banquet's conclusion as the empress dowager departed.[3]

The martial rites (*junli*) applied to specific occasions: review of the imperial army by the emperor, entry into battle led by the emperor as commander in chief, the army's triumphant return from combat, the appointment of generals, and the acceptance of prisoners of war. Following Emperor Kangxi's lead, Emperor Qianlong conducted his first Eight-Banner review in 1739 (cat. no. 33) with ten thousand participating soldiers. As part of the review, the emperors, military officials, and imperial troops demonstrated their archery prowess. Imperial noblemen and banner soldiers learned archery at a young age. In between their classes, princes practiced on the archery grounds in the outer court, while officials and soldiers practiced on the Nanyuan and Mulan hunting grounds.

The guest rites (*binli*) addressed ceremonial functions for receiving foreign ambassadors, regional kings, religious leaders, and Chinese officials from areas outside the capital. A rare handscroll (cat. no. 101) depicts the Pope's envoys presenting horses to the Yuan emperor in 1336. By the eighteenth century, New Year's Day had become a sensational event when guests from Asia, Central Asia, and Europe gathered in the Forbidden City to present tributes of regional goods and exotic animals to the emperor (cat. no. 24). According to the rites, guests were expected to kneel and touch their heads to the ground in front of the emperor. The rites specified that court officials provide guests with room and board; give them parting gifts of fur, silk, and silver; and escort them to the border or the coast.[4] The guest rites were codified to cultivate diplomatic and trading relationships between the court and foreign governments and glorified the empire.

During his 1793 visit to China, foreign envoy George Macartney (Irish, 1737–1806) refused to kowtow in front of Emperor Qianlong. Macartney hoped to convince China to open its trade ports to Great Britain, but Emperor Qianlong declined his request. Fifty years later, during the Opium Wars, Great Britain used the cannon to force open the door to trade with China. Even today, scholars debate the long-term effects of the 1793 clash between Chinese guest rituals and British diplomatic protocol.[5]

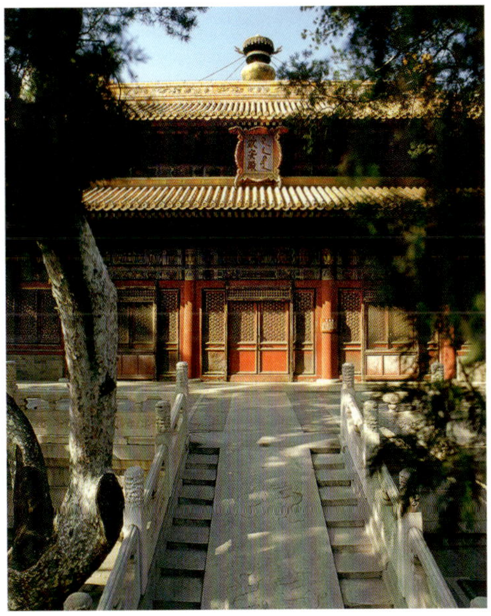

Fig. 2 Hall of Imperial Peace, 1982, © The Palace Museum

The misfortune rites were practices and customs relating to death and other tragedies, such as natural disasters and enemy attacks. Prayers and rituals expressed sympathy and provided comfort for the grieving. The inauguration of an emperor was usually a somber event because the entire court was still mourning the previous emperor. (Therefore, inaugural ceremonies did not include musical entertainment or elaborate banquets.) Funeral practices also addressed the afterlife, preparing tombs with great care and providing the deceased with clothes, food, wine, and blessings for the hereafter. Shortly after enthronement, rulers began to construct their tombs. Emperor Jiajing (r. 1522–66) spent several decades building and expanding the tomb of his father, Zhu Youyuan (1476–1519) (cat. no. 1), to fulfill the filial piety taught in Confucian philosophy.

Dharani Sutra coverlets (see cat. no. 124), one type of burial furnishings placed in the coffin, were intended to terminate the continued rebirth and take the deceased to heaven. That final destination is depicted in the portrait of Third Changkya Rolpe Dorje (1717–1786), where the enthroned spiritual leader (cat. no. 123) is surrounded by heavenly deities, flowers, and jewels in the Western Paradise of the Pure Land.

The Qing imperial rituals, rooted deeply in Confucius's teachings and carried over from Ming rule, integrated diverse cultural elements and developed into the most comprehensive model for ritual practices. An examination of the artworks presented in this catalogue furthers the study of ritual activities, shedding light on political, economic, and cultural life in the Qing court.

NOTES

1. Rawski 1998, 200–201.
2. *Da Qing Tongli* (1756) 1782, chap. 1.
3. ____, chap. 37.
4. ____, chap. 43.
5. See more guest ritual accounts in Hevia 2002, 227–28.

1 明嘉靖 朱祐杬像圖轴 绢本設色

Portrait of Zhu Youyuan, approx. 1524
Ming dynasty, Jiajing period (1522–66)
Hanging scroll; ink and color on silk
H. 108.3 cm (42.64 in.), W. 76 cm (29.92 in.)
Palace Museum, Gu.6210

When Emperor Zhengde (r. 1506–21) died without an heir in 1521, his cousin Zhu Houcong succeeded the throne as Emperor Jiajing (r. 1522–66). Soon after enthronement, Emperor Jiajing began to fight fiercely with court officials for the elevated status of his deceased father. The extended court dispute was known as "The Great Rites Controversy." After persecuting more than a hundred officials, Emperor Jiajing issued a dispensation that posthumously honored his father with imperial status. This portrait depicts Jiajing's father, Zhu Youyuan (1476–1519), who was renamed Emperor Xian. In 1524, Zhu Youyuan's grave was upgraded from a prince's tomb to an emperor's mausoleum. This portrait was most likely painted between 1521 and 1524.[1]

Here, Zhu Youyuan wears a court robe of imperial yellow satin embroidered with dragon roundels and the Twelve Imperial Symbols, a design made exclusively for the emperor in the late fourteenth century during the Ming dynasty. He wears a black gauze crown (*yishanguan*) and a pair of black leather shoes, and he sits on a throne covered with brocaded blankets, decorated with chrysanthemums and clouds. There are twelve dragon medallions embroidered on his robe: three on the front, three on the back, one on each shoulder, and two on each side of the lower garment. The robe features the Twelve Imperial Symbols: sun, moon, stars, mountain, dragon, and pheasant adorn the front and back of the upper robe, while designs of double goblets, weeds, fire, rice, axe, and bow are shown on both sides of the lower garment. A cut-silk (*kesi*) robe[2] similar to this design was excavated in 1956 from Dingling, the mausoleum of Emperor Wanli (r. 1573–1620) in the suburb of Beijing. LJ

1. He and Knight 2008, cat. no. 147, p. 259.
2. IOA 1990, 2:232, 239.

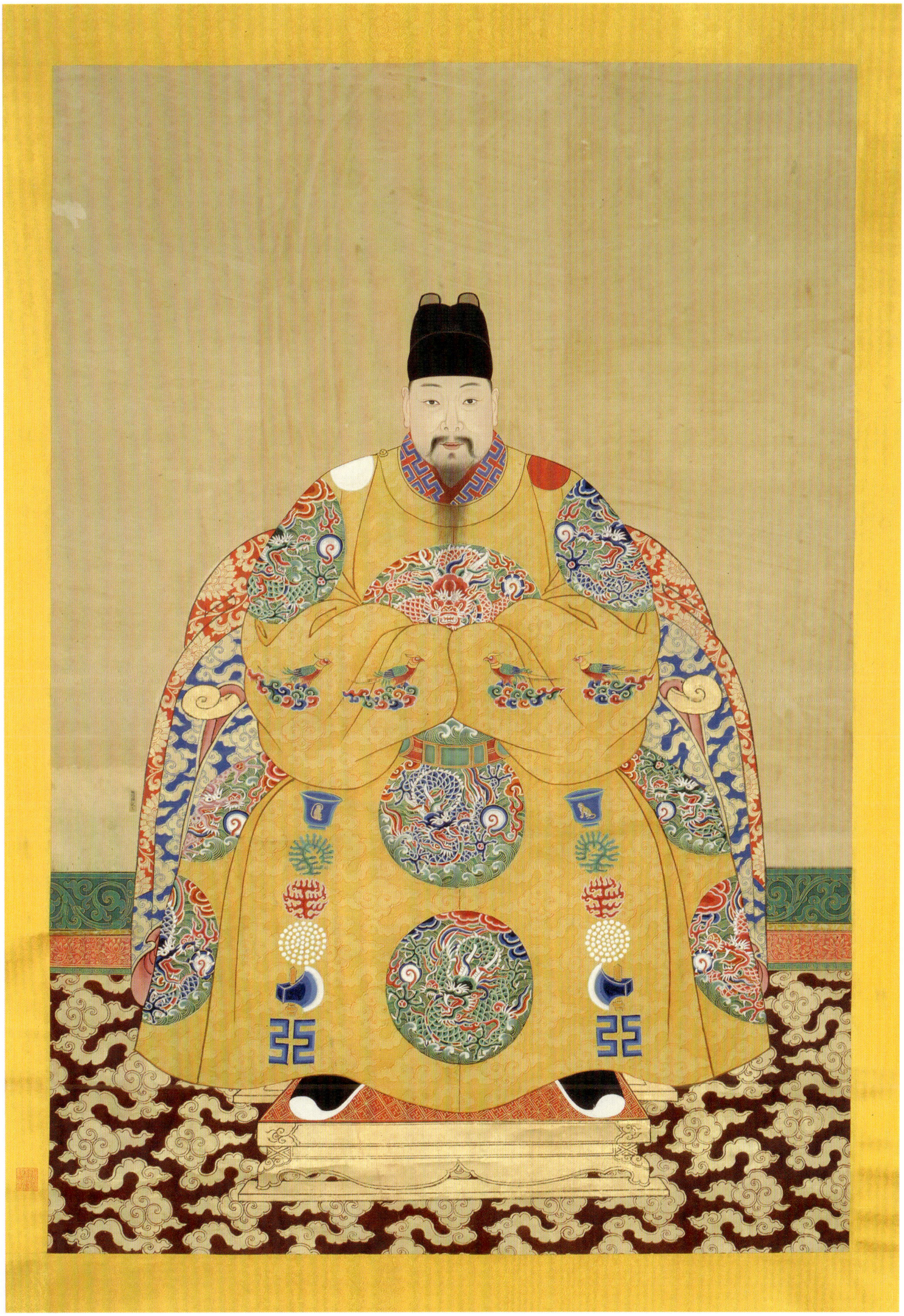

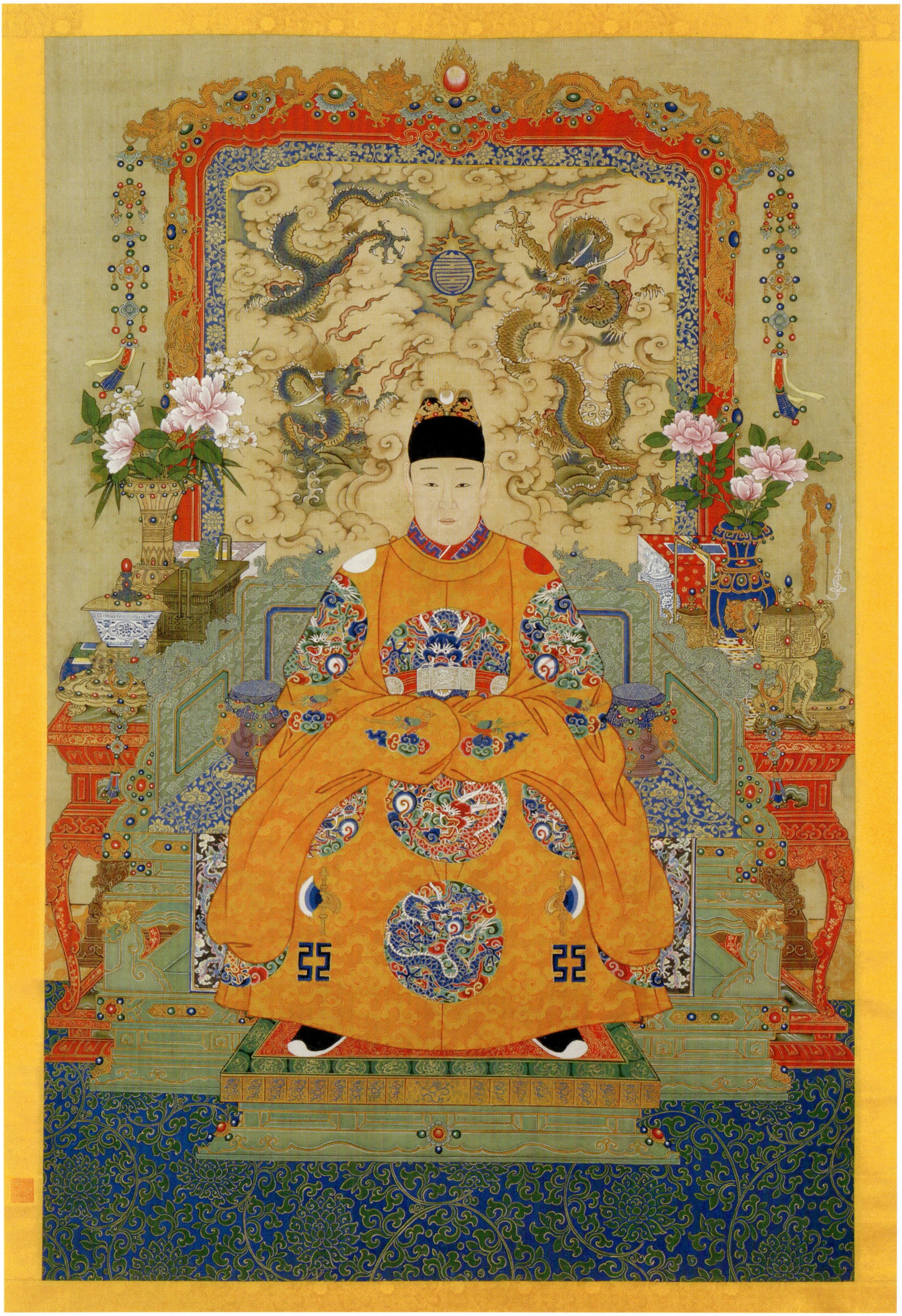

2 明天啟 朱由校朝服像軸 絹本設色

Portrait of Emperor Tianqi

Ming dynasty, Tianqi period (1621–27)

Hanging scroll; ink and color on silk

H. 112 cm (44.09 in.), W. 75.7 cm (29.80 in.)
Palace Museum, Gu.6209

This scroll depicts Zhu Youjiao, known as Emperor Tianqi, in a golden-yellow court robe, seated in front of a painted screen. A pair of gold dragons and a large cat's-eye stone embellish his black gauze crown, known as *yishanguan*. The embroidery on his robe features twelve dragon medallions and the Twelve Imperial Symbols—the fashion designated for an emperor in the early Ming dynasty.

The luxurious furniture surrounding the emperor represents his hobby of carpentry. Decorated with golden mounts and precious stone inlays, an enormous dragon throne sits before a screen mounted with dragons, jewels, and silk tassels. A pair of red lacquered tables display an array of the emperor's favorite objects, including a bronze incense burner, flower vases, an offering bowl, books, and scrolls. The two covered jars on the throne symbolize peace and stability. Their arrangement resembles that of large ceramic vases found in 1956 just outside the coffins at Dingling, the mausoleum of Emperor Wanli.[1] Like most of the Ming emperors' portraits, this scroll was created after Emperor Tianqi's death in 1627. With intricate details, the painting provides a rich visual source for the study of costumes, rituals, and court displays in the early seventeenth century.

Along with a large number of ancient portraits of Chinese emperors and empresses, this scroll was once stored in the Nanxundian, a palace hall in the outer court. A survey conducted in 1749 revealed that this imperial holding sustained serious damage. The paintings were documented and remounted according to instructions given by Emperor Qianlong (r. 1736–95). Portraits of emperors, empresses, and other imperial family members were mounted on yellow silk fabrics, and works depicting court officials were mounted on dark blue silk fabrics. LJ

1. IOA 1990, pls. 87 (WW2), 88 (DW3).

3 清乾隆 弘曆朝服像軸 絹本設色

Emperor Qianlong in Ceremonial Robe, 1740s
Qing dynasty, Qianlong period (1736–95)
Hanging scroll; ink and color on silk
H. 263 cm (103.4 in.), W. 176 cm (69.3 in.)
Palace Museum, Gu.6467

This portrait depicts Emperor Qianlong, known also as Hongli (1711–1799), the fourth son of Emperor Yongzheng (r. 1723–35) and the favorite grandson of Emperor Kangxi (r. 1662–1722). Emperor Qianlong ascended the throne at age twenty-five and reigned until age eighty-five, becoming the longest-reigning emperor in Chinese history. In this portrait, a seated Emperor Qianlong holds a lapis lazuli bead from his necklace, while he gently gazes at the viewer. The richly embroidered dragon garment, a sable crown decorated with gold and pearls, and the belt around his waist reveal his supreme status. Portraits of Emperor Qianlong tend to be similar in size, but this painting differs in its omission of a decorative carpet.

Like other portraits of Emperor Qianlong, this work is unsigned, unsealed, and undated. Compared to his inaugural portrait painted in 1736,[1] the emperor in this painting appears slightly older, dating the work around the 1740s when he was in his thirties. The fine facial features, which reveal the inner essence of the sitter, and the dazzling yellow pigments, which emphasize the robe's texture, make this one of the finest imperial portraits of the mid-Qing dynasty.

In 1834, Emperor Daoguang (r. 1821–50) relocated 121 paintings—hanging scrolls, handscrolls, and album leaves depicting his grandfather, Emperor Qianlong—from the Jingqige, a building in Qianlong's retirement compound (cat. no. 24), to the Hall of Imperial Longevity (Shouhuangdian), a Qing ancestral worship hall in the north of the Forbidden City in today's Jingshan Park.[2] Most likely, this scroll joined other imperial portraits in the hall where succeeding emperors paid homage to their ancestors on New Year's Day and on emperors' birthdays. LJ

1. CCTP 1996, 150.
2. Wang 2011a, 470–74.

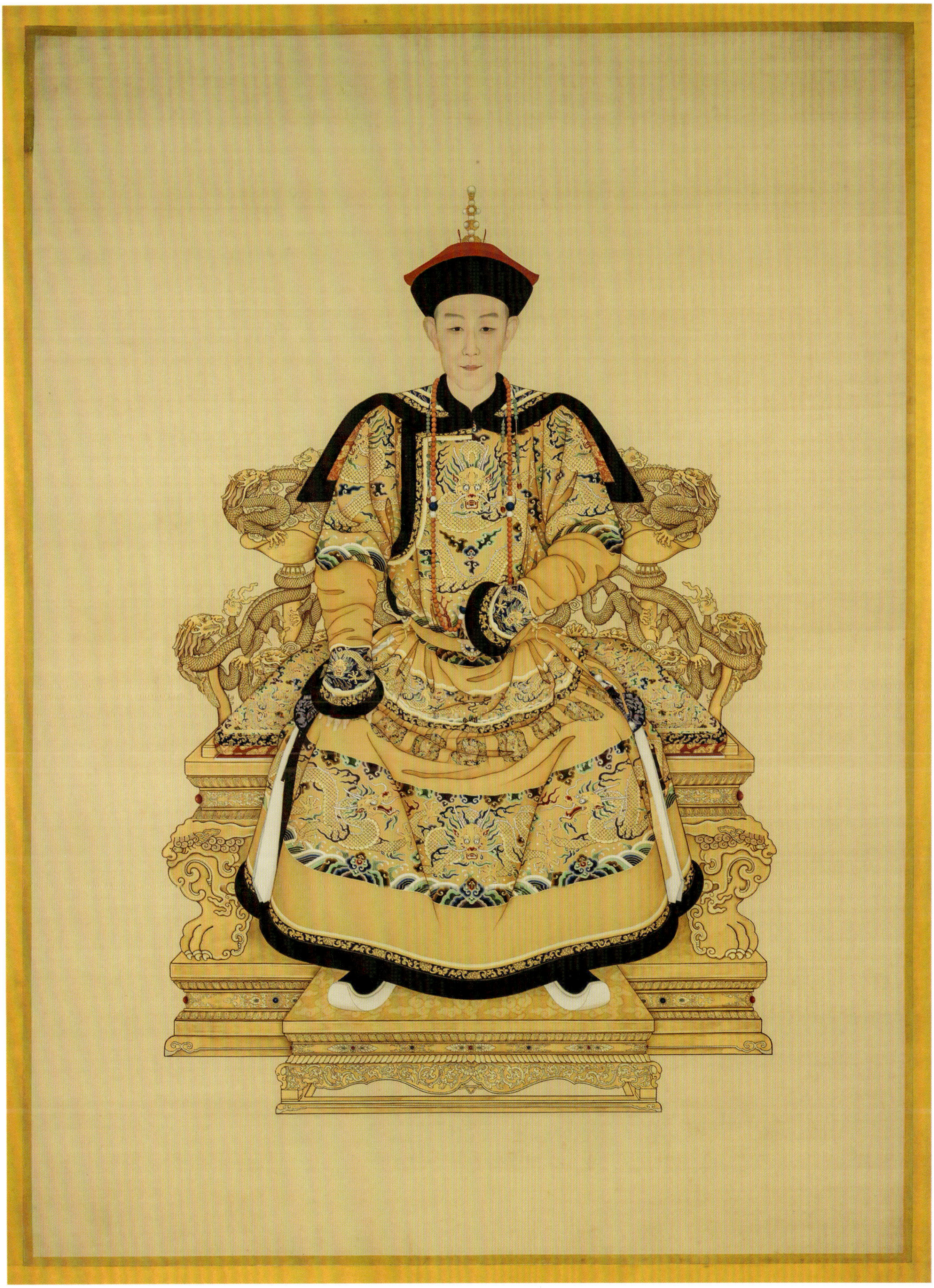

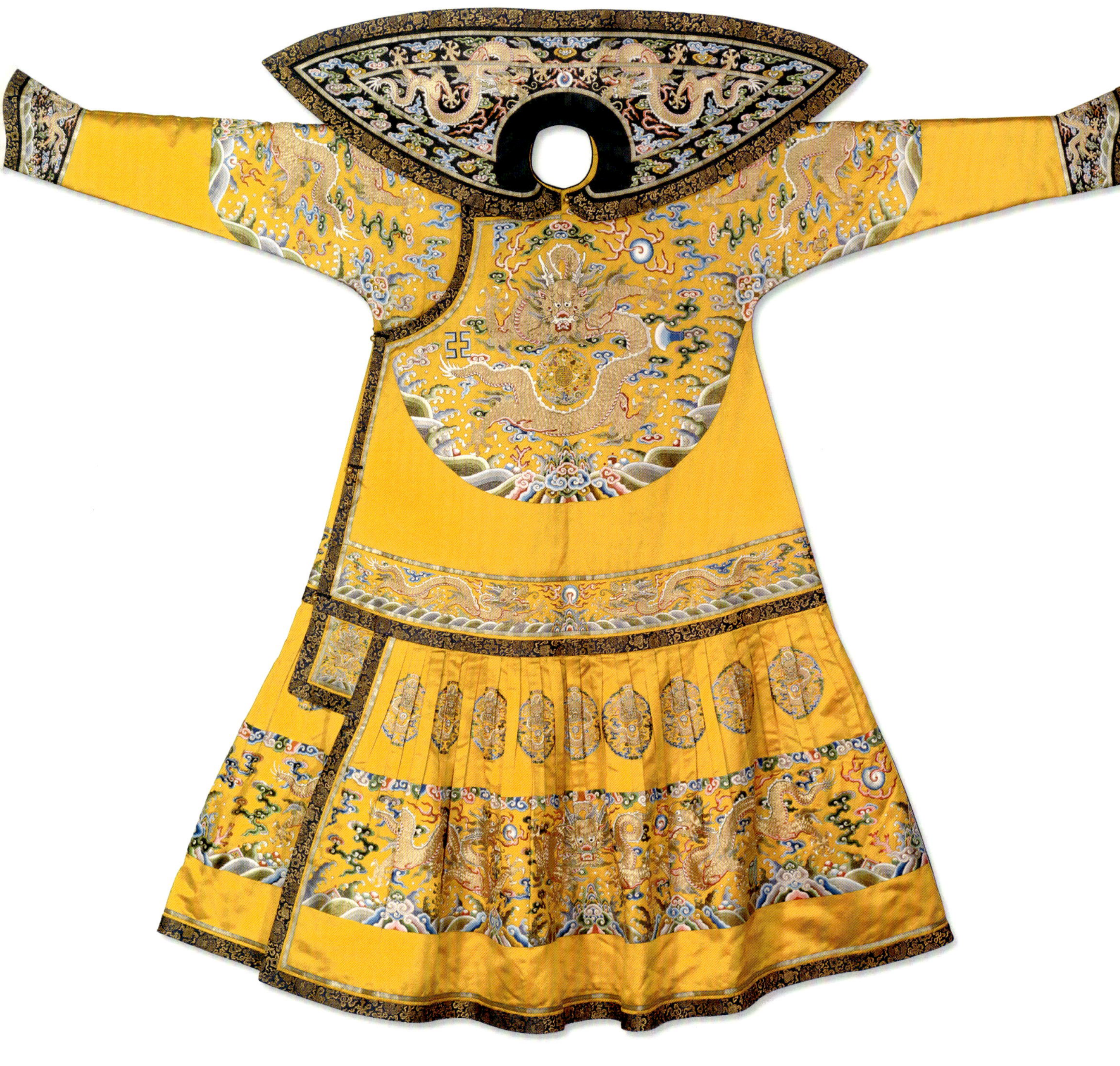

4 清乾隆 明黃色緞繡彩雲金龍紋棉朝袍

Imperial Yellow Robe with Dragons and Clouds

Qing dynasty, Qianlong period (1736–95)
Embroidered satin, ermine trim, twill-damask lining, cotton padding, coral, pearls, metal buttons
Body: L. 142 cm (55.91 in.); Overall sleeves: L. 196 cm (77.17 in.)
Palace Museum, Gu.42147

This luxuriously embroidered robe belonged to Emperor Qianlong. Made of imperial yellow satin, it has a sleeved tunic, a pleated apron, a right placket, padding with ermine trim, and a dark border woven in gold. The emperor wore the robe primarily in winter for rituals such as New Year's Day, birthdays, the winter solstice, and ritual sacrifices. The overall design reveals both Han and Manchu nomadic elements. Horse-hoof cuffs, a cape collar, and a folding apron were derived from the Qing nomadic costume tradition, whereas the dragons and the Twelve Imperial Symbols are Han stylistic motifs from the Ming dynasty (cat. no. 1).

Three imperial textile bureaus collaborated to produce this and other Qing imperial robes. The Hangzhou bureau specialized in the design and production of silk fabrics, such as gauze and tabby. The bureau in Jiangning (today's Nanjing) manufactured satin damask woven in gold thread and various brocaded fabrics. Famous for intricate embroidery and cut-silk (*kesi*) tapestry, the Suzhou bureau provided the fabric woven with gold-wrapped thread and the innovative stitching. LJ

Inscription, written in ink on a yellow tag attached to the collar: front of tag 高宗 *Gaozong* (Emperor Qianlong); back of tag
綉黃緞面片金邊袷朝袍一件,
珊瑚背雲二塊,珊瑚墜角四個,
加間飯塊正珠八顆
(An embroidered yellow satin robe with gold-foil border, two corals on ribbon, four corals at tassel ends, eight small round pearls.)

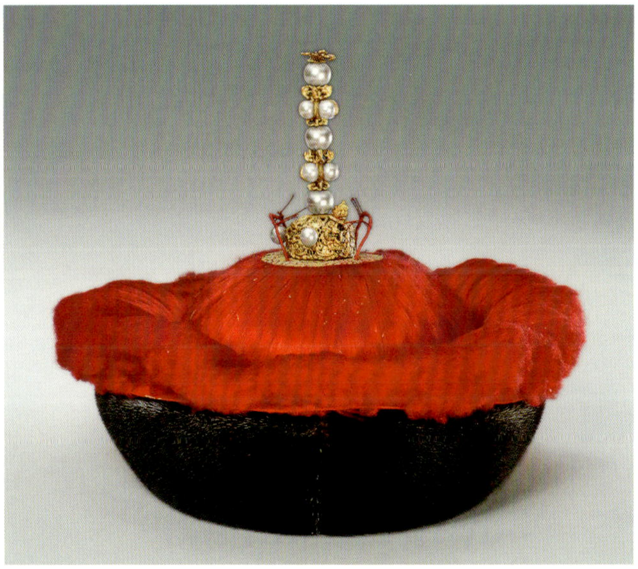

5 清乾隆 貂皮絨纓金龍頂皇帝冬朝冠

Emperor's Ceremonial Crown for the Winter

Qing dynasty, Qianlong period (1736–95)
Sable, silk floss, gold, pearl, gift bronze, silk threads
H. 24 cm (9.4 in.), Dia. 28 cm (11 in.)
Palace Museum, Gu.59739

The Qing court upheld a strict dress code that determined material, color, and decoration according to the status of the wearer. A gold-spiked insignia surmounts this crown's sable rim and red-floss top. The intricately decorated spike has four tiny dragons on each of the three levels, interspersed with a *dongzhu* pearl (the top pearl is missing). In keeping with an innovative style from the Yongzheng period (1723–35), two red silk archways flank the pierced gold base. These design components are indicative of a crown worn by an emperor during formal functions in winter. Velvet was an alternative to sable in the winter months, while material used in the summer ranged from woven straw to vines and silk (cat. nos. 46, 47).[1]

Treasured since the Song dynasty (960–1279), the dongzhu was considered a high-quality freshwater pearl, harvested from the Heilong River in northeastern China, a nomadic region and the home of the Qing's Manchu ancestors. The dongzhu pearl's production and distribution was administered by the Qing court. Large, round, glimmering pearls were reserved for making crowns and necklaces; those with irregular shapes were chosen to craft jewelry, sculpture, and decorative objects. LJ

1. Yunlu et al. (1766) 2004, chap. 4, pp. 101–11.

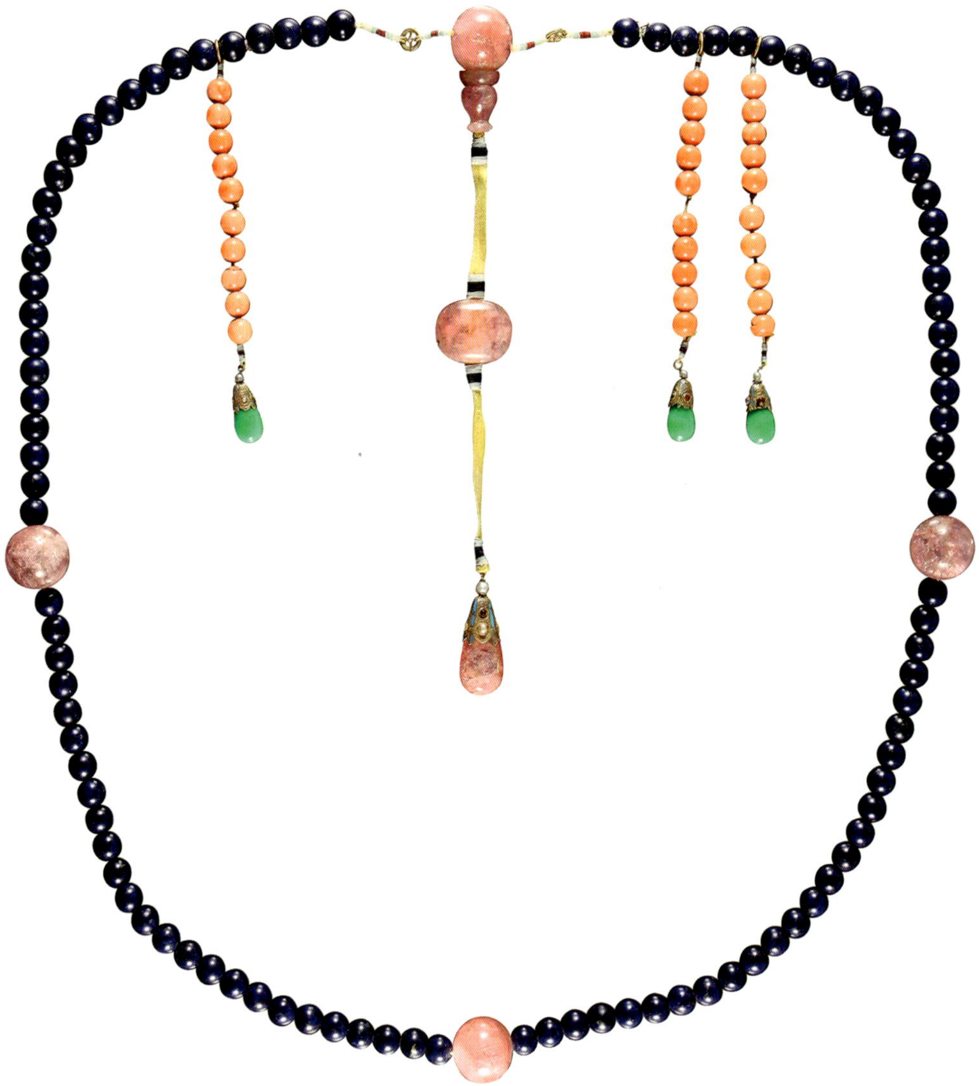

6 清乾隆 青金石朝珠

Ceremonial Necklace

Qing dynasty, Qianlong period (1736–95)

Lapis lazuli, tourmaline, jadeite, coral, gilt copper, silk

Circ. 144 cm (56.7 in.)

Palace Museum, Gu.225594

One of the first gemstones mined in the world, lapis lazuli—with its intense blue color and golden specks—has been treasured by makers of jewelry since the Shang dynasty (1600–1045 BC). Among this necklace's original 108 lapis lazuli beads, of which eight are now lost, four large tourmalines (*fotou*) alternate around the necklace. The top tourmaline connects to a gourd-shaped bead (*fotouta*) and an imperial yellow silk ribbon embellished in the center with a tourmaline plaque (*beiyun*). The necklace has three shorter strands (*jinian*), each comprising ten coral beads and a jadeite at the end of the string.

The emperor wore a lapis lazuli necklace with a blue dragon robe for his ritual services at the Altar of Heaven during the winter solstice (December 22–January 5). According to Qing costume rituals, the choice of stones and the color of the silk ribbon identify a necklace's owner. A lapis lazuli necklace with an imperial yellow ribbon, presented here, was designated for the emperor and crown prince.[1] LJ

1. Yunlu et al. (1766) 2004, chap. 4, pp. 107, 118, 125.

7 清嘉慶 明黃色珊瑚帯版吉服帶

Emperor's Ceremonial Belt

Qing dynasty, Jiaqing period (1796–1820)
Silk satin, embroidery, gold and silver threads, gold, gilt copper, coral, jadeite, ivory, pearl, turquoise

Belt L. 192 cm (75.59 in.)
Palace Museum, Gu.71892

Coral plaques decorate this belt made of imperial yellow silk satin. Its reverse side consists of red satin woven with golden thread to form dragon designs. Two rings carry white silk ribbons and a Manchu nobleman's essential accessories: four silk pouches, a fire flint, a gold toothpick case with turquoise inlay, and a portable knife case. The belt was worn outside a dragon robe with the fire flint on the left side of the owner and the knife on the right. According to *Illustrated Ritual Implements of the Imperial Dynasty,* published in 1766, the emperor wore such a belt during sacrificial services at the Altar of the Sun in Beijing.[1]

The pouches, known as *hebao,* were used for holding scent ingredients, medicine, and small objects. They are made of fine silk satin in the shape of a gourd or a shell with auspicious motifs and the character for longevity (*shou*) embroidered in metallic and multicolor silk threads. The exquisite design and craftsmanship are indicative of the Jiaqing period. LJ

1. Yunlu et al. (1766) 2004, chap. 4, pp. 108, 110.

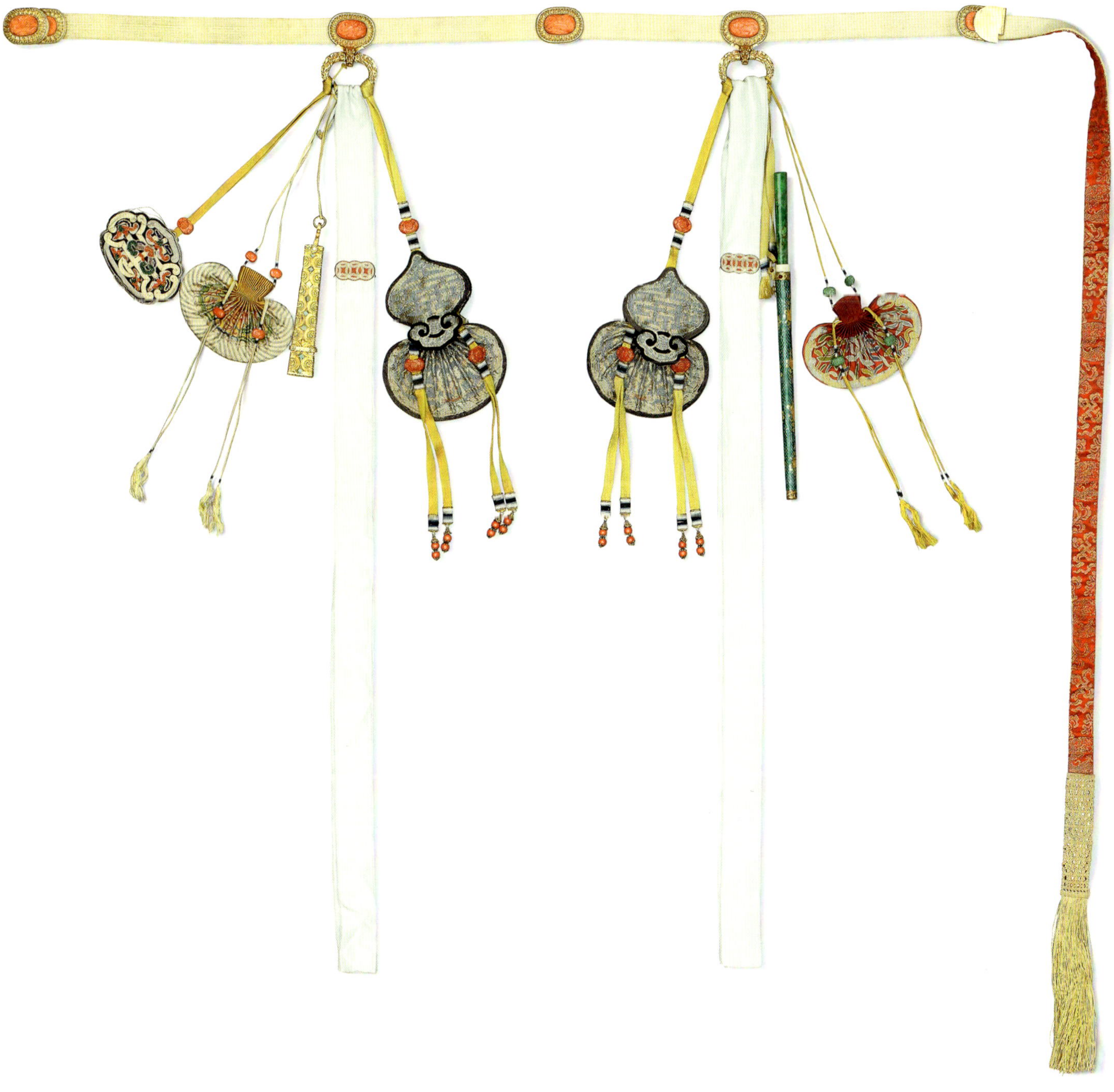

8 清乾隆 孝賢純皇后朝服像軸 絹本設色

Portrait of Empress Xiaoxianchun in Ceremonial Robe, 1736–38

Attributed to Lang Shining (Giuseppe Castiglione, Italian, 1688–1766)

Qing dynasty, Qianlong period (1736–95)

Hanging scroll; ink and color on silk

H. 194.8 cm (76.69 in.), W. 116.2 cm (45.75 in.)

Palace Museum, Gu.8769

Lady Fucha, born in 1712 to a prominent Manchu family, was married to Prince Hongli in 1727. Her husband ascended the throne as Emperor Qianlong in 1736, and she became empress in 1738. She was renowned for her frugality and was regarded as a model empress. In 1748, after a series of rites at Mount Tai and Confucius's Temple, she died at the age of thirty-seven in Dezhou, Shandong Province, during her return trip home.[1]

In this large full-length portrait, the empress sits on a dragon throne in an elaborate ceremonial robe. She gazes directly at the viewer. Fine facial features allude to her beauty, talent, and grace, and an elevated crown decorated with gold and pearls conceals her hair. She wears three strands of pearls and corals, a headband, a collar band, and a red silk ribbon. The rich jewelry, intricate embroidery, and splendid color reveal the noble status of the empress.

Although unsigned and undated, this painting was possibly completed between the emperor's enthronement in 1736 and the coronation of the empress in 1738.[2] The work's fine detail, colorful palette, and atmospheric perspective suggest that the portrait was painted by Giuseppe Castiglione (1688–1766), an Italian artist and Jesuit missionary known as Lang Shining. A native of Milan, he arrived in Beijing in November 1715 and began to serve in the court of Emperor Kangxi (r. 1662–1722). Unlike his later works, in which he rendered only faces and left background details to his assistants, this large portrait is believed to have been painted solely by Lang Shining.[3] This eighteenth-century portrait represents a new style of court painting, integrating Western oil-painting techniques with traditional Chinese ink-painting elements. LJ

1. Zhao et al. 1927, chap. 214.
2. Chen 2006, 99.
3. Nie 2001, 1–27.

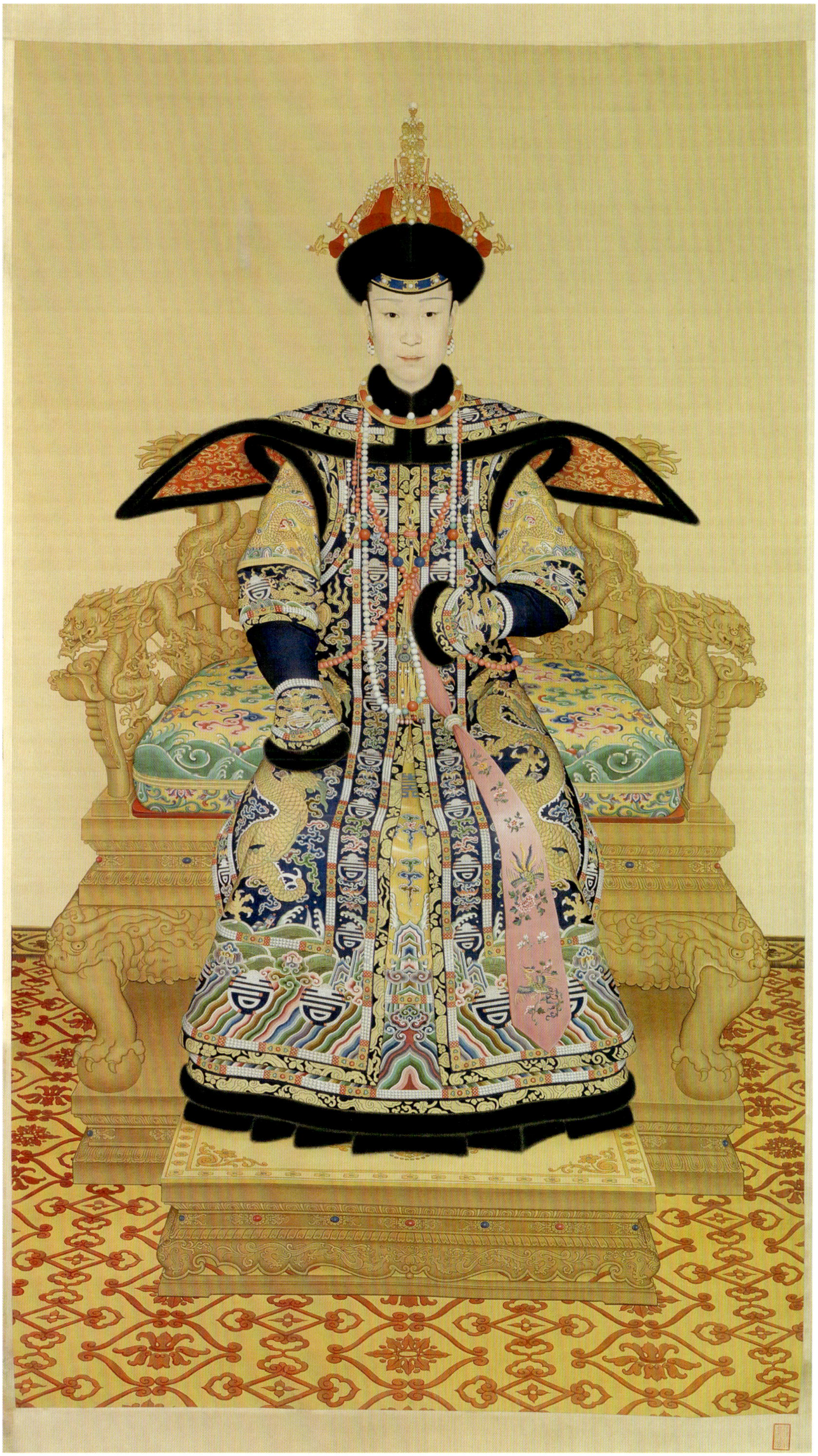

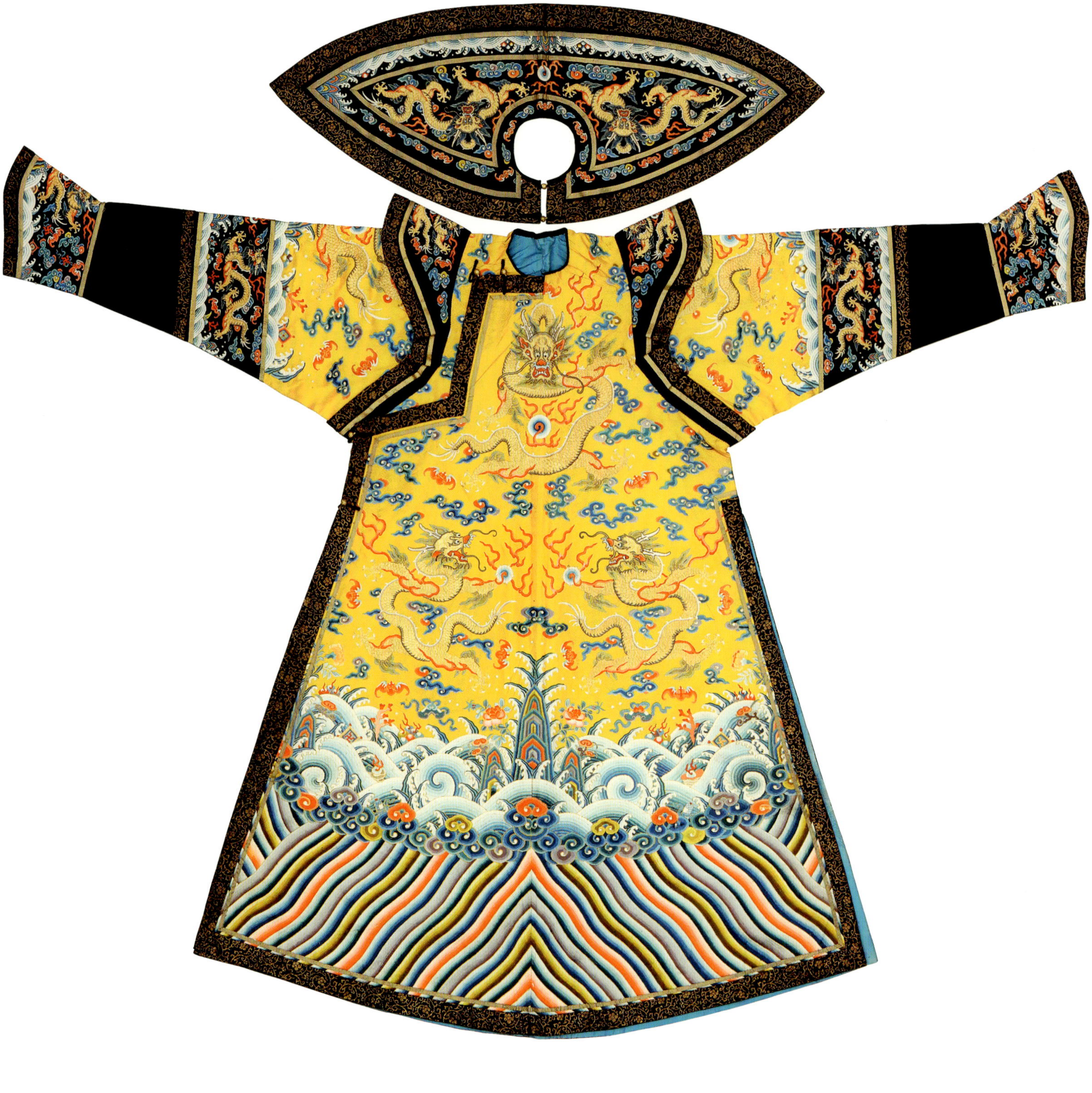

9 清嘉慶 明黃色紗繡五彩雲蝠金龍女夾朝袍

Imperial Robe with Dragons, Clouds, and Bats

Qing dynasty, Jiaqing period (1796–1820)

Gauze, embroidery, metal buttons

Body: L. 135 cm (53.15 in.); Overall sleeves: L. 194 cm (76.38 in.)

Palace Museum, Gu.42496

This lavishly embroidered yellow robe was considered the most formal court attire (*chaofu*) for the empress or the dowager empress. It formed a complete outfit (*lifu*) when worn along with a skirt underneath and a long tunic as an outer garment (cat. no. 8). Appropriate for spring or autumn, the robe was worn at some of the most important functions, including ancestor worship, imperial women's inaugurals, and formal family banquets. However, state sacrifices, inaugurations of emperors, and receptions for foreign envoys excluded women.

Made of fine yellow gauze, this A-line robe features a right placket, a round collar, tapered cuffs, reinforced shoulder pads, and an indigo satin trim woven with gold thread. The robe's design references Manchu nomadic culture, with cuffs shaped like horse hooves, pads around the collar symbolizing a saddle, and a cape collar shaped like a bow. The garment is lined with bluish-white gauze woven with dragon roundels.

The primary embroidered design depicts dragons, sixteen in total, arranged in confronting, striking, and ascending poses on the front and back panels and on the lining. Other auspicious motifs include the lotus, chrysanthemum, the Eight Treasures symbols, and ocean waves. The embroidery was rendered in a variety of stitches: long and short stitches (*taozhen*), satin stitches (*pingzhen*), parallel satin stitches (*qizhen),* connecting stitches (*gunzhen*), and couching stitches (*dingzhen*).

An inscription, written in ink on a cotton tag attached to the collar, notes a location for imperial storage in the Palace of Earthly Tranquility (Kunninggong) in the inner court. LJ

Inscription: 西暖殿 *xinuandian* (west-side hall)

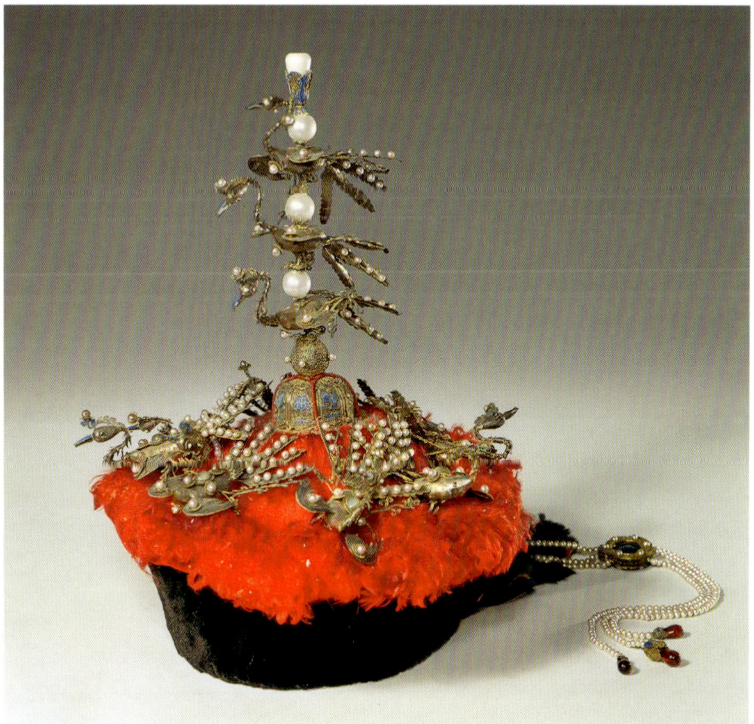

10 清乾隆 點翠鑲珠后妃朝冠

Crown for Imperial Women

Qing dynasty, Qianlong period (1736–95)

Sable, floss, cat's-eye stones, pearls, simulated pearls, gilt birch bark, gilt copper, feathers, glass, lapis lazuli, cotton

H. 37 cm (14.6 in.), Dia. 27 cm (10.63 in.)

Palace Museum, Gu.60084

A finial depicting three phoenixes decorated with large pearls surmounts this crown made of sable and red floss. Crouching on the red floss are seven phoenixes and one pheasant (*zhi*), all made of gilt birch bark and decorated with kingfisher feathers and pearls. Three strands of pearls hang from the tail of the pheasant. The strands feature a unifying lapis lazuli pendant and three glass beads. The choice of sable indicates that this crown was worn to formal ceremonies during the winter.

According to *Illustrated Ritual Implements of the Imperial Dynasty,* only an empress dowager, an empress, or an imperial royal consort could wear a hat decorated with cat's-eye stones and the grouping of seven phoenixes and one zhi, as featured in this crown. The pendant hanging from the back also identifies the specific status of the wearer. Traditionally, an empress dowager or empress would wear a pendant with five strands of pearls divided into three sections. A pendant that divides three strands of pearls into two sections, as presented here, was designed for an imperial royal consort (*huangguifei*) or a royal consort (*guifei*).[1] LJ

1. Yunlu et al. (1766) 2004, chap. 3, pp. 245, 263–64.

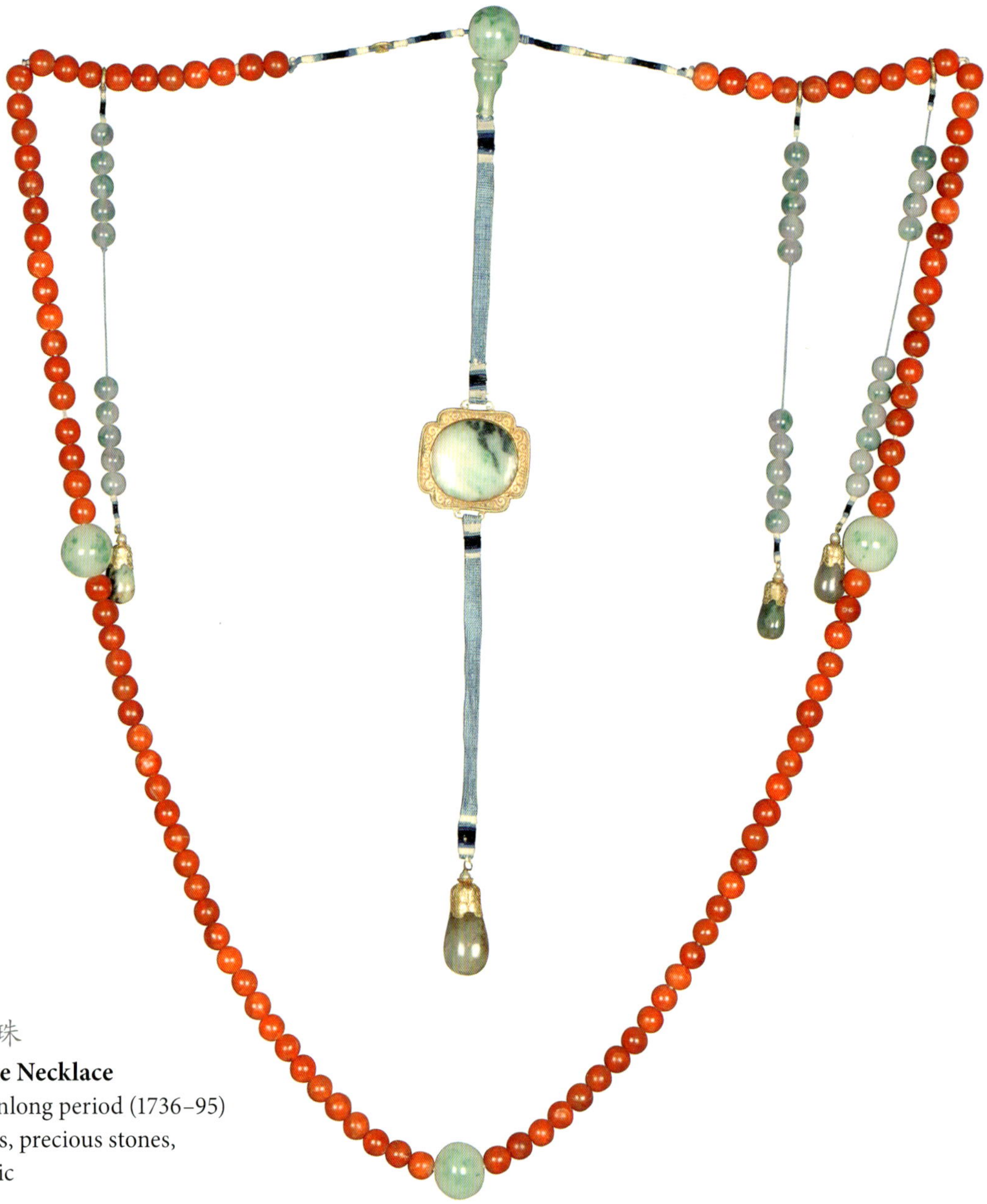

11 清乾隆 瑪瑙朝珠

Ceremonial Agate Necklace

Qing dynasty, Qianlong period (1736–95)
Agate, jadeite, glass, precious stones, gilt silver, silk fabric

Circ. 152 cm (59.8 in.)
Palace Museum, Gu.71772-2/27

Derived from a Buddhist rosary, this necklace consists of 108 agate beads, equally divided among four glass beads. A long blue silk ribbon with a large pendant and jadeite hangs in the middle, flanked by three small strands of ten glass beads and a jadeite each. This type of court necklace was worn with the strands of beads placed in the front and the long silk ribbon positioned in back. According to *Illustrated Ritual Implements of the Imperial Dynasty,* an agate necklace with a yellow ribbon was worn by an emperor during ritual services at the Altar of the Earth.[1] However, a necklace with a blue ribbon was not specified in the dress code.

As early as 1696, the Qing court established a glassmaking workshop under the supervision of European missionaries. Soon the workshop was able to make products that imitated precious stones, such as jadeite.[2] In 1730, Emperor Yongzheng (r. 1723–35) revised the clothing code, allowing colored glass as a replacement for precious stones traditionally used in various ritual jewelry. LJ

1. Yunlu et al. (1766) 2004, chap. 4, p. 107.
2. Feng 1996, 102.

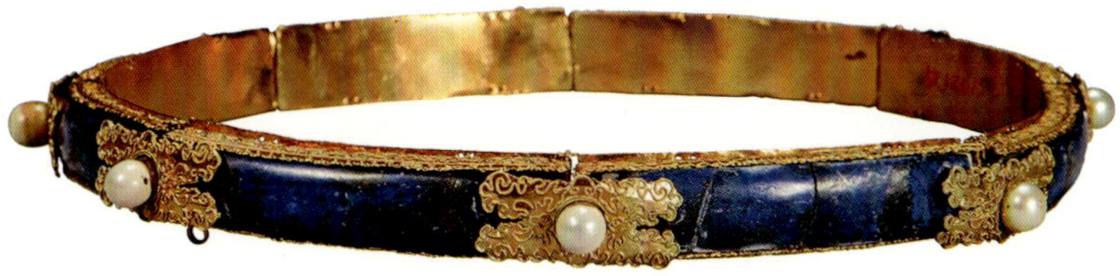

12 清乾隆 金鑲青金石金約

Gold and Lapis Lazuli Headband

Qing dynasty, Qianlong period (1736–95)

Gold, pearls, lapis lazuli

Outer Dia. 21.50 cm (8.46 in.)

Palace Museum, Gu.12015

This headband, a formal accessory for court fashion, was crafted with eight sections of lapis lazuli embedded in gold strips. Gold ornaments and stabilizing pearls join the sections. Originally, a three-strand pendant of pearls, now lost, hung from a loop on the back of the band. This headband was worn underneath a ceremonial crown, displaying the intense blue of the precious stones on the forehead. The number of sections of lapis lazuli on the headband conveys the owner's court status. According to the Qing ritual manual, headbands with eight sections belonged to an emperors' consorts.[1] Only the empress dowager or the empress wore a thirteen-section headband (cat. no. 8). LJ

Inscription, written in ink on yellow tag: 金鑲催生石頭箍一圍, 嵌無光東珠八顆, 共重六兩 (gold headband with lapis lazuli, encrusted with eight opaque *dongzhu* pearls, weight of six *liang* [223.8 grams])

1. Yunlu et al. (1766) 2004, chap. 6, p. 284.

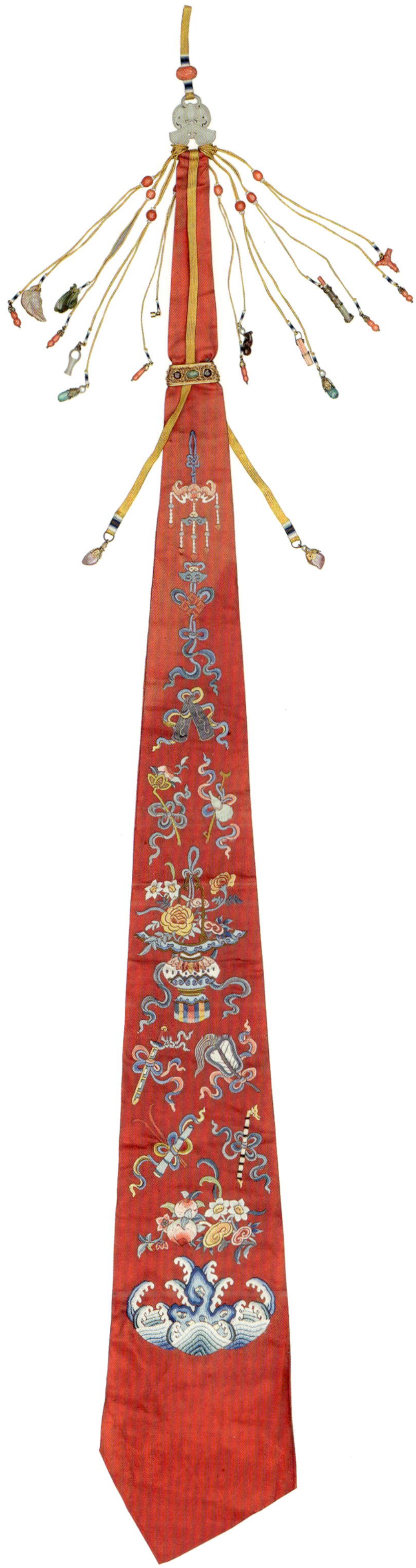

13 清 金箍鑲寶石紅緞彩帨

Ceremonial Ribbon with Gold and Precious Stones, 18th–19th century

Qing dynasty

Satin with embroidery, gold, silver, red rubies, jadeite, nephrite, tourmaline, turquoise, coral, seashells, pearls, goldstone

L. 110 cm (43.31 in.)

Palace Museum, Gu.12162

As part of a female's formal court attire, this ribbon, known as *caiyue,* was worn by attaching its top hoop to the second button of a court robe, as exhibited in the portrait of Empress Xiaoxianchun (cat. no. 8). Made of intense red satin and lined with yellow silk, the ribbon was reserved for celebrations such as birthdays or New Year's Day.

Accordingly, the tapered ribbon is densely embroidered with the Eight Daoist Immortals' magic attributes, known as Concealed Eight Immortals (*anbaxian*), consisting of castanet, gourd, lotus, flower basket, fan, sword, flute, and bamboo musical tube. Other motifs embroidered on the satin include bats, chimes, peaches fungi, mountains, and ocean waves, symbol of prosperity and immortality. Suspended from a jade chime on the top are various yellow strands of tassels and gemstones such as coral, turquoise, jade, and goldstone carved or in shapes of the same eight attributes. A small gold band encrusted with red rubies and jadeites serves as a loop on the top of the ribbon. LJ

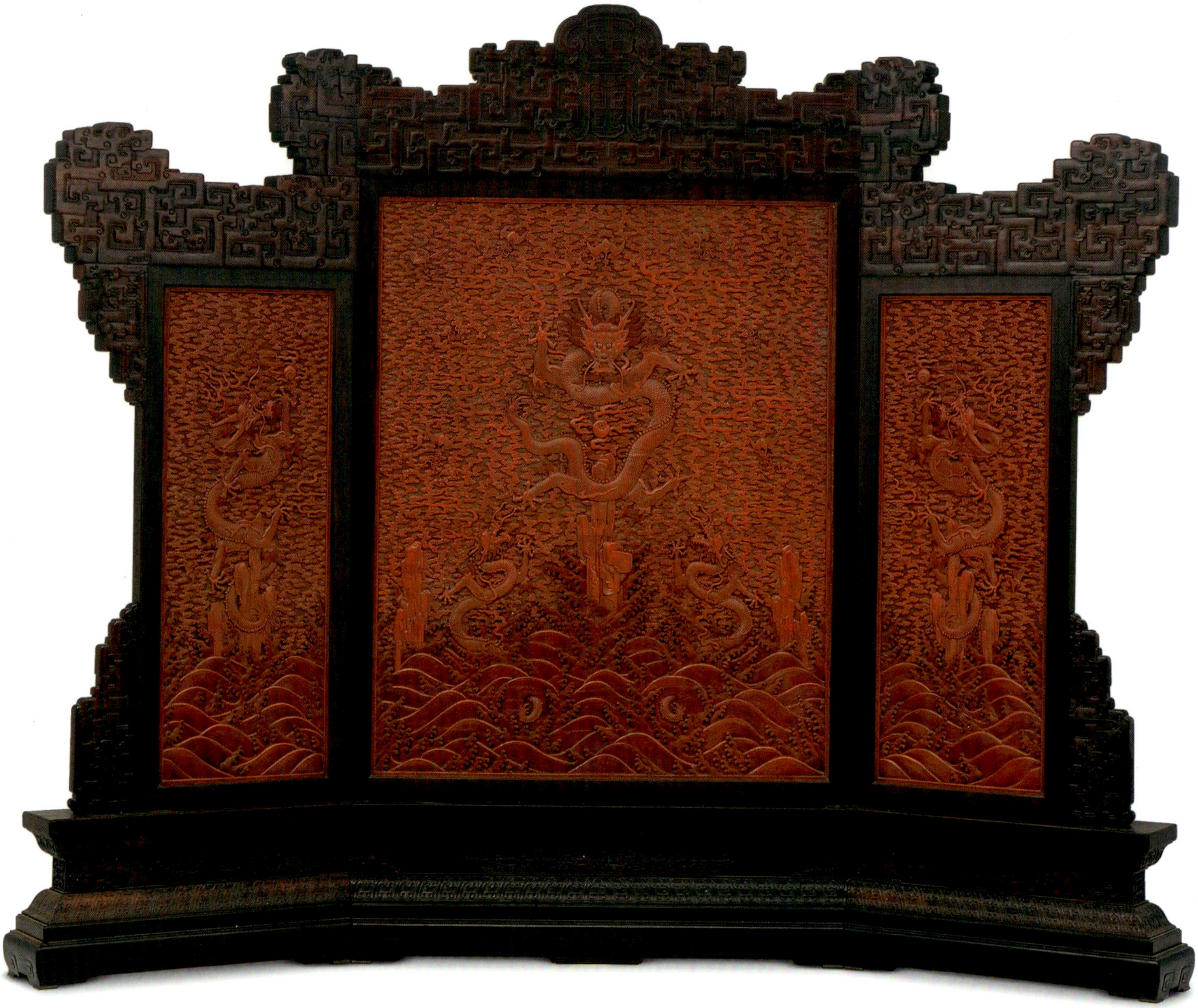

14.1 清乾隆 紫檀木剔紅雲龍紋圍屏
Screen with Dragons amid Clouds
Qing dynasty, Qianlong period (1736–95)
Carved red lacquer on *nanmu* wood, *zitan* frame
H. 264 cm (103.94 in.), W. 324 cm (127.56 in.)
Palace Museum, Xin.178206

14.2 清乾隆 紫檀木邊剔紅雲龍紋寶座 紫檀木漆面腳踏
Throne with Dragons amid Clouds
Qing dynasty, Qianlong period (1736–95)
Carved red lacquer on *nanmu* wood, *zitan* frame
Throne: H. 104 cm (40.94 in.), L. 130 cm (51.18 in.), W. 90 cm (35.43 in.)
Footrest: H. 14 cm (5.51 in.), L. 90 cm (35.43 in.), W. 33 cm (13 in.)
Palace Museum, Gu.208789

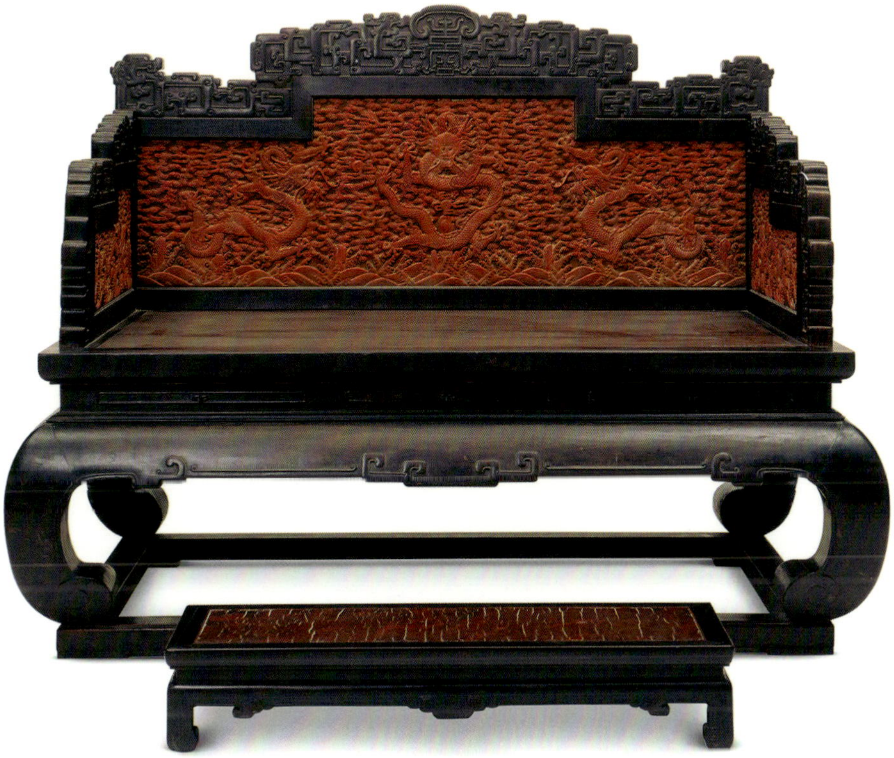

This red lacquered throne and its matching screen once furnished the Palace of Eternal Longevity (Yongshougong), one of the twelve residential chambers in the inner court. The screen was constructed with three *nanmu* panels and frames of *zitan* wood, a rare tropical hardwood from the rosewood family. In a scene carved on the center panel, a large dragon leads two smaller dragons (*canglongjiaozi*) amid clouds, symbolizing an emperor leading young princes. Similar carvings decorate the back and side panels of the throne, which is supported by curved legs.

A throne coupled with a screen behind it symbolized the emperor and provided a focal point in the center of primary halls in the Forbidden City. Although no Ming furnishings in this style survive today, some portraits of Ming emperors reveal a similar pairing (cat. no. 2). During the Qing dynasty, around 1682, Emperor Kangxi established throne rooms in the twelve chambers belonging to the empress and consorts. The rooms remained unchanged until 1742 when Emperor Qianlong refurnished them.[1] LJ

1. Wang 2011a, 109–10.

15 清乾隆 掐絲琺瑯甪端香熏

Censers in the Form of Mythical Animals

Qing dynasty, Qianlong period (1736–95)

Cloisonné enamel on copper alloy

H. 34.5 cm (13.58 in.), L. 22 cm (8.66 in.), W. 21 cm (8.27 in.)
Palace Museum, Gu.119749 and Gu.119750

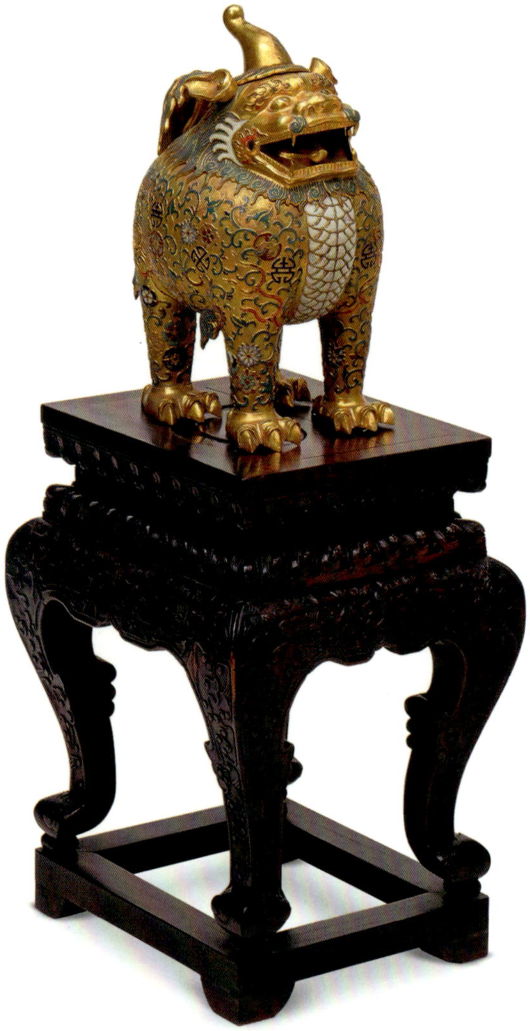

16 清乾隆款 掐絲琺瑯立鶴香爐

Pair of Incense Burners in Shapes of Cranes

Qing dynasty, Qianlong mark and period (1736–95)

Cloisonné enamel on copper alloy

H. 93 cm (36.61 in), Base Dia. 31 cm (12.2 in.)
Palace Museum, Gu.119526 and Gu.119527

Mark: 大清乾隆年製 (Made in the Qianlong reign of the Great Qing dynasty)

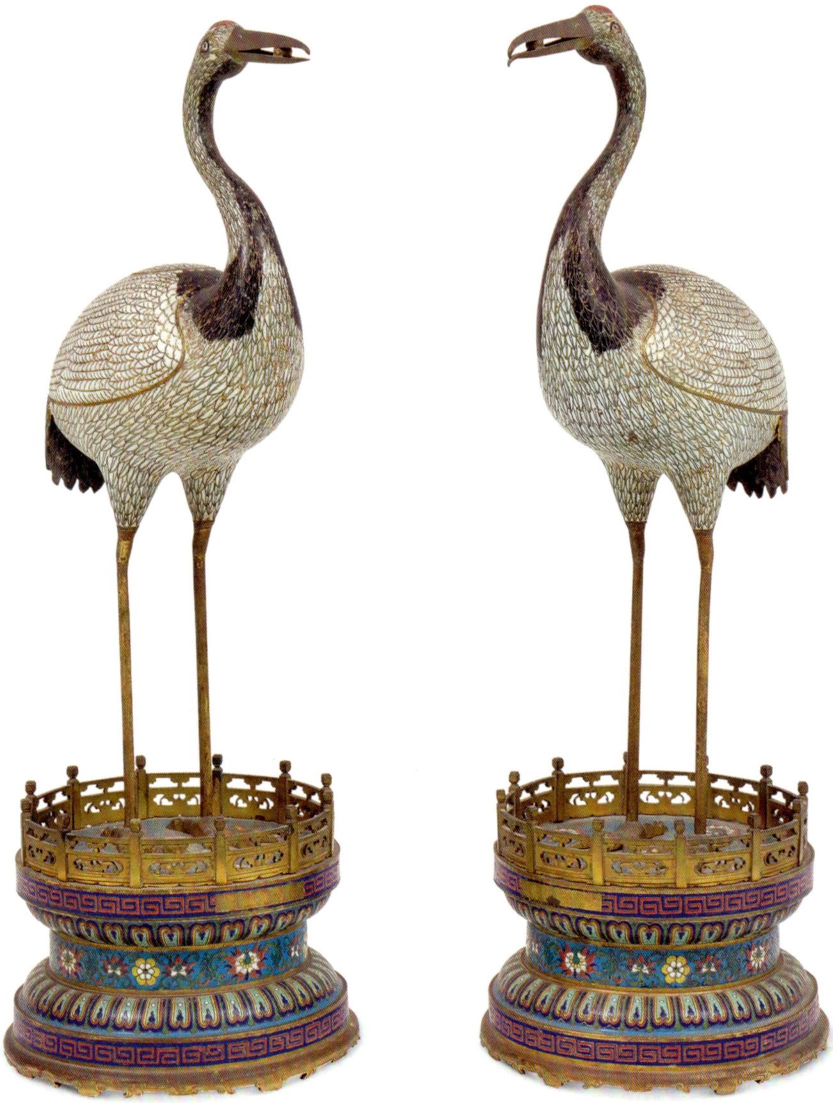

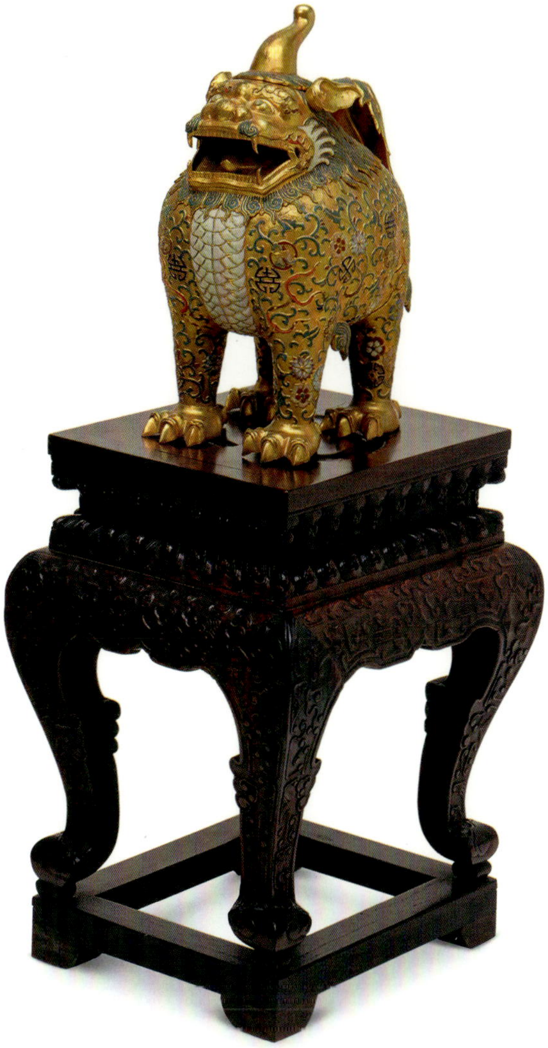

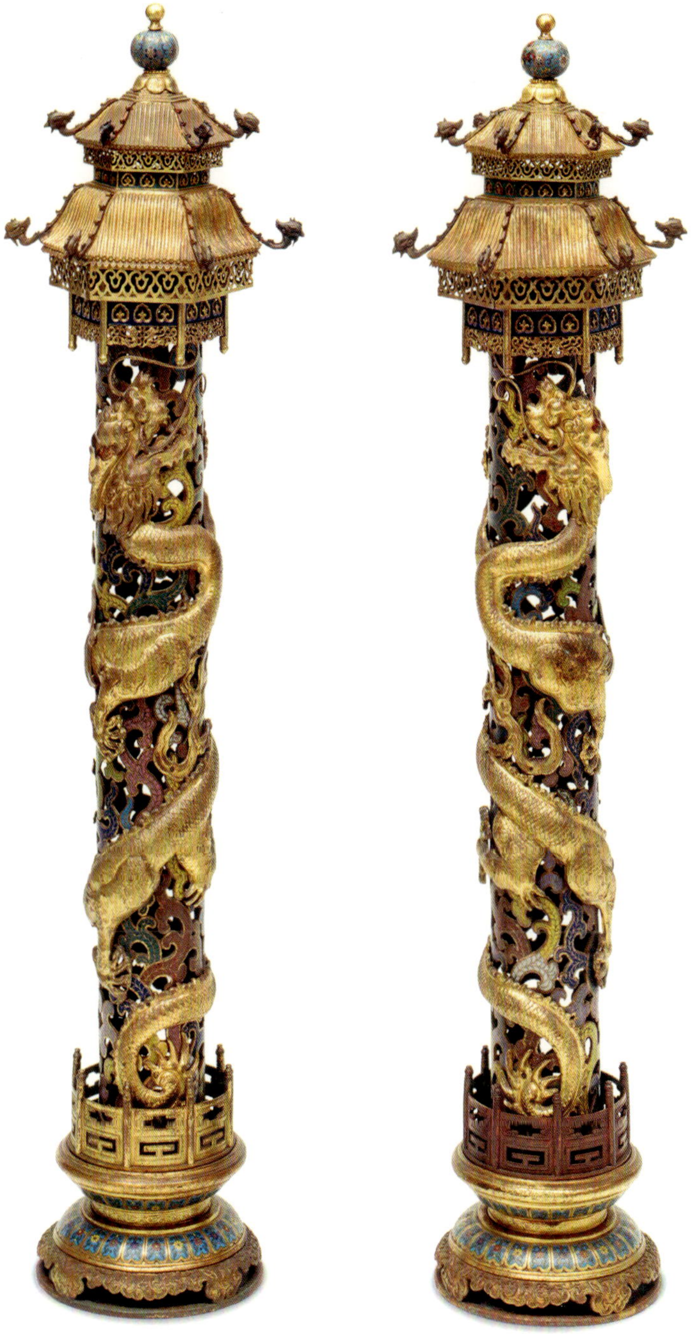

17 清乾隆 掐絲琺瑯鏤空勾蓮蟠龍紋香筒

Pair of Pavilion Incense Burners

Qing dynasty, Qianlong period (1736–95)

Cloisonné enamel on copper

H. 110 cm (43.31 in.)

Palace Museum, Gu.119364 and Gu.119366

These three sets are fine examples of incense burners that flanked the throne and screen in a palace hall. Made of cloisonné enamels on copper, the animals have hollowed bodies, open mouths, and removable parts. The *luduan* (center) has a lion's body with a unicorn head and is adorned with auspicious swastika motifs and longevity (*shou*) characters. In Chinese legend, this mythical beast runs ten thousand miles a day and speaks multiple languages. The pavilion incense burners (right) are crafted with openwork design of an ascending dragon. Luduan censers and pavilion burners were displayed exclusively for the emperor and symbolized justice, transparency, and imperial power. Inscribed crane burners (left) are extremely rare in the collection of the Palace Museum.

Incense was made primarily from plants, animal secretions, and resins, depending on the season and function. The most valuable types of incense used in the Ming and Qing palace include *nanmu*, agar wood, sandalwood, and frankincense. Incense in various forms, such as sticks, coils, cones, or balls, could be placed and lit inside the burner. Some incense that could not come in contact with direct heat would be placed on mica and heated indirectly by charcoal imbedded under ash. Such openwork burners were used for natural incense, such as sandalwood, or for lighting Tibetan incense, creating smoke that would ascend in soft clouds around the palace hall. LJ

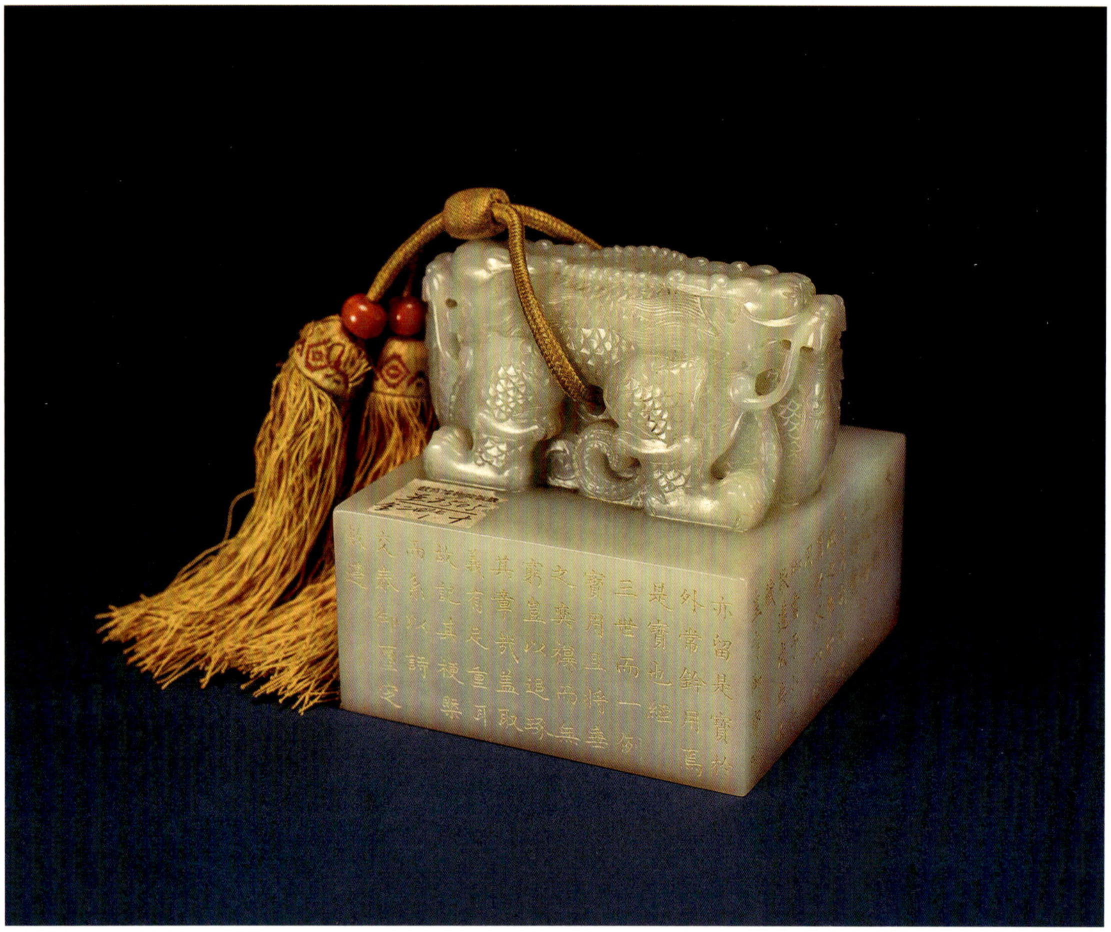

18 清嘉慶 青玉交龍紐"敬天勤民"寶璽

Emperor's Seal with Dragon Knob, approx. 1797
Qing dynasty, Jiaqing period (1796–1820)
Nephrite, gold pigment, silk, coral
H. 9.2 cm (3.62 in.), Base L. and W. 9.7 cm (3.82 in.)
Palace Museum, Gu.1166798

An emperor's seal represents the supreme power of the emperor and his empire. Engraved on white jade, this seal bears four Chinese characters in the seal script, *jing tian qin min,* which means "honor heaven, dedicated to the people." The carved knob features a pair of dragons, the symbol of the emperor. A poem by Emperor Qianlong is incised on the four sides. This seal was used when issuing imperial edicts to provincial officials.

Emperor Kangxi (r. 1662–1722) ordered the creation of the first "jing tian qin min" seal, which was made of wood. He used the four-character phrase as a guide to rule the country. When succeeding his father on the throne, Emperor Yongzheng (r. 1723–35) ordered another seal with the same characters carved out of jade. Like his father and grandfather, Emperor Qianlong (r. 1736–95) treasured the "jing tian qin min" seal and requested the inclusion of a poem in 1748. Unfortunately, in 1797, a fire struck the Palace of Heavenly Purity (Qianqinggong), and the seal was severely damaged. Immediately after the fire, Emperor Qianlong ordered the seal reproduced in the same style.

As Emperor Qianlong's poem states, the seal's value rests not in the jade but in the profound meaning of the characters. These words reflect Emperor Kangxi's idealistic governing philosophy. The seal became a model and symbol for his two successors, who sought harmony between divinity and society. LJ

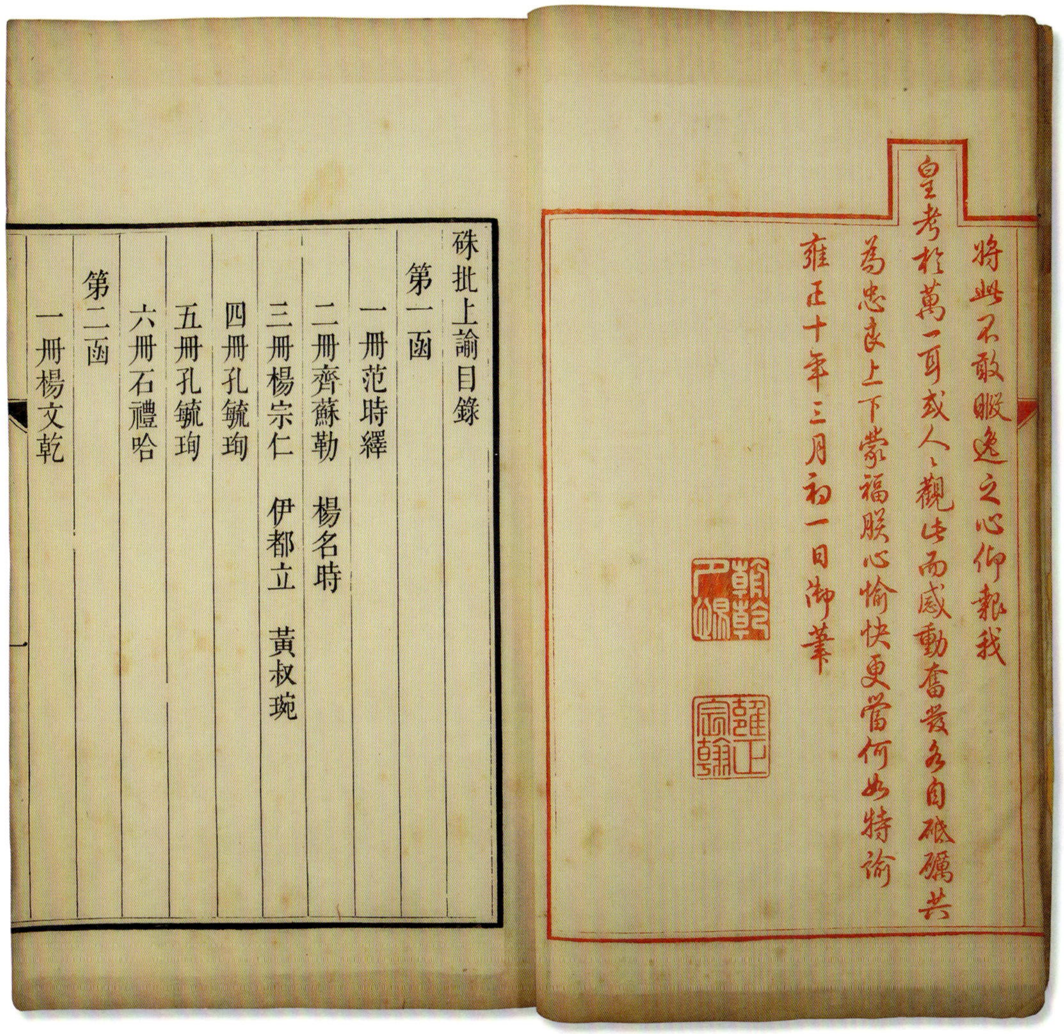

19 清雍正-乾隆 世宗胤禛敕编 硃批諭旨 一函六冊

Imperial Commentaries in Red Ink, 1732–38

Qing dynasty, Yongzheng period (1723–35)–Qianlong period (1736–95)

Six woodblock-printed books; black and red ink on paper

Book: L. 28.4 cm (11.2 in.), W. 18 cm (7.1 in.); Image: L. 20.5 cm (8.1 in.), W. 14.6 cm (5.1 in.)
Palace Museum, Shu.1222-1/112

Imperial Commentaries in Red Ink contains 112 volumes and 360 chapters of woodblock-printed books, featuring more than seven thousand official memorandums written by 226 court and provincial officials and reviewed by Emperor Yongzheng (r. 1723–35) from 1723 through 1732. In his first ten-year reign, Yongzheng reviewed twenty-two thousand documents and composed eloquent commentaries in memorandums of various lengths. The publication project, initiated by Emperor Yongzheng in 1732, was completed by his son Emperor Qianlong (r. 1736–95) after his father's unexpected death. This publication reveals Emperor Yongzheng's administrative activities and his governing philosophy, as well as his renowned calligraphy. The publication also provides a primary source for the study of the political, economic, diplomatic, military, and social activities of early eighteenth-century China. The memorandums are printed in black ink; Yongzheng's commentaries appear in red. Each volume includes a preface by Yongzheng and an epilogue by Qianlong. Court officials Yunlu (1695–1767) and Ortai (1677–1745) compiled the documents and had them printed at Wuyingdian Publishing House in the Forbidden City. This first edition represents the types of paper and ink used in early eighteenth-century printmaking for the court as well as the quality of woodblock carving, printing, and binding. LJ

20 清康熙 王翬, 楊晉, 冷枚等繪 南巡圖第十二卷 返回京師 絹本設色

Returning to the Capital from the series **Emperor Kangxi's Tour of the South,** approx. 1695–98
Wang Hui (1632–1717), Yang Jin (1644–approx. 1728), Leng Mei (approx. 1670–1742)
Qing dynasty, Kangxi period (1662–1722)
Handscroll; ink and color on silk
H. 67.6 cm (2.22 ft.), W. 2612.5 cm (85.7 ft.)
Palace Museum, Xin.147550

This monumental scroll belongs to a twelve-scroll series that documents Emperor Kangxi's second journey to southern China in 1689. Emperor Kangxi visited the South six times from 1684 to 1707, but paintings record only his second tour. After Emperor Kangxi stabilized the empire in the early part of his reign, his attention turned to economic development and the well-being of the people. The 1689 tour, which began on January 8, traveled along the Grand Canal from Beijing to the country's economic center in the Jiangnan region. There, in the southern area of the Yangtze River, he visited the cities of Yangzhou, Suzhou, Hangzhou, Shaoxing, and Jiangning (today's Nanjing). In 1691, Emperor Kangxi requested that the historical journey he made two years earlier be documented in a painting. Under the supervision of the court, Wang Hui, the most renowned landscape painter of the time, was chosen as the lead artist. A native of Changshu, Jiangsu Province, Wang Hui contributed landscape scenes, and his favorite student, Yang Jin, rendered figures, animals, and architecture.[1] Recent research has identified other artists who contributed to the series of scrolls, including Leng Mei (d. 1742), Wang Yun (b. 1652), and Song Junye (d. 1713).[2]

This scroll depicts the emperor's return to Beijing on March 19, 1689. The painting

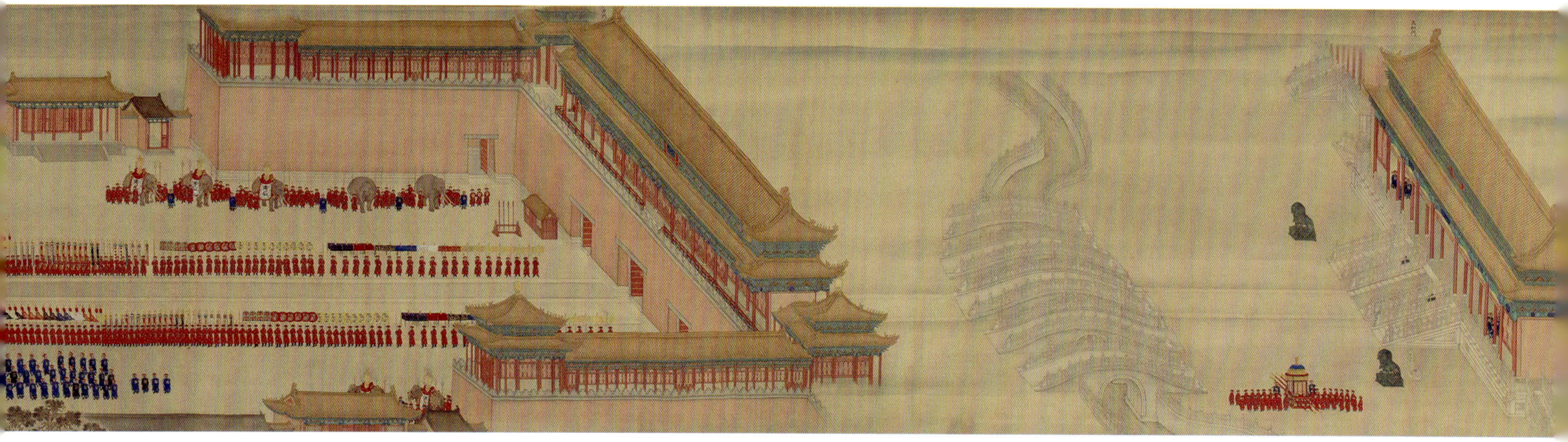

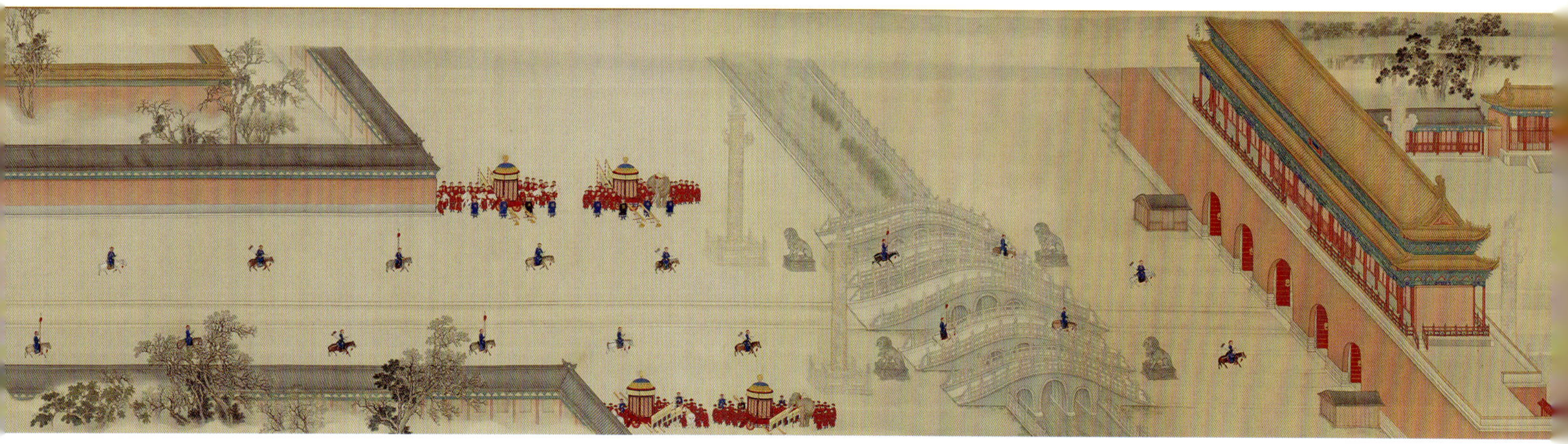

unrolls from right to left, showing the five-mile route from the imperial palace to Yongdingmen, the southern gate of Beijing. It begins with the vacant grounds of the Taihedian, where officials dressed in blue and imperial guards in red wait to greet the emperor at the Meridian Gate with ritual elephants, chariots, and banners on display on either side. Passing through the gates of Duanmen, Tian'anmen, Daqingmen, and Zhengyangmen, the procession begins with imperial guards and mounted horsemen. Outside Zhengyangmen, Emperor Kangxi sits in a sedan chair carried by eight bearers, preceded by the marching band and followed by imperial horsemen. The scroll ends with a parade of locals, including farmers, craftsmen, and merchants in the formation of four characters, *tian-zi wan-nian* ("long life of the Son of Heaven"), to celebrate the emperor's birthday on March 18. This significant painting realistically depicts not only the historical event and architectural landmarks on the central axis in Beijing but also seventeenth-century imperial ritual services in and around the Forbidden City. LJ

1. Yang 1993, 305–7, 332–36.
2. Nie 2008, 89

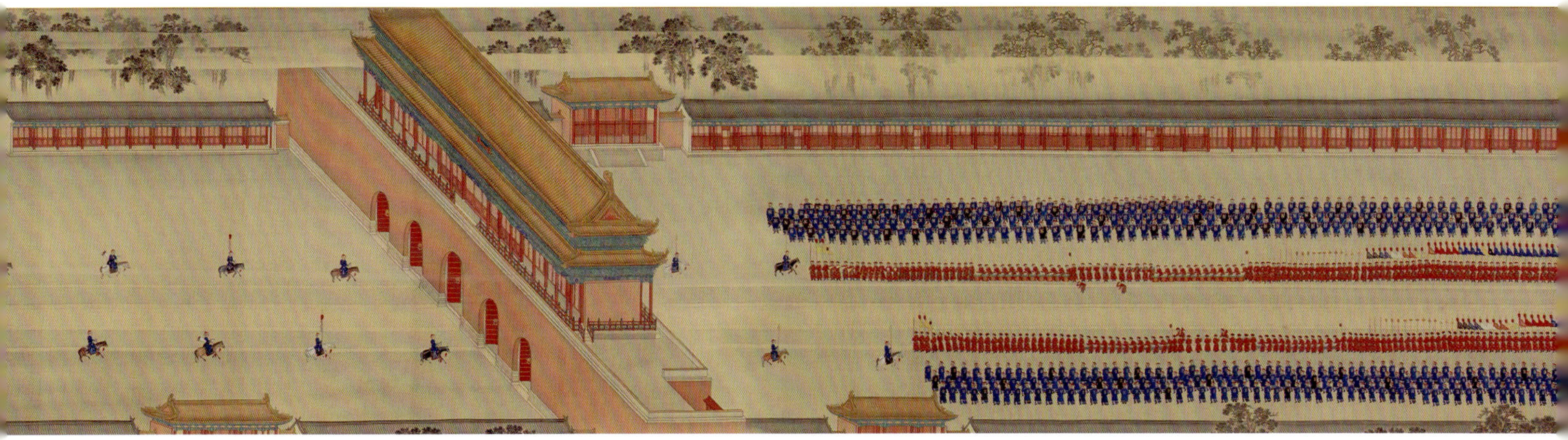

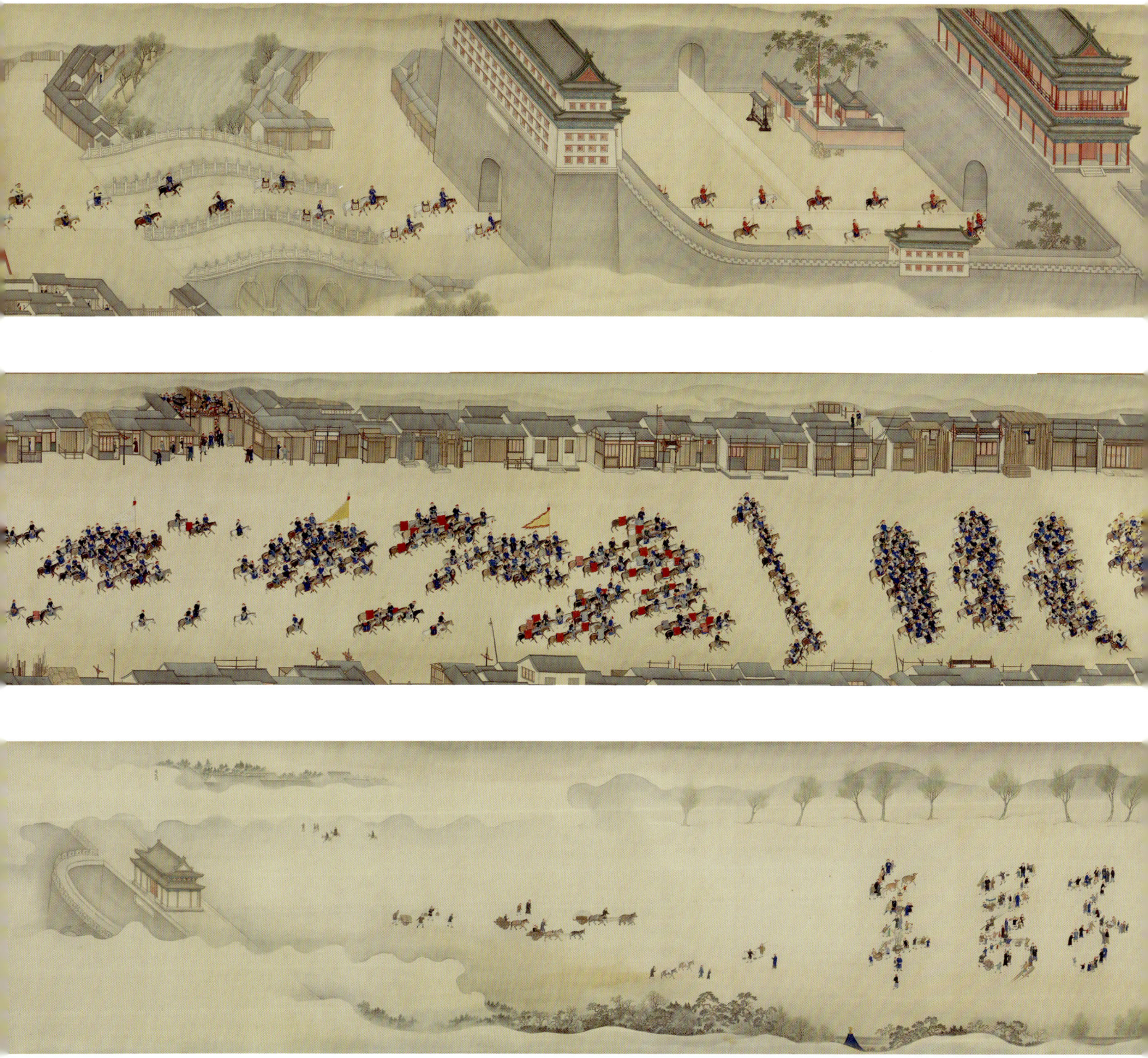

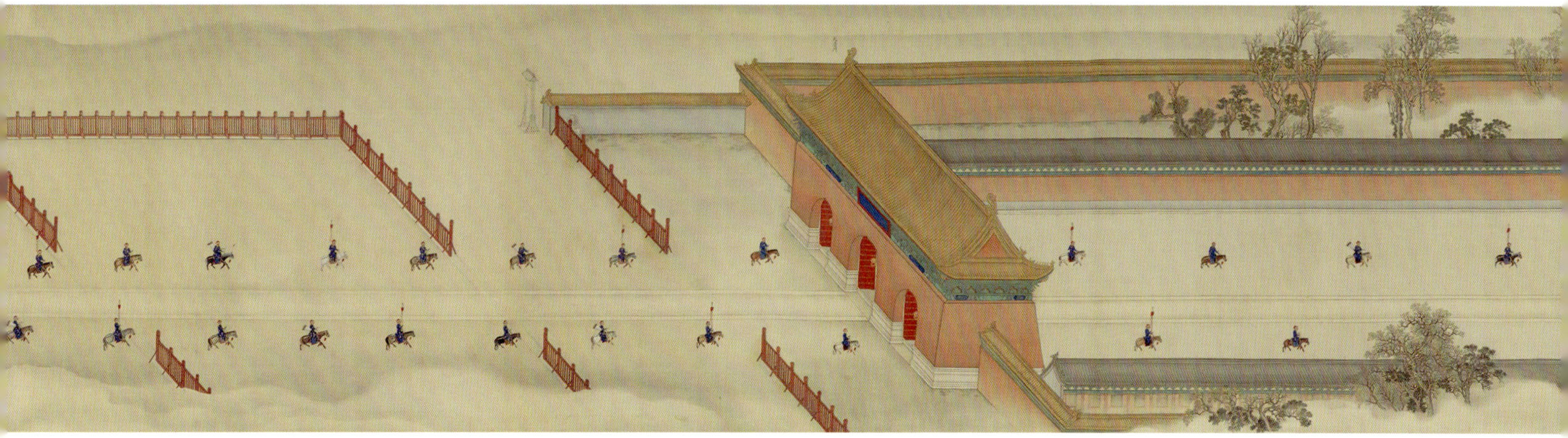

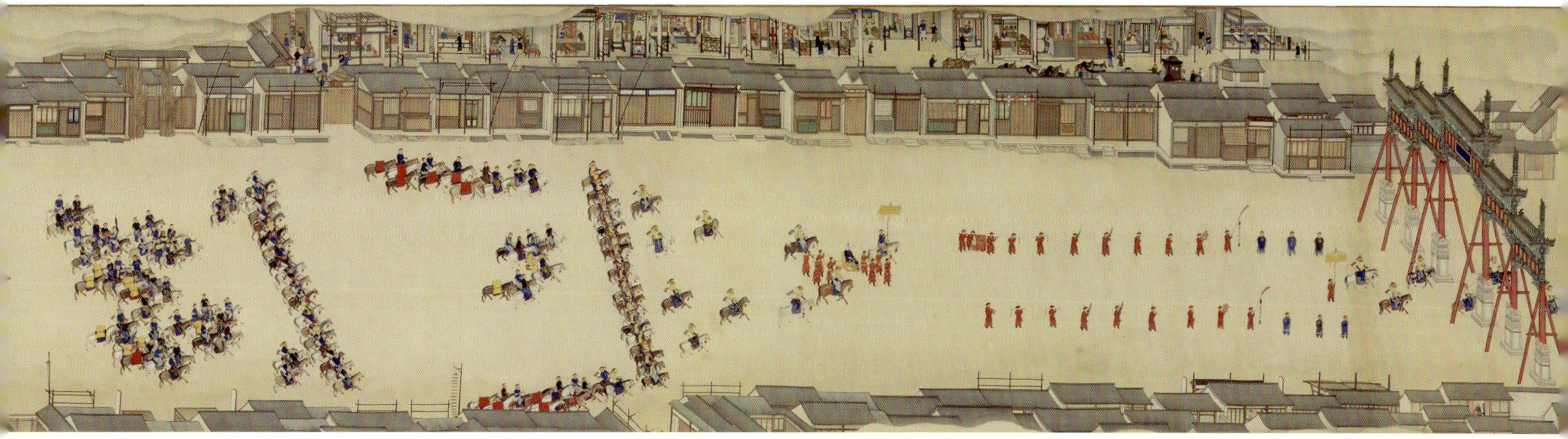

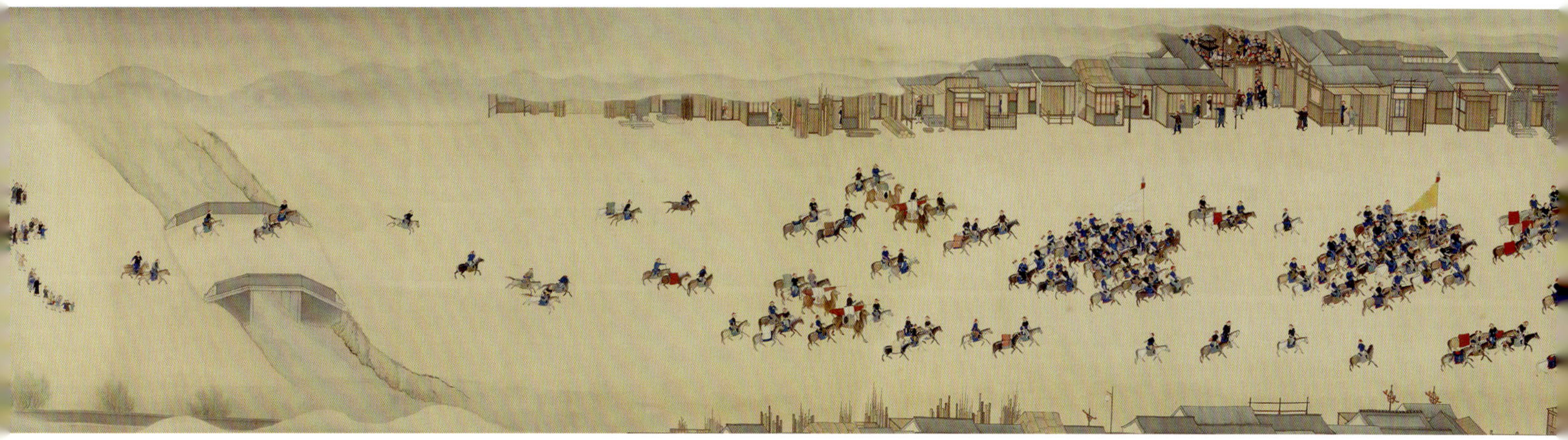

21.1 清康熙 胤禛耕織圖像冊 碌礡 絹本設色

Leveling the Farmland from the series **Farming and Weaving,** 1709–22
Qing dynasty, Kangxi period (1662–1722)
Album leaf; ink and color on silk
H. 39.4 cm (15.51 in.), W. 32.7 cm (12.87 in.)
Palace Museum, Gu.6634-5/52

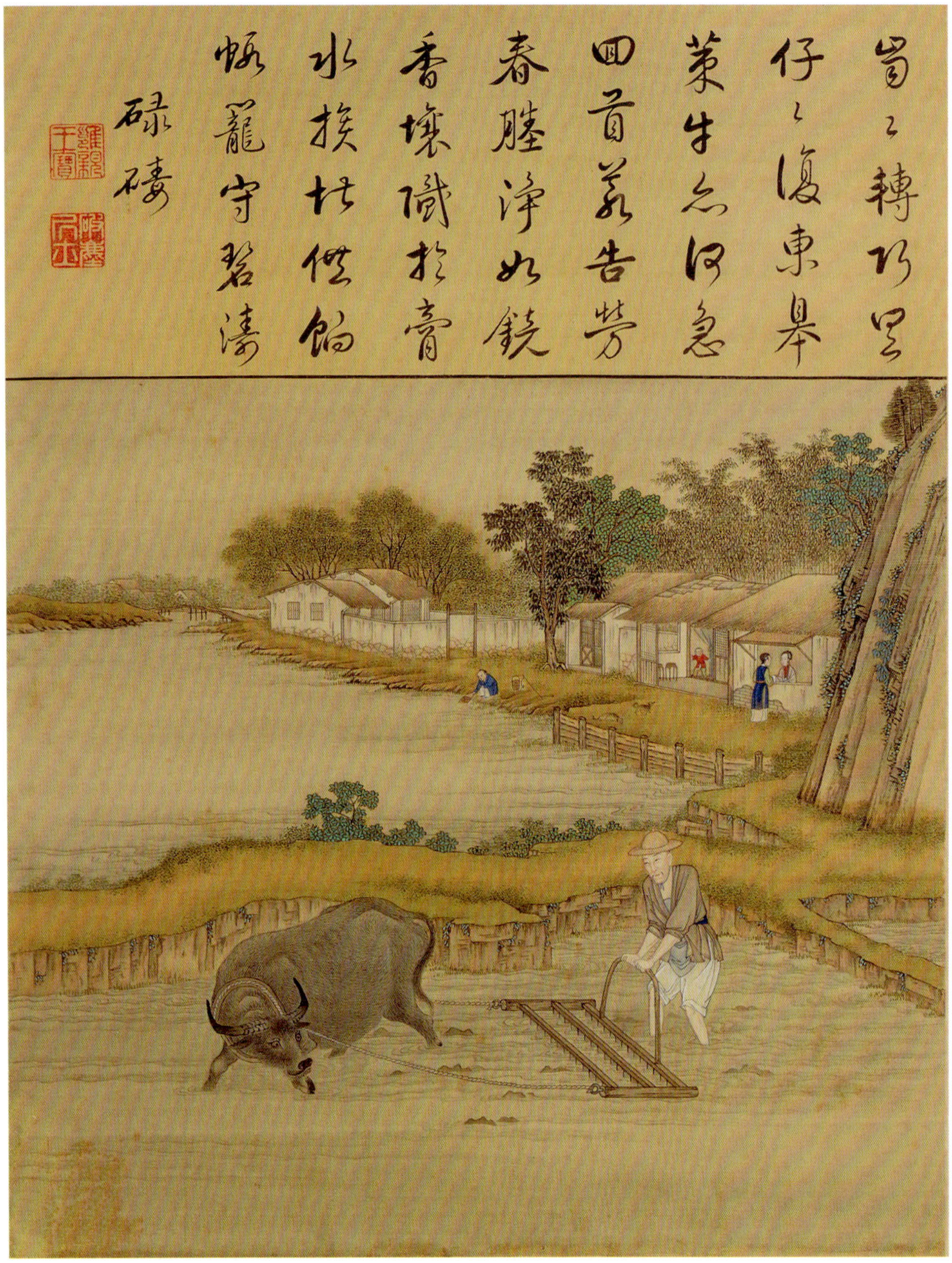

The series *Farming and Weaving* depicts countryside scenes in the Yangtze River Delta. Emperor Kangxi's son, Prince Yong (Yinzhen, 1678–1735), commissioned the forty-six paintings, equally divided between the subjects of farming and weaving. An earlier series consisted of woodblock prints and was produced in 1237 during the Song dynasty (960–1279). Many editions appeared in the centuries that followed to address the importance of agriculture and silk production.

Like the earlier editions, the paintings illustrate the farming process, from soaking seeds to irrigation and harvest, and the silk production process, from silkworm breeding to weaving, dying, and tailoring. Here, Prince Yong and his family are portrayed as commoners. Above, the prince engages a water buffalo in a muddy field. In the leaf shown to the right, his wife and consorts, dressed like village women, spool silk in a farmhouse as their children play. Socioeconomic themes, fine details,

21.2 清康熙 胤禛耕織圖像冊 絡絲 絹本設色

Spooling Silk from the series **Farming and Weaving,** 1709–22
Qing dynasty, Kangxi period (1662–1722)
Album leaf; ink and color on silk
H. 39.4 cm (15.51 in.), W. 32.7 cm (12.87 in.)
Palace Museum, Gu.6634-41/52

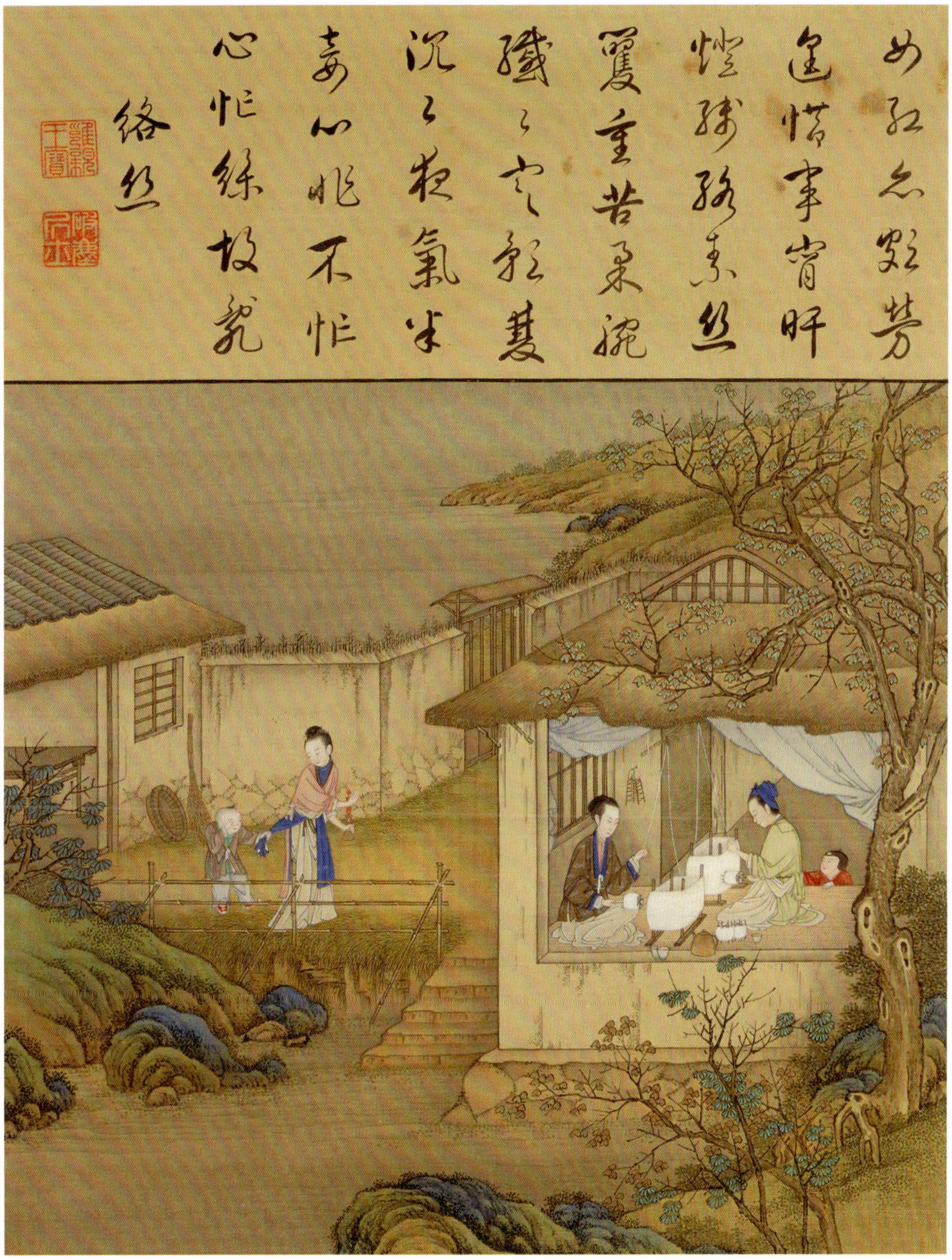

and evidence of Western influences on color and perspective make this series an excellent integration of painting, calligraphy, and poetry.

The area above each scene features a five-character poem written by Prince Yong in semicursive script followed by two seals. The seals, which reference "Prince Yong," help determine the age of these undated paintings as between 1709 and 1722, the year he ascended the throne as Emperor Yongzheng. Prince Yong offered this series as a gift to his father, Emperor Kangxi. He may have done so to win his father's favor after one of Prince Yong's brothers dishonored the title of crown prince in 1712, leaving the remaining brothers to vye for imperial honor. LJ

Seals: 雍亲王寶 *Yong qinwang bao* (the treasure of Prince Yong); 破塵居士 *Pochen jushi* (Lay Buddhist Beyond Worldly Affairs)

22.1 清乾隆 皇朝禮器圖式 皇帝冬朝服 內府繪本 絹本設色

Emperor's Robe from the series **Illustrated Ritual Implements of the Imperial Dynasty,** 1777–82
Originally compiled by Yunlu (1695–1767)
Emperor's preface inscribed by Liang Guozhi (1723–1786)
Qing dynasty, Qianlong period (1736–95)
Album leaf; ink and color on silk
Each leaf: L. 41 cm (16.14 in.), W. 39 cm (15.35 in.)
Palace Museum, Gu.6116-30/92-14

Illustrated Ritual Implements of the Imperial Dynasty is a court-sponsored multivolume work on state rituals that contains six sections: sacrificial offerings, scientific devices, ritual costumes, musical instruments, parade regalia, and arms and armor. The manual provides instructions on how to identify, produce, and use ritual implements. With similar design and color, the dragon robe illustrated here resembles Emperor Qianlong's embroidered dragon robe (cat. no. 4).

This ritual manual was compiled under the supervision of Yunlu (1695–1767), the sixteenth son of Emperor Kangxi and an officer in charge of ritual affairs in the court. In 1766, the court published a printed version of the manual, which was later included in the *Complete Library in Four Sections* (*Siku Quanshu*) in 1782.

The manual contains ninety-two volumes and thirteen hundred entries. Each entry features an illustration and a description, which includes a brief history, dimensions, mediums, design, and the designated owner. The descriptions were written in standard script (*kaishu*). Although undated, the series begins with Emperor Qianlong's original preface[1] of 1759 written by court official Liang Guozhi (1723–1786). Liang was summoned to Beijing in 1773 and appointed as the deputy chief editor of the *Siku Quanshu* in 1777.[2] This illustrated manual was most likely compiled alongside the *Siku Quanshu* project. LJ

1. Yunlu et al. (1766) 2004, chap. 4.
2. Zhao et al. 1927, chap. 214.

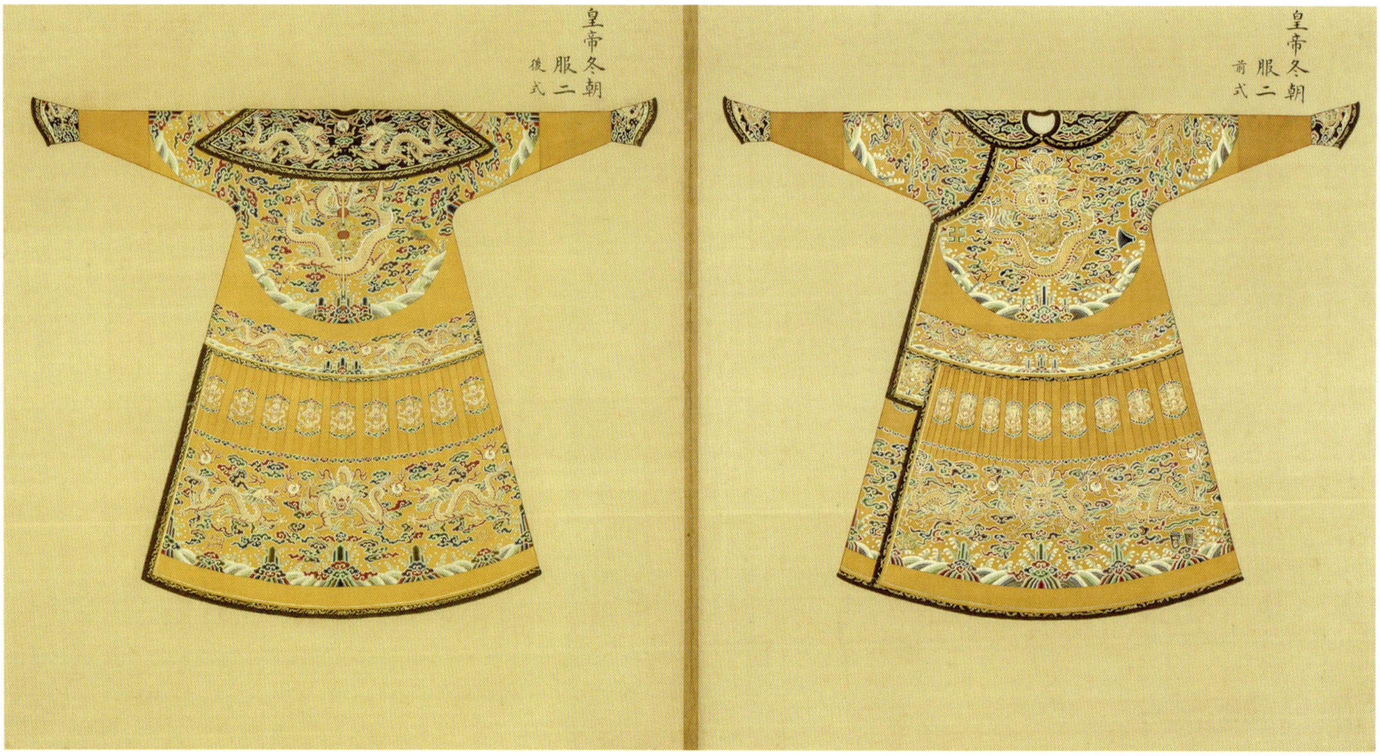

22.2. 清乾隆 皇朝禮器圖式 皇帝法駕鹵簿禮輿 内府繪本 絹本設色

Emperor's Ritual Carriage

Palace Museum, Gu.6116-68/92-20

This sedan chair, or palanquin, was constructed with a four-pillar chamber, a two-tier roof, and carrying poles lacquered in red. Golden dragons, a golden finial, and a canopy embroidered with dragons and clouds surmount the roof. The seventeen-foot-long carriage poles are painted with gold dragons and mounted with gilt-copper dragons. The chair was carried by placing the poles on the shoulders of sixteen bearers, eight on each side. The curtain, which opens in the front, conceals the carriage on three sides. Its fabric ranged from satin to gauze or wool, depending on the season. The windows were covered with blue gauze in the summer and glass in the winter. Calligraphy on the left describes the design and function of the carriage.

Illustrated Ritual Implements of the Imperial Dynasty records ten types of sedan carriages designed for the emperor to use for different functions. This carriage, named "Ritual Carriage," served as formal transportation for the emperor when visiting the Altar of the Sun, the Altar of the Moon, the Altar of Land and Grain, and Confucius's Temple to perform annual rites. LJ

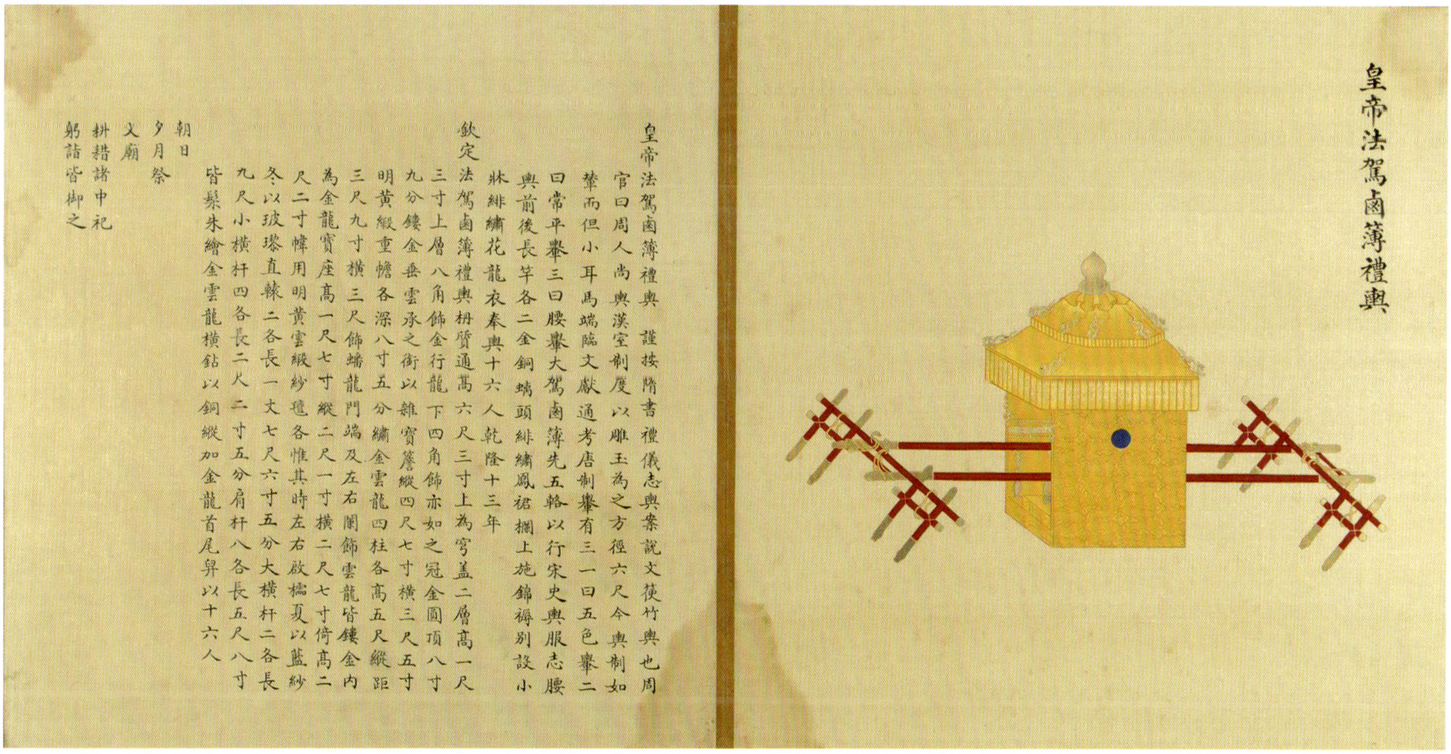

22.3 清乾隆 皇朝禮器圖式 皇太后儀駕萬壽輦 內府繪本 絹本設色

Empress Dowager's Longevity Carriage

Palace Museum, Gu.6116-69/92-1

This carriage or sedan chair, also known as the "Longevity Carriage," was made in 1751 for Empress Dowager Chongqing (1693–1777), mother of Emperor Qianlong (r. 1736–95), in celebration of her sixtieth birthday. Accompanied by her son, the empress dowager was carried in the sedan chair by twenty-eight men and traveled twelve miles from Changchunyuan, her summer residence, to the Forbidden City. The carriage, as described in the inscription, was also used at the empress dowager's seventieth birthday celebration in 1761.

Having the same structural design as the emperor's highest-ranking carriage, the "Golden Carriage" (*jin'nian*), this ten-foot-high palanquin is fashioned with a four-pillar chamber covered with yellow silk satin. The lavishly decorated roof boasts gold dust, jade plaques, and a golden finial.[1] The character for longevity (*shou*), fashioned in clerical script, is embroidered on the satin, and the title "Empress Dowager's longevity carriage" is written in standard script to the right of the image. LJ

Seal: 乾隆御覽之寶 *Qianlong yulan zhibao*

1. Yunlu et al. (1766) 2004, chap. 11, pp. 545–46; chap. 12, p. 553.

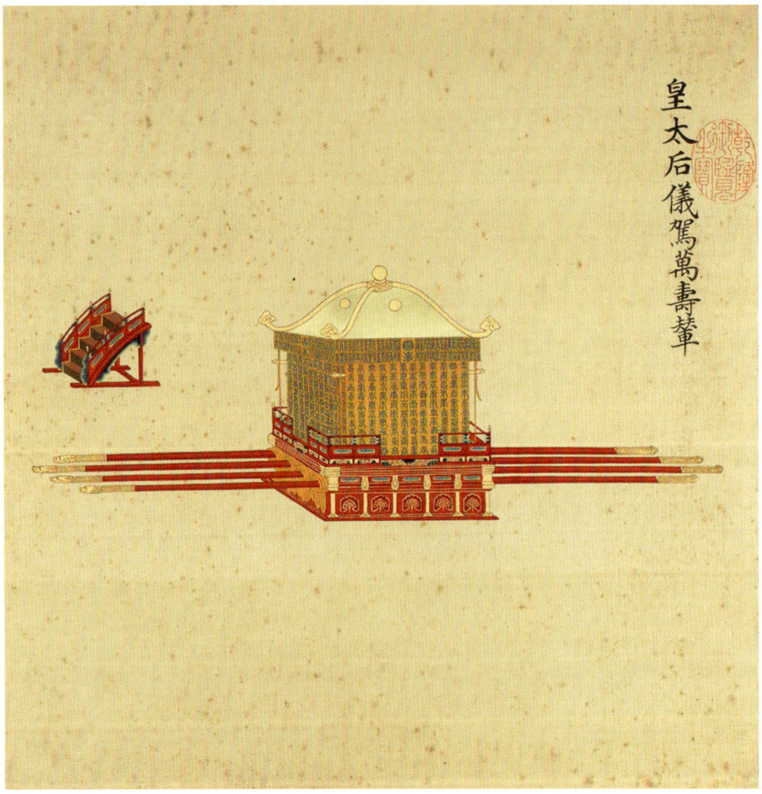

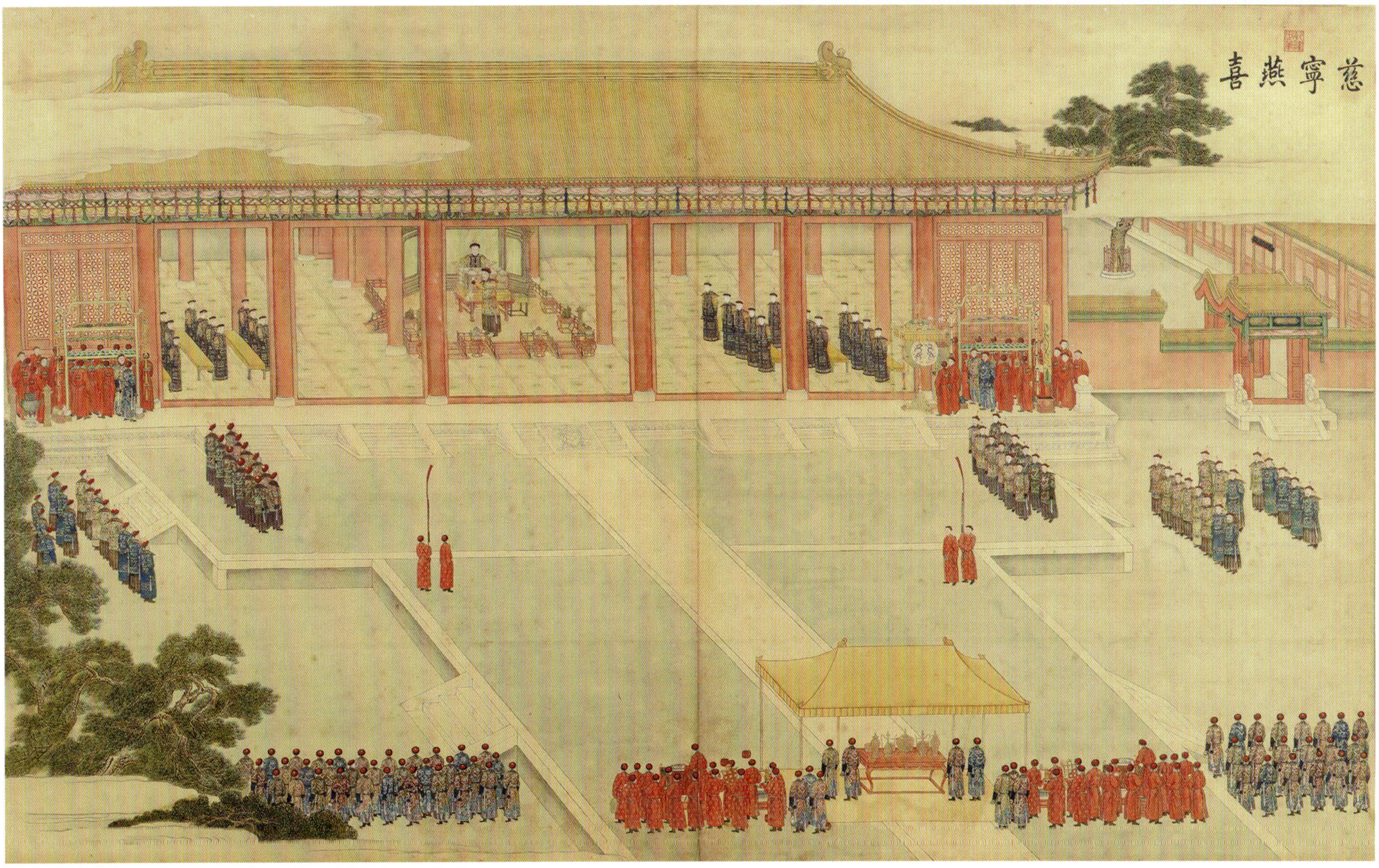

23 清乾隆 臚歡薈景圖冊 慈寧燕喜圖 絹本設色

Banquet at Cining Palace from the series
Scenes of Bliss and Celebrations, approx. 1761
Qing dynasty, Qianlong period (1736–95)
Album leaf; ink and color on silk
H. 97 cm (38.19 in.), W. 161.2 cm (63.46 in.)
Palace Museum, Gu.9198-4/8

Empress Dowager Chongqing (1693–1777) was the wife of Emperor Yongzheng (r. 1723–35). Born into a Manchu noble family, she gave birth to her only son, Hongli, in 1711. When Hongli ascended the throne as Emperor Qianlong (r. 1736–95), he hosted grand celebrations for his mother's birthdays at the Cining Palace.

This album leaf, from an eight-leaf series, illustrates a banquet ritual at the Cining Palace to celebrate the empress dowager's birthday. The painting unfolds to show a red palace hall with a yellow-glazed roof and a wide opening leading to a courtyard. Inside, Empress Dowager Chongqing, the central figure, sits behind a dinner table, while Emperor Qianlong, with cup in hand, offers a toast. To the left and right of the entrance, musicians play sets of ritual bells and chimes. Across the courtyard, under a yellow canopy, a table displays ritual vessels. In the middle of the courtyard, two men hold the *xizhu,* an instrument to conduct the ensemble. In keeping with rituals, imperial family members stand inside, while court officials remain in the courtyard.

Although this painting is undated, the structure of the palace roof provides a clue as to when it was produced. The Cining Palace, built originally in 1536, was used primarily as a site for celebrations during the Qing dynasty. In 1769, in preparation for the empress dowager's eightieth birthday, the palace was renovated, and its roof was upgraded to a two-tier design (fig. 1, p. xiv). The Qing historical paintings always pursued a realistic depiction with intricate details. Therefore, this painting, which depicts a single-tier roof, was made before the renovation, on the occasion of the empress dowager's seventieth birthday in 1761. LJ

Seal: 乾隆御筆 *Qianlong yubi*

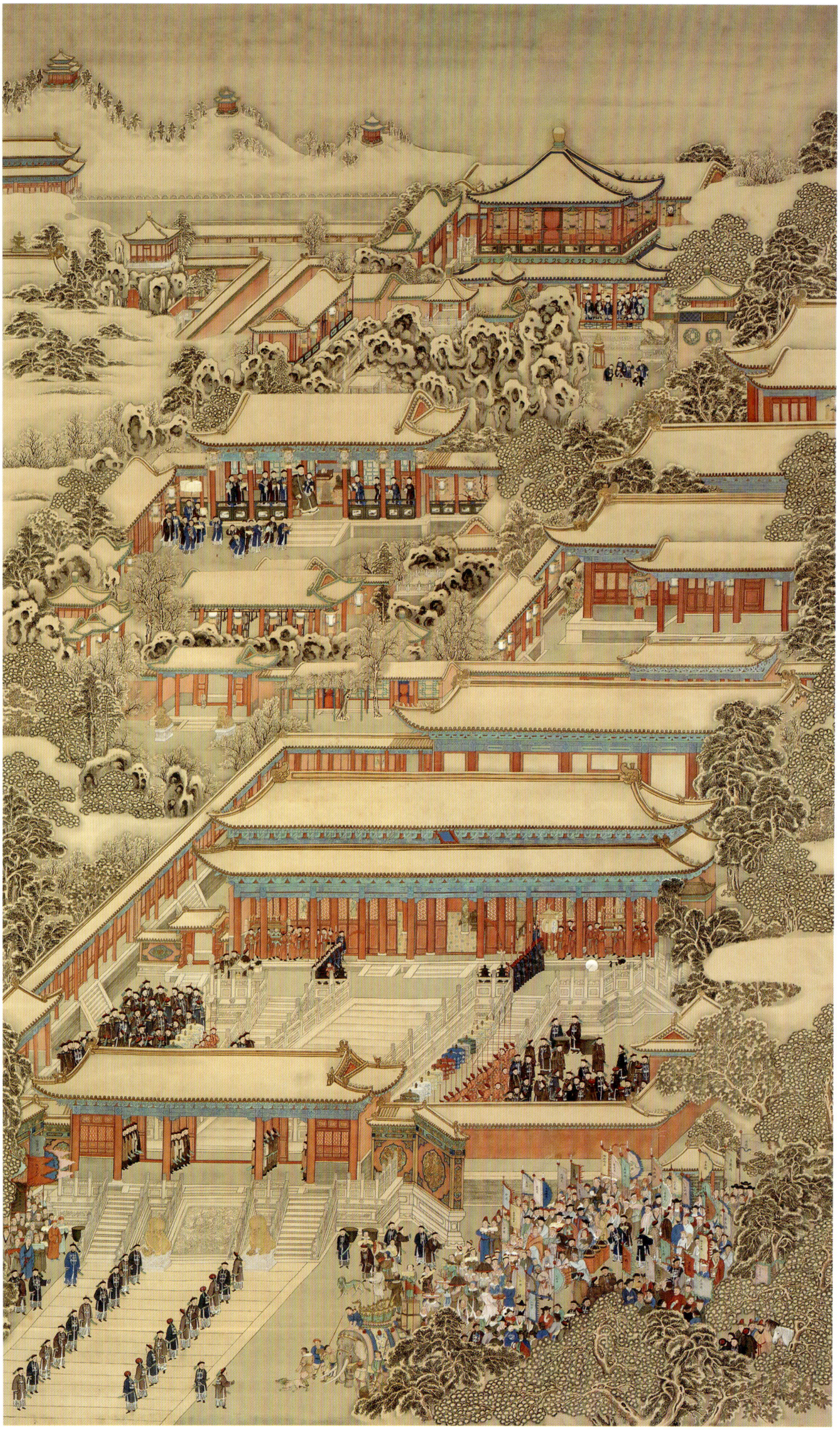

24 清乾隆 姚文瀚、賈全、謝遂等繪 萬國來朝圖軸 絹本設色

Arrival of Envoys from Thousands of Regions, approx. 1779
Attributed to Yao Wenhan, Jia Quan, and Xie Sui
Qing dynasty, Qianlong period (1736–95)
Hanging scroll; ink and color on silk
H. 365 cm (143.70 in.), W. 219.5 cm (86.42 in.)
Palace Museum, Gu.6271

Imperial family members, court officials, and foreign envoys gathered in the Forbidden City annually to celebrate New Year's Day. Four paintings in the Palace Museum depict this event. The earliest one, dated 1761, shows the three major halls in the outer court.[1] This scroll depicts the emperor's snow-blanketed retirement complex, which was built in the inner court in 1770s, in honor of Emperor Qianlong's seventieth birthday.

In the foreground, the imperial guards line up outside the gate, where two gilt-bronze lions stand watch as well. Guests from neighboring states and foreign lands, including Korea, Burma, Kazakhstan, and France, are in attendance. They arrive with tributes, such as precious goods, elephants, and exotic animals. Behind the gate, in the Hall of Imperial Supremacy (Huangjidian), sets of ritual bells and chimes are on display. Other primary buildings in the complex are the Palace of Tranquil Longevity (Ningshougong), the Hall of Spiritual Cultivation (Yangxingdian), and the Hall of Joyful Longevity (Leshoutang). In the Hall of Following Instincts (Suichutang), pictured in the upper left, Emperor Qianlong sits holding a child and looking out on the Qianlong Garden. In the upper right, the garden's courtyard features a large rocky hill in front of the Pavilion of Viewing Destiny (Fuwangge), where imperial women and children play with fireworks. Beyond are the pavilions on the Longevity Hills outside the Forbidden City.

According to the Zaobanchu imperial workshop archives, this painting was created in 1779 for the clerestory window of the Hall of Spiritual Cultivation, the emperor's most elaborate residence hall in the complex. The painting is attributed to Yao Wenhan, Jia Quan, and Xie Sui,[2] a new generation of court painters active in the latter half of the eighteenth century. LJ

1. Rawski and Rawson 2005, cat. no. 83.
2. ZGDYLSDAG 2005, 44: 35.

25.1–2 清光緒 慶寬繪 載湉大婚典禮全圖冊 第七冊 皇后鳳輿入宮圖 絹本設色

Empress's Phoenix Carriage Entering the Palace from the series
Complete Illustrations of the Guangxu's Imperial Wedding, approx. 1889
Qing dynasty, Guangxu period (1875–1908)
Album leaf of vol. 7; ink and color on silk
Each image: H. 61 cm (24 in.), W. 111 cm (43.70 in.)
Palace Museum, Gu.5887-7/9

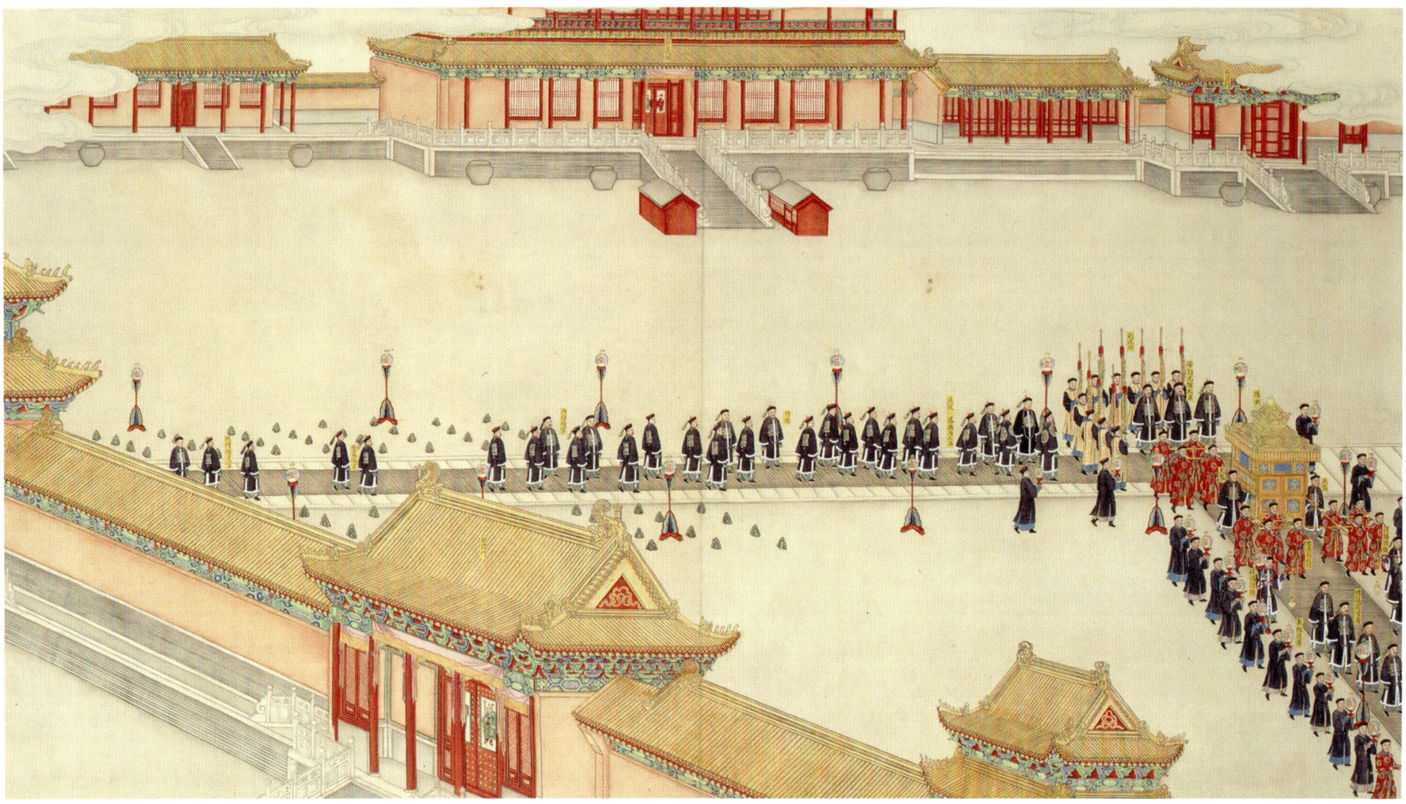

This series, which contains 144 leaves in nine volumes, depicts Emperor Guangxu's wedding in the Forbidden City. Emperor Guangxu (1871–1908) married Empress Longyu (1868–1913), cousin of Empress Dowager Cixi, becoming the fourth Qing emperor to wed in the imperial palace since 1644 but the only one whose wedding is documented in a painting. Commencing in December 1888 and concluding in February 1889, the wedding celebration included prewedding rites (proposal and presentation of gifts to the bride's family), a wedding ceremony (inauguration of the empress and arrival of the empress), and postwedding rites (wedding announcement and banquet).

These two leaves show the wedding procession entering the palace in the early morning hours on January 27, 1889. Led by imperial guards holding lanterns, the empress's procession has just passed through the Gate of the Hall of Supreme Harmony (Taihemen). Decorated with the phoenixes and attended by sixteen bearers, her carriage crosses the square with the Hall of Central Harmony (Zhonghedian) and the Hall of Preserving Harmony (Baohedian) to the left of the procession.

The empress was inaugurated on the same day. When she arrived at the palace, a ceremonial ritual display of her tablets and seal (cat. no. 25.3) took place at the

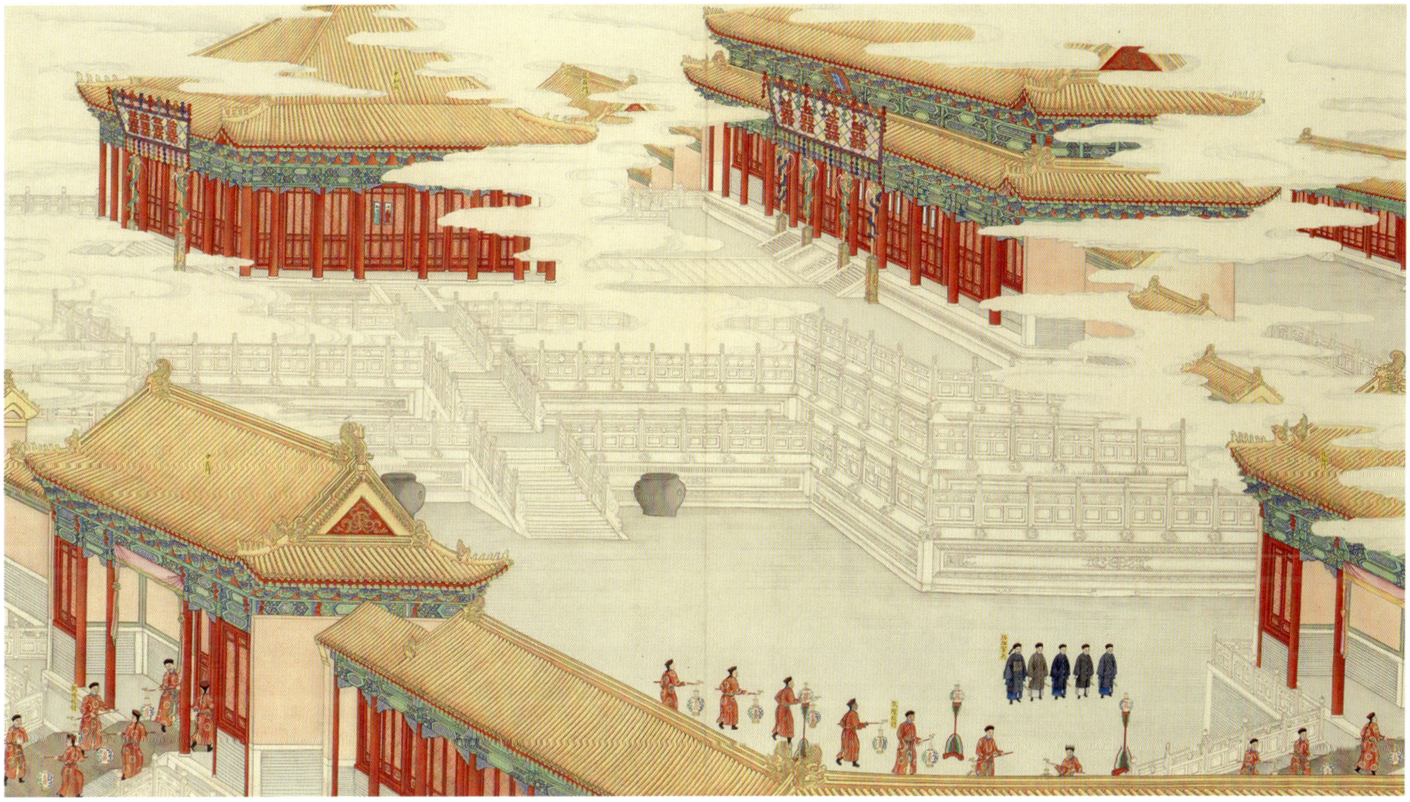

25.3 清光緒 慶寬繪 載湉大婚典禮全圖冊 第八冊 陳設冊寶圖 絹本設色

Display of the Empress's Tablets and Seal from the series

Complete Illustrations of the Guangxu's Imperial Wedding, approx. 1889

Qing dynasty, Guangxu period (1875–1908)

Album leaf of vol. 7; ink and color on silk

H. 61 cm (24 in.), W. 111 cm (43.70 in.)

Palace Museum, Gu.5887-8/9

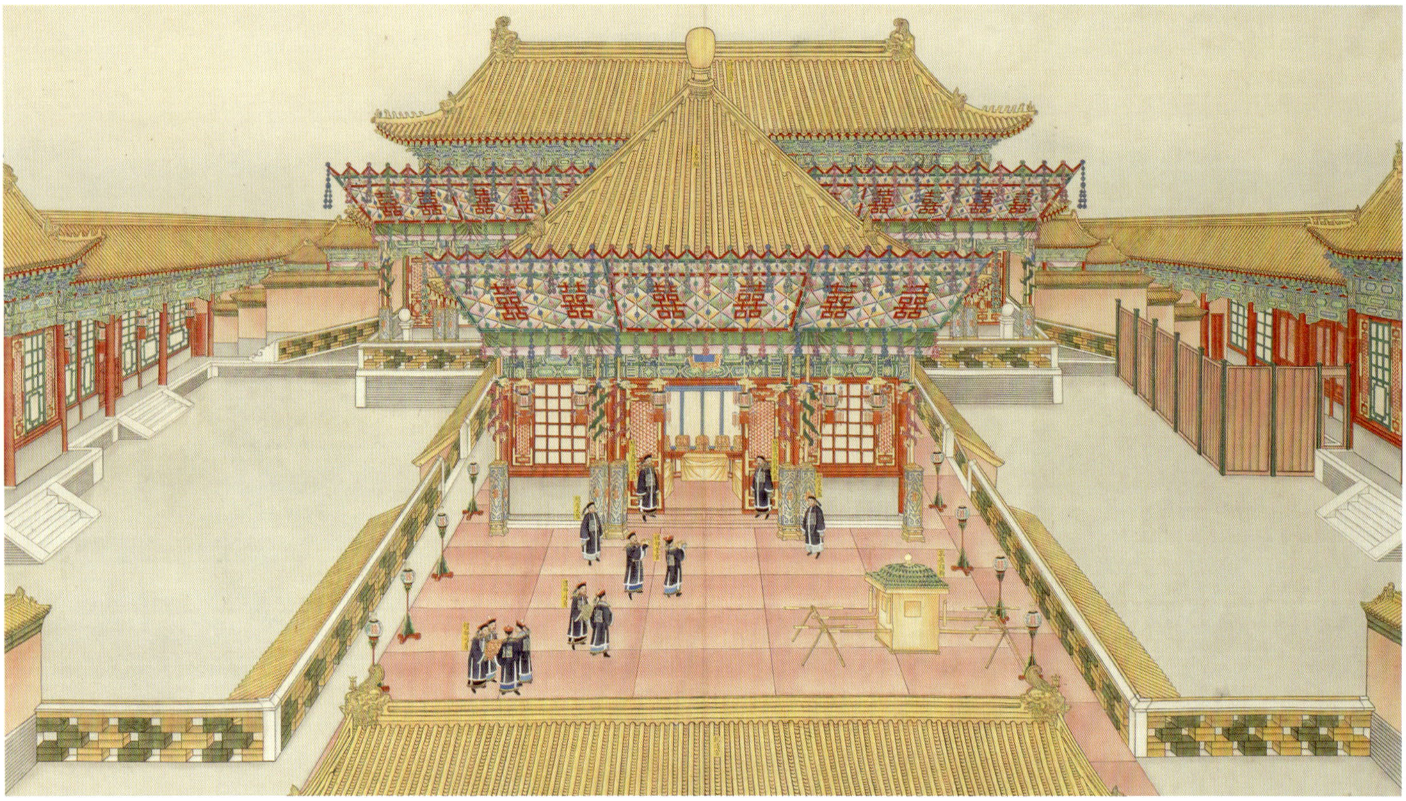

Hall of Union (Jiaotaidian). Ritual officials, carrying the gold tablets and gold seal, walk toward the hall. The empress's Peacock Carriage, which has a roof decorated with peacock feathers, sits parked in the courtyard.

The marriage was announced to the public on February 4, 1889. The next leaf (cat. no. 25.4) shows the announcing document, held in the beak of a phoenix that is being lowered from the Gate of Heavenly Peace (Tian'anmen), the Forbidden City's front entrance. A kneeling officer from the Ministry of Rites (Libu) receives the document, which was then transferred, in the Dragon Carriage parked behind, to the Libu for printing and national distribution.[1]

On February 15, 1889, the emperor hosted a state banquet, which was the highlight of the wedding (cat. no. 25.5). In this scene, officials and guests gather in front of the Hall of Supreme Harmony, watching traditional Manchu dancing, known as Qinglongwu, on the platform. Ritual musical instruments are placed on each side of the hall, and performers are dressed in animal hides and masks to portray beasts or horsemen who hunt and shoot. Other performers (Mongolian, Uighur, and Burmese musicians and Korean acrobats) stand to the right.

25.4 清光緒 慶寬繪 載湉大婚典禮全圖冊 第八冊 頒詔圖 絹本設色

Submitting the Wedding Announcement from the series
Complete Illustrations of the Guangxu's Imperial Wedding, approx. 1889
Qing dynasty, Guangxu period (1875–1908)
Album leaf of vol. 8; ink and color on silk
H. 61 cm (24 in.), W. 111 cm (43.70 in.)
Palace Museum, Gu.5887-8/9

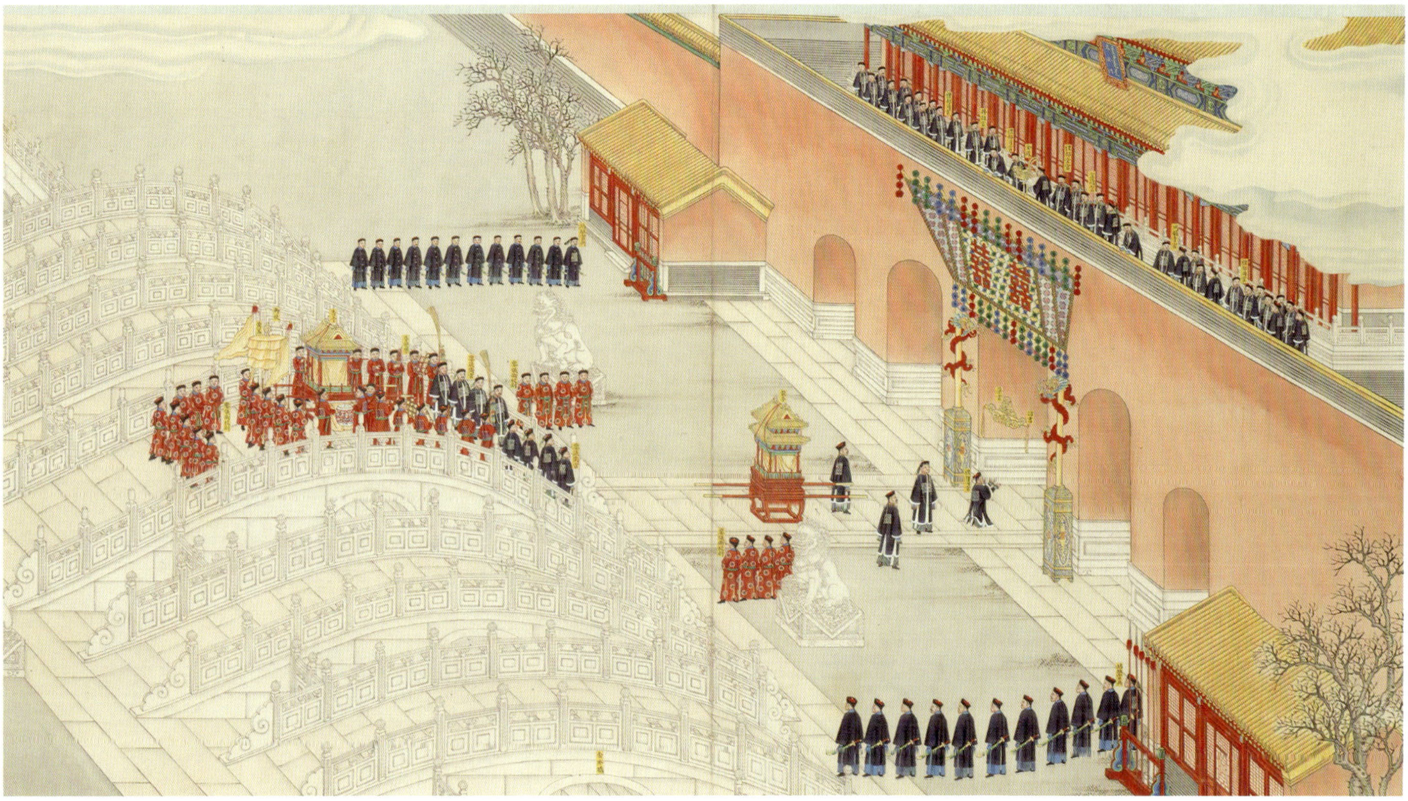

This album series features unique compositions, bird's-eye views, accurate perspectives, and realistic depictions. Lead court painter Qingkuan (1848–1927) and his assistants created the albums. Born in Tieling, Liaoning Province, Qingkuan served as a painter at the residence of Prince Chun (1840–1891), the father of Emperor Guangxu, before being employed as a court officer and painter. Using bright colors and fine lines, the artists faithfully illustrated the grand ceremonial wedding events, rendering architectural structures, thousands of figures, processions, and ritual services. The album remains an invaluable resource for the study of court rituals, functions of imperial buildings, and the display of ritual implements in the late Qing dynasty. LJ

1. GGBWY 2006.

25.5 清光緒 慶寬繪 載湉大婚典禮全圖冊 第八冊 賜晏圖 絹本設色

Emperor's State Banquet from the series
Complete Illustrations of the Guangxu's Imperial Wedding, approx. 1889
Qing dynasty, Guangxu period (1875–1908)
Album leaf of vol. 8; ink and color on silk
H. 61 cm (24 in.), W. 111 cm (43.70 in.)
Palace Museum, Gu.5887-9/9

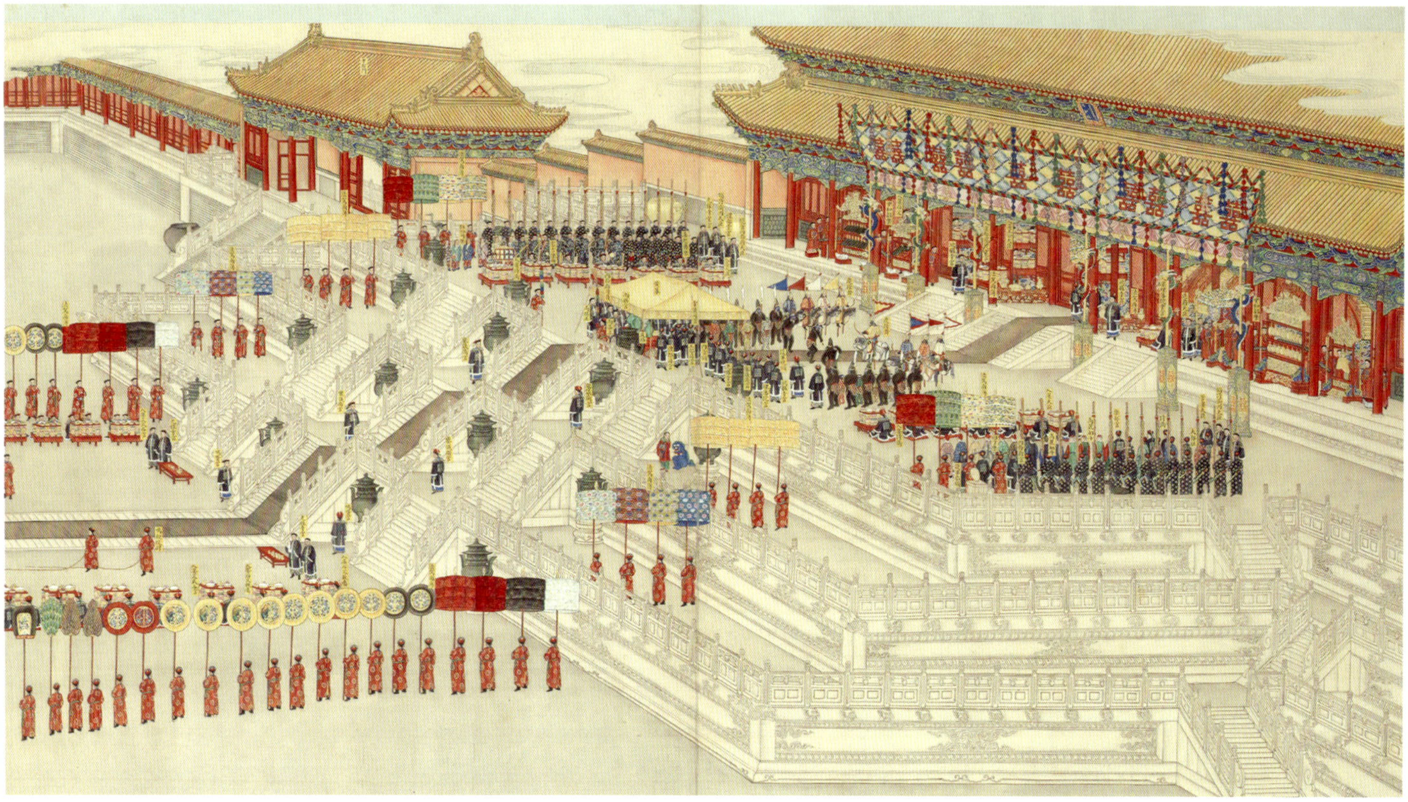

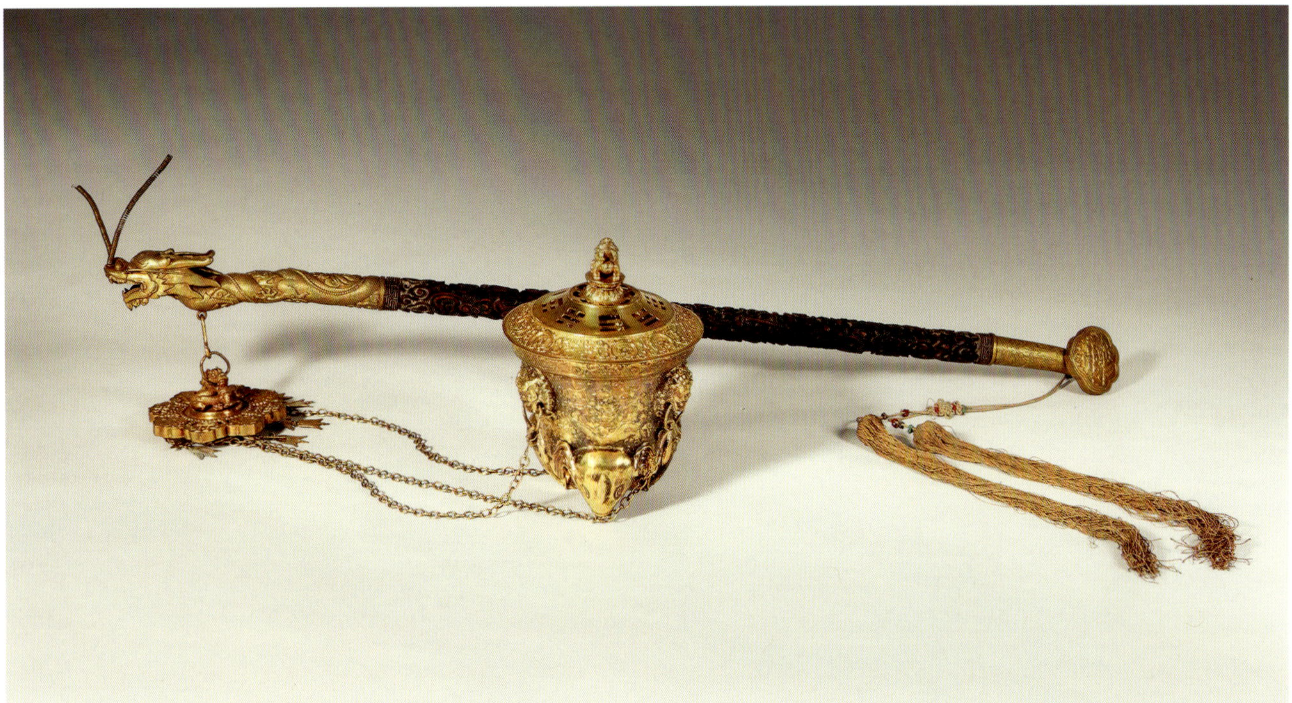

26 清同治十一年 金云龍纹象首足兽耳銜環提爐

Portable Incense Burner, 1872

Qing dynasty, Tongzhi period (1862–74)

Gold, wood, silk

Burner: H. 25 cm (9.84 in.), Rim Dia. 16.5 cm (6.38 in.)
Handle: L. 105 cm (41.34 in); Overall: H., including chain, 68 cm (26.77 in.)
Palace Museum, Gu.141447

In September of 1872, at the age of seventeen, Emperor Tongzhi (r. 1862–74) married Empress Xiaozheyi, and this ceremonial burner was specially crafted for the wedding with an abundance of gold. Its design features dragons and clouds chiseled into the burner's exterior, three legs fashioned as elephant heads, and Daoist symbols pierced in the lid. The burner hangs from a three-chain disc, cast with eight characters of *xi*, a blessing for happy matrimony. In addition, the wooden handle's carved motifs of bats amid clouds symbolize happiness and good fortune. A gold dragonhead mounts the front end of the handle, and a *ruyi* mushroom motif adorns the other end.

According to Qing rituals, an incense burner was on display at the grand ceremony (*fajia*) as one of the Eight Gold Objects: two burners, two incense boxes, two vases, a washbasin, and a water jar.[1] An illustration of Emperor Guangxu's wedding depicts a burner resting on a lacquered stand and a ritual official carrying the handle in front of the Cining Palace.[2] LJ

Inscription: 同治十一年八成金二兩平重112兩9錢 (Made in the 11th year of the Tongzhi reign, eighty percent pure gold, weighing 112.9 *liang* [4,211 grams])

Marks: 聚華 *Juhua*, 義和 *Yihe* (two local gold workshops in Beijing)

1. Yunlu et al. (1776) 2004, chap. 10, pp. 448–52.
2. GGBWY 2006, 101.

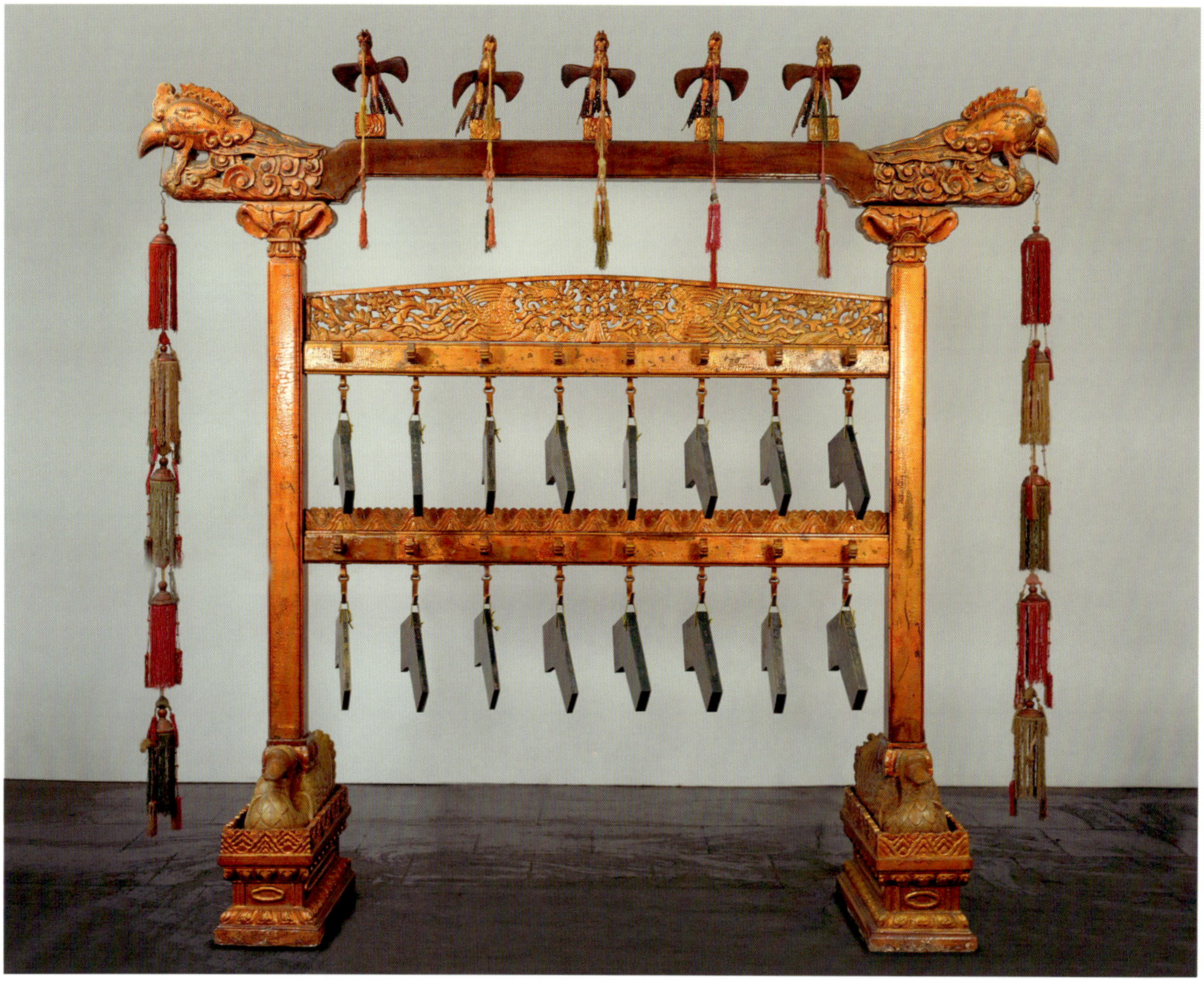

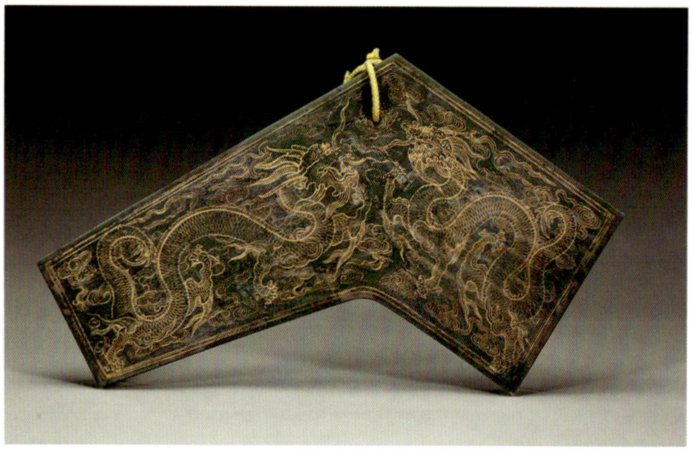

27 清乾隆二十九年 碧玉描金云龙纹编磬

Set of Sixteen Chimes, dated 1764
Qing dynasty, Qianlong period (1736–95)
Nephrite, gold lacquer on wood, silk
H. 340 cm (133.8 in.), W. 350 cm (137.8 in.)
Palace Museum, Gu.169354-1-15/15 and Gu.169360

Among the most celebrated percussion instruments, stone chimes were played alongside bronze bells (cat. no. 28) during state events as early as the Western Zhou dynasty (1050–771 BC). The sixteen jade chimes in this set are painted in gold with dragons and clouds on both sides. While uniform in size, the chimes, which are struck with wooden mallets, vary in thickness and tone, and thicker chimes produce higher notes. The name of each chime's corresponding note is indicated on the chime itself. Carved from precious Hetian jade, the chimes' solid forms and smooth surfaces ensure resonance. Green jade chimes such as these were used for rituals at the Altar of Heaven and the Altar of Land and Grain. The chimes of *lingbi*, finely grained limestone from Lingbi, Anhui Province, were played during other sacrificial and banquet ceremonies.[1] Similar to the bronze bells, these jade chimes hang in two rows from a lacquered wooden stand. Five phoenixes sit across the lintel with a phoenix head at each end. The middle crossbar is carved with a pair of phoenixes. LJ

Inscription, carved on the side of each chime: 乾隆二十九年製 (Produced in the 29th year of the Qianlong reign)

1. Yunlu et al. (1766) 2004, chap. 8, p. 372.

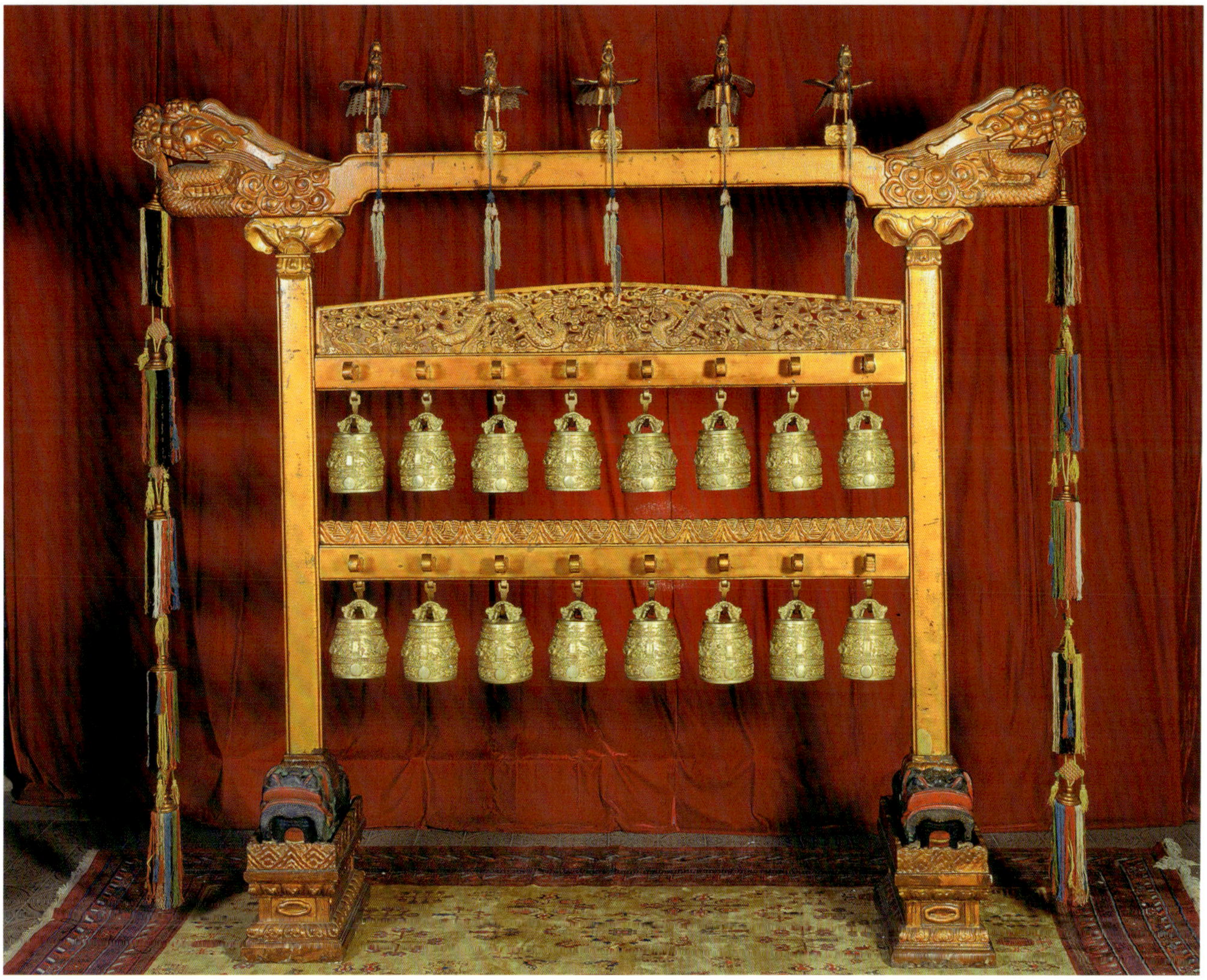

28 清康熙五十二年 銅鍍金雙龍紐雲龍紋編鐘

Set of Ritual Bells, dated 1713

Qing dynasty, Kangxi period (1662–1722)

Gilt bronze, gold lacquer on wood, painted design, silk

H. 340 cm (133.8 in.), W. 350 cm (137.8 in.)
Palace Museum, Gu.169500-1-16/16

The history of bronze bells can be traced back to the Western Zhou dynasty (1050–771 BC) when they were the most important ritual instruments used for formal state events. The bodies of the sixteen gilt-bronze bells in this set were cast with dragons amid clouds, and their knobs with a pair of dragons. With varying inner diameters, heights, and wall thickness, the bells produce distinct musical notes and, when struck along the rim, emit rhythmic tones. Each bell's tone name is cast on its back.[1]

Suspended from a lacquered wooden stand supported by a pair of crouching lions, this set of bells was played outside a palace hall during events such as the emperor's enthronement, sacrifices, and state banquets. With silk tassels hanging from their beaks, five phoenixes stand across the lintel, flanked by sculpted dragonheads. Carved into the lower crossbars are a pair of dragons, mountains, and waves. LJ

Inscriptions, tone names cast on the back of each bell and the following cast on the front of each bell: 康熙五十二年製 (Cast in the 52nd year of the Kangxi reign)

1. Yunlu et al. (1776) 2004, chap. 8, pp. 364–65.

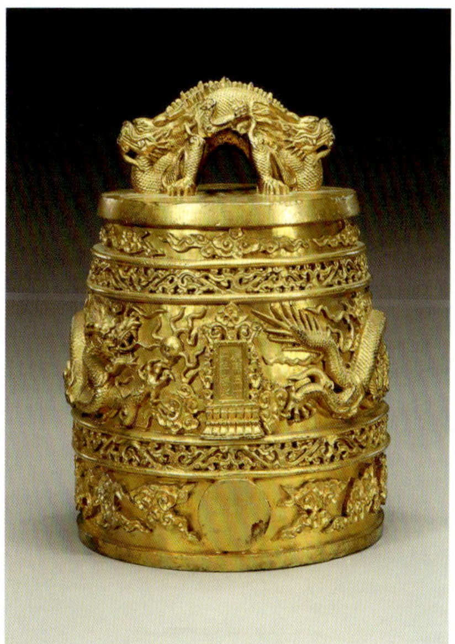

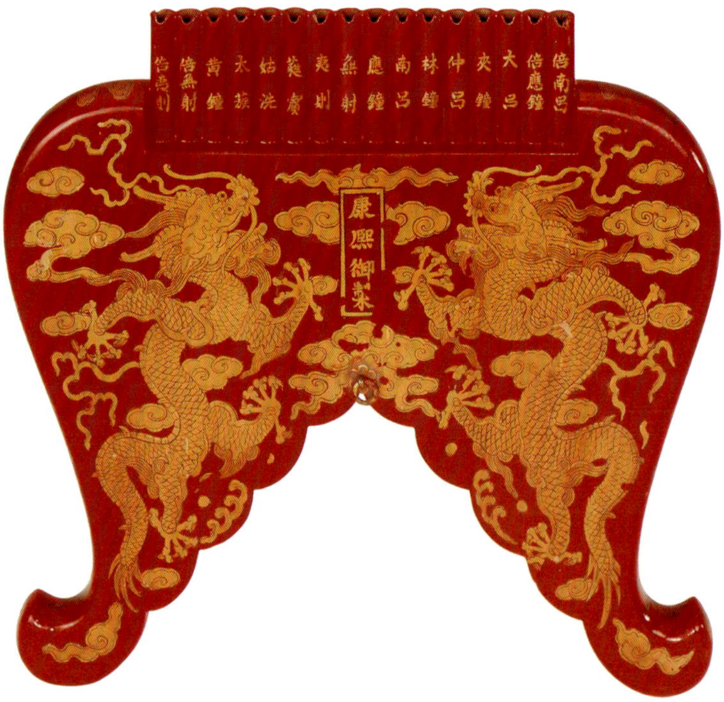

29 清康熙 紅漆描金雲龍紋木櫝竹管排簫

Wind Instrument with Dragons amid Clouds, 1713–18
Qing dynasty, Kangxi period (1662–1722)
Lacquer on wood, bamboo, gilding
H. 34 cm (13.27 in), W. 36.5 cm (14.09 in.)
Palace Museum, Gu.169650

This elegant wind instrument (*paixiao*) possesses a unique design, symmetrical form, and distinct craftsmanship. Sixteen bamboo stems of different lengths were assembled in a row and partly enclosed in a wooden case. The shortest pieces with the highest tones were placed in the center, with the progressively longer pieces arranged outward to the left and right of center (eight *yang* tones on the right; eight *yin* tones on the left). Noted on each pipe is its corresponding musical tone. Gold leaf with a pair of ascending five-clawed dragons amid clouds form a vibrant decoration against red lacquer. Originally, a silk tassel, now lost, was attached to a ring between the legs. In the early eighteenth century, the Kangxi court conducted an extensive survey of musical instruments and ancient ritual music. Following this investigation, Emperor Kangxi ordered the production of musical instruments for state rituals. The project started in 1713 and was completed in five years. Straight and even bamboo stems were acquired from Suzhou and Nanjing. The image of this paixiao was selected by the Chinese Musical Association as the state's musical emblem in 1956. LJ

Inscription: 康熙御製 (Made in the imperial Kangxi period)

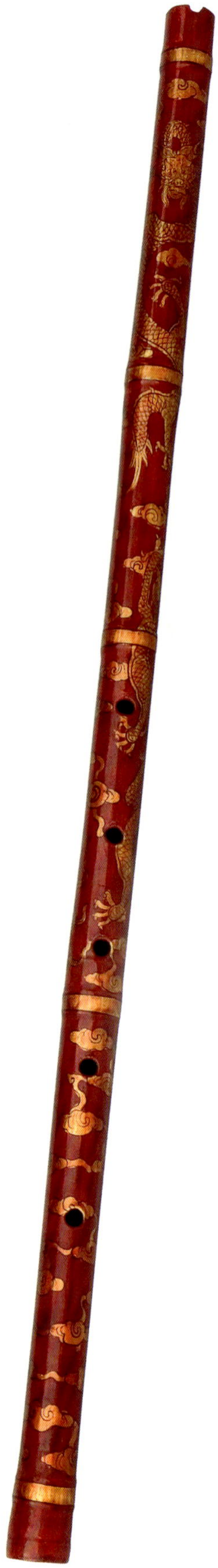

30 清乾隆 紅漆描金雲龍紋竹簫

Flute with Dragons and Clouds
Qing dynasty, Qianlong period (1736–95)
Red lacquer on bamboo, gold pigment
L. 57.2 cm (22.52 in.), Bottom Dia. 1.9 cm (0.75 in.)
Palace Museum, Gu.169702

On this vertical end-blown bamboo flute, known as *xiao*, dragons and clouds are painted in gold against a red lacquered background. The flute has five finger holes along the tube and two sound holes, one on either side. Originally, silk tassels were attached to the sound holes. The court flutist joined the ensemble to play for a variety of ritual services connected to such activities as grand court ceremonies, sacrifices, farming, hunting excursions, banquets, and cultivating silkworms, as well as triumphant music. LJ

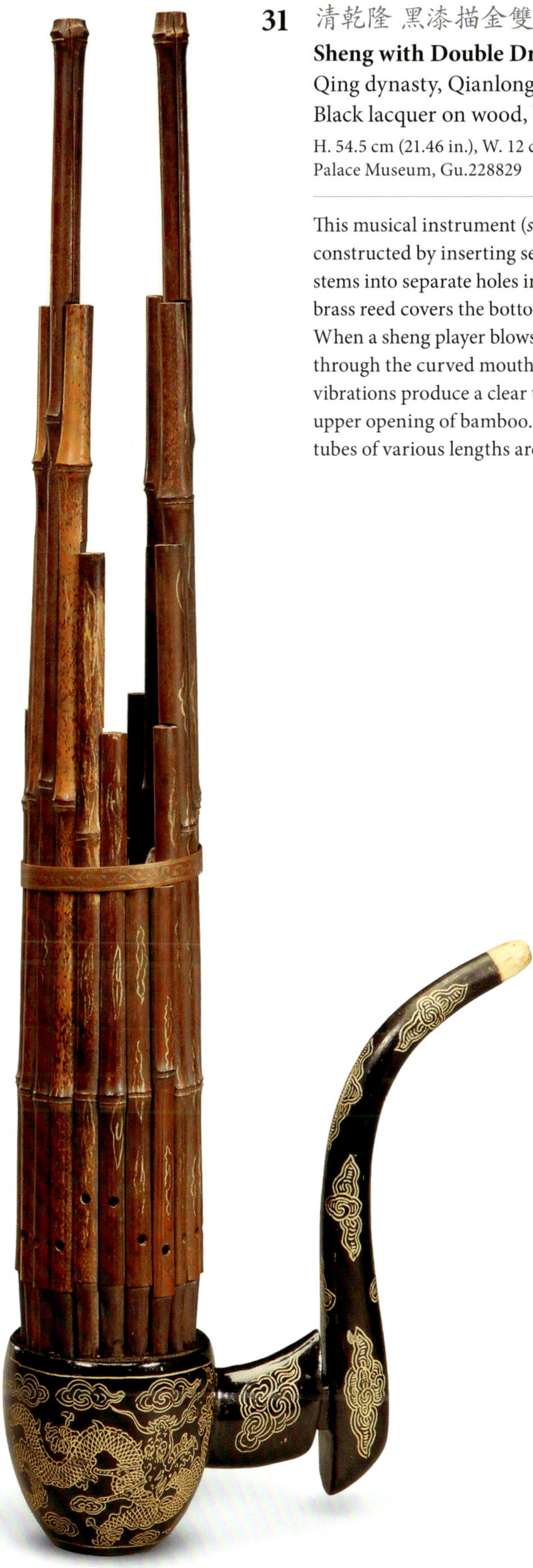

31 清乾隆 黑漆描金雙龍戲珠紋木門笙

Sheng with Double Dragons and a Pearl

Qing dynasty, Qianlong period (1736–95)

Black lacquer on wood, bamboo, gold pigment, ivory

H. 54.5 cm (21.46 in.), W. 12 cm (4.72 in.)

Palace Museum, Gu.228829

This musical instrument (*sheng*) was constructed by inserting seventeen bamboo stems into separate holes in a pipe bowl. A brass reed covers the bottom of each stem. When a sheng player blows and inhales through the curved mouthpiece, the vibrations produce a clear tone through the upper opening of bamboo. The assembled tubes of various lengths are meant to resemble the body and wings of a phoenix. The pair of dragons painted in gold on the black lacquer background signifies it was an imperial instrument. The sheng was commonly played at sacrificial services.[1] LJ

1. Yunlu et al. (1766) 2004, chap. 8, p. 379.

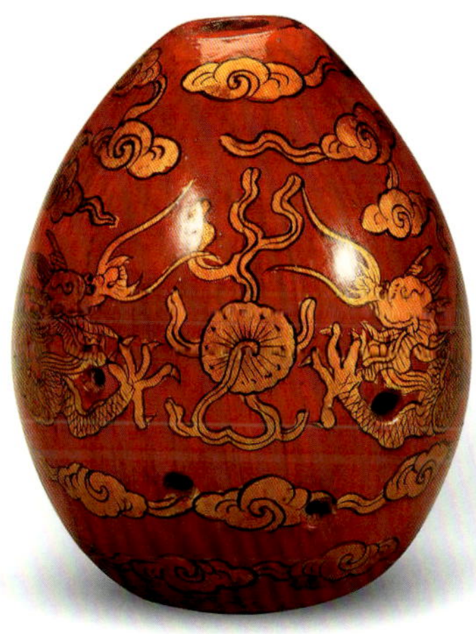

32 清乾隆 紅漆描金雲龍紋塤

Xun with Design of Dragons and Clouds

Qing dynasty, Qianlong period (1736–95)

Lacquer on clay, gold, pigment

H. 8 cm (3.3 in.)

Palace Museum, Gu.170152

This egg-shaped instrument (*xun*) has a hollow clay body pierced with seven holes: one blow hole on top, four sound holes in the front, and two finger holes on the back. Painted in gold and color, the scene depicts a pair of five-clawed dragons playing with a pearl amid clouds set against a red background. A musician held the base of the xun in both hands, wearing a long silk tassel on his finger. The xun was played during sacrifices and banquets, and often two musicians joined together to increase the depth and volume of music. LJ

33 清乾隆 弘曆盔甲乘馬圖軸 絹本設色

Emperor Qianlong on Horseback, 1758

Attributed to Lang Shining (Giuseppe Castiglione, Italian, 1688–1766)

Qing dynasty, Qianlong period (1736–95)

Hanging scroll; ink and color on silk

H. 430 cm (169.29 in.), W. 228 cm (89.76 in.)

Palace Museum, Gu.6488

This historical portrait depicts Emperor Qianlong at his first review of the grand parade of the Eight-Banner Army. During the event, which took place in Nanyuan, ten miles south of Beijing in November 1739, the young, ambitious emperor wore his ceremonial armor and helmet (cat. no. 37.1) and carried a sword, bow, and arrows, while riding his favorite white horse, Wanjishuang (Thousands of Auspiciousness), a gift from Khalkha Mongolian nobles.[1]

Nearly twenty years later, in 1758, Emperor Qianlong summoned Lang Shining, the Italian Jesuit court painter, to create this painting for the Huafangzhai, a newly constructed building on the eastern shore of the imperial garden in today's Beihai Park.[2] In this quiet complex, Emperor Qianlong often met with lead court painters or practiced archery with officials in the courtyard. Contrast of light and dark, a three-dimensional perspective, and intricate brushwork for the armor and the horse reveal Lang's distinctive style. For some of his larger works, Lang rendered the primary forms, such as the emperor's face and the horse, and his assistants completed the landscape and the armor. This painting blends Western technique and Chinese traditional mediums, a characteristic of mid-Qing dynasty court paintings. LJ

Inscription and date: 南苑大閱紀事一律 (An eight-line poem on the Nanyuan Grand Review) and 戊寅仲冬御筆 (Written by Emperor Qianlong in the midwinter of the *wuyin* year, 1758)

Seals: 惟精惟弌, 乾隆宸翰, 五福五代堂古稀天子寶, 八徵耄耋之寶, 信天主人.

1. Nie 2008, pl. 2–1.
2. *Da Qing Shilu* 1964.

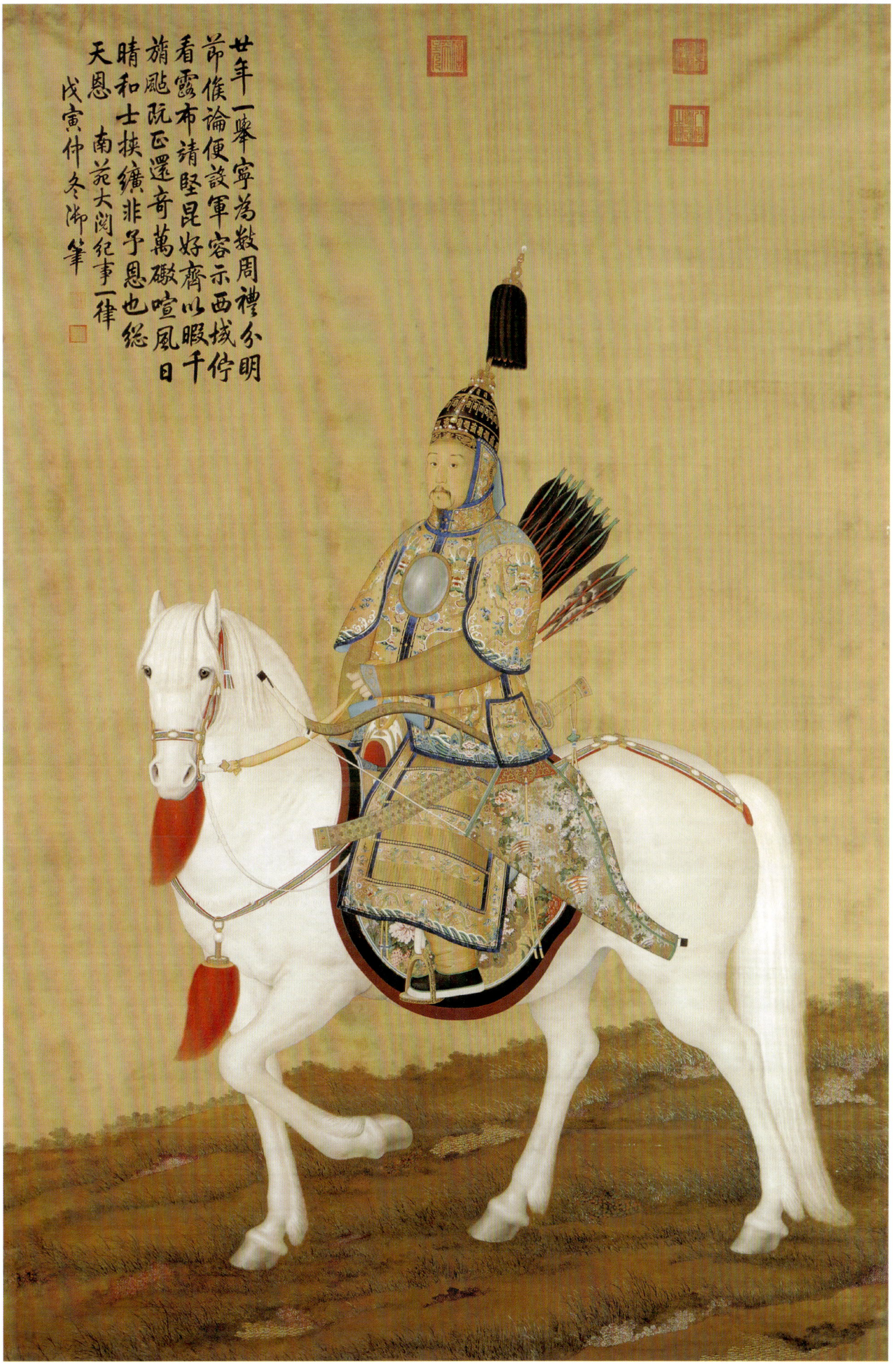
廿年一舉寧為數周禮分明
節備論便設軍容示西域佇
看露布靖堅昆好齊以暇干
旍颭既正還奇萬礮喧風日
晴和士挾纊非予恩也總
天恩 南苑大閱紀事一律
戊寅仲冬御筆

34 清乾隆 郎世寧繪 自在駒圖軸 絹本設色

Horse Zizaiju, 1743

Lang Shining (Giuseppe Castiglione, Italian, 1688–1766)

Qing dynasty, Qianlong period (1736–95)

Hanging scroll; ink and color on silk

H. 250.5 cm (98.62 in.), W. 270.5 cm (106.5 in)

Palace Museum, Gu.5355

Lang Shining was a trained portrait painter from Italy. He arrived in Beijing in 1715 as a young Jesuit missionary, and his artistic talent led him to a successful career as a court painter for more than fifty years under three Qing emperors: Kangxi (r. 1662–1722), Yongzheng (r. 1722–35), and Qianlong (r. 1736–95). Although Lang painted many different subjects in court, his horse paintings won him the greatest recognition in Chinese art history.[1]

According to Lang's own signature, this life-size portrait of the imperial horse named Zizaiju (which translates to "at ease with oneself") was painted in 1743 for the Qianlong emperor. The horse was a tribute from Mongolia, and Lang included the painting in his set of portraits called *Ten Imperial Horses (Shijuntu).* Here, Lang successfully combined his Western training with conventional Chinese methods and values to give his subject both substance and character. Lang's unique blend of style was particularly suited for the imperial need of providing visual records of imperial events, including inauguration portraits, imperial portraits, tours of the South, rituals, imperial hunting trips, and tribute horses or other animals.

Lang often collaborated with or taught other Chinese and European painters in the Qing court. One of his followers was Ai Qimeng (Ignatius Sickeltart, Bohemian, 1708–1780), who collaborated with Lang in 1772 and created a second set of *Shijuntu.* In this later set, Lang painted only three horses and Ai the remaining seven. This work, painted when Lang was fifty-six, is based on a realistic sketch and apparently met the approval of the Qianlong emperor. HMS

Inscriptions: The painting includes the horse's name written in three languages (Chinese, Manchurian, and Mongolian), a poem written by Emperor Qianlong in both Chinese and Manchurian, and an official inscription by Liang Shizheng.

Signature and date: 乾隆癸亥孟春海西郎世寧恭畫 (Respectfully painted by your servant Lang Shining from the "Western Sea" in the first month of Qianlong *guihai* year, 1743)

Seals: 臣郎世寧 *chen Lang Shining*; 恭畫 *gonghua*

1. Nie 1988, Yang 1988, Liu 1988, Wang 2007, 12–18.

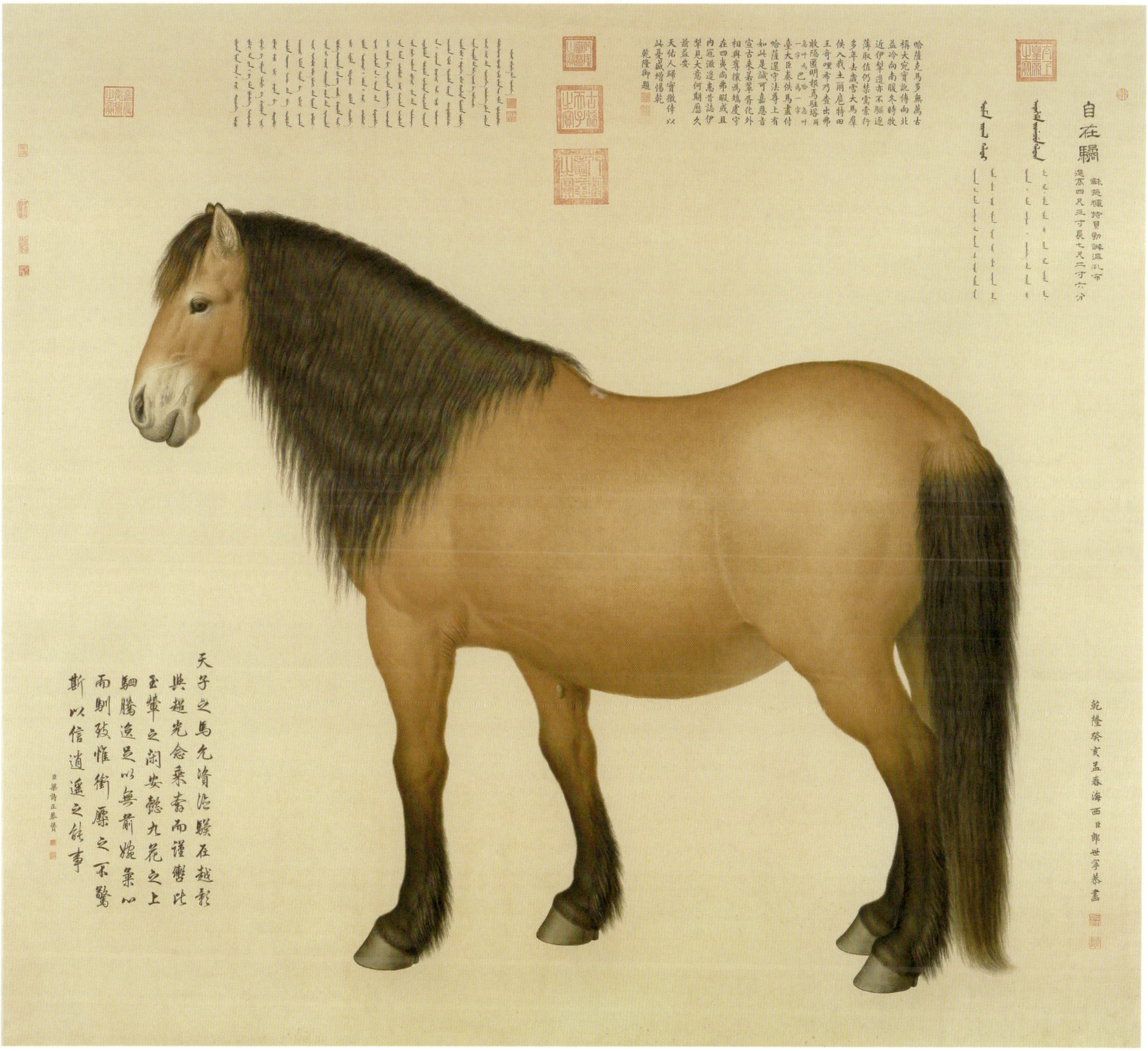

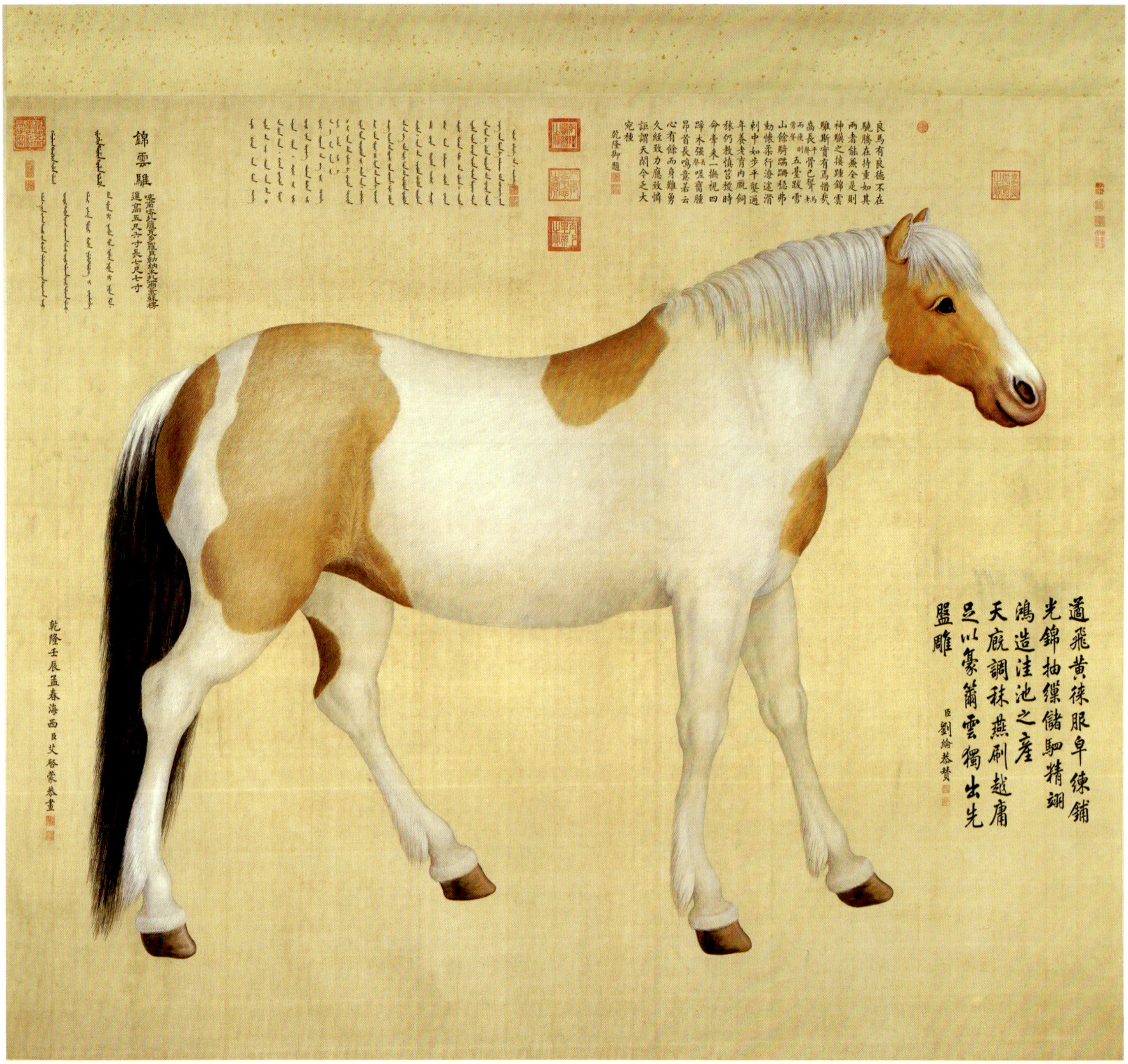
錦雲騅

35 清乾隆 艾啟蒙繪 錦雲騅圖軸 絹本設色

Brilliant Cloud, 1772

Ai Qimeng (Ignatius Sickeltart, Bohemian, 1708–1780)

Qing dynasty, Qianlong period (1736–95)

Hanging scroll; ink and color on silk

H. 229 cm (90.16 in.), W. 276 cm (108.66 in.)

Palace Museum, Gu.5017

Ignatius Sickeltart, renamed Ai Qimeng, was a Jesuit missionary from Bohemia (part of present-day Czech Republic) who came to Beijing in 1745 and entered the imperial court as a painter. To meet imperial approval, Ai studied with Lang Shining (Giuseppe Castiglione, Italian, 1688–1766) and learned to paint in a style that harmoniously blended Western perspectives with Chinese aesthetic principles.[1]

Ai, who specialized in depicting birds and animals, was best known for his paintings of horses, including this life-size portrait of Brilliant Cloud (Jinyunzhui), one of Emperor Qianlong's favorite horses. The painting, dated 1772, belongs to a set of portraits called *Ten Imperial Horses (Shijuntu)*—a collaboration between Ai, who created seven of the ten, and Lang Shining. Their version, which included Ai's spectacular *Brilliant Cloud,* was kept in the Hall of Tranquil Longevity (Ningshougong), as documented in *Shiqu baoji xubian.* An earlier version of these portraits was created by Lang Shining and, as documented in *Shiqu baoji chubian,* kept in the Yushufang Imperial Study.

Even when using the Chinese painting tools and materials of brush and silk, Ai applied the Western technique of layering color washes to build volume and convey the textures of the horse's skin and hair. As a result, Ai's horse is far more realistic than horses portrayed in traditional Chinese paintings. HMS

Inscription: The painting includes the horse's name written in three languages (Chinese, Manchurian, and Mongolian), a poem written by Emperor Qianlong in Chinese and Manchurian, and an inscription by Liu Lun.

Signature and date: 乾隆壬辰孟春海西臣艾啓蒙恭畫 (Respectfully painted by your servant Ai Qimeng from the "Western Sea" in the first month of Qianlong *renchen* year, 1772)

Seals: 臣艾啓蒙 *chen Ai Qimeng;* 筆沾恩雨 *bizhen enyu*

1. Nie 1984.

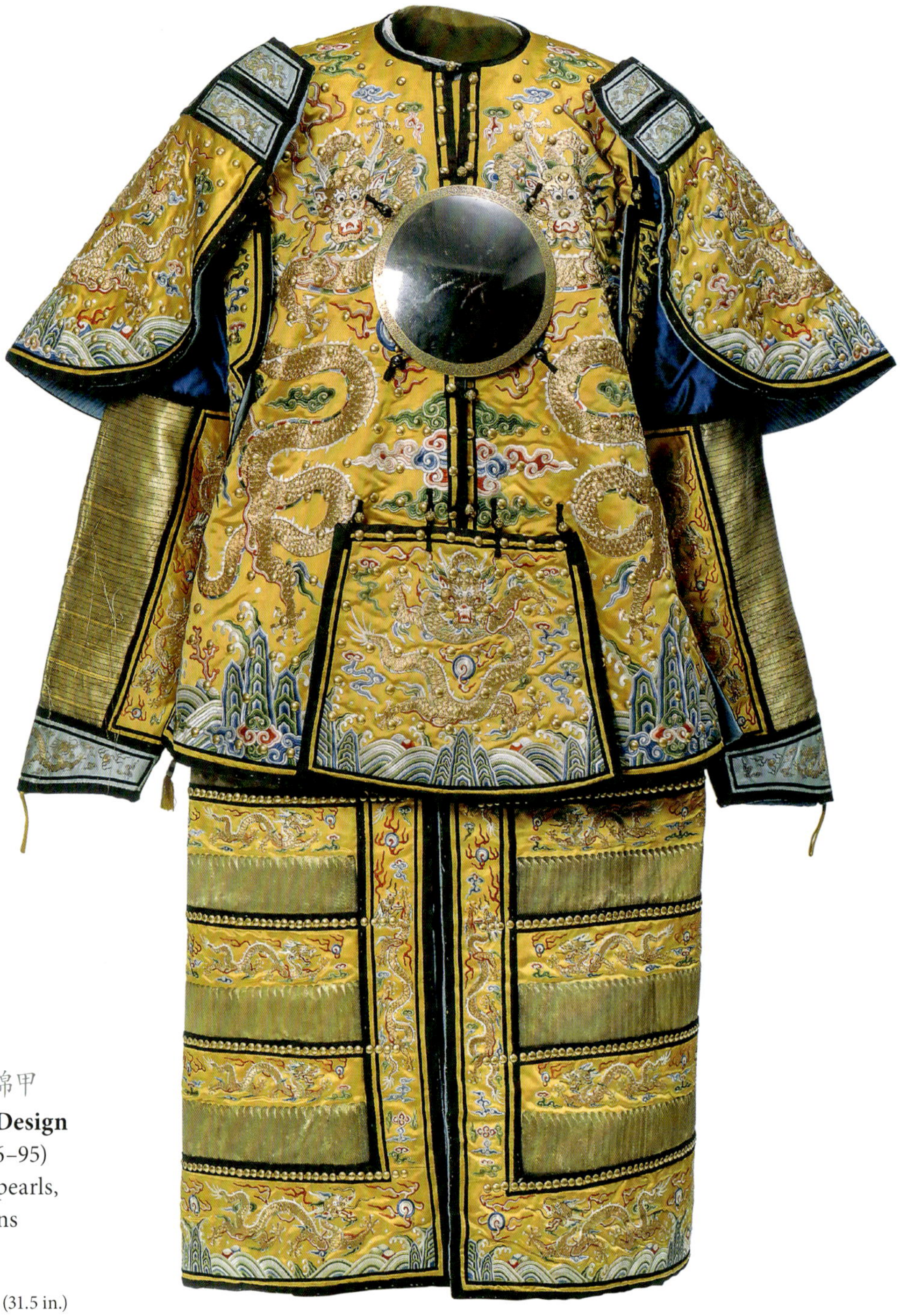

36 清乾隆 明黄緞繡金龍紋銅釘棉甲

Ceremonial Armor with Dragon Design
Qing dynasty, Qianlong period (1736–95)
Satin with embroidery, gold thread, pearls, gilt copper studs, steel, copper buttons
Upper garment: L. 78 cm (30.71 in.)
Overall sleeves: L. 208 cm (82 in.)
Lower garment: L. 78 cm (30.71 in.), W. 80 cm (31.5 in.)
Palace Museum, Gu.171798

Assembled with six protective panels, the jacket for this imperial armor guards the shoulders, the underarms, the belly, and the left side of the body. Three pearls are encrusted on each shoulder panel. All of the individual panels are connected by buttons or tied by cords. Other protective features of this armor include a smooth steel roundel over the chest and a steel plate on the back decorated with dragons and clouds.

The materials include imperial yellow satin, thin padding, and a blue tabby lining, all stabilized with metal studs. The outstanding embroidery on the armor includes five-clawed dragons in gold thread, multicolor flaming pearls, and other auspicious motifs, such as clouds, ocean waves, and mountains. On the sleeves, golden horizontal plates are woven in gilded strips to imitate overlapping metal scales. Emperor Qianlong wears an almost identical suit of armor in his portrait (cat. no. 33). LJ

37.1 清乾隆 黑漆嵌金飾珍珠乾隆帝御用盔

Ceremonial Helmet for Emperor Qianlong

Qing dynasty, Qianlong period (1736–95)

Black lacquer on leather, sable, gold, pearls, red silk floss

H. 31.5 cm (12.4 in.), Mouth Dia. 21 cm (8.27 in.)

Palace Museum, Gu.171125

37.2 清乾隆 皮盔纓

Helmet Finial

Qing dynasty, Qianlong period (1736–95)

Leather, cowhide, lacquer, diamond, gold-leaf, pearls, sable, embroidered satin, gold and silver threads

H. 30 cm (12 in.)

Palace Museum, Gu.171813-9/9

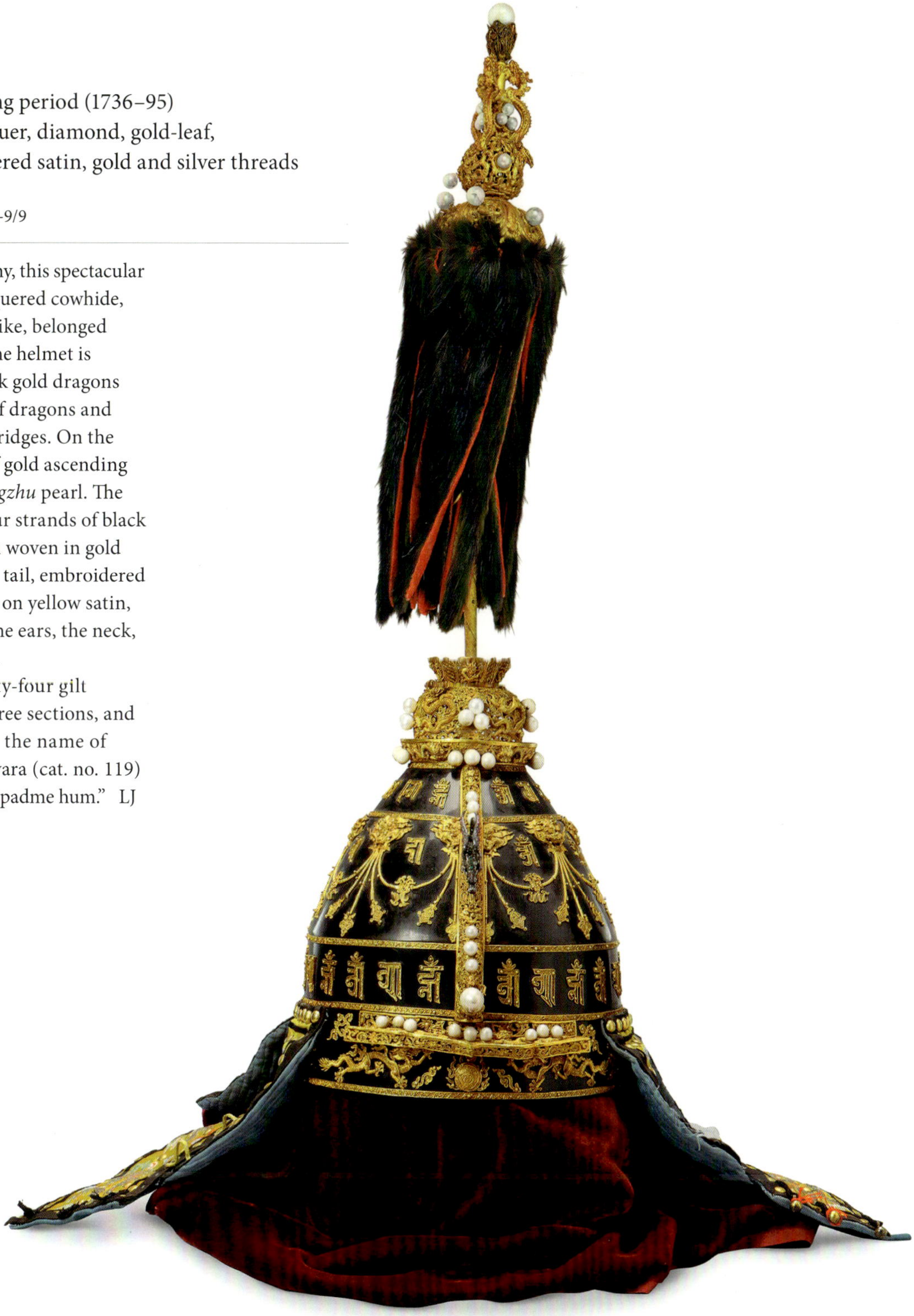

As an emblem of monarchy, this spectacular helmet, shaped with lacquered cowhide, fabric flaps, and a gold spike, belonged to Emperor Qianlong. The helmet is surmounted by openwork gold dragons and pearls, with gold-leaf dragons and a diamond snake on the ridges. On the top of the finial, a pair of gold ascending dragons hold a large *dongzhu* pearl. The finial features twenty-four strands of black sable lined with red satin woven in gold thread. The flaps and the tail, embroidered with dragons and clouds on yellow satin, are designed to protect the ears, the neck, and the back of the head.

The helmet bears forty-four gilt Sanskrit characters in three sections, and the inscription includes the name of bodhisattva Avalokiteshvara (cat. no. 119) and his mantra "om mani padme hum." LJ

38 清乾隆 鑲銅鍍金鏨雙龍紋木馬鞍

Saddle with Stirrups

Qing dynasty, Qianlong period (1736–95)

Wood, gilt iron, nephrite, silk velvet, cotton, damask lining, cotton wadding, metal fittings, iron stirrups, silk straps

H. 34 cm (12.60 in.), L. 62 cm (24.41 in.), W. 32 cm (12.6 in.)

Palace Museum, Gu.171493

This custom-made saddle was designed to fit the contour of a horse's back, providing a stable seat for a mounted archer. Made of wood and noted for its concave shape, this saddle possesses a high pommel in the front and a cantle in the rear. The pommel has a gilt-iron overlay with an openwork design of floral scrolls and encrusted green nephrite. Silk velvet and cotton cloth enclose the saddle's surface. A saddle cloth made of embroidered yellow satin with dragon and cloud designs rests on top. The extra cushioning served as a shock absorber and provided comfort for both horse and horseman. A pair of gilt-iron stirrups with dragon designs hangs from the saddle by leather straps. The stirrups free the rider's hands and aid in mounting the horse as well as balancing the rider.

Qing leaders considered riding and archery to be necessary skills for all imperial Manchu family members. The emperors, especially in the early and mid-Qing dynasty, emphasized the production of riding equipment, including elaborate saddles. LJ

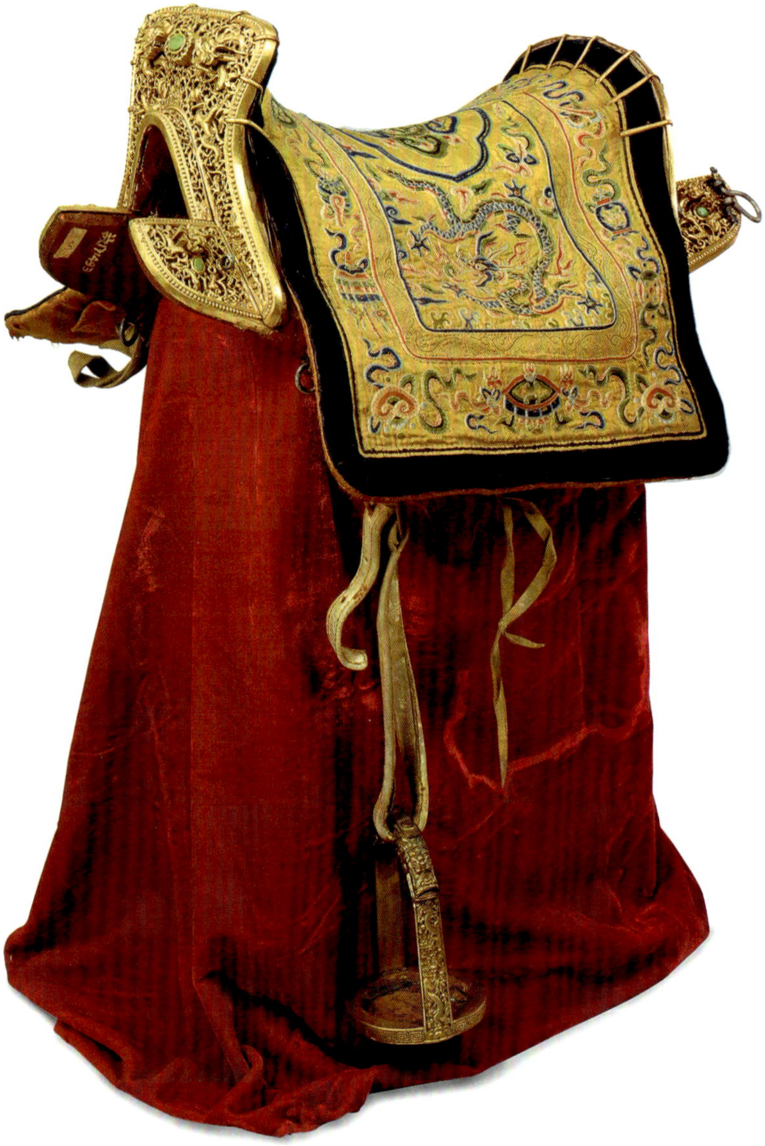

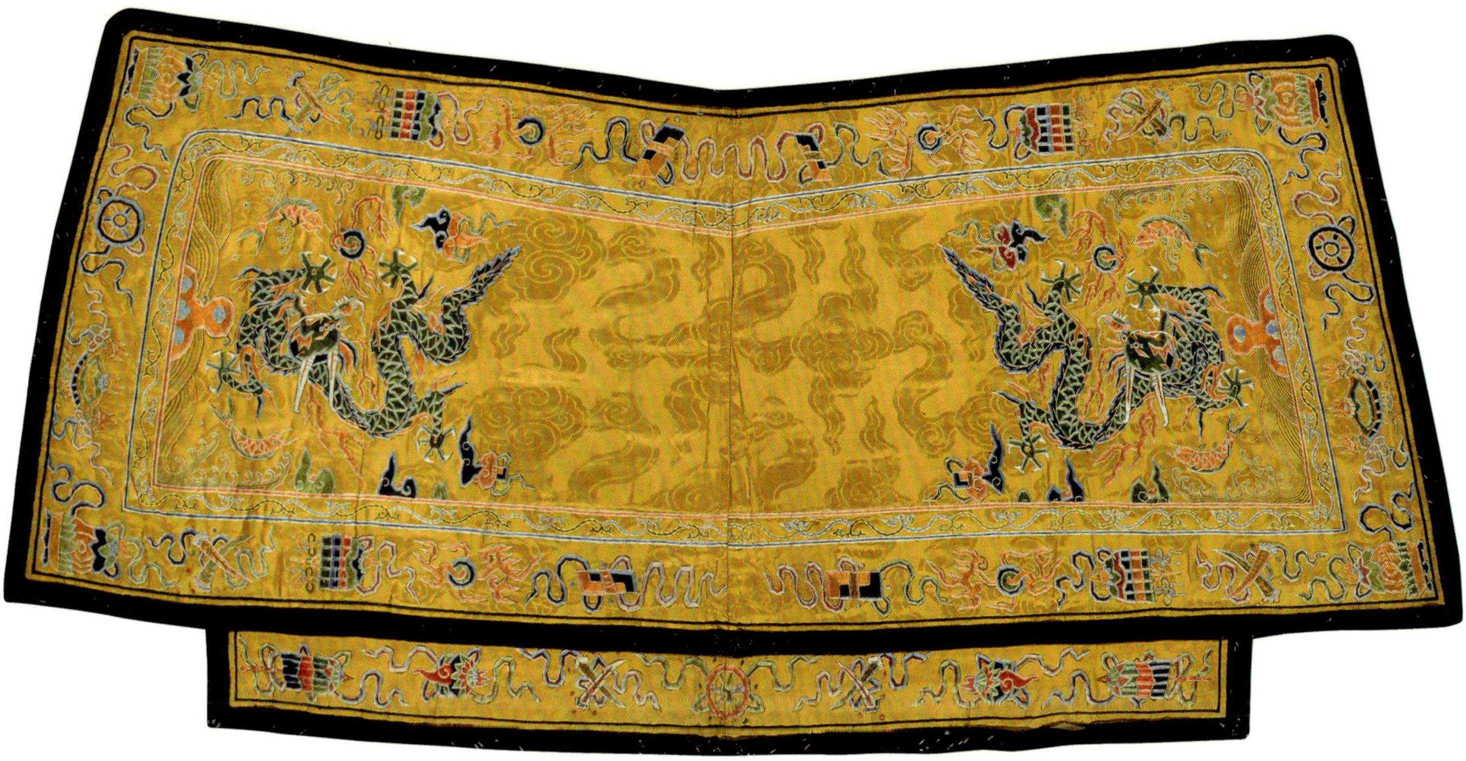

39 清順治 黃色緞繡雲龍八寶紋鞍韂

Saddle Pad with Dragons, Clouds, and Eight Treasures

Qing dynasty, Shunzhi period (1644–61)

Satin with embroidery, cotton lining and wadding, velvet edge

L. 125 cm (49.21 in.), W. 85 cm (33.46 in.)
Palace Museum, Gu.212430

The saddle pad, or saddle blanket, protected the horse's body from abrasion caused by the rider or his stirrups. Such a pad was placed directly on the horse's back, underneath a saddle, and was stabilized by a girth around the horse's barrel. Made of yellow satin, this double-edge saddle blanket was tailored to fit the contour of an imperial horse. When draped over a horse, the blanket displayed an embroidered dragon on each side, surrounded by the Eight Treasures (parasol, fish, vase, lotus, conch, knot, banner, and wheel).

This blanket belonged to Emperor Shunzhi, as indicated by the inscription written in ink on a wooden panel attached to the blanket. Emperor Shunzhi, known as Shizu, was the first Qing emperor to rule China after the Qing conquered the Ming dynasty (1368–1644). LJ

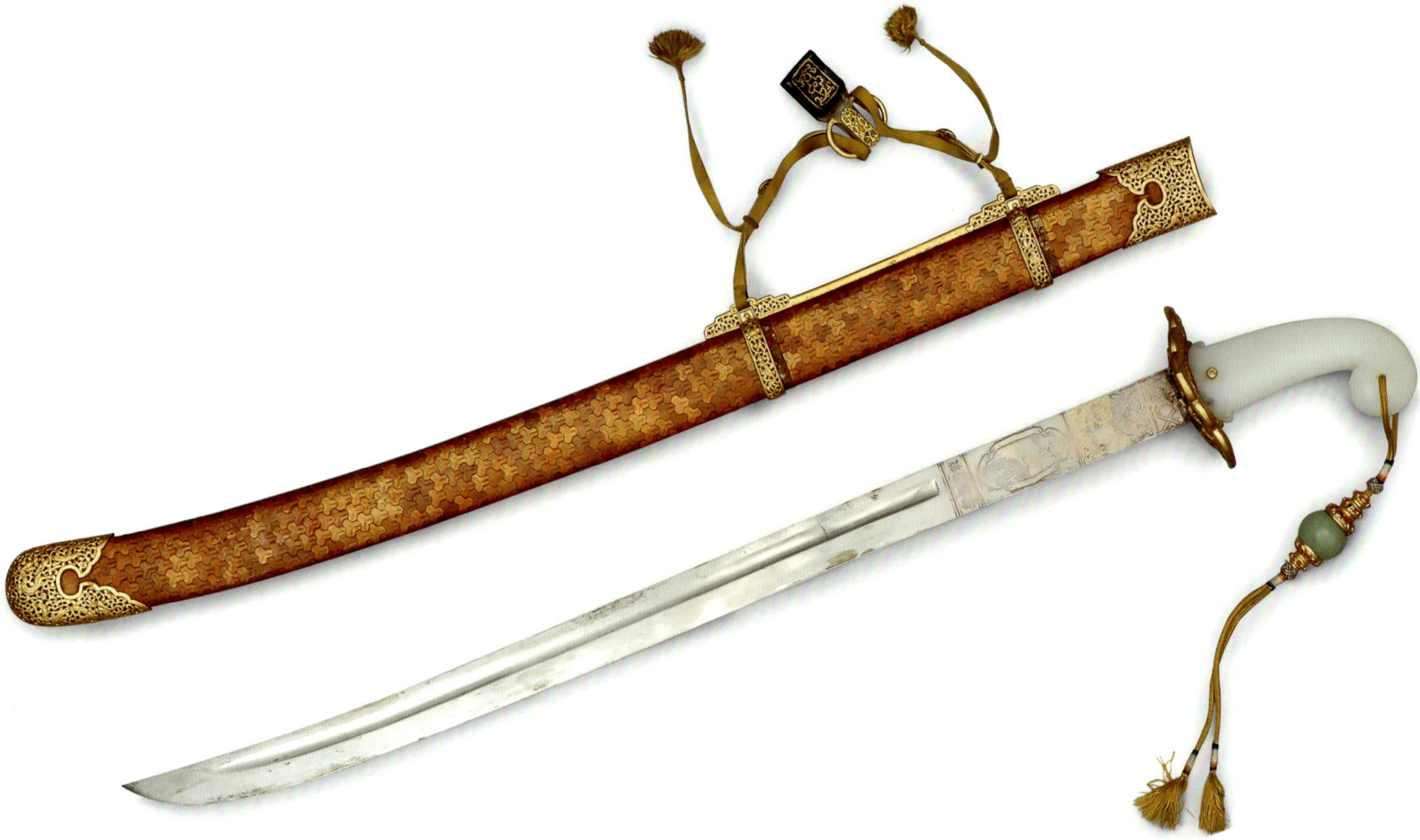

40 清乾隆 玉柄金桃皮鞘"寒鋒"腰刀

Sword "Cold Blade," 1757

Qing dynasty, Qianlong period (1736–95)

Steel, silver, gold, copper, gilt iron, gilt bronze, wooden scabbard, *jintao* bark, leather, nephrite, precious stones, silk cord, turquoise

L. 96 cm (37.8 in.)

Palace Museum, Gu.170406

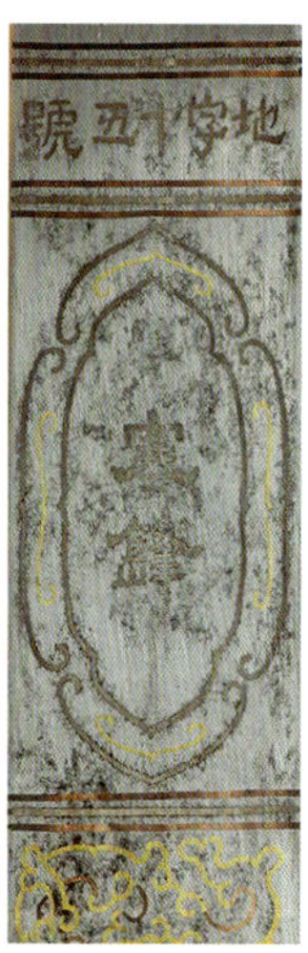

An example of excellent craftsmanship, this sword represents Emperor Qianlong's fascination with blade weapons. From 1748 through 1795, the emperor commissioned four orders of ninety knives and swords from the Zaobanchu imperial workshop. One of sixty from the first order completed by 1757, this sword has a long blade and weighs eighteen *liang* (671 grams).

The handle was carved out of one piece of pure white jade from Hetian, in today's Xinjiang region, and decorated with precious stones. Ornamenting the silk cord is a turquoise bead, believed to ward off danger and illness. Openwork designs of dragons and clouds decorate the gilt-iron hand guard and the wooden sheath. The latter is covered with trefoil-patterned *jintao* bark, derived from a type of peach tree from southern China and chosen for its natural golden color. This type of sword was carried by Emperor Qianlong during imperial reviews of the army (cat. no. 33), autumn hunts, or inspection tours. LJ

Inscriptions: inlaid in copper on reverse, 乾隆年製 (Made in the Qianlong reign); inlaid in silver, 寒鋒 *Hanfeng* (Cold Blade) and the number fifteen in the Earth category

41 清乾隆 玉嵌料石柄銅葉鞘匕首

Dagger

Qing dynasty, Qianlong period (1736–95)
Steel, nephrite, precious stones, gold,
gilt copper scabbard

L. 45 cm (17.72 in.)
Palace Museum, Gu.170686

Like the sword (cat. no. 40) made by the imperial workshop for Emperor Qianlong, this dagger has a double steel blade. Inspired by the Mughal style, the jade handle is inlaid with pearls and precious stones such as rubies, which were believed to ward off misfortune and became a traditional decoration for treasured weapons. The jade on the handle was from Hetian, located in today's Xinjiang region in northwestern China and known for its high-quality nephrite in colors ranging from white to green and black. A gilt-copper sheath of openwork floral design covers the dagger. LJ

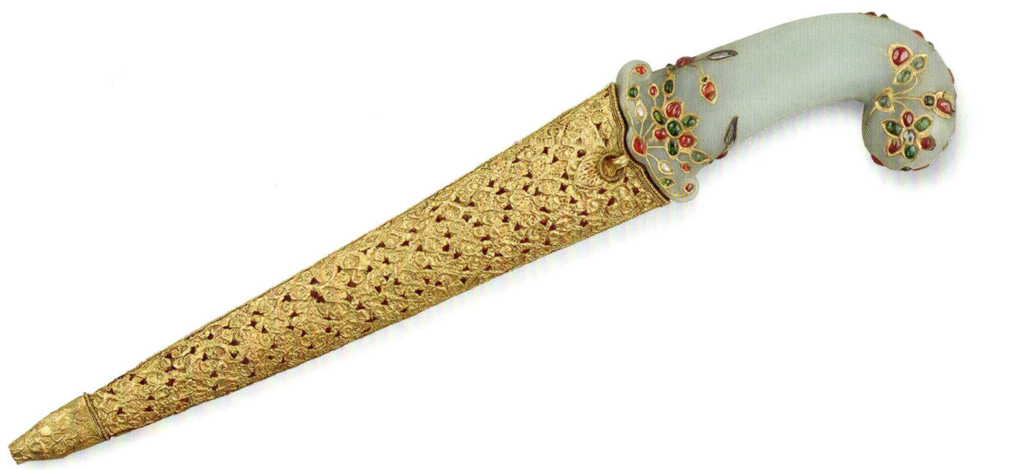

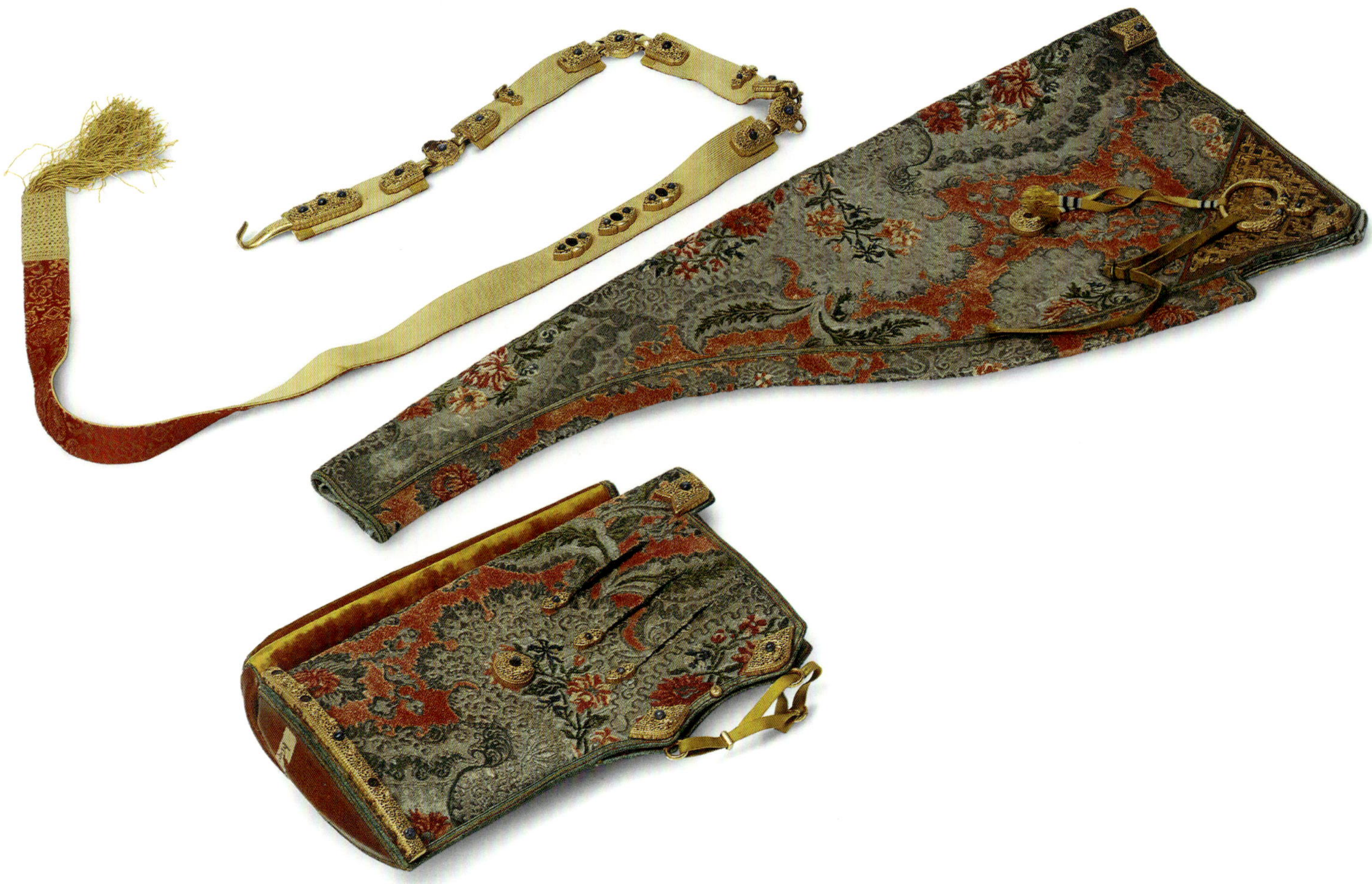

42 清乾隆 金銀絲花緞嵌藍寶石櫜鞬

Bow Case and Arrow Quiver

Qing dynasty, Qianlong period (1736–95)
Satin with gold and silver threads, leather, blue rubies, gilt metal fittings

Arrow quiver: H. 36 cm (14.17 in.), W. 21 cm (8.27 in.)
Bow case: L. 81 cm (31.9 in.)
Palace Museum, Gu222012

43 清 牛角樺皮弓

Bow

Qing dynasty (1644–1911)
Wood, oxhorn, birch bark, silk strings, bone, pigment

L. 162 cm (63.78 in.)
Palace Museum, Gu.172026

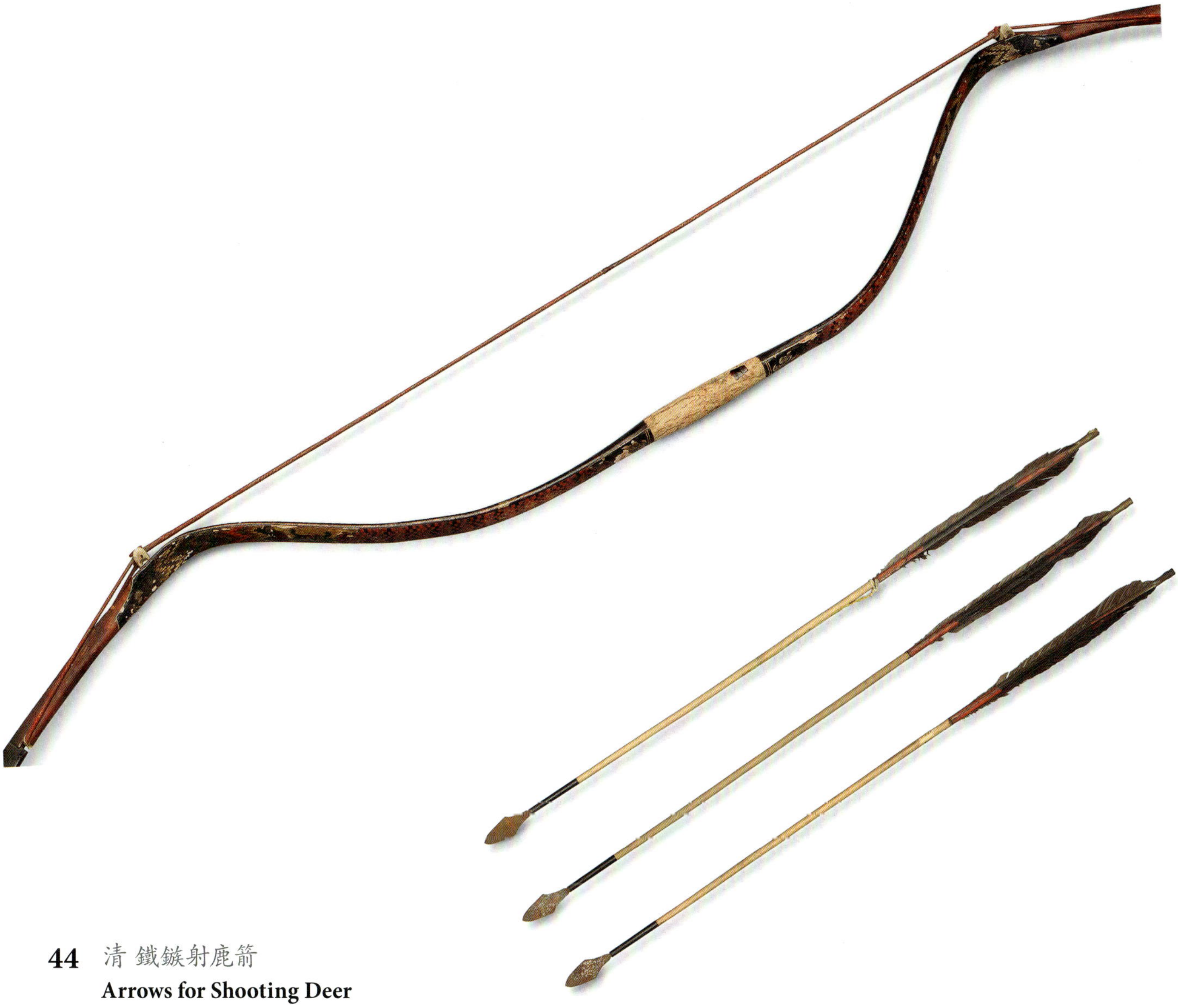

44 清 鐵鏃射鹿箭

Arrows for Shooting Deer

Qing dynasty (1644–1911)

Iron, aspen wood, peach bark, birch bark, feather, pigments

L. 98 cm (38.58 in.)

Palace Museum, Gu.170974-1-3/5

This hunting equipment was used by emperors during grand military reviews and autumn hunts. Lined with velvet and trimmed in leather, the bow case (cat. no. 42) is woven with floral and foliage designs. Made of the same material, the quiver, or arrow case, folded into multiple compartments, and gilt-iron studs stabilized the arrows. Hanging on a waist belt, the quiver was placed on the right side and the bow case on the left. A portrait of Emperor Qianlong mounted on a horse (cat. no. 33) illustrates the ease with which these objects were handled.

Made of durable, moisture-resistant birch wood, the composite bow (cat. no. 43) consists of slender limbs and a silk bowstring. Its belly, the side facing the archer, is coated with a thin layer of black oxhorn, which returns the bow limbs to their original position after the archer releases the arrow. The back of the bow, the side facing the target, is made of birch bark painted with floral and geometric designs and incised with *shou* and swastika symbols, blessings for longevity and good luck. Other functional features are oxhorn mounts at the ends and bone knobs to attach the bowstring. A piece of Amur cork functions as the bow handle, ensuring a comfortable grip in cold weather.

The arrow shafts (cat. no. 44) are made of aspen wood painted in red and black, wrapped with dark peach bark at the front. Fletching, the feathers glued onto the ends of the shaft, act as airfoils to stabilize the arrow in flight.[1] LJ

1. Yunlu et al. (1766) 2004, chap. 10, pp. 453–54.

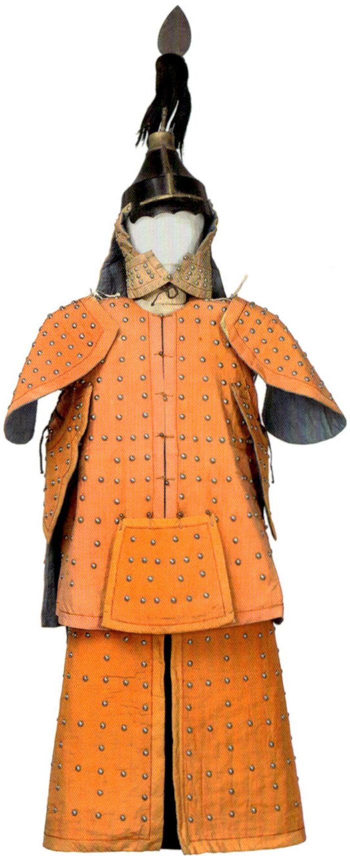
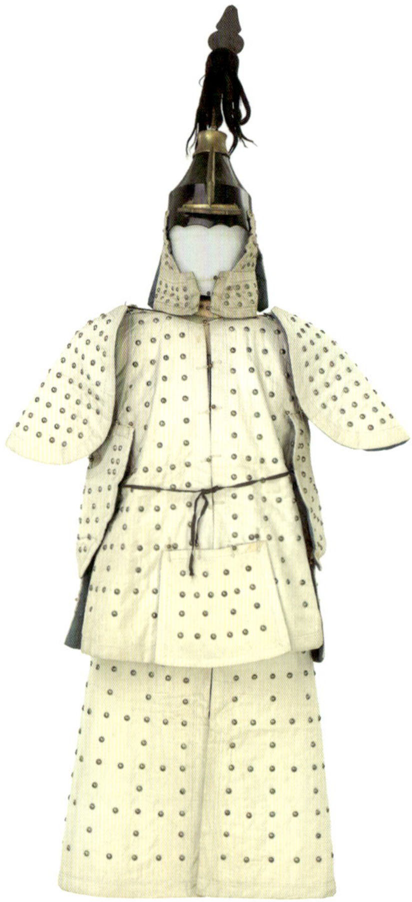
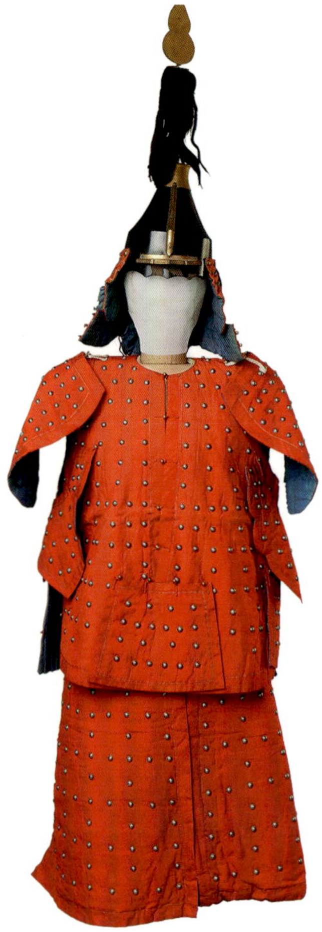
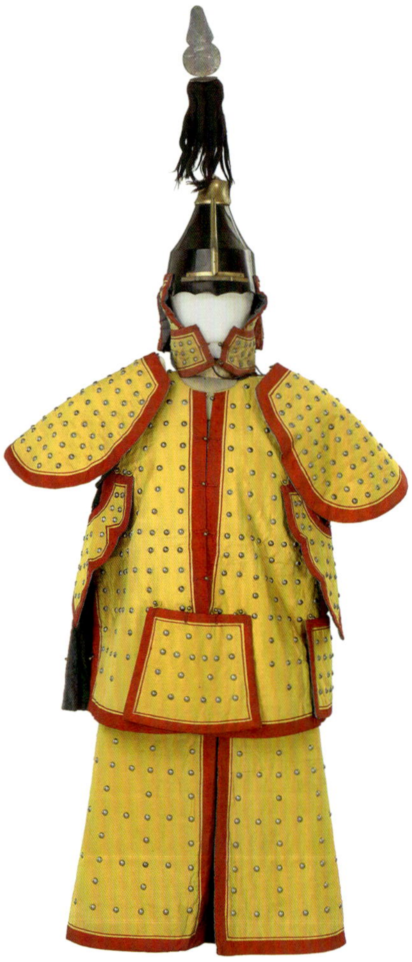
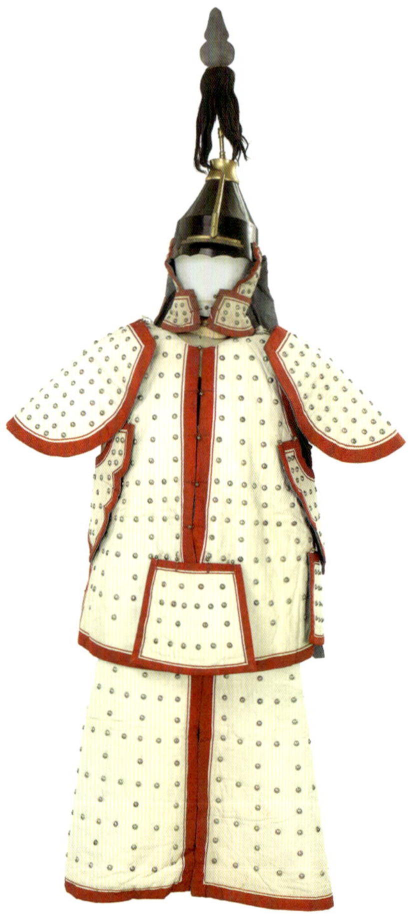
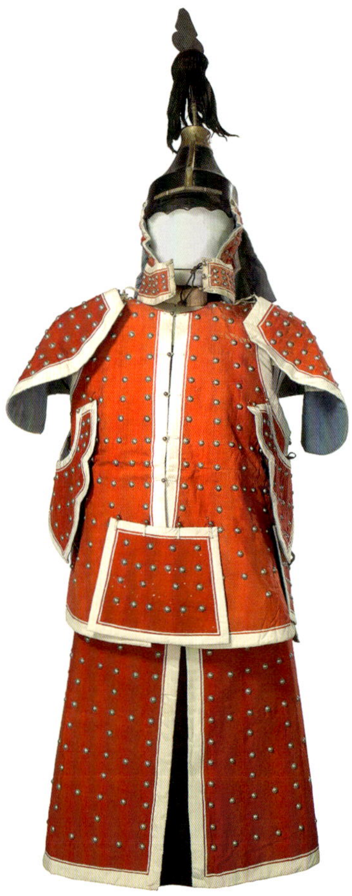

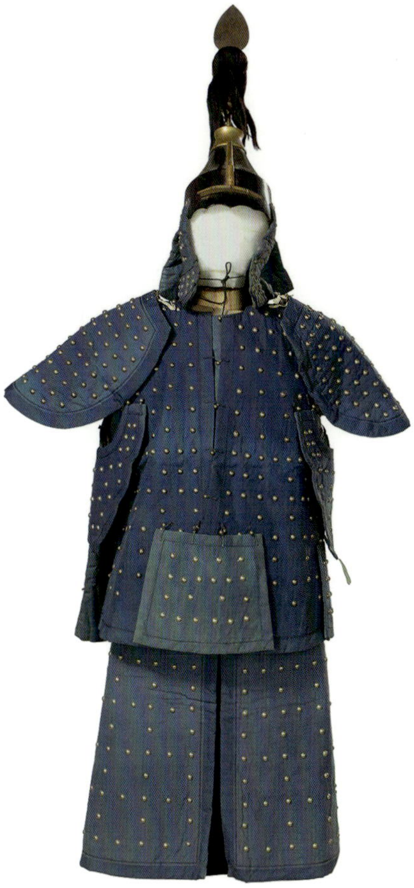

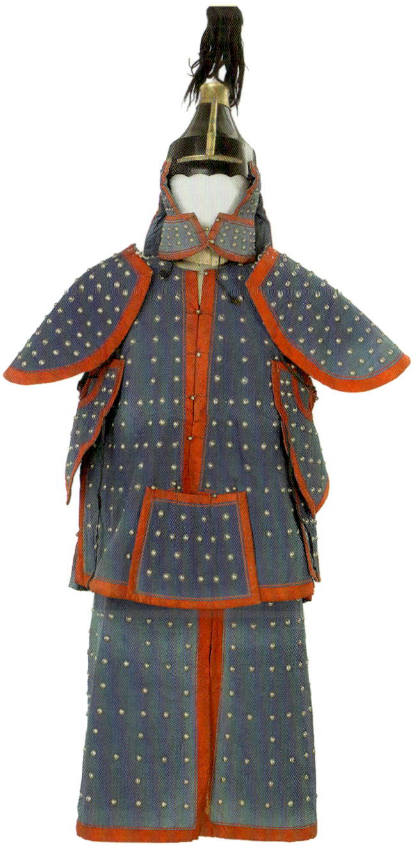

45 清乾隆 八旗盔甲

Eight Sets of Armor for Imperial Army

Qing dynasty, Qianlong period (1736–95)
Armor: silk tabby, cotton lining, silk padding, copper studs
Helmets: lacquered leather, gilt copper, metal fittings,
silk and cotton flaps, red tassels, yak hair

Tunic: L. 74 cm (29.13 in.)
Apron: L. 76 cm (29.92 in.)
Helmet: H. 32 cm (12.6 in.)
Palace Museum, Gu.170987-4/800, Gu.171988-4/730, Gu.170989-4/744, Gu.170990-4/743, Gu.170991-4/731, Gu.171992-4/712, Gu.170993-4/722, Gu.170994-4/724

Created in 1601, the Eight Banners was a system of organization for the Manchurian military forces, made up primarily of Manchu, Han, and Mongol soldiers, but also including Koreans, Uighurs, Tibetans, and Russians. Its branches and banners were defined by four solid colors of yellow, blue, white, and red. By 1615, in response to an expanding military, four colored edges were added to the existing solid color, making a total of Eight Banners. In the mid-seventeenth century, the metal-scale armor was used for the battlefields. In the eighteenth century, after decades of peace, the metal was replaced by silk padding and satin, reducing the armor's weight for the grand review and ceremonial events.

Each uniform consists of a jacket, a four-piece apron, and a helmet. The jacket includes a tunic, a pair of shoulder covers, and two underarm panels, as well as front and left panels. Lined with blue cotton fabric, the armor has silk padding and copper studs that stabilize the material. The helmet, made of lacquered leather, features three protective flaps and yak hair that hangs from the insignia. In keeping with Ming tradition, the Qing court established imperial workshops in Hangzhou and Suzhou to provide uniforms for the court. These eight sets of armor are products of the Hangzhou Textile Bureau (Hangzhou zhizaoju). LJ

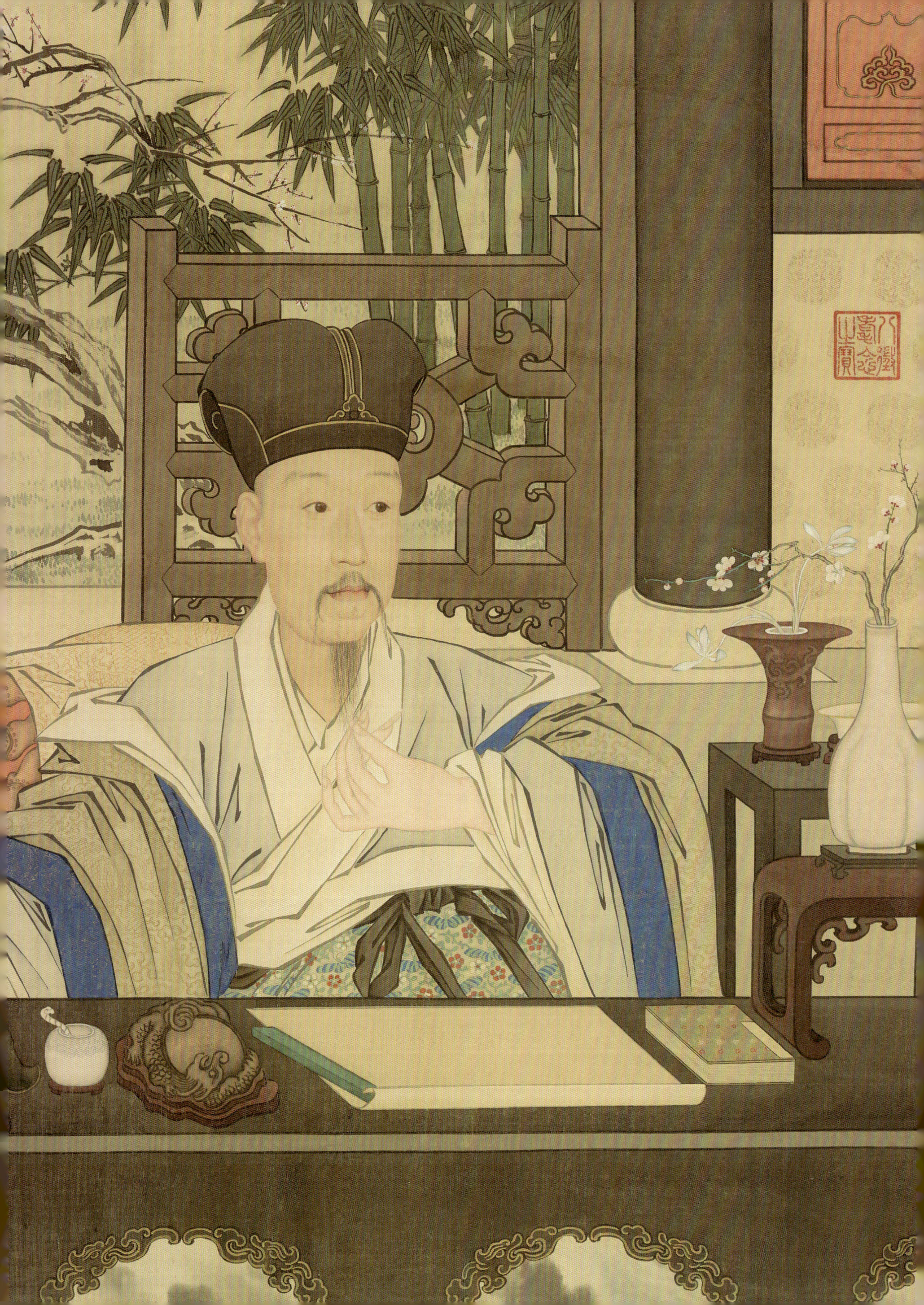

雅藝悅性

Court Arts in the Inner Quarters

He Li

After overthrowing the Mongol-ruled Yuan dynasty (1279–1368), the Ming court sought the esteem of the Han Chinese, the country's ethnic majority. Political and economic changes brought on by Ming rule affected court life and art. Regionally, Ming founders took practical measures to ensure Chinese supremacy, implementing a systematic policy to restore China to the superior status it enjoyed during the Tang dynasty (618–907). A renewed popularity of Chinese culture integrated classicism with Confucianism, Tibetan Buddhism, and Daoism. The Ming court's diplomatic strategy included seven court-sponsored naval expeditions from 1405 to 1433 to "manifest power on the seas, as well as to demonstrate Chinese prosperity."[1] The fleet, commanded by Zheng He (1371–1433), reached as far as the eastern coast of Africa by way of the Indian Ocean and ushered in an intellectual revolution for the otherwise self-contained Chinese civilization.

After 270 years, the Ming dynasty fell to the Manchus, a nomadic minority that established its kingdom in 1618 in the northwest region. While the Manchus carried their faith and religion into the heartland of China, they realized that governing the large nation, with its dominant Han culture, required garnering the support of its people. The Manchus, rulers of the new Qing dynasty, were compelled to embrace Han Chinese culture. Emperor Kangxi (r. 1662–1722) not only set an excellent example as an assimilated Chinese sovereign but also maintained a keen interest in developing European ties. His diplomatic relations with Louis XIV (1638–1715) of France encouraged numerous European Jesuits to enter the service of the Qing court.

Emperor Kangxi's fascination with European culture and technology intensified in 1693, when his recurring malaria was cured by quinine provided by five French mathematicians, headed by Bai Jin (Joachim Bouvet, 1659–1730) and sent by Louis XIV to the Qing court in 1688.[2] With the Jesuits' involvement, Emperor Kangxi launched institutional plans in 1693 to restructure the Imperial Household Department (Neiwufu) to explore European aesthetics, particularly materials used by Western artists. The fourteen workshops under the Imperial Household Department specialized respectively in enamel, gold, jade, lacquerware, packing and mounting, chariot fittings, metal fittings, helmets, paintings, stove casting, clocks, drawings, artillery, and glass. The workshops were located throughout the Forbidden City, the Garden of Perfect Brightness (Yuanmingyuan), the residence of Prince Yi (Yunxiang, d. 1730), and certain areas of Beijing. Much of the workshops' successes were due to the court's subsidies, as well as collaborations between Jesuit artists and Chinese specialists who were selected from all over the county by the Imperial Household Department.[3]

The European aesthetic also inspired Emperor Kangxi's successors, emperors Yongzheng and Qianlong, in their vision of the arts. From 1723 to 1733, Yongzheng instructed Jesuit artist Lang Shining (Giuseppe Castiglione, Italian, 1688–1766) to paint more than twenty works with auspicious allegories.[4] In the Qing Painting Academy, Lang personally taught Chinese students the oil-painting methods used to render perspective. Lang collaborated with Nian

Xirao (d. 1738) in 1729 on the Chinese translation of a textbook on the principles of Western art. European influences shaped methods, styles, and even subjects. Yongzheng himself set a precedent for Chinese court painting when he sat for a self-portrait dressed like a European aristocrat on a hunt, wearing a curly wig and breeches with tight stockings.[5]

Qianlong had a passion for the broader realms of Western architecture, music, oil painting, clocks, glass, and enamel. His meetings with Lang and Jiang Youren (Michel Benoist, French, 1715–1774) resulted in plans for the great zodiacal fountain erected in Garden of Perfect Brightness,[6] merely one of his many enthusiastic projects involving European influence on an extraordinary scale. Court art during his reign took bold steps, even portraying golden-haired European women in low-cut gowns.[7]

The royal Qing art collection, as shown in this catalogue, drew from an array of sources; some were made at the imperial workshops in Beijing or commissioned by the Imperial Household Department to local workshops, while others were tributes from regional and foreign governments. The tributes from Jiangnan, a large area in the southeastern region encompassing cities such as Suzhou, Yangzhou, Nanjing, and Hangzhou, enjoyed a reputation of superiority for many years.

Gold and metalwork with gilt and enamel decoration were held in high esteem and much enhanced the prestige and value of the imperial collection. Mining of gold and silver was monopolized by the state. The inflow, storage, and expenditure of gold and silver were managed through detailed inventories by the Storage Office, one of seven major units in the Imperial Household Department. The use of gold and silver was rigidly restricted by rank, as evidenced by the regulations on types and numbers of utensils, which were precisely allocated according to each user's status.

The major jade works were made of nephrite, a variety of mineral compound that was widely available in China. The best quality nephrite came from what is today's Xinjiang region in the northwest. Jadeite, or *feicui* in Chinese, is harder than most nephrite. Despite the fact that credible records on collecting jadeite date back to the eleventh century, the earliest archaeological evidence to date has been only a bracelet that was found in a late Ming tomb and dated 1586–1646.[8] The Burmese tributes of jadeite to the Qing court came from Yongchang, Yunnan Province, as documented in the 1733 imperial inventory; the Chinese source of jadeite began to be mined (mainly in Yunnan), crafted, and traded around the 1500s.[9] The imperial jade workshop employed skillful jade cutters from Suzhou and Yangzhou to handle delicate works; these craftsmen were oriented in classical methods and given assignments by subject.

Major ceramic works were produced by the government's imperial workshop in Jingdezhen, Jiangxi Province. The Qing court manufactured ceramics in Jingdezhen under the supervision of Zang Yingxuan (served 1680–88), Lang Tingji (served approx. 1705–12), and later Nian Xirao (served approx. 1728–35) and Tang Ying (served 1728–56). Nian and Tang succeeded in producing the most perfectly executed ceramics. Tang Ying often presented his drawings of sample wares to the Imperial Household Department for approval. The emperors sometimes responded in writing, giving recommendations or disapproving the plans altogether. Once the products were delivered to the Forbidden City and reviewed by His Majesty or the appointed officials, the Imperial Household Department would note their distribution.

Known as the "exotic" or "foreign" colors in Chinese, European enamel, which reached China in the sixteenth century, was a glassy compound containing boride and arsenic acid that melted at low temperature, making the colors soft and opaque. Until the late 1600s, the enamels used in the imperial workshop to produce luxury items were mostly imported. Around 1700, the

Guangzhou imperial workshop in the South was the primary producer of enamels. By the 1720s, the workshop succeeded in producing nine new colors modeled after those from Europe. Precious and costly, the early eighteenth-century enamels were carefully allocated by the Imperial Household Department to meet demand.

Both the Ming and Qing courts preferred hardwoods for furniture and architecture. The furniture in the Ming palace was made predominantly of rosewood (*huanghuali*), with its beautiful veins, and China fir (*shanmu*), which furniture makers liked for its compatibility with lacquer. During the Qing period, three types of wood prevailed: rosewood, *nanmu*, and sandalwood; the latter eventually dominated imperial furniture.[10] By the seventeenth century, the Qing court began to import hardwoods from South Asia to supplement the exhausted domestic supplies.

The imperial lacquerware workshop incorporated diverse methods that had flourished in the South. Qing lacquer carving was especially sophisticated in its technical precision and complicated design. Rich textures included a range of sharp, smooth, shallow, deep, and textile- or painting-like effects. Its intricacy and delicacy drew inspiration from the art of bamboo carving in Jiangnan. In fact, the imperial workshop summoned a number of bamboo-carving artisans from Jiangnan to carve lacquer.[11]

Court life during the period under Qing emperors Kangxi, Yongzheng, and Qianlong experienced unprecedented prosperity and exuberance in architecture and the arts, at heights never to be reached again. In subsequent decades, increasing unrest, open rebellions, foreign intrusions, and civil wars created turbulence and chaos that did not cease until the 1940s.

NOTES

1. Mingshi (ca. 1739) 1969, chap. 6, p. 7105; chap. 304, p. 7841.
2. Collani 2005, 17.
3. *Da Qing Huidian* (1886) 1963, vol. 5, chap. 98, p. 15.
4. Nie 2009, 368–72.
5. CCPT 1996, 120.
6. Liu 1963, 36–58.
7. National Palace Museum 1969, 62–69.
8. Yang 2006, 277–78.
9. Ibid., 8, 280–83; *ZGDYLSDAG* 2005, File ID: Gongzhong jindan Yong0016.
10. Zhu 1985 A,B; Evarts 2010.
11. *ZGDYLSDAG* 2005, 9: 158–59; ZGQQQJ 1993, 6: 15.

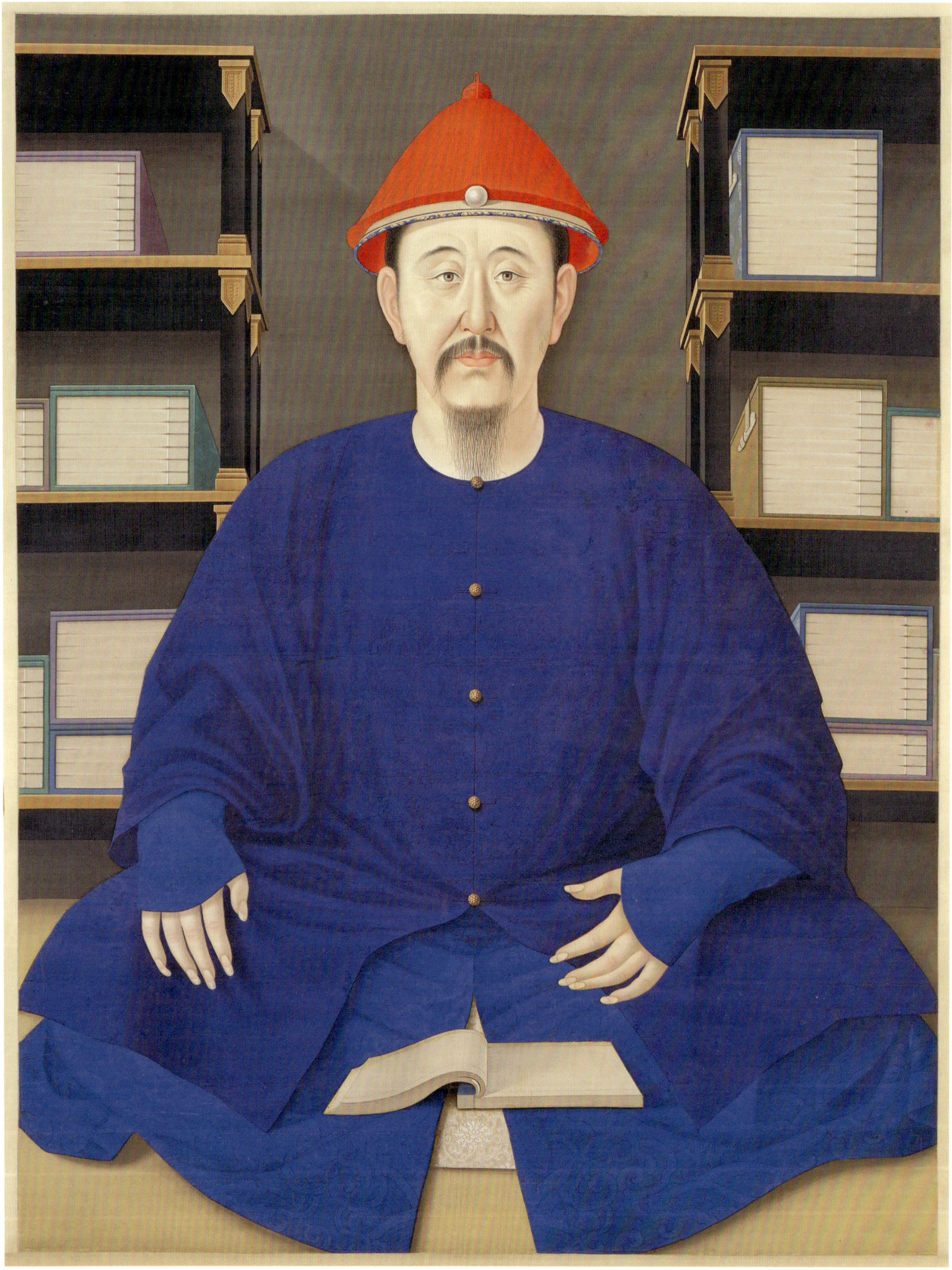

46 清康熙 玄燁便服讀書圖軸 絹本設色

Emperor Kangxi Reading

Qing dynasty, Kangxi period (1662–1722)

Hanging scroll; ink and color on silk

H. 137 cm (53.94 in.), W. 106 cm (41.73 in.)

Palace Museum, Gu.6411

This work depicts Qing-dynasty emperor Kangxi reading in a studio. A major figure in the development of modern China, Emperor Kangxi learned the rudiments of Western technology from European Jesuit missionaries, some of whom, sent by King Louis XIV of France (1638–1715), served as court artists. The diplomatic exchanges between Louis XIV and Emperor Kangxi led to increased numbers of Jesuits in the Forbidden City in the late 1600s, and the resulting cultural interaction influenced Chinese art.

Stimulated by this new environment, court artists—both Jesuit and Chinese—produced a considerable amount of artwork, and their integrated techniques characterized Qing-dynasty art. While Qing court painters had to abide by rules for portraying royal subjects with adequate dignity, Emperor Kangxi welcomed diverse artistic creations and European influences in Chinese court art. Together, European and Chinese artists experimented with combining techniques to portray animals, still life, and people.

This work, probably by a European Jesuit painter, is an eminent example of court portraits that combine techniques. The scene shows Emperor Kangxi in a symmetrical setting that conveys a sense of solemnity and formality in keeping with the strict principles of court portraits. Soft light emanates from the left, casting gray shadows on the wall, the book, and the emperor's face and hands. Intense colors—the cobalt blue of his outer robe, the lighter blue of his inner clothing, and the red hat with a pearl in its center—were all calculated to appeal to the emperor. HL

47 清雍正 胤禛持并蒂蓮半身像圖軸 絹本設色

Emperor Yongzheng Holding Double-Headed Lotus

Qing dynasty, Yongzheng period (1723–35)

Hanging scroll; ink and color on silk

H. 79 cm (31.1 in.), W. 62.4 cm (24.6 in.)
Palace Museum, Gu.6448

This painting features Emperor Yongzheng (1678–1735) dressed in a Manchu robe. A branch with two lotus blossoms rests in his hands. The flower is a Daoist icon known as "twin lotus blossoms from the same root" and a literary symbol for "a loving couple in eternal harmony." During the Yongzheng period, the flower was a good omen, particularly in official memorials, where it symbolized the emperor's virtue; the lotus blossom was thought to foretell successful days to come. This symbolism pervaded court art at the time, including the work of Jesuit court painter Lang Shining (Giuseppe Castiglione, Italian, 1688–1766) who produced the masterpiece *A Collection of Auspicious Signs* (1723).[1]

A generous patron of the arts, Yongzheng was increasingly fascinated with a pursuit of mystical Daoism, Tantric Buddhism, and auspicious symbolism. Unlike his father, who enjoyed extravagant travels to the South, Yongzheng stayed in the capital. He allocated enormous funding from the state treasury to have artwork produced and to have his manor, the Garden of Perfect Brightness (Yuanmingyuan), decorated. Yongzheng's Western-influenced aesthetic was enhanced by his involvement with Jesuit court artists.

The emperor modeled for artists, acting less like an imperial ruler and more like a collaborator in the artistic process. Many paintings depict Yongzheng in Han Chinese attire at leisure as an emperor, military general, scholar, farmer, patriarch, admirer of flowers, Daoist priest, Buddhist monk, and even an aristocratic European hunter.[2] The work here conveys the emperor's sophisticated, multifaceted personality. HL

1. Lin 2009, 315, 374–89.
2. CCTP 1996, 14:120, fig. 18.7.

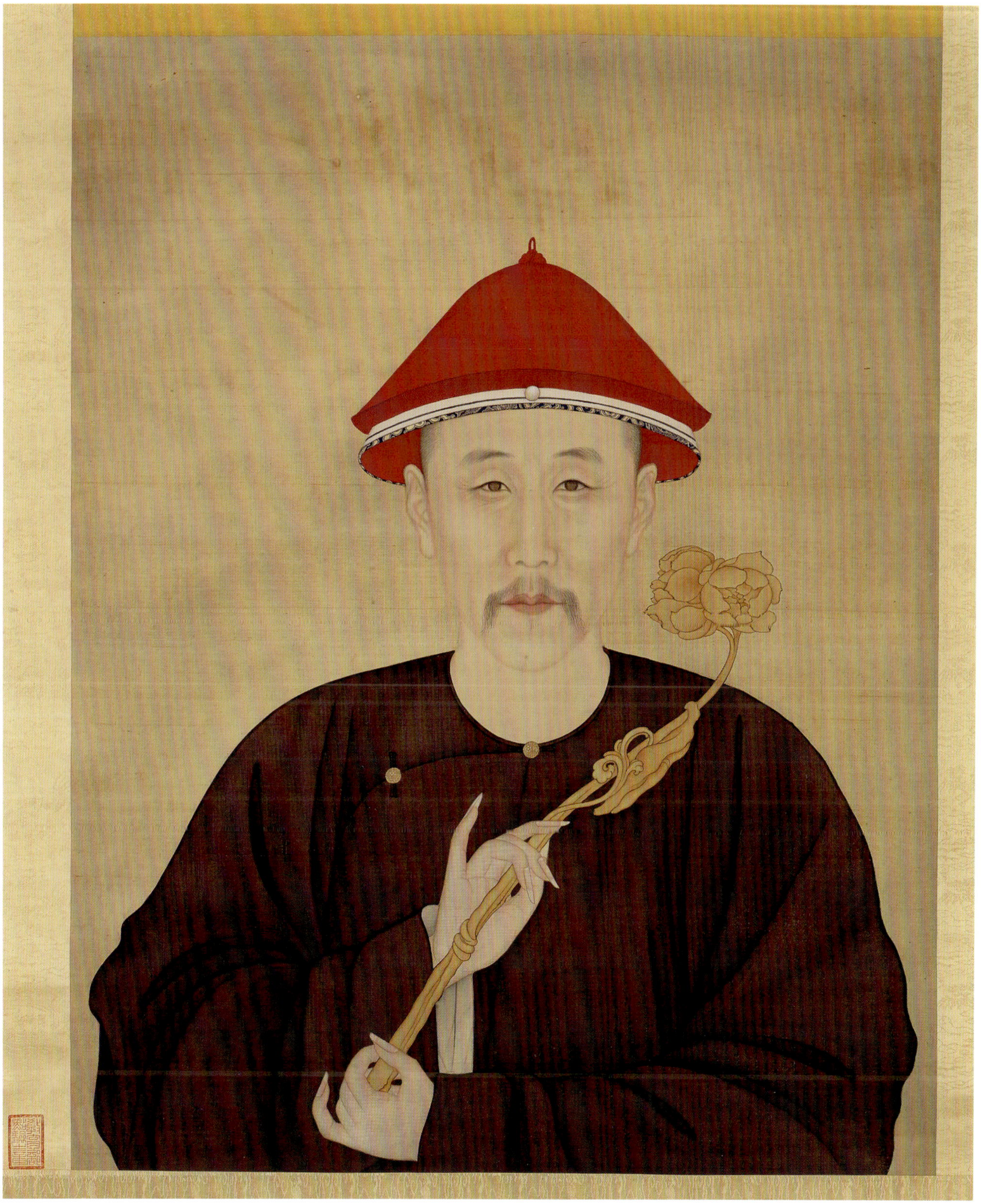

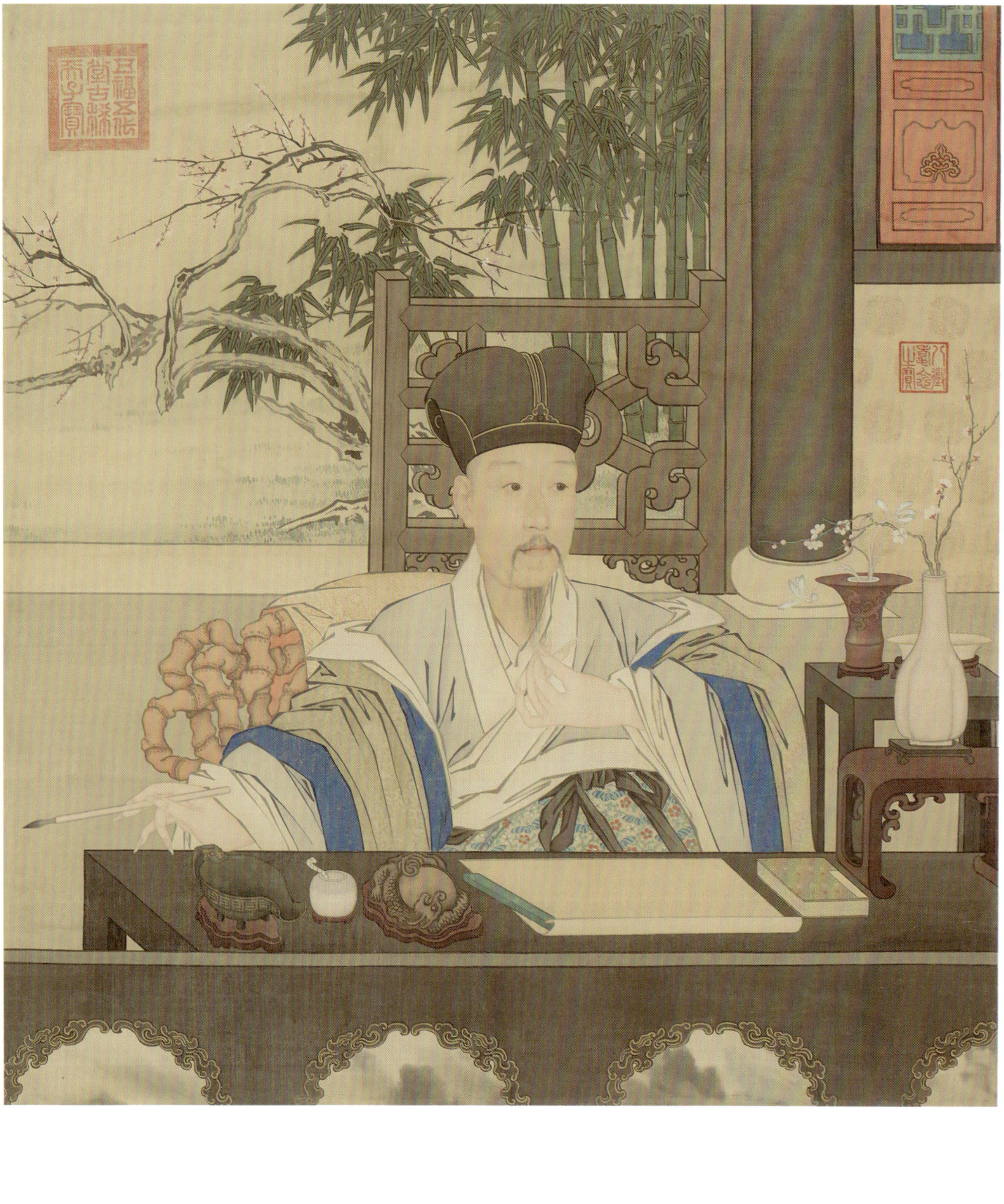

48 清乾隆 弘曆古裝像圖軸 絹本設色

Emperor Qianlong Writing in His Studio

Qing dynasty, Qianlong period (1736–95)

Hanging scroll; ink and color on silk

H. 101 cm (40 in.), W. 95.7 cm (34.54 in.)
Palace Museum, Gu.6524-1/2

Poet, calligrapher, and art connoisseur, Emperor Qianlong (1711–1799) is best known as a highly educated, versatile ruler. The forty thousand verses and poems he wrote earned him a reputation as the most literary and indeed the most prolific emperor in Chinese history. Expressing these sensibilities, this portrait features the emperor dressed in Han-style clothing with a stylish literati hat and plum-patterned gown. His left hand calmly toys with the thin whiskers on his chin, while his right hand holds a brush delicately poised to write or paint. Featuring writing implements that convey a literati atmosphere and symbolize the virtues of a scholar, the scene exudes the sophistication and elegance for which Emperor Qianlong was known.

Successfully combining European and Chinese elements required coordination between painters. Lang Shining (Giuseppe Castiglione, Italian, 1688–1766) and Jin Tingbiao (Chinese court painter approx. 1760) were well respected for their collaborative studio method. Here, the emperor's face, which is sensitively shaded, is attributed to Castiglione or another European painter, while the attire and setting were likely done by Jin.[1] Jin's brushwork seems to echo Castiglione's style, as the surrounding light colors bring attention to the emperor's contemplation.

This painting was originally made along with a hanging scroll depicting a ravishing woman who looks into a mirror.[2] If, as is commonly believed, the two paintings were created together to express an erotic theme of "genius and beauty,"[3] such a pairing was rare and meant that Emperor Qianlong allowed or even commissioned the artists to depict him in an unconventional manner that fell beneath imperial standards of dignity. HL

Seal of Qianlong: 八徵耄念之寶 *Bazheng maonian zhibao* (Treasure of an Elder with the Eight Sensibilities)

1. CCTP 1996, 200.
2. Ibid. 1, 200–201.
3. Zhang 2002, 106–7.

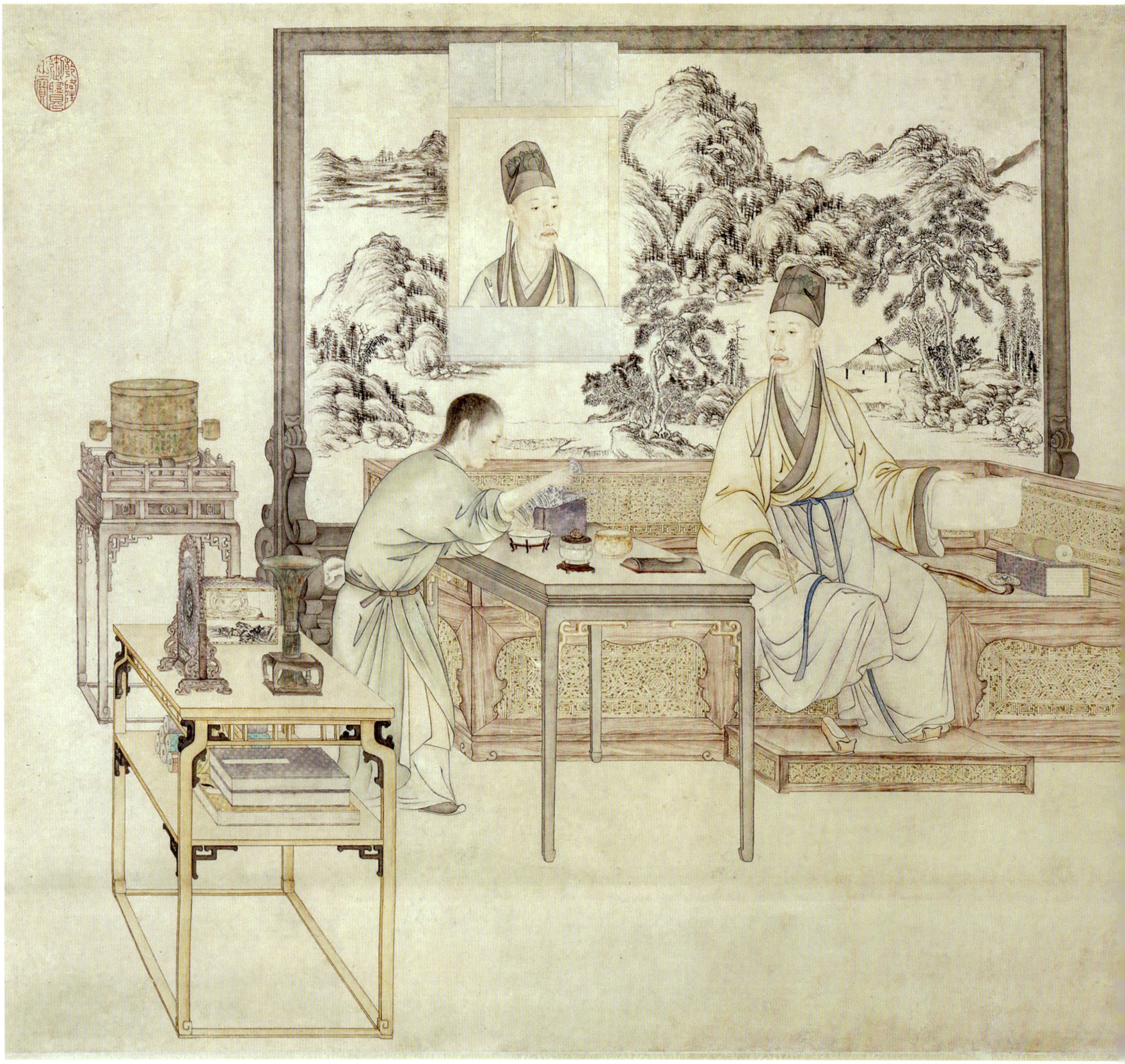

49 清乾隆 弘曆題"是一是二"圖軸

One or Two? Emperor Qianlong Enjoying Antiques

Qing dynasty, Qianlong period (1736–95)

Hanging scroll; ink and color on paper

H. 76.5 cm (30.12 in.), W. 147.2 cm (57.95 in.)

Palace Museum, Gu.6493

This unique painting from the imperial collection contains a double portrait. Qianlong appears in Han attire. He sits on a couch and is surrounded by antiques. On the screen behind him hangs his portrait, done in an identical likeness. This portrait-within-a-portrait suggests a critique of the emperor-scholar by his higher self—a puzzle made even more fascinating by Qianlong's verse in the painting:

> Are they one or are they two?
> Neither contiguous nor distant
> Perhaps Confucian, perhaps Mohist
> Why worry? Why ponder?

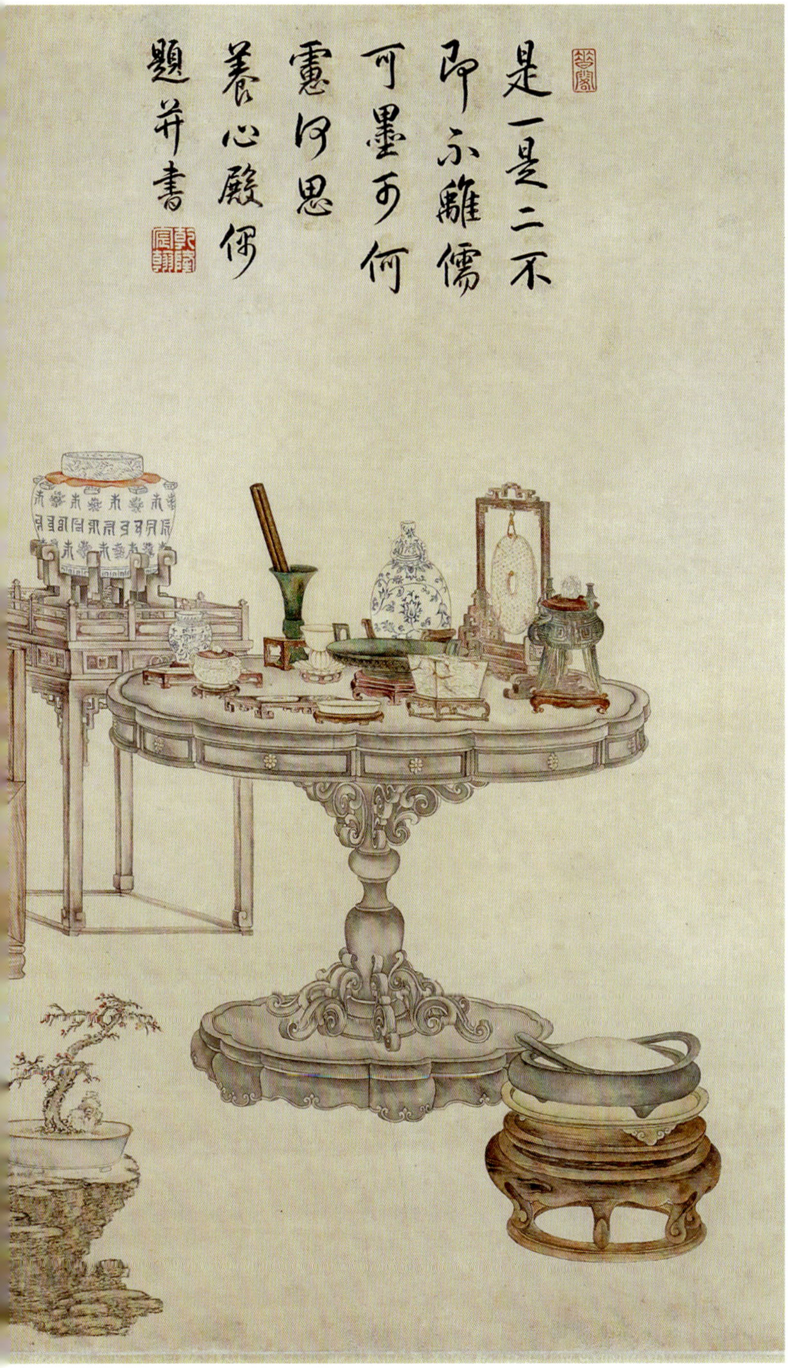

The two philosophical schools the Qianlong emperor mentions offer contradictory principles of government. Confucius (551–479 BC) emphasized the importance of ritual and social order, whereas Mozi (approx. 400s BC) advocated frugality and technology over formality and ritual. The emperor presents both views in this work rather than declaring one absolute answer.

Historical evaluations of Emperor Qianlong's verses suggest influences of Tibetan Buddhism.[1] Attesting to the emperor's interest in Tibetan Buddhism, a number of *thangkas* portray him as the manifestation of Buddhist figures.[2] However, as evidenced by the clues on his headdress, Tibetan Buddhism was not the only inspiration for Emperor Qianlong's contemplation. The inner cap in the shape of lotus blossoms represents Daoist icons worn by prominent figures. The outer hat reflects an older literati style used by Daoist gods or priests.[3]

Spanning thousands of years and made of a range of materials, the antiques surrounding Emperor Qianlong portray him as an intelligent guardian of treasures. The Qianlong emperor showed pride not only in his collection but also in his outstanding accomplishments in Chinese classical education. Yet as a satirist, he wanted to appear as a skeptic who did not settle all questions but conveyed their complications in a regal setting. HL

Inscription: 養心殿偶題並書 (Spontaneously composed and inscribed in Hall of Intellectual Cultivation)

Seal: 乾隆宸翰 *Qianlong chenhan*

1. Rawski and Rawson 2005, 439.
2. Zhang 2002, 52, 113; CCTP 1996, 202–4.
3. Little and Eichman 2000, 122, 175, 18, 191, 328.

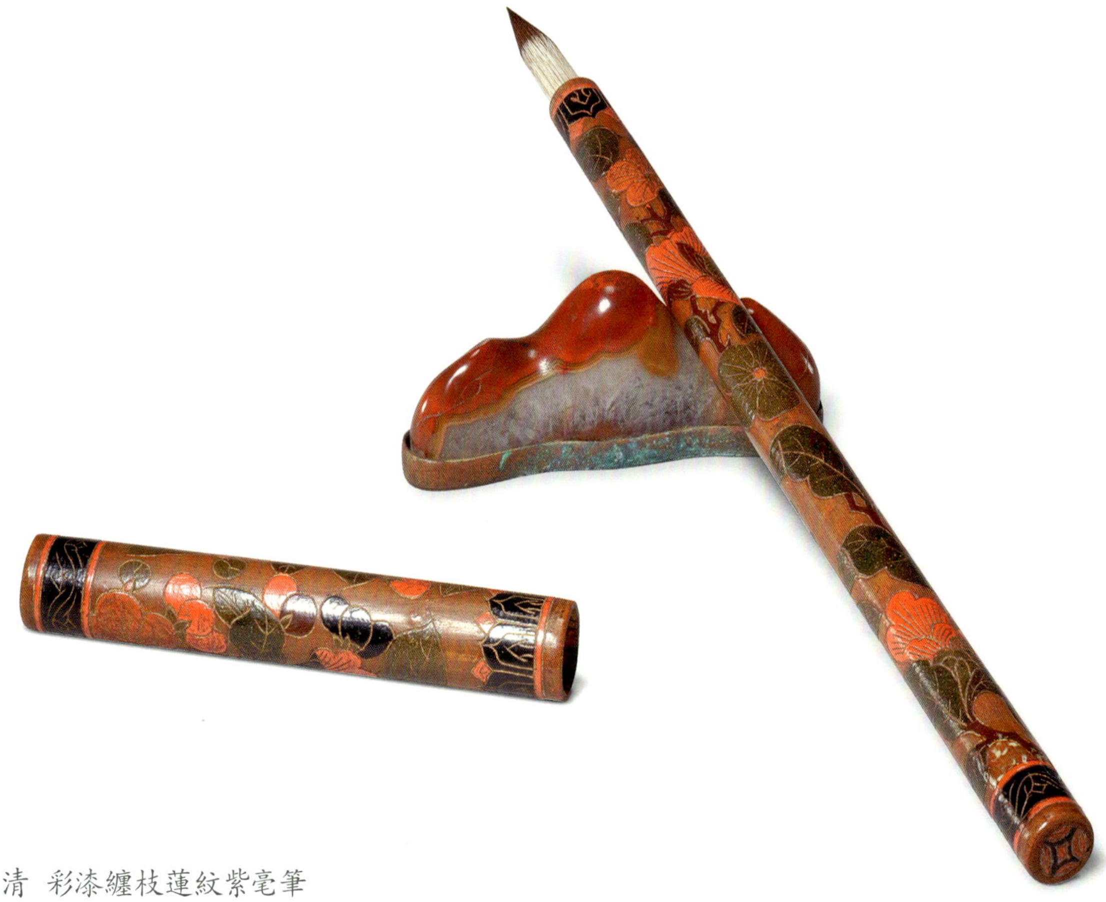

50 清 彩漆纏枝蓮紋紫毫筆

Brushpen with Lotus Scrolls

Qing dynasty (1644–1911)

Wood painted with multicolored lacquer, hair

Brush: L. 20.2 cm (7.95 in.), Dia. 1.1 mm (0.043 in.)
Cap: L. 9.2 cm (3.62 in.); Hair: L. 3.5 cm (1.38 in.)
Palace Museum, Gu.132743

Brush making has two general traditions. The first involves twisting a flat row of rabbit hair with fleece and then rolling it into a solid cylindrical tuft to be used as the core. The core is wrapped with another layer of rabbit hair and then inserted into the handle. The second tradition involves mixing a few human hairs, fleece, and rabbit hair, and arranging them into a flat row. The roots of the hairs are then attached to a narrow piece of hemp paper, and the whole row is then rolled up to form the brush.

The two most prominent brush makers were named after their locations of origin. The Xuan brush originated in the town of Xuan (Anhui Province) during the Tang dynasty (618–907). The dark-colored Xuan brush, known as Purple Hair (*zihao*), contained hairs from rabbits, deer, and sheep, which tended to be stiff and straight. When the Song court resettled its capital in the Southeast in 1127, the center of brush making began to shift from Xuan southward to Shanlian in the Hu prefecture, Zhejiang Province.

The Hu brush was renowned for its exquisite execution and for fastidiously selected materials, particularly its superb fleece. Its shaft was made of materials unprecedented in variety and extravagance—gold, silver, metal, jade, gemstones, bamboo, porcelain, horn, ivory, hawksbill shell, and hardwood. As documented in local chronicles, the completion of each brush involved over one hundred processes, including selection, cleaning, tying, shaping, and decorating the shaft. This brush, with its purple tip and bamboo shaft carved with lotus scrolls, is a fine example of the Hu productions. HL

51 清"玉筍"銘斑竹管畫筆

Brushpen with Inscriptions

Qing dynasty (1644–1911)

Mottled bamboo shaft with ivory rims and sheep-fur tip

Shaft: L. 21 cm (8.27 in.), Dia. 1 cm (0.39 in.)
Cap: L. 12.5 cm (4.92 in.), Dia. 1.1 cm (0.43 in.)
Hair: L. 4.4 cm (1.73 in.)
Palace Museum, Gu.133122-6/10

The shaft and cover of this brush are made of a special species of bamboo with natural dark-brown mottles. Made of a bundle of sheep fleece, the brush is especially clean and absorbant, making it effective for both calligraphy and painting, especially in freehand strokes. The beauty of this bamboo is regarded so highly that the shaft is labeled *yu* (jade) for its exquisite coloring and *sun* (cone-shaped bamboo root) for its fluid form.

The process of making this brush and cover began with incising the inscription, then filling in the engraved area with colors of blue and green, and lastly mounting the handle and cover with pretrimmed ivory. The materials selected for the tip and handle identify the brush as a Hu product.

Hu brushes surpassed Xuan ones in quality and quantity and maintained their dominance in the market until modern times. HL

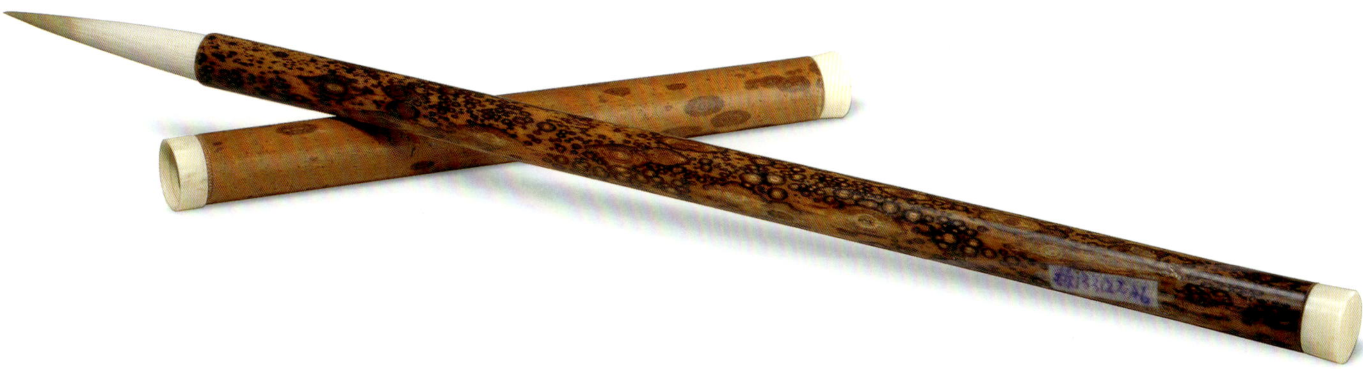

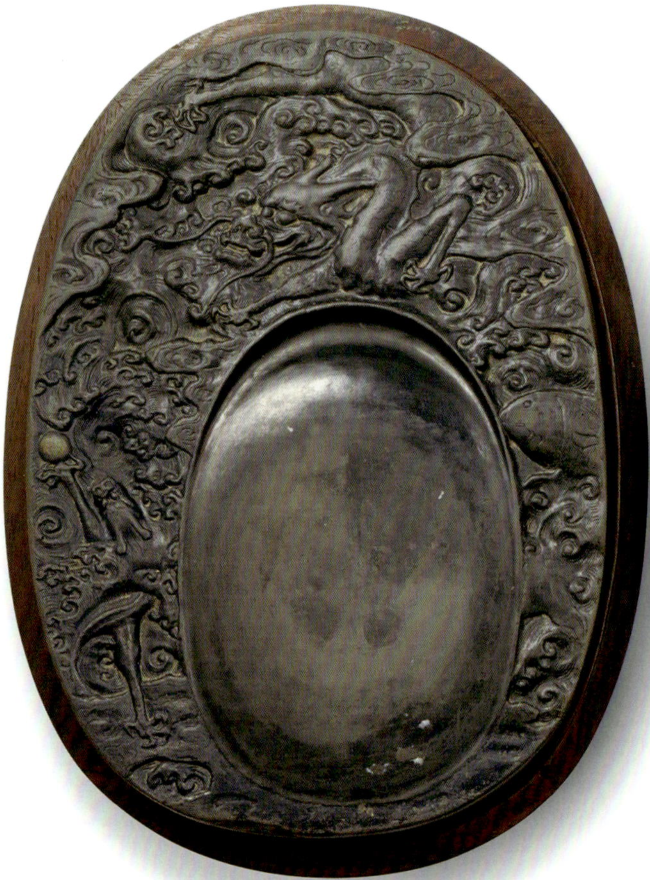

Inkstone

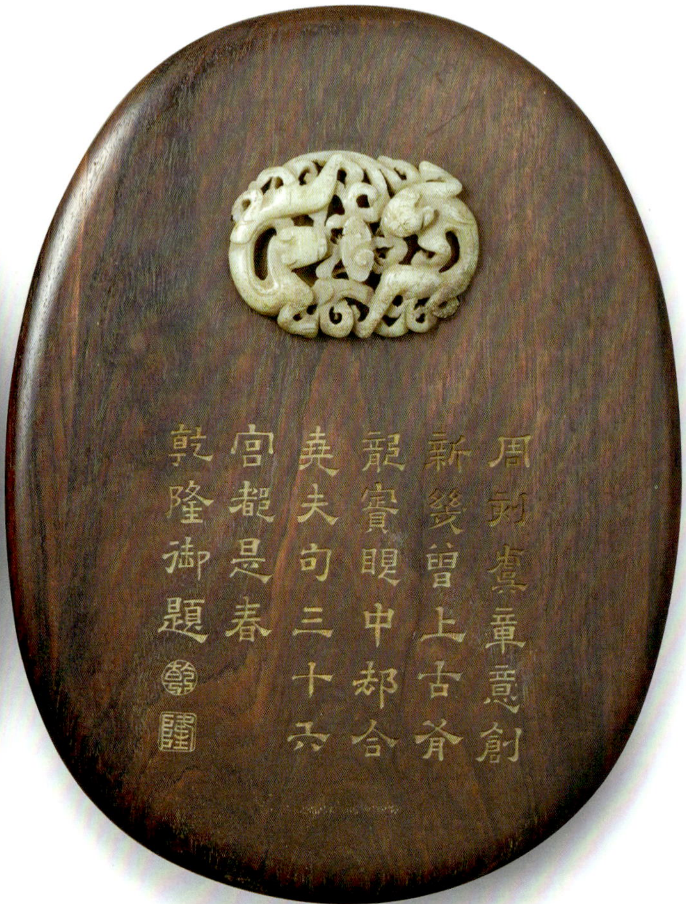

Container lid

52 清乾隆銘 端石魚龍硯

Inkstone with Emperor Qianlong's Inscription, 1778

Qing dynasty, Qianlong period (1736–95)

Duan stone, sandalwood *zitan,* nephrite

H. 7 cm (2.76 in.), L. 25.8 cm (10.16 in.), W. 19.3 cm (7.60 in.)
Palace Museum, Gu.133959

This oval inkstone was owned and used by Emperor Qianlong himself. Ink can be made on this inkstone through a slow process of grinding a dry ink stick in water. The inkstone has a concave area in the center for grinding, and the border's carved design depicts a dragon turning in the ocean. The dragon plays with a flaming pearl formed by an eyelike cavity. The walls are incised with the Twelve Imperial Symbols.

On the bottom of the inkstone, thirty-six protruding column-like carvings, each with an eyelike cavity on top, represent the legendary suns rising from the East Ocean in immortal paradise. The emperor's poem titled "For the Old Duan Inkstone with Twelve Imperial Symbols," which was dedicated to this inkstone in 1778,[1] is carved around the bottom edge as well as on the matching sandalwood lid. Also on the lid, a jade ornament with a double-dragon design represents the high standard of imperial Qing style.

A late seventeenth-century study described stones found along the Duan River, in Zhaoqing, Guangdong Province.[2] Their whitish "plantain leaf–shaped veins" and eyelike cavities were praised as "superb" and "glimmering." The ink made from these stones did not harm brushes, did not stick to hands, was long lasting, and required three-tenths less water. HL

Inscription: carved around the rim of the base: 周刻虞章意创新，几曾上古有龙宾，眼中却合尧夫句，三十六宫都是春，乾隆戊戌仲夏御题 (Inscribed by the emperor in midsummer of Qianlong *wuxu* year, 1778)

Seal: 朗润 *Langrun*

1. National Palace Museum 1976, vol. 8, chap. 52, p. 22.
2. Gao (ca. 1688) 1958.

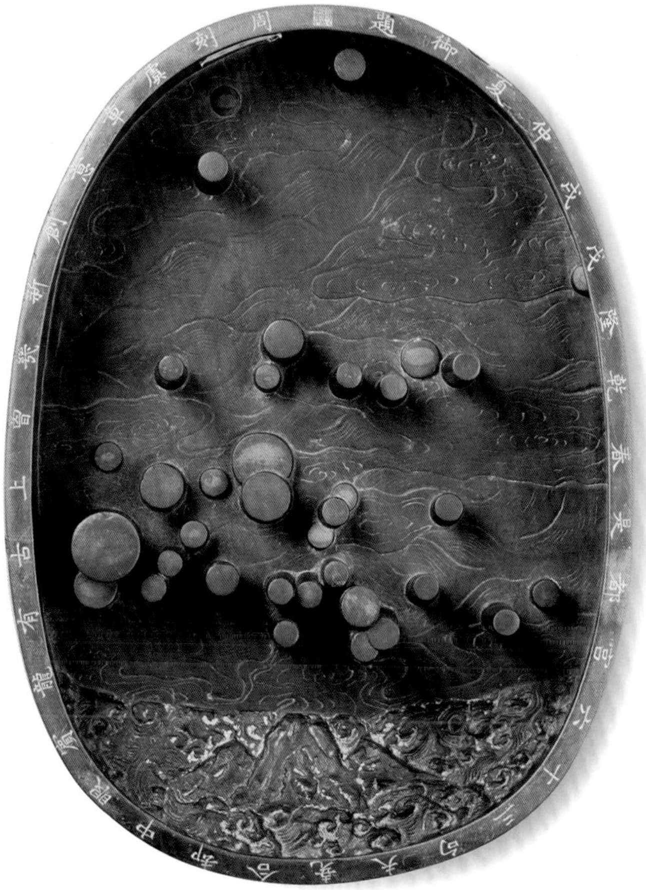

Underside of inkstone

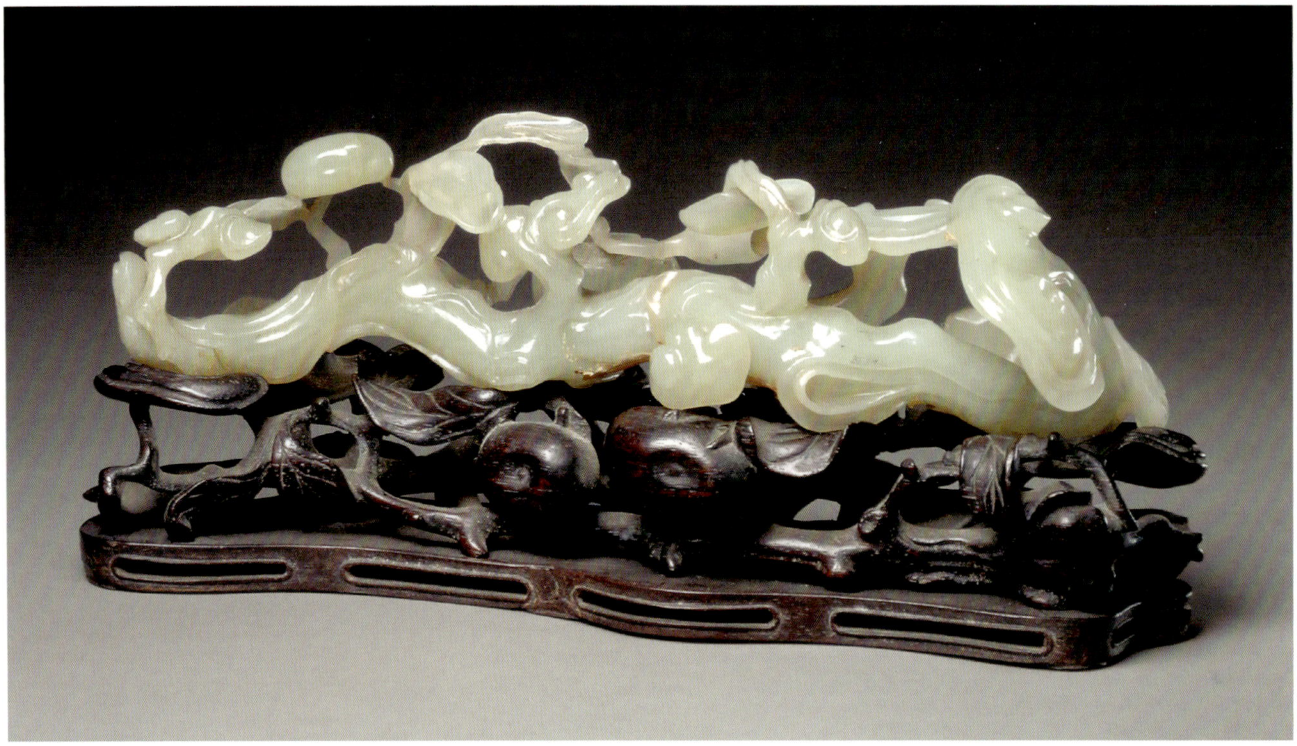

53 明 青玉靈芝花筆架

Brush Rest in the Form of Lingzhi Fungus

Ming dynasty (1368–1644)

Nephrite, wooden stand

Overall: L. 19 cm (7.48 in.), W. 6 cm (2.36 in.); Bottom support: H. 8.5 cm (3.35 in.)
Palace Museum, Gu.135592

An artist working at a scholar's table would place his brushes on rests such as this. Many brush rests, for their exquisite workmanship, are considered decorative art or literati symbols. This fine example made of nephrite, a type of jade, presents an intricate design intertwined with representations of the fungus *lingzhi,* a Chinese symbol of longevity. Lustrous, pure, and clean, the nephrite was intentionally selected as material aesthetically suitable for a scholar's desk.

Archaeological evidence shows that early brush rests were made of various stones. Their natural shapes resembled mountain peaks and gullies and served nicely as brush holders. An example of such evidence is a crystal brush holder with five peaks found in a scholar's tomb in the southeastern province of Zhejiang and datable from 1127 to 1279.[1] An age-old reverence for mountains as a connection to spiritual energy inspired artists to include them in their works. By the third century BC, the image of the mountain had been designated as one of the Twelve Imperial Symbols placed on an emperor's ceremonial uniform. The interest in jade objects as mountain symbols grew among the ruling class, who not only collected them but also buried them with the dead. HL

1. *ZGYQQJ* 1993, pls. 113, 114.

54 清乾隆 青玉乾隆御題蘭亭修禊圖山子

Boulder with the Scene of Gathering at the Orchid Pavilion, 1747

Qing dynasty, Qianlong period (1736–95)

Nephrite, wooden stand

H. 11.7 cm (4.61 in.), L. 40.2 cm (15.83 in.), W. 7.7 cm (3.03 in.); Stand: H. 16. cm (6.30 in.)
Palace Museum, Gu.96150

A solid boulder, representing a mountain, functions here as a paperweight, a symbolic and decorative piece for a studio. Depending on the material's scale, a boulder typically combined its natural form with meticulous surface treatment and detailed depictions of historical scenes. In this unusual work, rough form and natural "imperfections" counter the jade workers' superior skills. The boulder's front side provided a smooth surface for storytelling.

The Sage of Calligraphy, Wang Xizhi (303–379), inspired this depiction, made centuries after his time. Wang and his elite circle of forty-one scholars gathered at the Orchid Pavilion (Lanting) located in Shaoxing, Zhejiang Province, for a spring purification festival in the year 353. They competed for wine with recitations of calligraphic poems. Wang's original "Preface to the Orchid Pavilion Compilation" has been lost since the eighth century, but its reproductions have been studied throughout history.[1] As a paragon of nobility and scholarly pleasure, the elegant gathering has endured as a popular subject for art. Even Emperor Qianlong copied Wang's verse and ordered that it be added to this jade work in 1747. HL

Inscriptions, on front and back: 蘭亭 *Lanting* (Orchid Pavilion); 乾隆丁卯嘉平月既望御題 (Inscribed by the emperor on the 16th day of the 12th month in the *dingmao* year of the Qianlong reign, 1747)

Seals: 太 *tai*; 王卜 *wangbu*

1. Harrist and Fong 1999, 18–22; Ouyang and Fong 2008, 152–53.

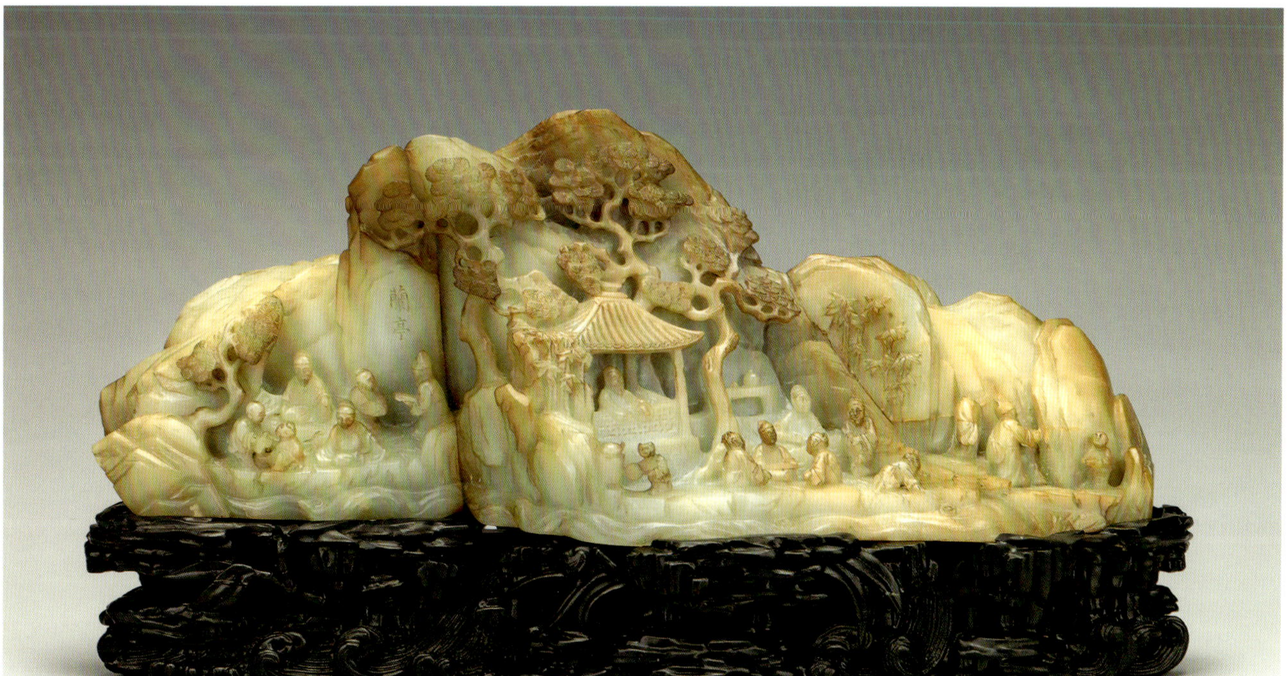

55 清乾隆 黄釉描金楸叶式笔掭

Leaf-Shaped Brush Dip

Qing dynasty, Qianlong period (1736–95)

Jingdezhen porcelain with yellow glaze and overglaze gold decoration

H. 1.4 cm (0.55 in.), L. 12.5 cm (4.92 in.), W. 6.5 cm (2.56 in.)
Palace Museum, Gu.152603

Porcelain brush dips made exclusively for emperors were produced regularly in Jingdezhen. Here, two overlapping foliate designs form two shallow beds where ink and colors can be mixed with water. Its elegant stems and striated veins are enlivened by richly shaded marigold and gold enamels.

In the Kangxi era, lighter scholars' tools replaced the traditional ponderous inkstones. This shift was due, in part, to the influential painting style known as sketching nature. The elegant and graceful painted depictions of flowers and foliage also decorated porcelain pots and sculpted three-dimensional forms.

The imperial porcelain workshop in Jingdezhen launched a delightfully decorative scheme for adorning porcelain that reached its height during the eighteenth century. Figures, animals, fruits, nuts, flowers, and plants were crafted in ceramic forms with an amazing fidelity that Tang Ying described as "lifelike" or *xiangsheng*.[1] Tang Ying, the supervisor at the Jingdezhen workshop, was the key person responsible for their execution. Workshop documents record that, in 1739, Tang designed a series of brush dips with new and traditional glazes based on imperial productions of the Song and Ming dynasties.[2] HL

1. Tang 1735; Zhang 2007, 279.
2. *ZGDYLSDAG* 2005, 9: 141–142.

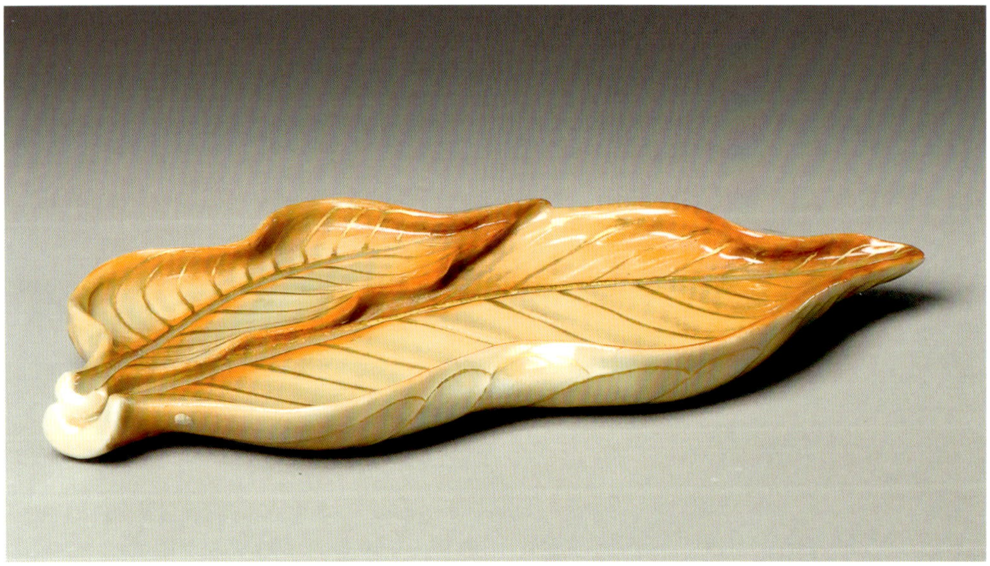

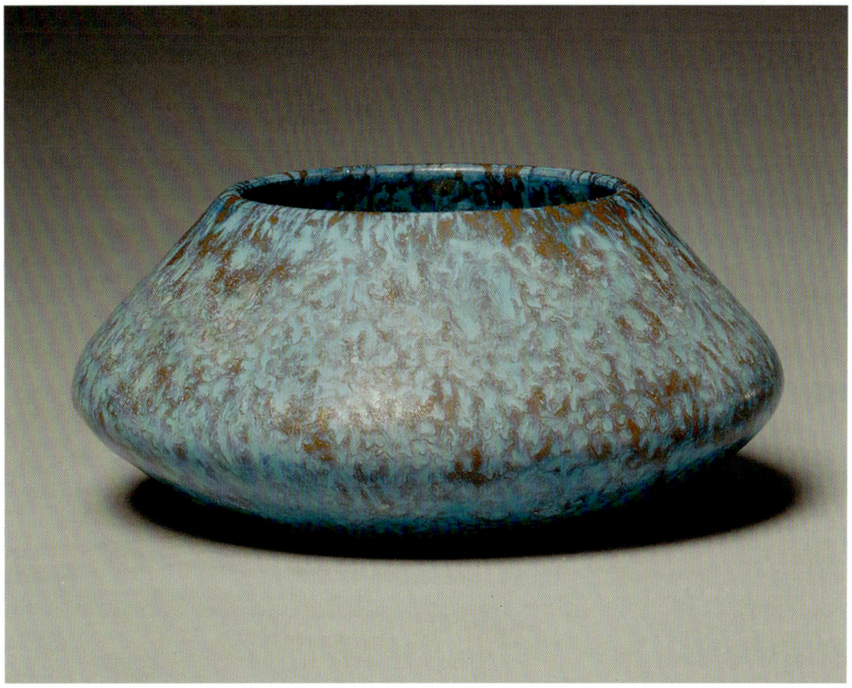

56 清雍正款 爐鈞釉水丞

Water Vessel

Qing dynasty, Yongzheng period (1723–35)
Jingdezhen porcelain with suffused Lujun glaze
H. 4.5 (1.77 in.), Mouth Dia. 5 (1.97 in.), Foot Dia. 4.8 cm (1.89 in.)
Palace Museum, Gu.148959

This type of squat vessel was commonly found on a scholar's desk and held water for making ink or washing brushes. While form remained conventional, glaze styles changed with a new emphasis on brilliantly contrasting colors. Named "furnace-mutation" glaze, or Lujun, by Tang Ying in 1735, the thick, opaque glaze reveals turquoise blue drippings suffused with strong reddish speckles. Tang drew inspiration from the traditional Jun glaze invented in Henan Province in the twelfth century and created a variety of flambé—multicolor glazes. According to Tang, Lujun produced a kind of "dripping glaze"; its color was reminiscent of a mix between the Shiwan and Yixing.[1]

The glaze was coated over the prefired body for the second firing. The intense reds that appeared during the firing process won the reputation of "sorghum red" at that time. Made for the imperial family, Lujun glazed ware was highly costly and challenging to produce. The formula is believed to be a mixture of sodium sulfate, cobalt, copper, and stones in the quartz family.[2] Part of the technique was lost after the mid-eighteenth century. As seen in late Qing Lujun glaze, only bluish speckles are visible. HL

Inscription: 雍正年製 (Produced during the Yongzheng reign)

1. Tang 1735.
2. National Palace Museum 1981, 15–34.

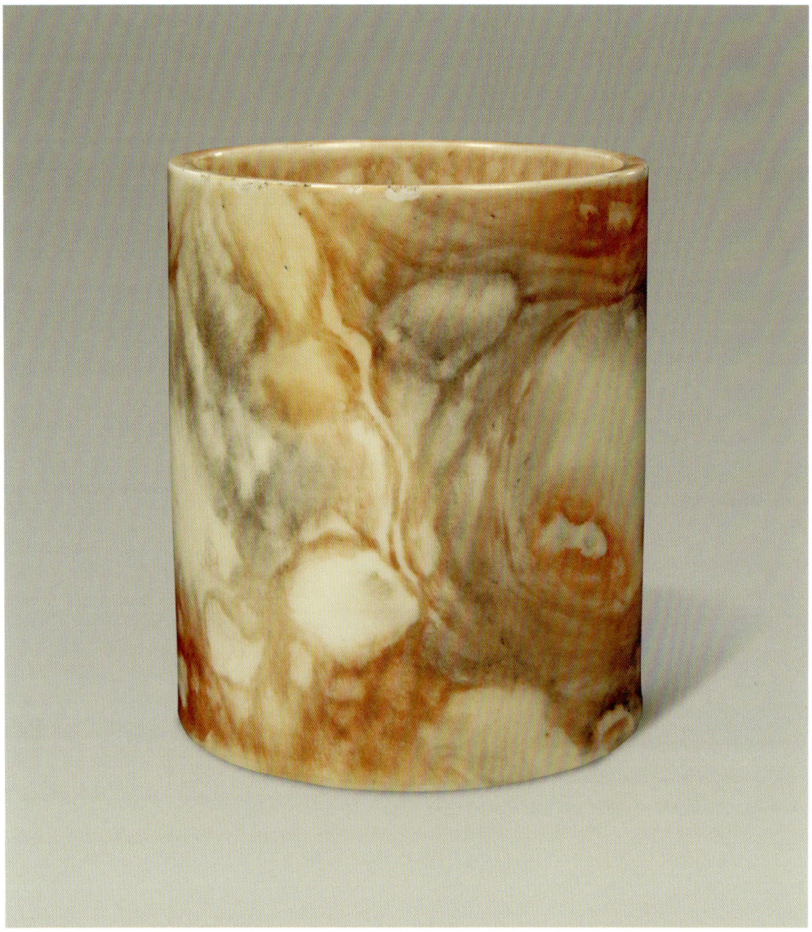

57 清乾隆 仿石紋釉筆筒

Brush Holder with Glaze Imitating Stone

Qing dynasty, Qianlong period (1736–95)

Jingdezhen porcelain with overglaze polychrome decoration

H. 9.7 cm (3.23 in.), Mouth Dia. 8.2 cm (3.82 in.)
Palace Museum, Xin.152283

This cylindrical pot on a foot ring held brushes on a scholar's table. Both the inside and outside body are decorated with a layer of opaque glaze and swirls of amber, brown, and gray, giving the impression of marble stone. The design was hand painted on the fired ware and then fired for a second time. The marble-like glaze demonstrates the changing trends in porcelain decoration in the eighteenth century.

In the seventh and eighth centuries, during the Tang dynasty, artisans invented a technique known as "blending clays." Clay of two different colors was twisted into patterns to create rhythmic marble or feather-like patterns. This aesthetic concept remained an inspiration in the ceramic industry until modern times.

In the 1700s, polychromes of "marble" glazes made their debut. The glazes were among many milestones achieved at the imperial workshop under Tang Ying's supervision. Perhaps inspired by his work and his time with fellow potters, Tang expressed the following in a poem, which appears on a square brush holder he made in 1755: "crouching into high mountains and never coming out . . . only within moss and white stone."[1] HL

1. Zhang 2007, 179–85, 381.

58 清 白玉碧玉圍棋子 黑漆描金花卉盒

Encirclement Chess *(Weiqi)*

Qing dynasty (1644–1911)

Chess pieces: greenish and whitish nephrite

Containers: lacquer on wood with gold decoration

H. 6.5 cm (2.56 in.), Top Dia. 5.7 cm (2.24 in.), Max. Dia. 1.5 cm (0.59 in.), Smallest Dia. 1.3 cm (0.51 in.), D. 0.4 cm (0.16 in.)
Palace Museum, Gu.93563

Weiqi is an ancient board game played with pieces in two different colors on a board of 361 squares set in nineteen rows that run both vertically and horizontally. Chess was institutionalized as part of royal education and was an official game played at court during the Tang dynasty (618–907) or even earlier. Early chess boards, made of wood or stone, evolved over thousands of years, expanding from eleven intersecting lines to thirteen, fifteen, seventeen, and eventually nineteen by the Eastern Han era (AD 25–220). Chess pieces, which varied in number, were made of wood or stone, including jade, and changed from square shaped to round.

During the Ming and Qing periods, emperors would occasionally order stylish pieces from the imperial workshop in Jingdezhen. In 1746, Emperor Qianlong ordered Tang Ying to make porcelain chess pieces with the classical *ge* type glaze.[1] This jade set was classical in its oblate form, consisting of 185 white and 180 green pieces, stored in black lacquered containers decorated with gold floral designs. HL

1. *ZGDYLSDAG* 2005, vol. 14, Jiangxi shaozao, 440–41.

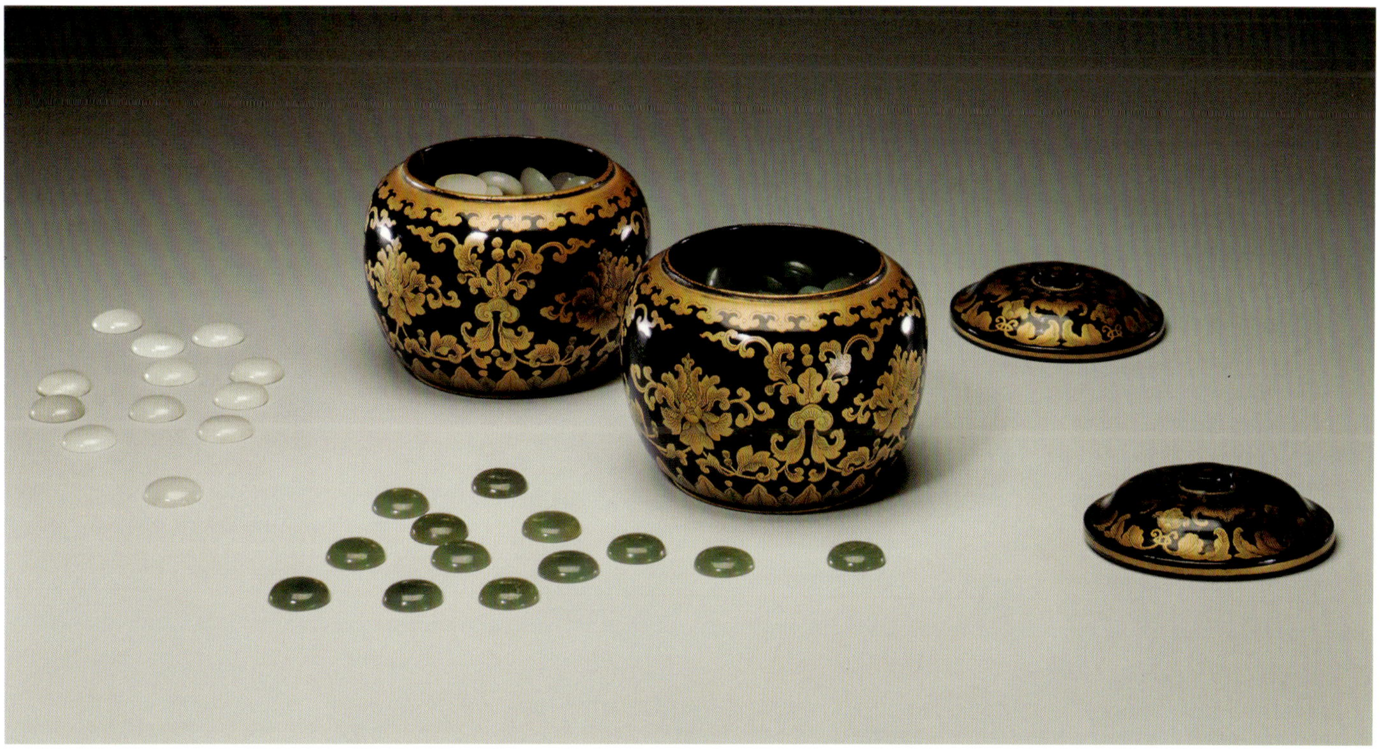

59 明万曆 王舜臣製 黑漆桐木"蕉林听雨"琴

Seven-Stringed Zither with Inscriptions, 1616
Wang Shunchen (act. 1600s)
Ming dynasty, Wanli period (1573–1620)
Lacquered paulownia wood, nephrite, silk
L. 124.6 cm (49.06 in.), Top W. 19.2 cm (7.56 in.), Bottom W. 14.4 cm (5.67 in.), D. 5.1 cm (2.01 in.)
Palace Museum, Xin.150804

Music in early Chinese philosophy was a representation of the universe, and a proper rendition of ritual music could bring good fortune and transmit the feelings of the sage kings to the gods. Bells and strings were the major instruments played at state rituals, while the zither enjoyed special favor among nobles.

The zither's growing popularity resulted in the development of different schools of music. Many scores and melodies for the zither were composed and collected. In the 1600s, when this zither was produced, the outstanding book by the prominent Gao Lian (act. late 1500s) had identified a new form of zither fashioned after a plantain leaf,[1] as presented in this zither.

A particularly beautiful characteristic of this *qin,* or seven-stringed zither, is its smooth and lustrous black lacquer with radiating reddish tones. On its underside, minor crackles resemble snakeskin. Numerous studies of zithers dated from the 700s to the 1600s assert that such crackles were caused by vibrations transmitted by sound and compounded by hundreds of years of play. Thus, the form, depth, and size of the crackles help determine the zither's age.[2]

Besides the obvious features that indicate the zither's age, an original inscription that is visible inside the instrument and four inscriptions that were added later identify ownership over a nearly four-hundred-year period. HL

Inscriptions, from top to bottom: 蕉林听雨 (Listening to the rain in a plantain forest; 万曆丙辰秋 錢唐王舜臣製 (Produced by Wang Shunchen from Qiantang, fall of Wanli *bingchen* year, 1616); a four-line poem written by Prince Cheng (1752–1823) with a seal of 成親王 *Cheng Qinwang*; a four-line poem written by Prince Cheng in 1817 with a seal of 皇十一子 *Huang shiyizi*; a four-line poem written by Zuo Zongtang 左宗棠 (1812–1885) in 1876 with a seal of 清宫太保 *Qinggong taibao*

1. Gao (1591) 1968, 244.
2. Zheng 1991.

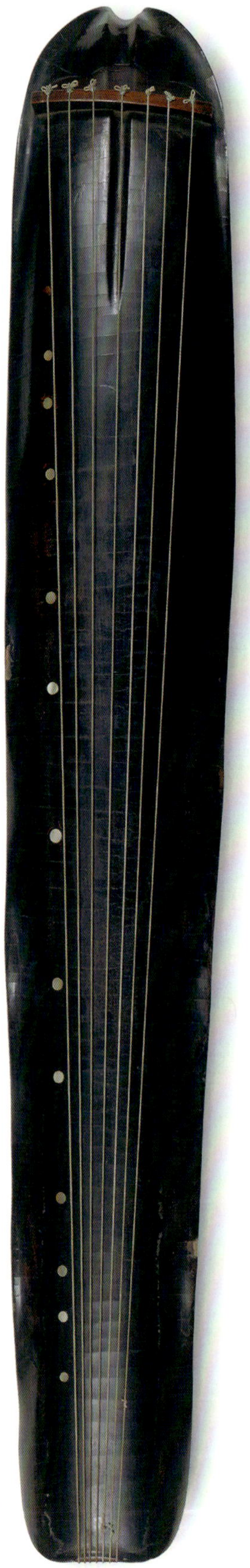

Top View

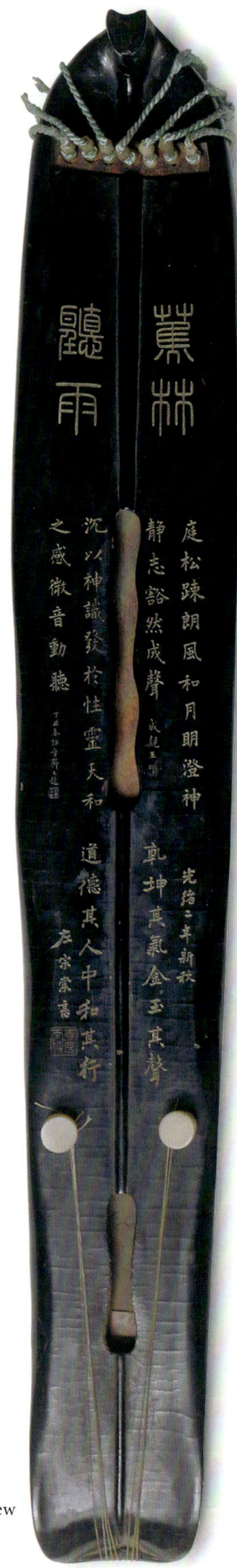

Bottom View

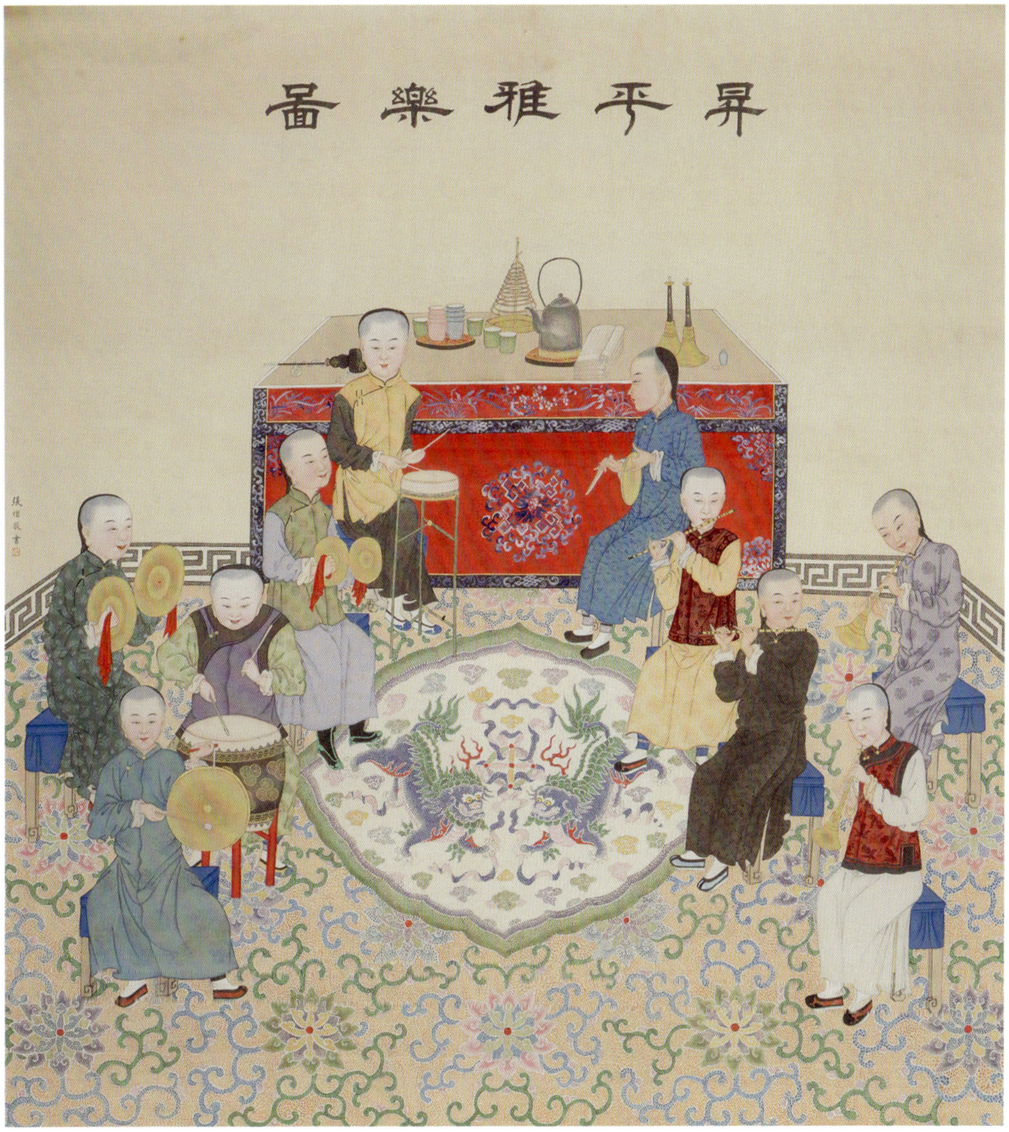

60 清晚期 張愷繪 昇平雅樂圖軸 绢本设色

Scene of Elegant Music, late 19th century
Zhang Kai (act. 1860–1900)
Qing dynasty, Guangxu period (1875–1908)
Hanging scroll; ink and color on silk
H. 129.7 cm (51.06 in.), W. 120.1 cm (47.28 in.)
Palace Museum, Gu.8540

This painting boldly displays its title in classical clerical script above performers of a style of ancient chamber music known as Elegant Music, which adopted melodies from Central Asia. The Sui court (581–618) revived Elegant Music, using it for ritual practices,[1] and established the twelve-tone, equal-temperament of musical scales used by the Tang dynasty (618–907) and its neighboring states. For over a thousand years, Elegant Music frequently sparked revivals in court rites and influenced music throughout Asia. Qing court music was managed by officials of the Southern House (Nanfu) from the musically advanced South. Nanfu was reorganized in 1827 and renamed the Department for Differences and Balance (Yiping shu).

The scene depicted here by the court painter Zhang Kai, the head of the Qing Painting Academy, was taken from a rehearsal of the imperial orchestra on a stage made to look like a furnished room. Seated around a rug that depicts cavorting lions, ten brightly attired musicians play gongs, drums, cymbals, flutes, and Chinese trumpets. On the lacquer table behind the musicians, a pile of music scores, sets of snuff, tea, tobacco, and incense accentuate the festive spirit of the gathering. HL

Signature: 張愷敬書 (Respectfully painted by Zhang Kai)

Seal: 愷 *Kai*

1. Suishu (ca. 651) 1969, chap. 13–15, pp. 2376–82.

61 明萬曆四十年 丁雲鵬繪 玉川煮茶圖軸 紙本設色

Depiction of Yuchuan Brewing Tea, 1612
Ding Yunpeng (1547–after 1628)
Ming dynasty, Wanli period (1573–1619)
Hanging scroll; ink and color on paper
H. 137.3 cm (54.6 in.), W. 64.4 cm (25.35 in.)
Palace Museum, Xin.145178

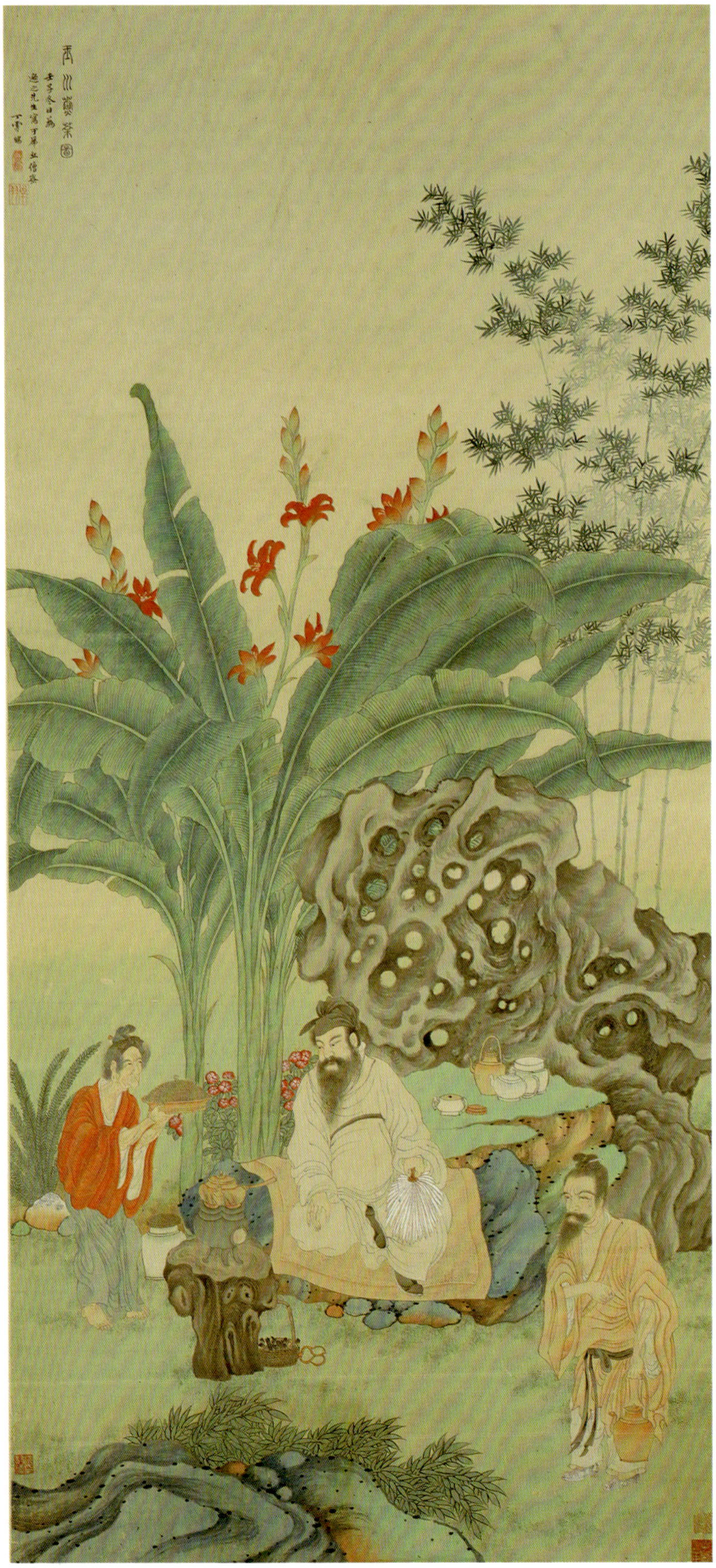

This artist's chief source of inspiration was a classic Tang-dynasty legend about tea practices. The word *yuchuang* (Jade River), inscribed on the painting, identifies the sitter as Lu Tong (d. 835), who called himself Son of the Jade River. The Tang-era eccentric referred to the Long River as "Jade River" because its clear water enticed him to brew tea.[1] Lu had declined the honorable call to serve at the Tang court and instead sought to distance himself from the capital's increasingly bureaucratic ways. He lived in seclusion around Mount Song of Henan Province, where the cold streams of the Long River motivated him to pursue tea brewing.

Here, the famous painter Ding Yunpeng envisions Lu's life of seclusion in a bamboo-and-rock garden with plantains. Dressed in typical Tang-style clothing, Lu awaits his tea and stares anxiously at the teapot on the stove. His maid carries a tray, while a male servant returns with a kettle from the riverside. The wrinkled faces, distorted bodies, and shabbily dressed figures reveal the artist's tastes and sensibilities. The overall rendering and figures' exaggerated reverence imbues the tea party with a sense of humor. HL

Inscription: 壬子冬日为逊之先生寫于虎丘僧寮, 丁雲鵬 (Painted by Ding Yunpeng for Master Xunzhi—Wang Shimin, 1592–1680—in the monk's living quarters at Huqiu Monastery on a winter day in the year *renzi*, 1612)

Seals: 雲鵬 *Yunpeng*; 南羽 *Nanyu*

1. *Xin Tangshu* (ca. 1060) 1969, chap. 176, p. 4052.

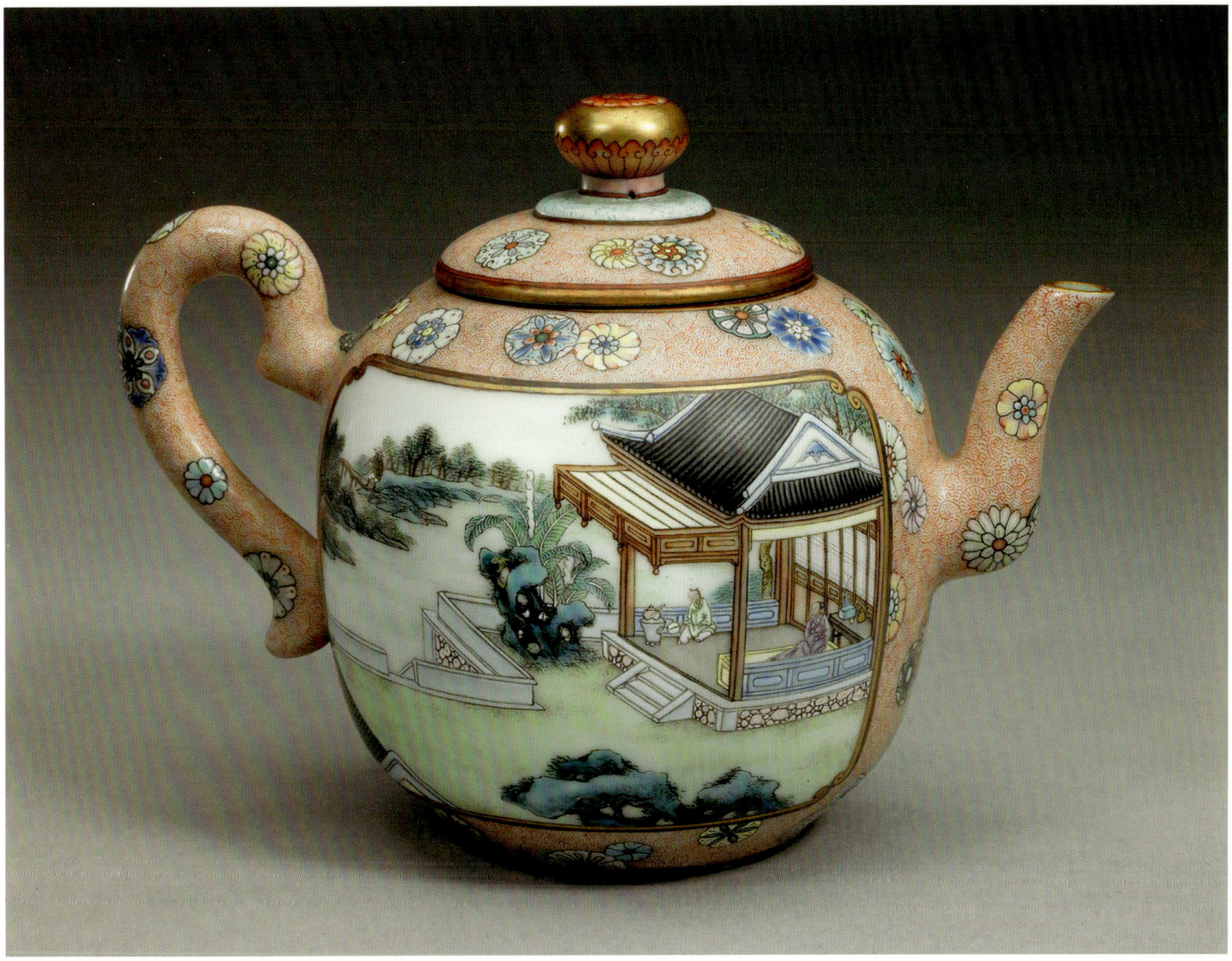

62 清乾隆款 粉彩開光乾隆題詩人物茶壺

Teapot with Emperor Qianlong's Poem and Scene of Making Tea

Qing dynasty, Qianlong period (1736–95)

Jingdezhen porcelain with clear glaze; enamel decoration painted and fired at the imperial workshop, Beijing

H. 12.6 cm (5 in.), Top Dia. 5.5 cm (2.2 in.), Bottom Dia. 6.3 cm (2.5 in.)
Palace Museum, Gu.154836

Qing-dynasty teapots, like the one seen here, combined painting and calligraphy and were decorated with "exotic" enamel (*yangcai*) and "powdery" enamel (*fencai*). A rectangular-lobed panel on this pot features Qianlong's poem "Making Tea in the Rain: Compiled while Boating on Water Studio." The poem reads, "the bamboo stove by the tea bowl is reflected in clear torrents as seen in the painting by Mi Fu (1051–1107)."[1] Opposite the poem is a panel with a spring landscape and a pavilion open on three sides. The emperor relaxes on a platform while observing a servant making tea. Shades from the powdery enamels and colors of light blue, lavender, and apricot create an elegant scene that echoes the southern landscapes found in literati painting.

The surface between the two panels is in the yangcai enamel style. With bright flowers scattered over a finely incised lacelike background, this exquisite scheme was inspired by woven textiles that Tang Ying, supervisor at the Jingdezhen imperial workshop, had advocated since 1737. In imperial reports, he called the setting with lobed panels "replenishing panels on brocade," and he called the background "replenishing flowers on brocade," both of which are traditional textile terms.[2] HL

Mark, written in underglaze blue on the base: 大清乾隆年製 (Produced during the Qianlong reign of the Great Qing)

1. National Palace Museum 1976, vol. 2, sec. 1, chap. 9, p. 9.
2. Zhang 2007, 168, 283.

63 清乾隆 樺木雕手提乾隆御題詩文茶具格 (紫砂壺、紫砂罐、銅心竹殼爐、茶具格)

Portable Cabinet with Tea Set and Stove, approx. 1751

Qing dynasty, Qianlong period (1736–95)

Lacquered *hua* wood (Betulaceae) cabinet; copper alloy stove encased in woven bamboo; high-fired ceramics teapot and container

Teapot: H. 16 cm (6.3 in.), Mouth Dia. 5 cm (1.97 in.), Foot Dia. 5.9 cm (2.32 in.)
Tea container: H. 14.5 cm (5.7 in.), Mouth Dia. 5.6 cm (2.2 in.), Foot Dia. 5.9 cm (2.32 in.)
Stand: H. 31.3 cm (12.32 in.), W. 32.4 cm (12.76 in.), D. 19 cm (7.48 in.); Stove: H. 23 cm (9 in.)
Palace Museum, Gu.123203

This tea set, made in the mid-eighteenth century, integrates court and literati styles and was produced in Yixing, a town in Jiangsu Province, in southeastern China. Tea elites, whose writing and painting greatly promoted tea connoisseurship and touted the local Yixing teapot, favored the water of the nearby Hui stream on Mount Hui. The Hui stream was named "second-best water in the world" by the Sage of Tea, Lu Yu (733–804); he considered water from the Chu region in his native Hubei Province the best.[1]

Emperor Qianlong composed poems about the legendary tea parties at Hui. Lines in one of his poems, written in 1751, offer evidence that this tea set copied the "bamboo oven from Mount Hui" that was fashioned "over four hundred years ago."[2] The poem was carved at the bottom of the bamboo box containing the metal oven. Lightweight and portable, the set could be used to make tea quickly for Emperor Qianlong, who enjoyed the hot beverage whatever the season and wherever the location.

Designed for Emperor Qianlong's travel procession, the cabinet could be lifted by the metal handle on top. The drawers on the upper level stored bowls, ladles, or snacks. Teapots or containers could be stored in the lower compartments. The stove is one of only four well-preserved tea stoves in the Palace Museum collection. The upper stove was designed for the use of charcoal and served as a kindling chamber. The lower ash box on the pedestal has a pit door in the front, and ash would pass through a metal grid fixed between the stove and the box.

Both the clay teapot and the clay container were also made in Yixing. Another Qianlong verse regarding the Mount Hui legacy is scribbled on the teapot. Unglazed Yixing pots like this one were ideal for bringing out the perfect flavor and fragrance of teas.

Yixing stoneware has influenced ceramists worldwide since the late seventeenth century. Early reproductions of Yixing-style red-brown stoneware appeared between 1710 and 1717, made by Johann Bottger, a German chemist at the ceramic factory at Meissen, near Dresden. HL

Inscription: 乾隆辛未年倣惠山聽松庵竹爐成詩以詠之

1. *Xin Tangshu*, (ca.1060) 1969, chap. 196, p. 4087; Chen 1992, 628–29.
2. National Palace Museum 1976, vol.3, sec. 2, chap. 26, p. 21.

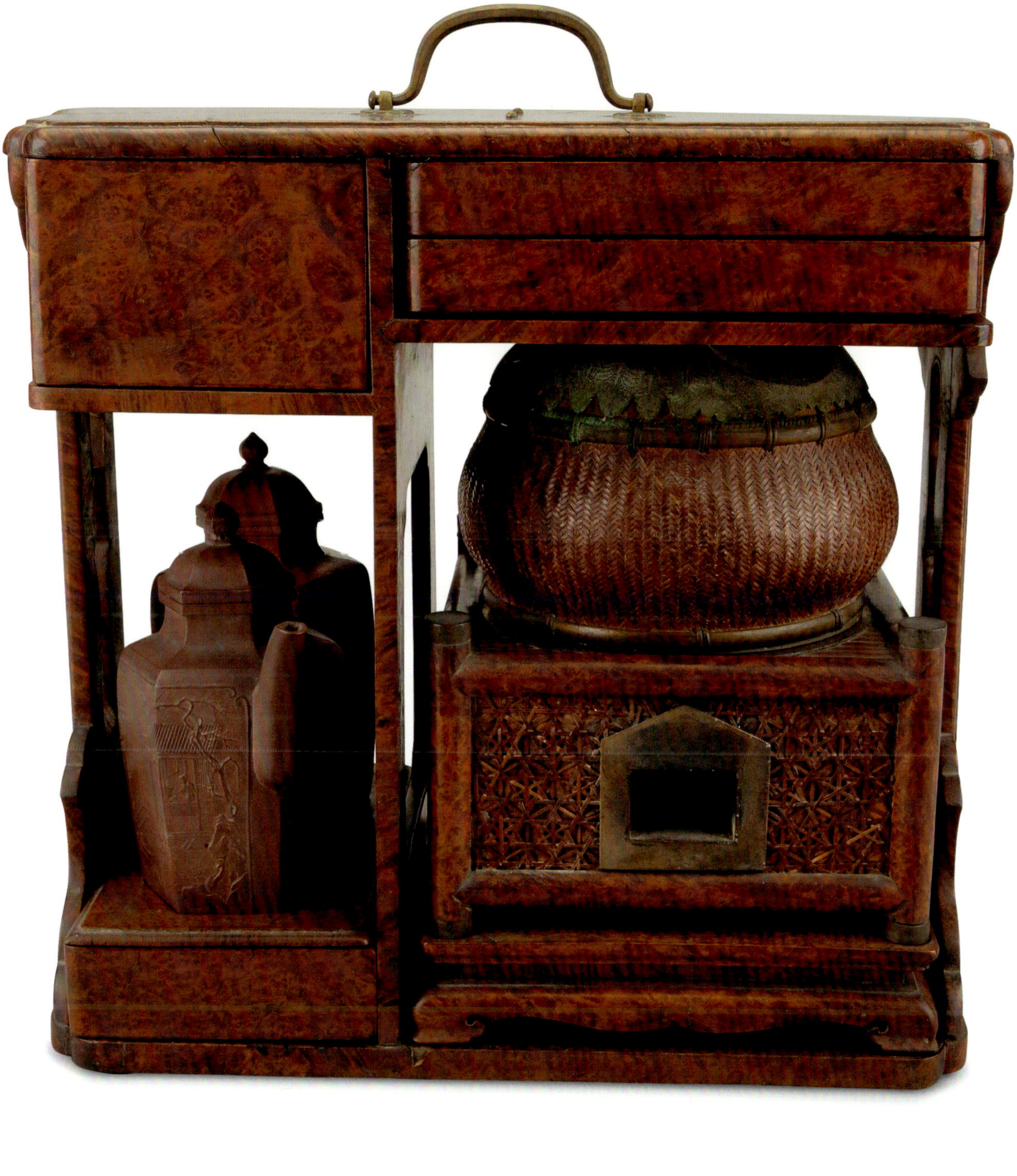

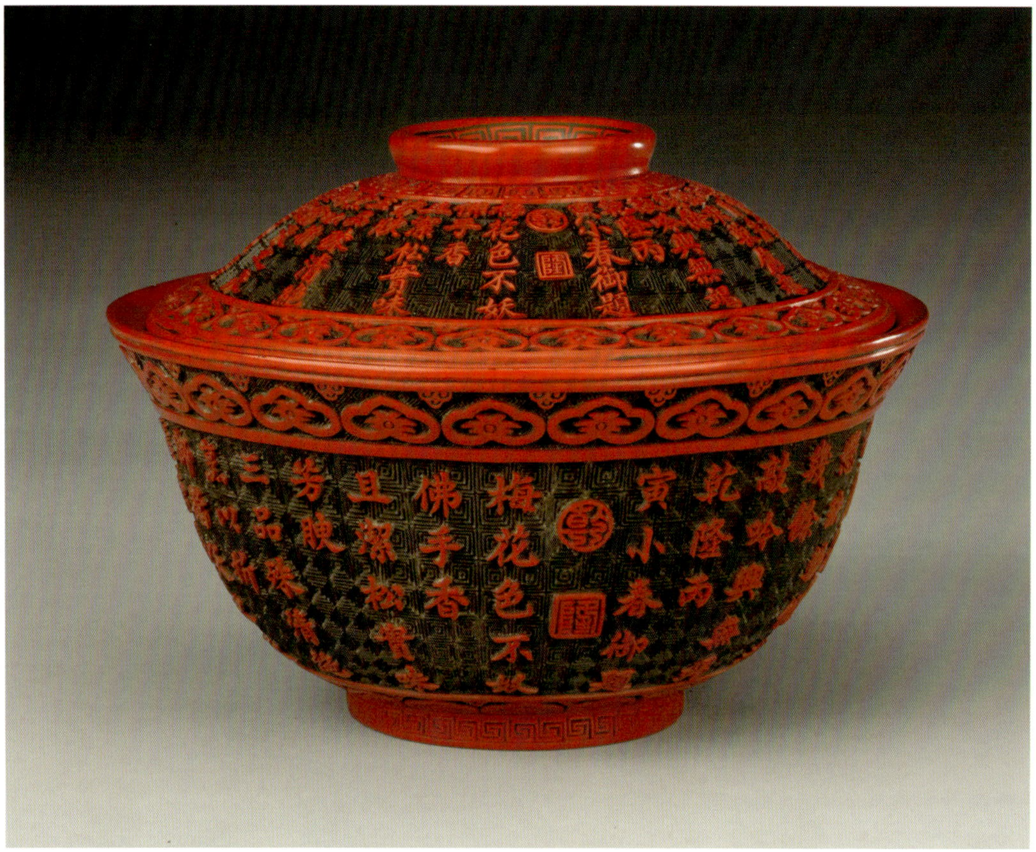

64 清乾隆 剔紅漆器乾隆御題三清茶詩如意紋蓋碗

Covered Bowl with Emperor Qianlong's Poem, 1746–80

Qing dynasty, Qianlong period (1736–95)

Carved red and black lacquer on wood

H. 8.5 cm (3.35 in.), Rim Dia. 12.7 cm (5 in.), Bottom Dia. 8.5 cm (3.35 in.)
Palace Museum, Gu.109555

As Emperor Qianlong describes in the poem on this bowl, his favorite tea in winter was Three Purities tea, or *sanqing cha*: pine nuts, plum-blossom petals, and the fruit known as Buddha's hand citron mixed together and steeped in melted snow. Emperor Qianlong was directly involved in the conceptual scheme and design for this particular lacquer bowl made in 1746.[1] The carving technique, designed to reveal multicolored or single-colored layers of lacquer, was derived from a particular style that emerged in the Southeast during the Song dynasty, a style that also inspired painted lacquer and porcelain with underglaze and overglaze decoration. The compositional arrangement of this bowl became the standard for royal tea bowls for two hundred years.

In symbolic and allegorical language extolling vitality and blessings, Three Purities tea appears frequently in Qianlong's compositions. In 1780, on the Ming painting *Tea* by Wen Zhengming (1470–1559), Qianlong inscribed his desire to commission tea ware decorated with his poem and an illustration of the tea's three ingredients, intending to bestow them on officials and academicians at tea banquets in the Palace of Double Splendor (Chonghuagong), located in the northwestern end of the Forbidden City.[2] HL

Inscription: 乾隆丙寅小春御題 (Written by the emperor, in the 10th month of the year *bingyin,* 1746)

1. National Palace Museum 1976, vol. 2, sec. 1, chap. 36, p. 17; *ZGDYLSDA* 2005, vol. 15, Jiangxi shaozao, 99.
2. National Palace Museum 1976, vol. 8, sec. 4, chap. 74, pp. 7–8.

65 清嘉慶 白地礬紅彩嘉慶御題詩如意紋蓋碗

Covered Bowl with Emperor Jiaqing's Poem, approx. 1797
Qing dynasty, Jiaqing period (1796–1820)
Jingdezhen porcelain with overglaze monochrome decoration
H. 8.1 cm (3.2 in.), Mouth Dia. 15.7 cm (6.2 in.), Foot Dia. 4.7 cm (1.85 in.)
Palace Museum, Gu.161232-2/22

Long after his rule, the theme of Qianlong's poem titled "Three Purities Tea" reappeared in a variety of tea ware made of lacquer, metal, or porcelain. This bowl, with a shape that resembles a full moon, includes a poem by Emperor Jiaqing with the following opening lines:

> Fine tea comes with the
> first-season tribute,
> the tea washes over the poem
> under the full moon.[1]

This bowl was reproduced in 1904 for Qianlong's fifth-generation descendant, the Guangxu emperor (r. 1875–1908).[2] HL

Inscription: 嘉慶丁巳小春月之中浣御製 (Written by the emperor in the middle of the 10th month of the year *dingsi* of the Jiaqing reign, 1797)

Mark, written in red in three lines on the base: 大清嘉慶年製 (Produced during the Jiaqing reign of the Great Qing)

1. GGBWY 2000, vol. 1, chap. 15, 286.
2. CCTP 2009, 52.

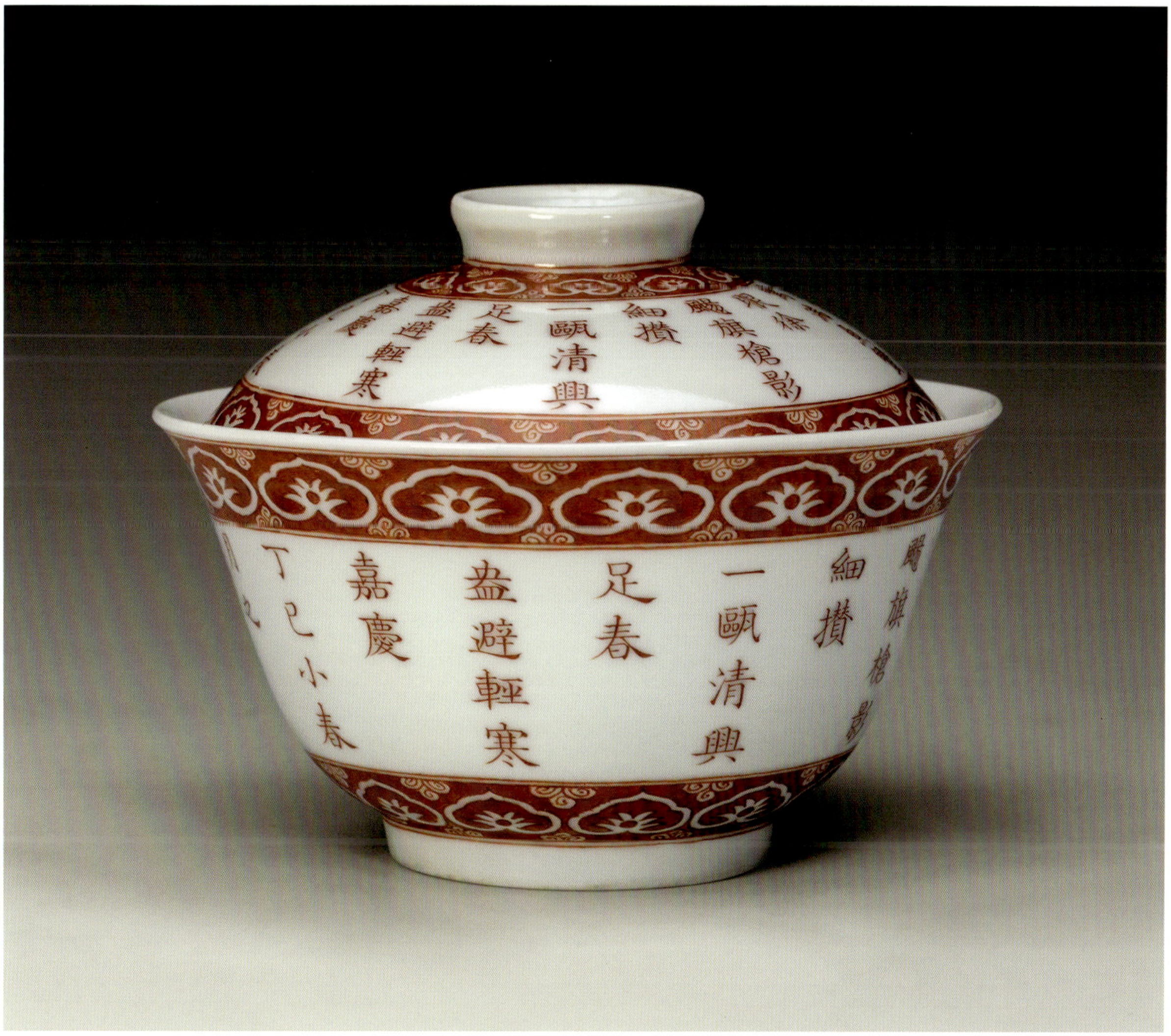

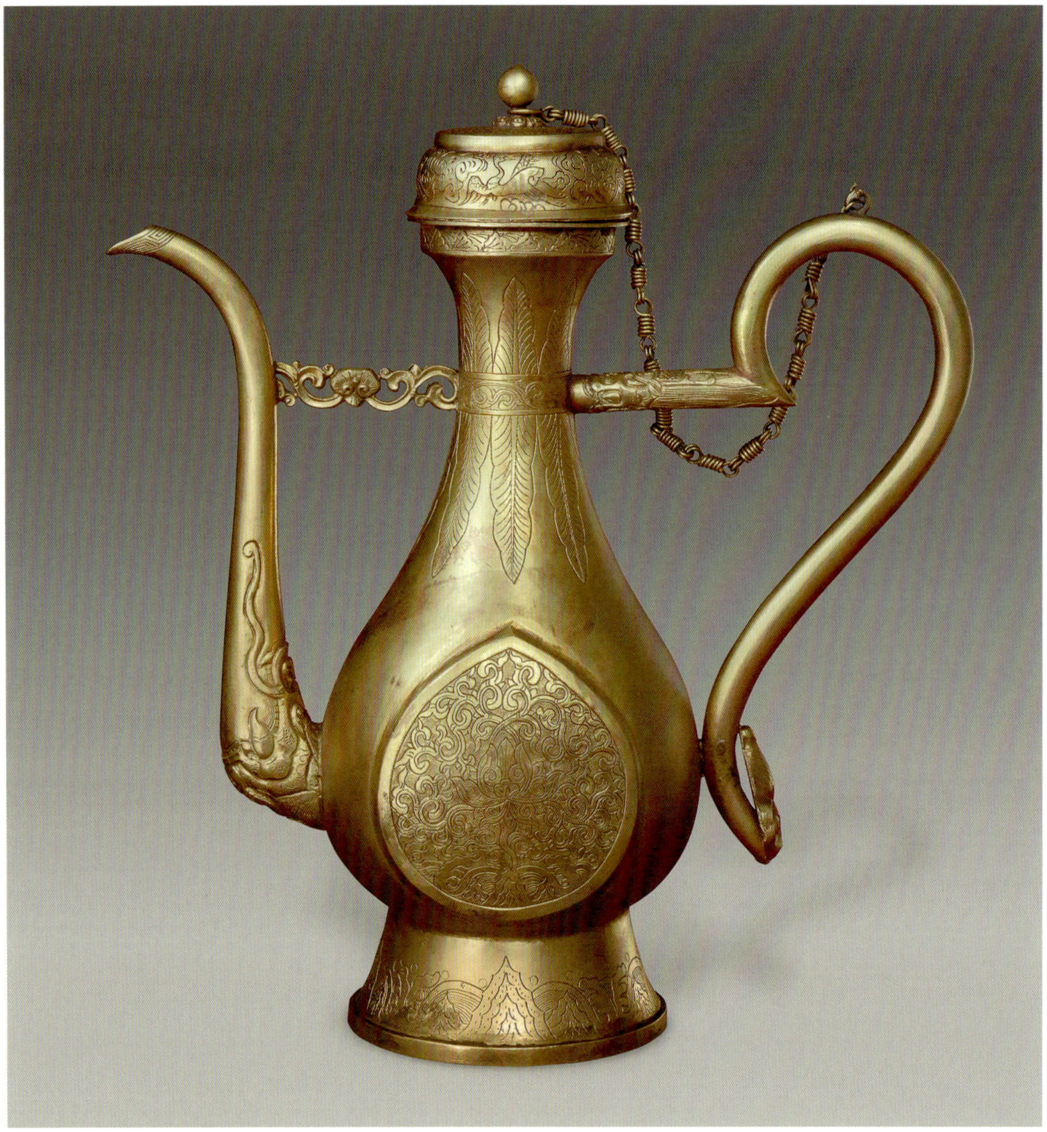

66 清 金鏨花杏葉纏枝花獸首流口執壺

Ewer with Apricot-Leaf Design

Qing dynasty (1644–1911)

Gold with engraved and applied decorations

H. 27.2 cm (10.63 in.), W. 24.5 cm (9.65 in.)
Palace Museum, Gu.11453

A prime example of Qing dynasty metalwork, this ewer represents the confluence of two passions of the aristocrat: wine and gold. Topped with a pearl-shaped finial, its sharply angled design connects the curving spout and S-shaped handle with the body. At the center, a shallow incised design of swirling lotuses, which represent an abundant spring, fill an apricot leaf in the shape of a peach, which is a symbol of longevity.

In the eleventh century, Chinese goldsmiths began to seek inspiration from traditional arts. Excavated wine pots were consistently found with ceramic ewers that had curving spouts and S-shaped handles.[1] This long-surviving form was developed by Ming potters into new designs, in which a peach shape was set on both sides of a pot.[2] The golden ewers were chased with a plain peach-like design to denote imperial use. An inscription, "the tin apricot-leaf teapot," on metal wares from the Ming emperor Wanli's tomb (1619) helps identify this design as an "apricot-leaf."[3]

The Qing court continued to manufacture golden ewers with elaborate engravings of the same design to underscore the splendor of the Manchu monarchy. HL

Inscription, engraved on base: 二十九兩九錢 (29 *liang* and 9 *qian*) [approx. 1,115 grams]

1. *Wenwu* 1980; 1995.
2. ZGTCQJ 2000, vol. 13, pls. 96, 151.
3. Mei and Tao 2004, 94; IOA 1990, vol. 2, pls. 147, 149, 185.

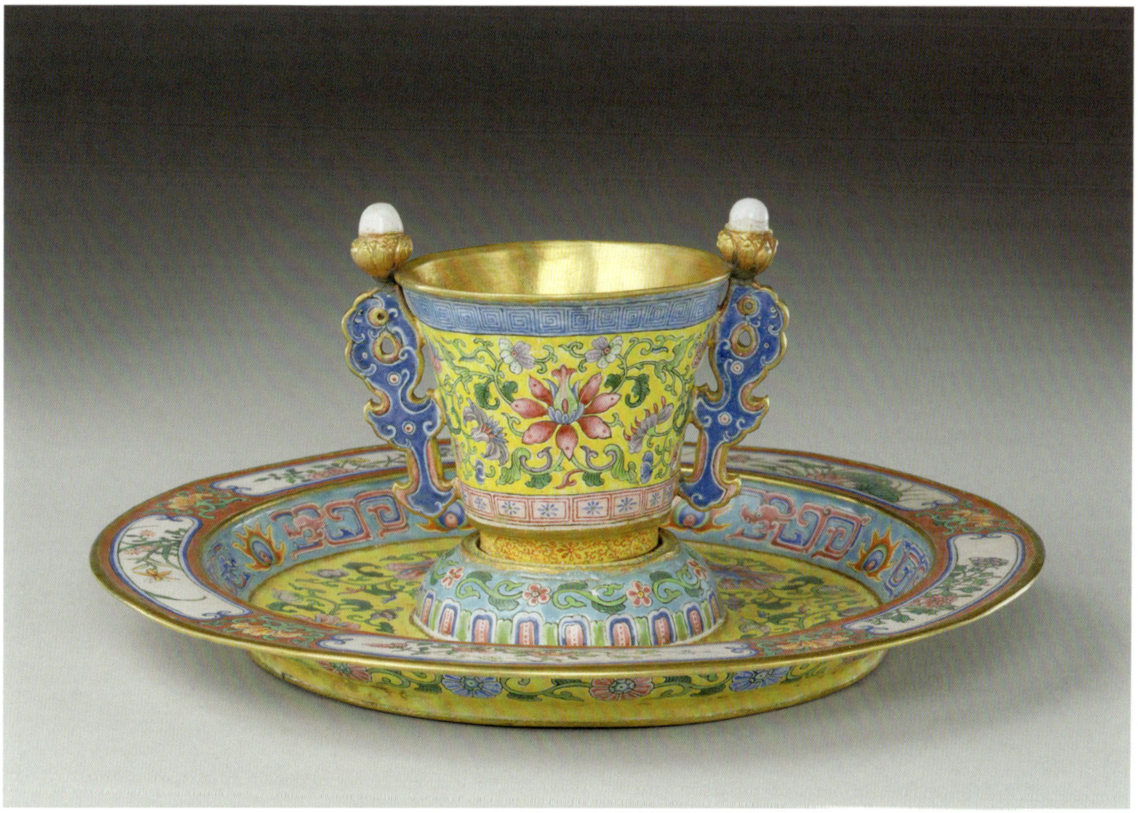

67 清乾隆款 金胎畫琺琅錦地開光花卉夔龍雙耳杯盤

Wine Set of Cup and Saucer

Qing dynasty, Qianlong period (1736–95)

Gold with polychrome enamels, two pearls on handles

Overall H. 9.7 cm (3.82 in.), Cup Dia. 9.7 (3.82 in.), Saucer Dia. 20.3 cm (7.99 in.)
Palace Museum, Gu.11582

The extraordinary painting on this cup and saucer marks it as one of the most exceptional wine sets produced at the imperial workshop. The exteriors of the cup and saucer are decorated with floral motifs in lavish gold, turquoise, cobalt blue, cerulean, green, white, pink, and purple on a lemon-yellow background. With its brilliant color scheme, asymmetrical cascading, and classic designs on the handles and saucer, this set typifies the Qing court's enamel style, influenced by Louis XVI designs. Many elaborate works like it were for decoration only.

In 1716, when the Imperial Household Department (Neiwufu) recruited nationwide for workshop artisans, Canton governor Yang Lin sent Pan Chun, Yang Shizhang, and two pupils to the capital to experiment with enamel.[1] Soon thereafter, Prince Yi (Yunxiang d. 1730), who was Emperor Kangxi's thirteenth son and the minister of revenue, gave Tang Ying advice on formulas for "exotic" enamel. The imperial workshop successfully created its own enamels modeled after European colors. Highly precious and costly, the enamel made by the imperial workshop was carefully allocated by the Imperial Household Department to meet demand. HL

Mark, written in blue enamel on base: 乾隆御製 (Produced for His Majesty Qianlong)

1. Lü 1981; Zhang 1983, 29.

68 清乾隆十一年 乾隆款剔紅飛龍宴盒

Flying-Dragon Banquet Box, approx. 1746
Qing dynasty, Qianlong period (1736–95)
Multicolor lacquer with carved design
H. 25.3 cm (10 in.), L. 51 cm (20 in.), W. 21.5 cm (8.46 in.)
Palace Museum, Gu.109961

Multipurpose tableware became popular in the mid-eighteenth century, when Emperor Qianlong favored such works for their detail and intimacy. Such qualities are seen in this lacquer box, which stored metal bowls like the two pictured on the right. Designed to glorify the empire, the box contains heavenly symbols: the dragon and phoenix alongside bats flying above ocean waves, flower blossoms, and stylized meander patterns. The gilded wire mesh affixed to each side is a special characteristic that was inspired by woven bamboo mesh belonging to a lacquer box from the Ming dynasty.

This lacquer box is a rare survivor of the emperor's commission in 1743. An entry in the imperial archive states that the size, thickness, depth, design, and quantity of bowls had to follow the emperor's exact specifications. Emperor Qianlong's detailed requirements were passed on to Tang Ying with a sample lacquer box and ten silver bowls, instructing him to produce two copies of the box and thirty copies of the bowls. The project took almost three years to carry out, and finally in 1746, the artist submitted the presentable boxes and bowls to the court.[1] HL

Inscription and marks, carved on the box: 弼輔聖, 福祿, 乾坤, 長春, 如意; carved and filled with gold, on the bottom—大清乾隆年製 (Produced in the Qianlong reign of the Great Qing dynasty) and 飛龍宴盒 (Flying Dragon Banquet Box)

1. *ZGDYLSDAG* 2005, vol. 11, falangzuo, 745; Zhang 1989, 16.

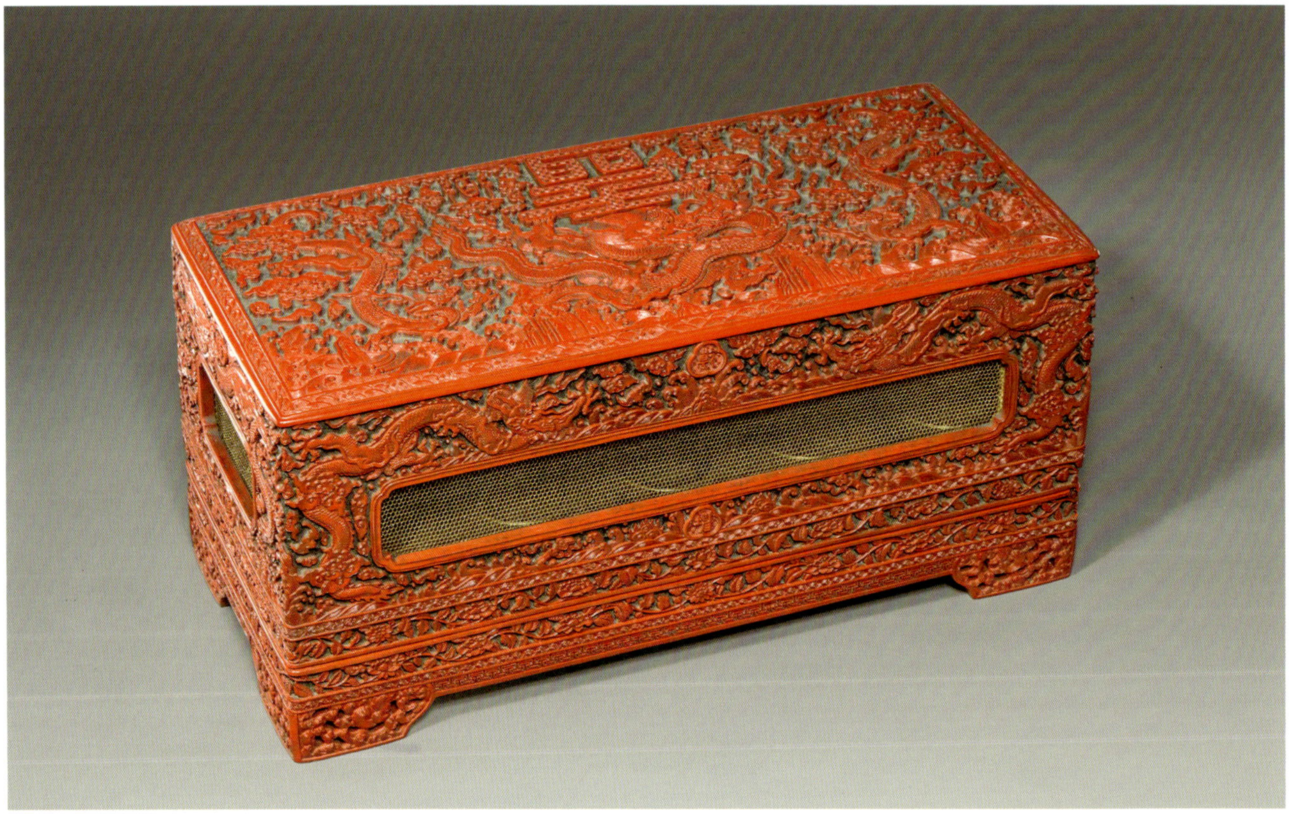

69.1 清乾隆 掐絲琺琅寶相纏枝花萬壽無疆碗

69.2 **Pair of Bowls with Characters and Flower Scrolls,** approx. 1746

Qing dynasty, Qianlong period (1736–95)

Copper alloy with gilding and polychrome enamel inlays (cloisonné)

H. 6 (2.36 in.), Mouth Dia. 11.5 cm (4.53 in.)
Palace Museum, Gu.236345 and Gu.236348

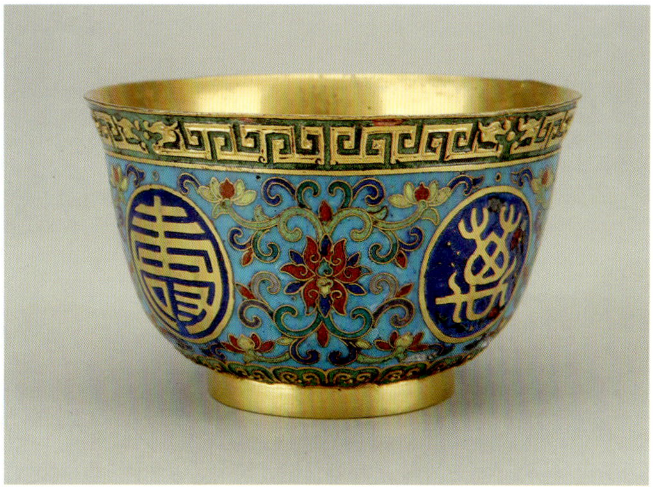

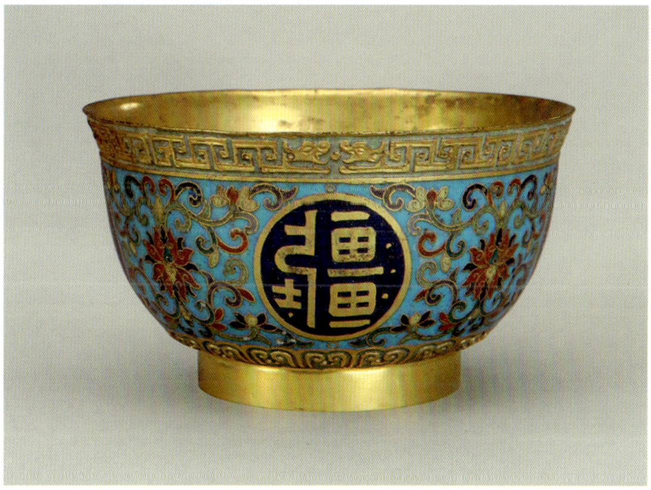

These nearly identical bowls were decorated with a rich turquoise ground and floral scrolls in tones of red, purple, yellow, and blue. Alternating with the flowers and branches are four large roundels that enclose a gilded character against cobalt blue. Together, the characters compose an ancient phrase coined exclusively for emperors: "longevity without limits."

This style of cloisonné was commonly used during the Qianlong period. The execution of cloisonné involved filling colored enamels into connected cells encircled by fine metal wire and arranged in a variety of patterns. The enamel substance, which was readily combined with colorants, was fused to the metal through firing, yielding brilliant colors.

The two other common methods involve filling prechased concave areas with enamel or painting enamel directly onto design surfaces of metal, porcelain, Yixing clay, and glass. Enameled wares were fired in a muffle kiln at a temperature between 700 and 800 degrees Celsius (1,292–1,472 degrees Fahrenheit). Colorants were made up of metallic oxides, including copper green, manganese purple, cobalt blue, iron red, pink produced by colloidal gold, and opaque white produced by arsenate. This complex process required the combined skills of the metallurgist, coppersmith, painter, and engraver. HL

Mark, carved on base: 子孫永寶
(To be forever treasured for generations)

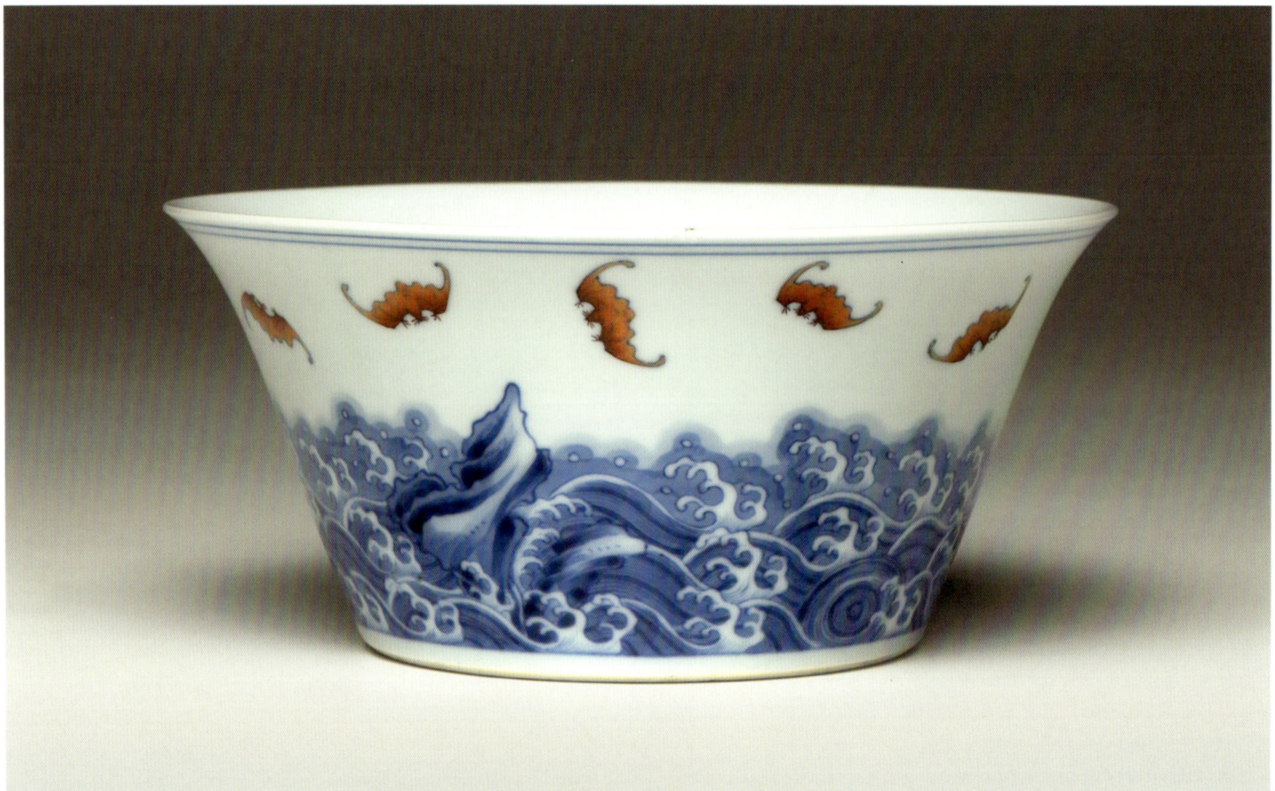

70 清雍正款 青花加紅彩福山壽海碗

Bowl with Bats, Waves, and Rocks

Qing dynasty, Yongzheng period (1723–35)

Jingdezhen porcelain with underglaze cobalt blue decoration and overglaze red enamels.

H. 8.3 cm (3.25 in.), W. 17.8 cm (7.01 in.)

Virginia Museum of Fine Arts, Special Oriental Art Purchase Fund, 72.37.1

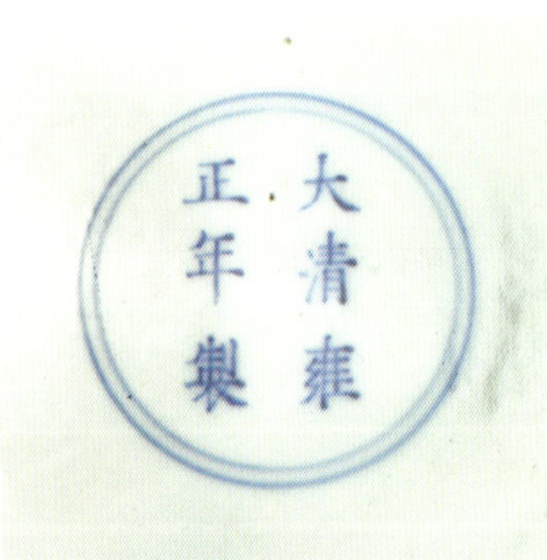

This bowl has a flat base on a foot ring, a deep vault, and a flaired rim. The exterior scene, set against a white background, depicts twelve red bats flying above blue waves and mountain rocks. The decorative motifs symbolize happiness (bats) and immortality (mountain rocks).

The technique, which integrates underglaze blue and overglaze color enamels, was developed in the Jingdezhen kilns during the Ming and Qing dynasties. In this technique, the design is first outlined in cobalt blue on the clay body and then fired at a high temperature. Next, the outlined spaces are filled with red enamel, and the body is fired again at a low temperature. The contrast of the pure cobalt blue, the gradation of red enamels, and the white clay body makes this bowl a fine example of porcelains produced at the imperial kiln at Jingdezhen in the early eighteenth century. LJ

Mark: 大清雍正年制 (Made in the Yongzheng reign of the Great Qing dynasty)

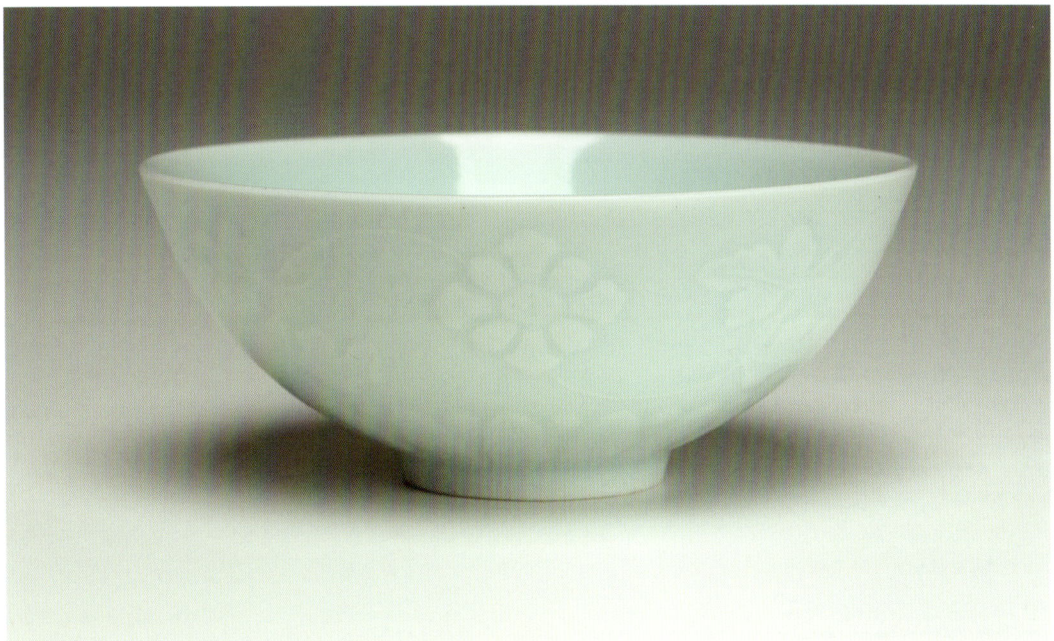

71 清雍正款 冬青釉纏枝菊花紋碗

Bowl with Chrysanthemum Design

Qing dynasty, Yongzheng period (1723–35)
Jingdezhen porcelain with molded and incised decoration under celadon glaze

H. 4.6 cm (1.81 in.), Mouth Dia. 11.5 cm (4.53 in.)
Virginia Museum of Fine Arts, Gift of Frank Raysor in celebration of VMFA's 75th anniversary, 2009.359

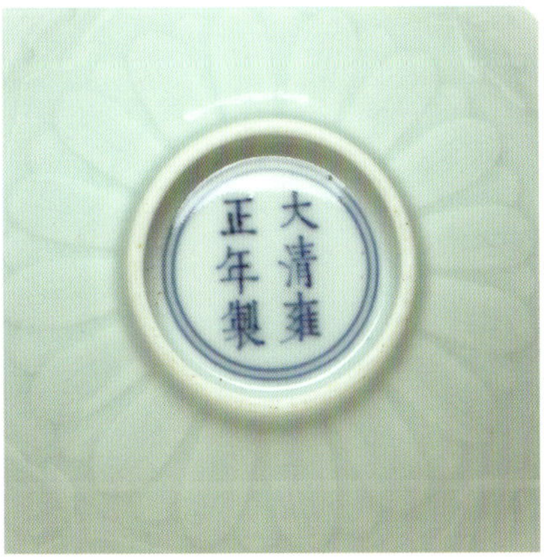

The evenly glazed surface and precisely molded decoration on this small bowl make it one of the finest of its kind produced at the imperial kiln in Jingdezhen in the early eighteenth century. Mold-impressed designs of chrysanthemums and leafy scrolls with incised details decorate the exterior, and chrysanthemum petals encircle the base. The bowl's interior features an incised design of a chrysanthemum in full bloom. The entire vessel is covered with a light green glaze, derived from the celadon glaze of Longquan ware in the Song dynasty (960–1279).

The celadon glaze and molded floral design on this vessel reveal Emperor Yongzheng's fascination with monochrome glazed ceramics and molded designs from the twelfth century. During his short reign, the emperor appointed court officials to manage imperial production in Jingdezhen, a center for ceramics in Jiangxi Province. Court official Tang Ying (1682–1756) began his service in 1728 and supervised the entire ceramic production to meet the emperor's specific requirements for shapes, designs, glazes, and marks. LJ

Mark: 大清雍正年制 (Made in the Yongzheng reign of the Great Qing dynasty)

72 清乾隆 仿雕漆紅釉瓷碗

Bowl Imitating Carved Lacquer

Qing dynasty, Qianlong period (1736–95)

Jingdezhen porcelain with gilding and red glaze

H. 4.5 cm (1.77 in.), Mouth Dia. 13 cm (5.12 in.), Foot Dia. 8.2 cm (3.23 in.)
Palace Museum, Gu.154531

As owner, patron, and adviser, Emperor Qianlong sought comfort in the arts as an escape from political life and took pleasure in showcasing a variety of ceramic products. The emperor, interested in developing new styles, asked Tang Ying to experiment with a new type of porcelain that demonstrated sophistication by employing innovative and novel decorations. The thoroughly cutting-edge styles combined mediums to yield works reminiscent of metal, wood, bamboo, or lacquer.

In this marvelous example of visual illusion, the bowl's gilt interior was designed to look like gold, and the exterior imitates a particular type of red lacquer with its series of designs rendered in shallow relief: geometric meanders along the top rim, a dominating floral brocade, and flower petals along the bottom rim. Even the base was coated with a glaze resembling red lacquer with no mark, unlike ordinary porcelain works that commonly bear a reign mark on a white ground. HL

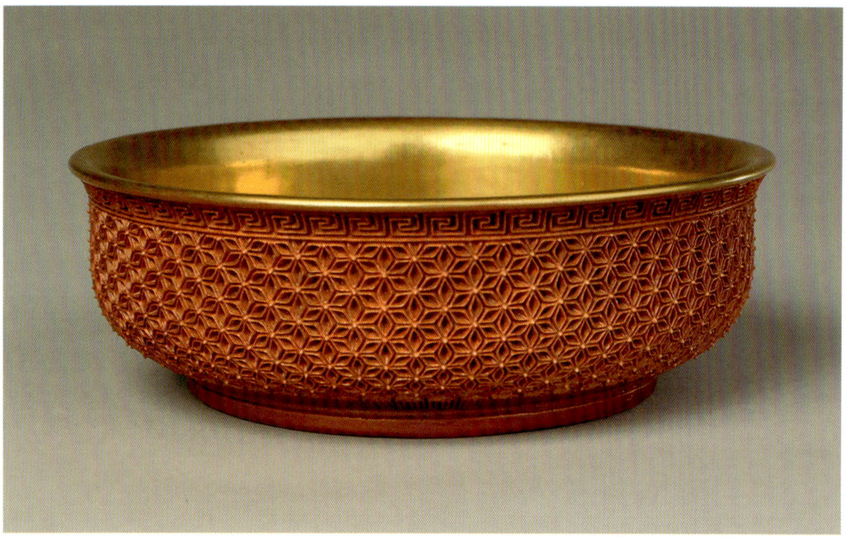

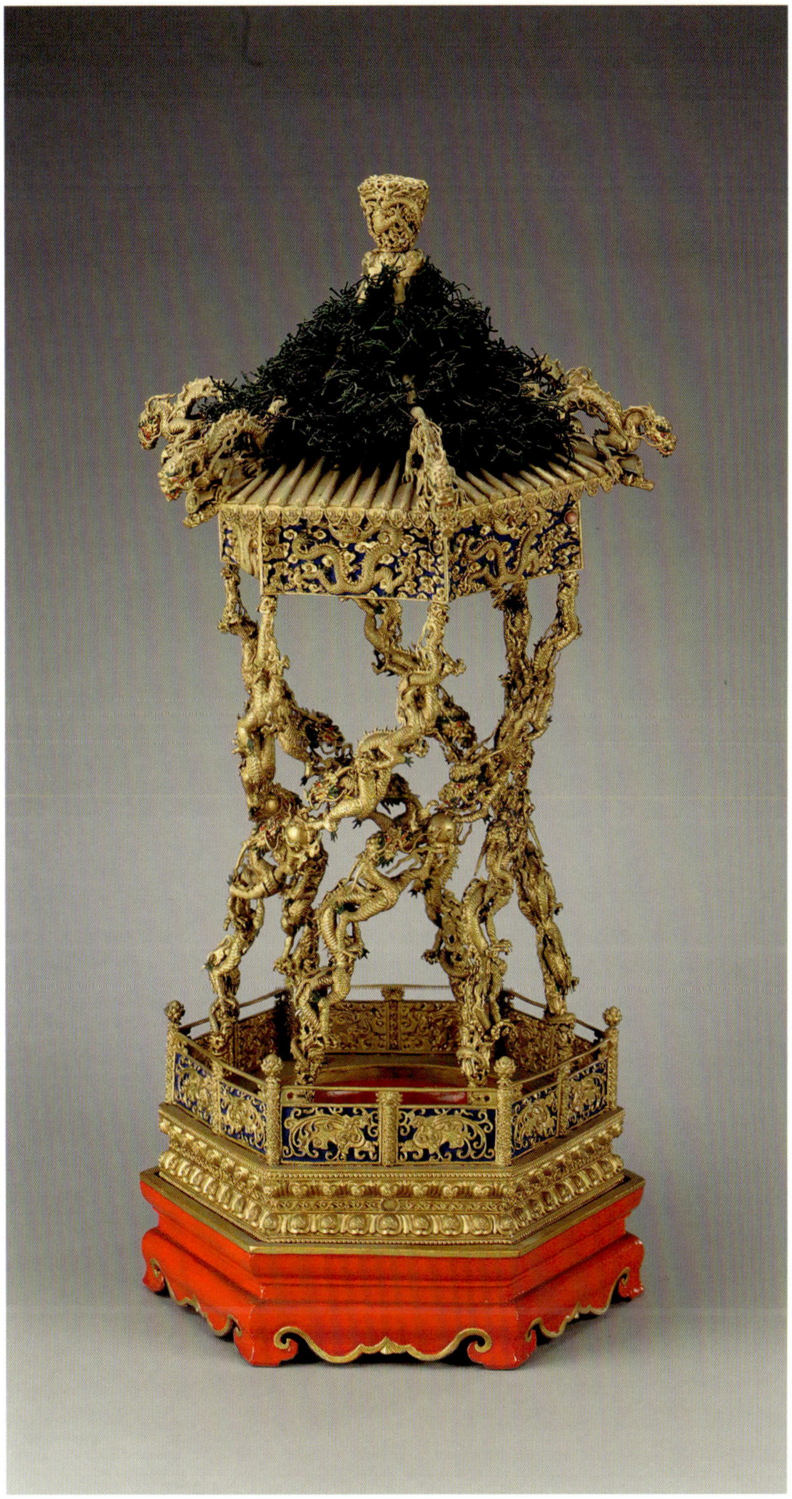

73 清 銅鍍金松棚果罩

Fruit Container in the Shape of a Hexagonal Pavilion

Qing dynasty (1644–1911)

Copper alloy with gilding and inlays of turquoise stone and polychrome enamel, lacquered wooden stand, silk cords

H. 67 cm (26.38 in.), Dia. 34 cm (13.39 in.)
Palace Museum, Gu.178580

Tableware with enamel decorations epitomized the level of luxury at court banquets in the eighteenth century. In this innovative container, probably for fruit or snacks, various types of materials form a hexagonal pavilion with six openwork columns, each entwined by two dragons playing with flaming pearls. On the pavilion's rooftop, six dragonheads extend outward from the facets, and green silk cords represent spring pines. The malachite brings out the bright turquoise and enamel pieces imbedded in the dragons' eyes and eyebrows. In contrast, a wooden pedestal lacquered in red is mirrored to support the base of the pavilion. These delicate details were rendered with craftsmanship that combined chasing, engraving, beading, weaving, and braiding. HL

74 清 孝欽顯皇后(慈禧太后)龍袍吉服像軸 紙本设色

Empress Dowager Cixi Taking Snuff, approx. 1860s–70s
Qing dynasty, Tongzhi period (1862–74) or Guangxu period (1875–1908)
Hanging scroll; ink and color on paper

H. 199.5 cm (78.54 in.), W. 101.2 cm (39.84 in.)
Palace Museum, Gu.6361

This painting was recorded in the imperial inventory as a portrait of Empress Xiaoqinxian, best known as Empress Dowager Cixi (1835–1908). Cixi rose from low-ranking concubine of Emperor Xianfeng to honored imperial consort when she gave birth to a son, the future Emperor Tongzhi.[1] With the support of the court's conservative factions, Cixi managed to take full control of the government—ruling from "behind the screen" during the reigns of emperors Tongzhi and Guangxu. Her influence had an adverse effect, however, that greatly intensified national poverty, worsened class conflicts, and weakened the military, all leading to the unrest that culminated in the fall of the Qing dynasty in 1911.

Cixi lived a life of extravagance. Shown here as a radiant middle-aged woman dressed opulently in embroidered and woven textiles, Cixi sits on a couch beneath an old pine tree in a courtyard and dabs her middle finger in snuff. Her yellow garment's design of a dragon over the Eastern Ocean in the Daoist paradise identifies it as ceremonial attire (*jifu*) that an empress or honored consort wore only for important occasions. Over her left shoulder, a striking ensemble of peonies and nine peaches symbolize good fortune and longevity, suggesting an upcoming birthday celebration for Cixi. The scene's inclusion of snuff reflects the substance's popularity among nobility in the late nineteenth century. HL

1. *Qingshi* (1913–27) 1971, vol. 5, chap. 215, p. 3500.

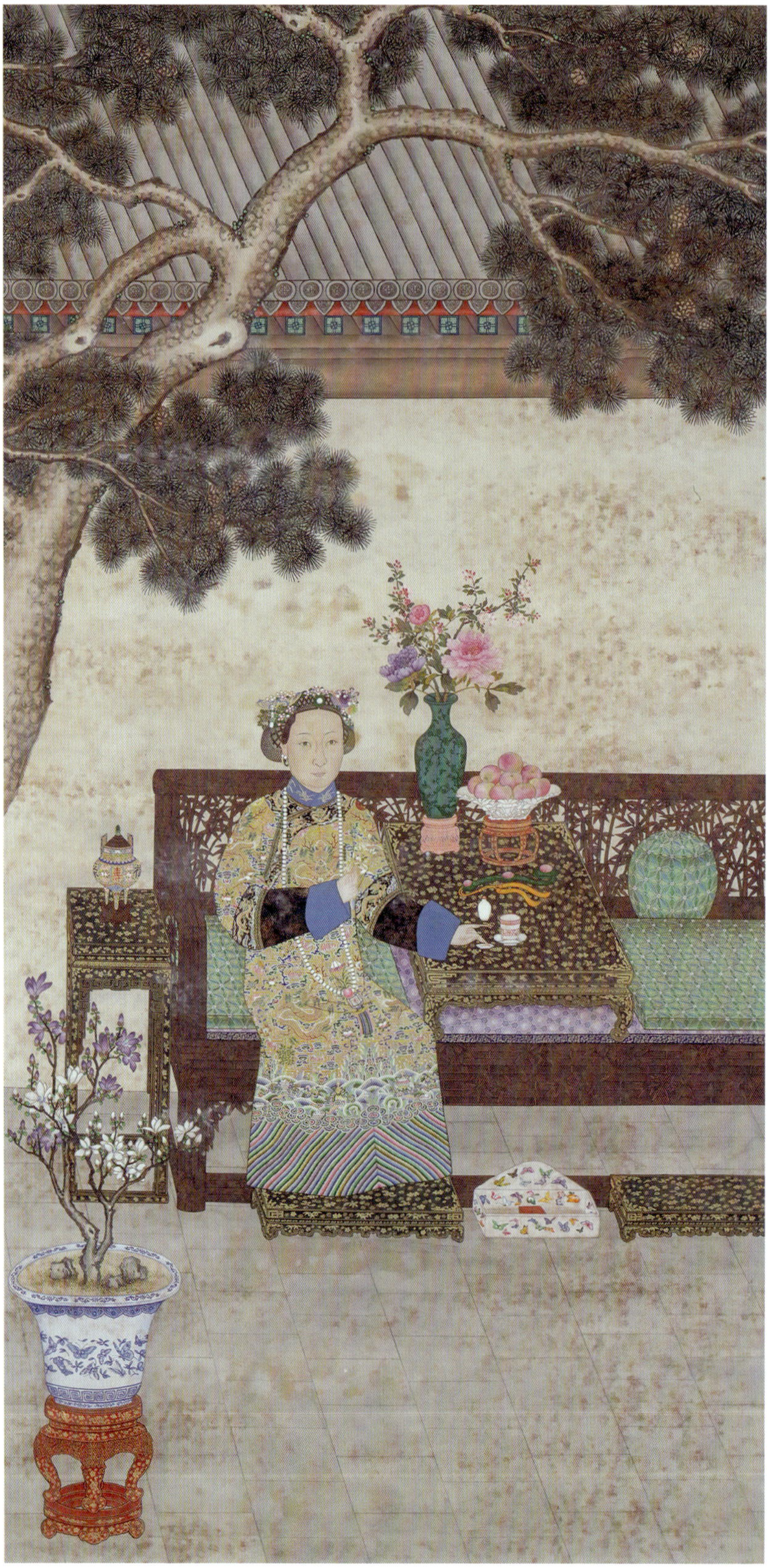

75 清光緒 明黃緙絲十二章金龍紋龍袍

Robe with Dragons and Twelve Imperial Symbols

Qing dynasty, Guangxu period (1875–1908)

Cut-silk (*kesi*) tapestry with silk and metallic threads, copper buttons

L. 142 cm (55.90 in.), W. 182.9 cm (72.01 in.)

Virginia Museum of Fine Arts, Gift of Brigadier General John S. Letcher, 81.33

The design on this robe combines nine dragons and Twelve Imperial Symbols, making it the highest-ranking garment worn by an empress dowager or empress. Red bats, blue *shou* characters amid stylized coiling clouds, and the Eight Auspicious Symbols (*bajixiang*) above blue waves suggest it was produced in the late nineteenth century. The robe features a round collar, straight silhouette, side slit, Manchu hoof cuffs, and gold trim. The symbols woven into the fabric indicate this was an official robe, suitable for the most important court functions, namely New Year's Day and the birthdays of the emperor and the empress dowager.

A weaving technique involving cut silk (*kesi*) is a unique and time-consuming process first developed during the Tang dynasty (618–907). This technique attained its highest quality during the eighteenth century when the Suzhou textile workshops, under the supervision of the Imperial Household Department (Neiwufu), produced cut-silk robes as well as hanging scrolls (cat. no. 86). With marvelous colors and density of designs, this robe represents the last phase of imperial cut-silk weaving of the Qing dynasty. LJ

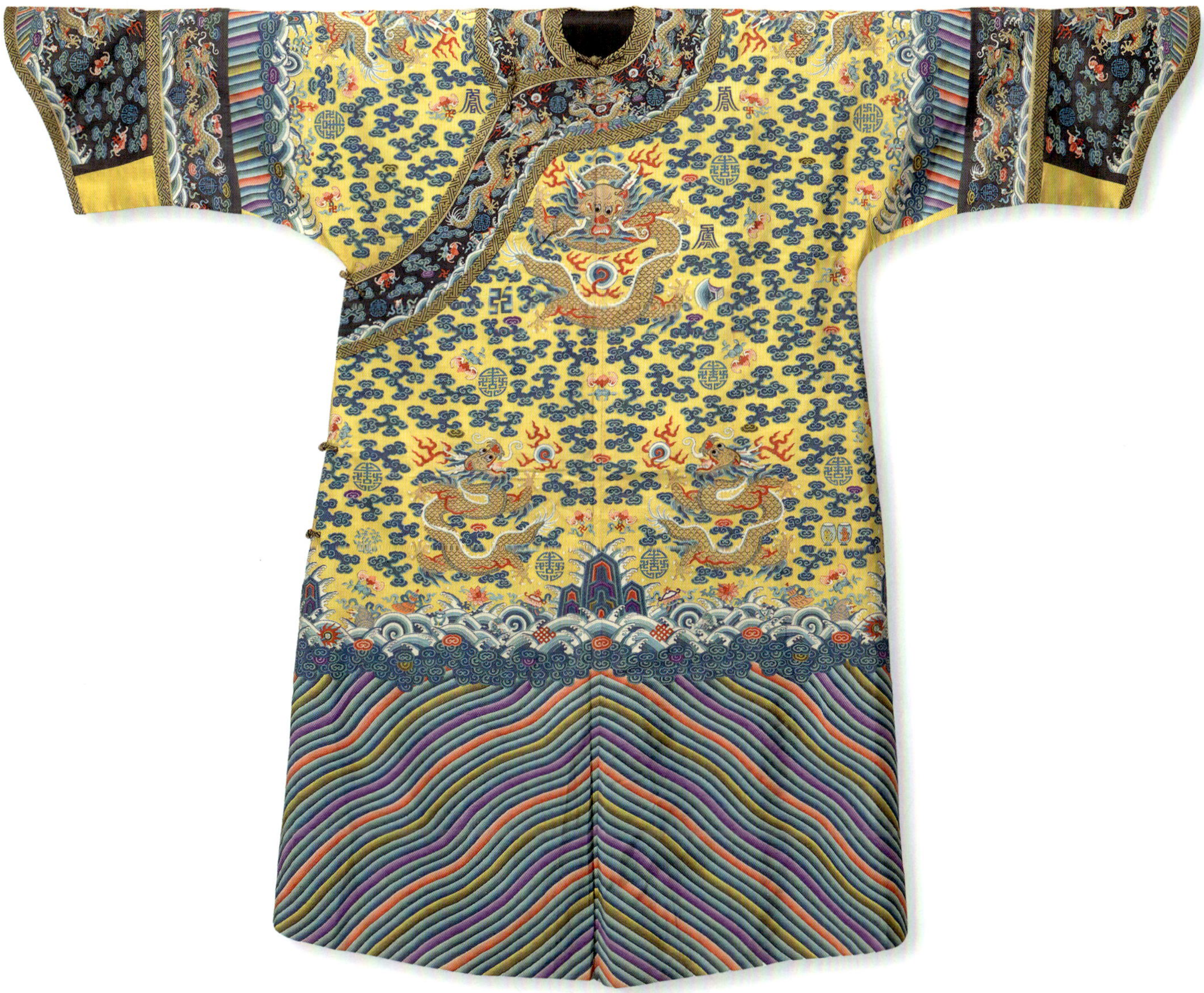

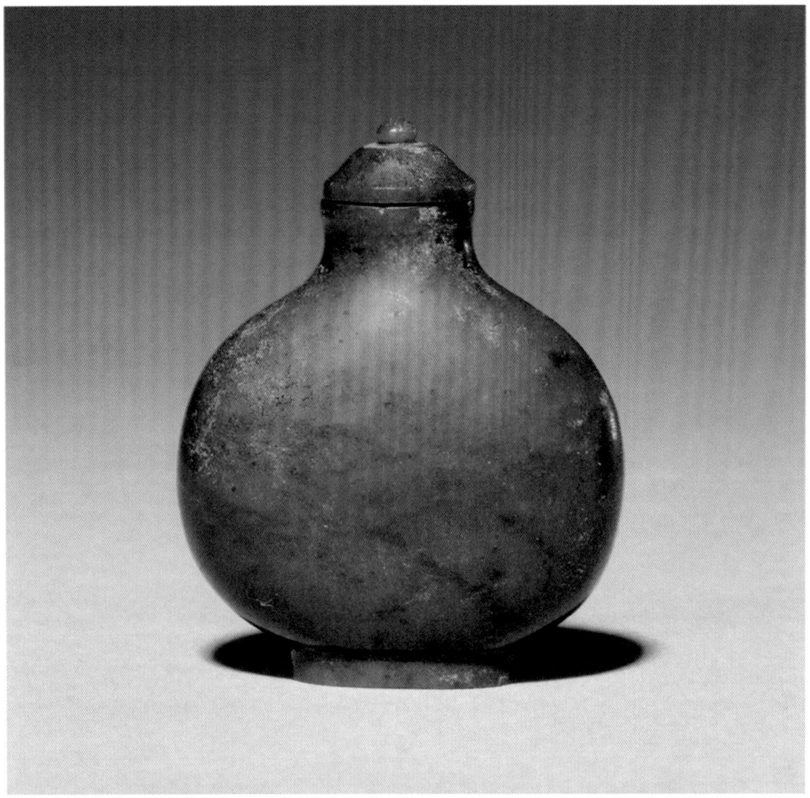

76 清乾隆款 碧玉鼻煙壺

Snuff Bottle

Qing dynasty, Qianlong period (1736–95)

Nephrite, ivory

H. 5.7 cm (2.25 in.), Mouth Dia. 2 cm (0.8 in.), Foot Dia. 2.4 cm (0.94 in.)
Palace Museum, Gu.93248

Perhaps Emperor Kangxi (r. 1662–1722), during his first inspection tour of the South, was among the first in China to receive the gift of scented powdered tobacco, or snuff, from European missionaries in 1684 in Jiangning (today's Nanjing).[1] Snuff rapidly became fashionable among Chinese aristocrats. Immediately, the imperial workshop redesigned the European snuffbox in the shape of the Chinese medicine bottle. The resulting snuff bottle usually had a matching cap attached to a cork and a tiny spoon.

The mid-eighteenth century witnessed an expansion of the Qing empire northwest into the region of Xinjiang, increasing the capital's supply of jade. Cut and allocated according to purity and color, fine stones were often desired for snuff bottles. The design of these small bottles benefited from the characteristics and textures of this material's superior quality.

Made of dark green jade with black mottle, this carefully finished piece is elegantly fashioned. Its simple, fluid contours and smooth, polished surface give the flask an appropriate balance, with an emphasis on the beauty of its color. A lid shaped like a straw hat, also worked from the dark green jade, is attached to a tiny ivory spoon. HL

Inscription, on the base: 乾隆年製 (Produced during the Qianlong reign.)

1. CCTP 2002, 137.

77 清乾隆款 銅胎畫琺琅母嬰山水圖鼻煙壺

Snuff Bottle with Mother and Boy Listening to Bamboo Flute

Qing dynasty, Qianlong period (1736–95)

Brass with multicolor enamel, ivory spoon, gilt brass lid

H. 6.3 cm (2.5 in.), Mouth Dia. 1.6 cm (0.63 in.), Foot Dia. 1.7 cm (0.67 in.)

Palace Museum, Gu.116551

In the eighteenth century, Jesuit missionaries introduced the Forbidden City to baroque and rococo styles. Decorative arts of the Qing court effectively moved away from the classical style and toward colorful and dramatic images that combined elaborate Chinese brushwork with a Western approach.

Inspired by European compositions of the Madonna and Christ Child, the subject here is a young mother and her son. She offers him a long ribbon, and the gesture carries the symbolic meaning of fertility and prosperity, as the word *dai* is a Chinese homonym that means both "ribbon" and "generation." A boy seated opposite plays a bamboo flute, a traditional depiction that celebrates peace. In the exquisitely painted textures of the hair and drapery, as well as the harmonious tones of subtle colors, the brushwork and color palette are impressive in their embrace of baroque and rococo styles. In terms of composition, the close-up view of the large seated bust against rural scenery reveals European influence.

Not all of the snuff bottles in the Qing imperial collection were used functionally; some were used as collectibles or awarded on occasions such as royal birthdays, the New Year, and festivals. HL

Inscription, written in blue enamel, on the base: 乾隆年製 (Produced during the Qianlong reign)

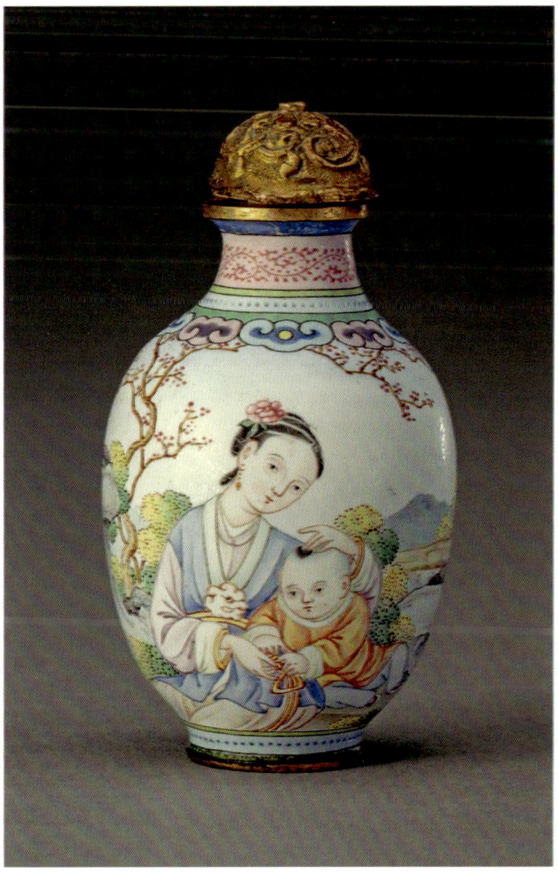

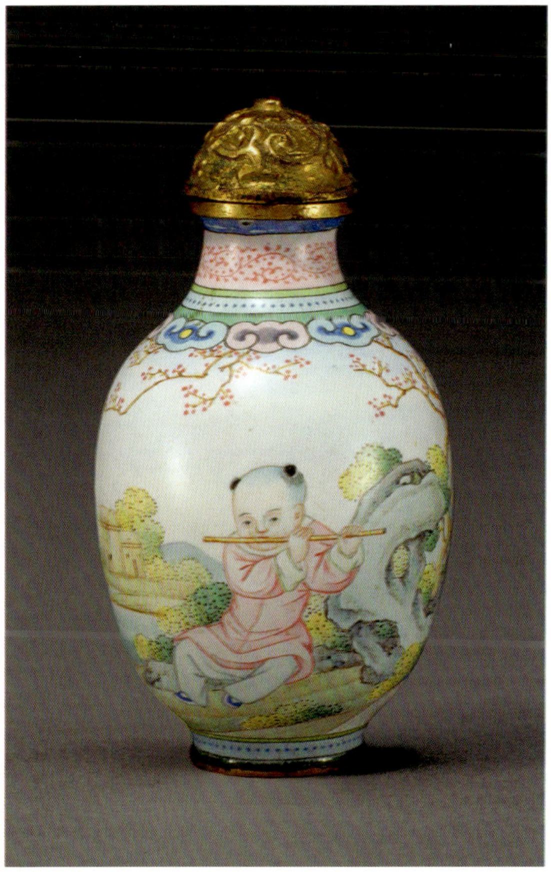

78 清雍正款 青花纏枝花紋花澆

Ewer with Flower Designs

Qing dynasty, Yongzheng period (1723–35)
Jingdezhen porcelain with underglaze cobalt blue

H. 25 cm (9.84 in.), Mouth Dia. 5 cm (1.97 in.)
Foot Dia. 9 cm (3.54 in.)
Palace Museum, Gu.149493

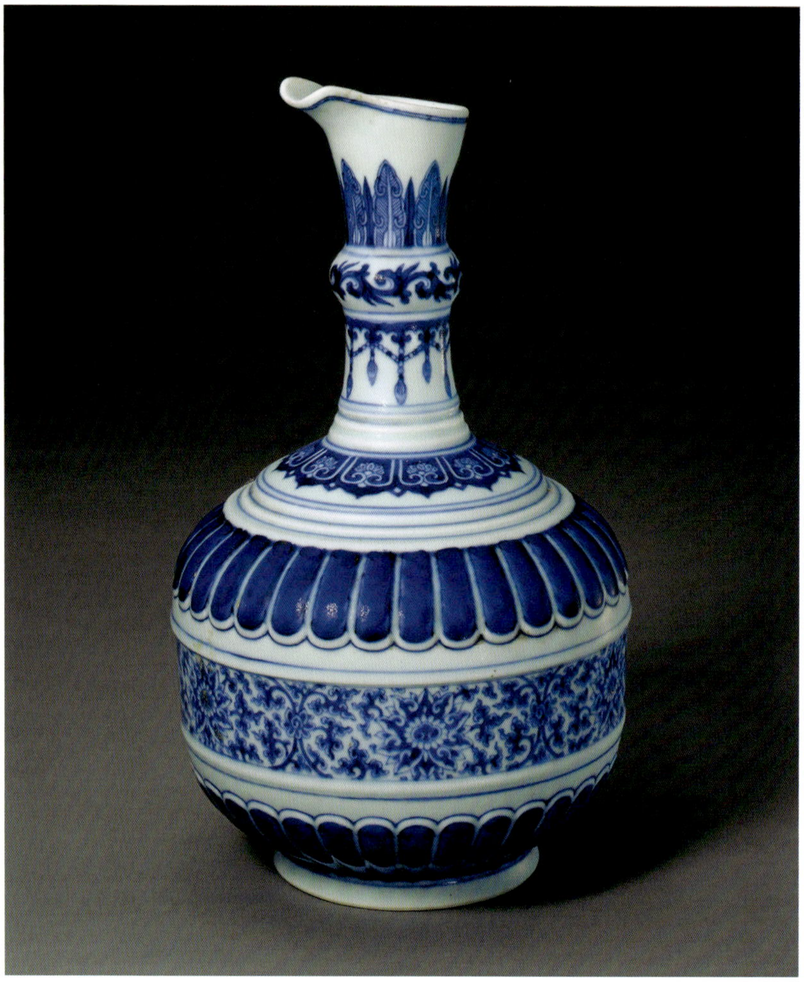

Traditionally known as a flower-watering vessel, this work represents a new production achieved by the Jingdezhen imperial workshop. Rather than being functional, these decorative amphora-shaped vessels were displayed in cabinets or on shelves.

The vessel's shape was directly inspired by ancient Islamic metalwork made popular in the Ming court when Zheng He's naval explorations between 1405 and 1433 expanded trade. The popularity was short lived, however, as the Ming court soon lost interest in diplomatic relations with the Islamic world and no longer ordered the Jingdezhen workshop to design amphora-like pieces, which were used primarily for diplomatic affairs and foreign markets. Three hundred years later, during the Qing dynasty, amphora-like wares were given new life as a result of the Yongzheng court's revival of early fifteenth-century tastes.

Classical floral ornamentation in cobalt blue, which was introduced to Chinese ceramics during the Tang dynasty (618–907), decorates the exterior of this vase. Several friezes encircling its neck, shoulder, and body present stylized patterns that resemble relief decorations on Islamic metalwork. Its precisely designed composition, even application of cobalt, and shape bear witness to the artistry and craftsmanship of the Yongzheng era. HL

Mark, written in underglaze cobalt blue at the base: 大清雍正年製 (Produced during the Yongzheng reign of the Great Qing)

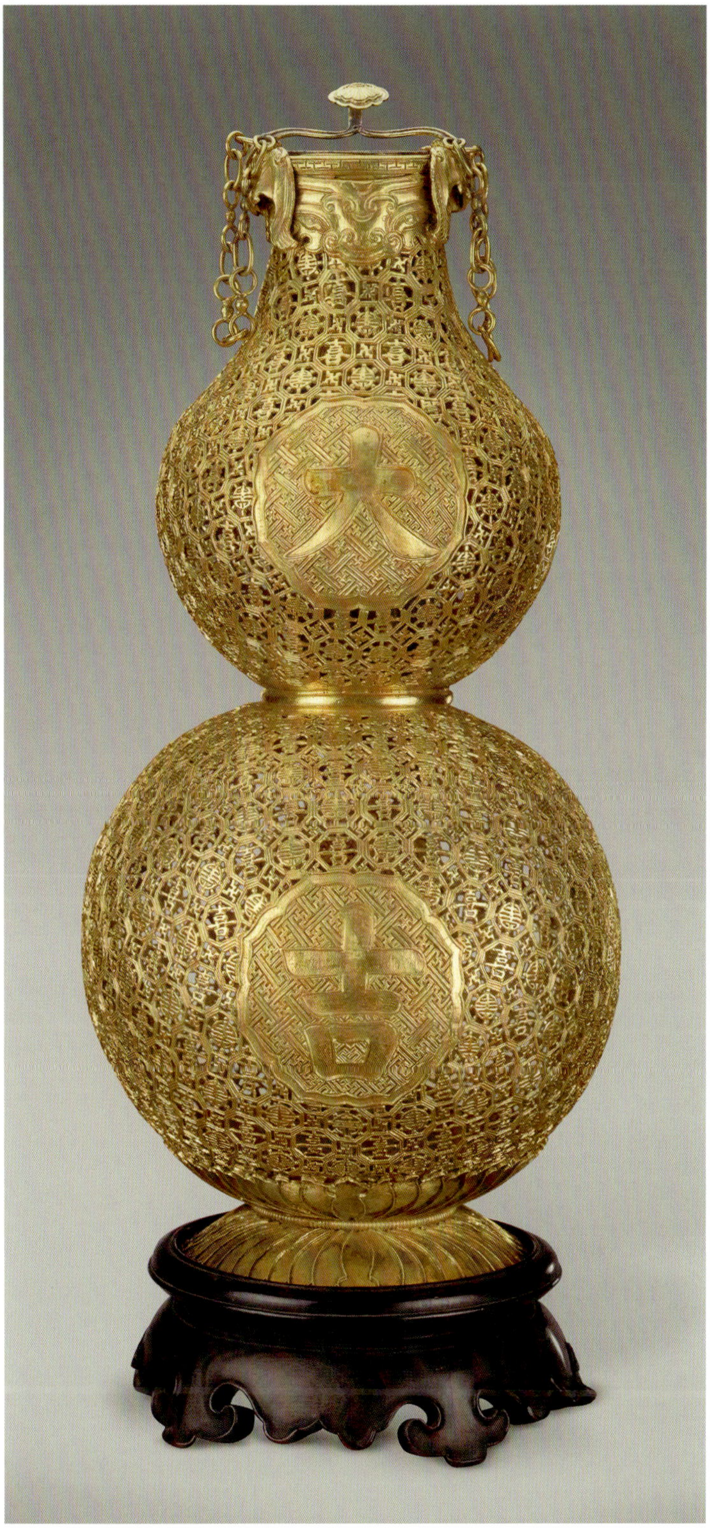

79 清 金鏤空葫蘆式香熏

Fumigator in the Shape of a Double Gourd, approx. 1750–1850
Qing dynasty (1644–1911)
Gold exterior, silver interior, sandalwood

H. 42 cm (16.54 in.), Mouth Dia. 7.3 cm (2.87 in.)
Foot Dia. 13.3 cm (5.24 in.), Weight 2,340 grams
Palace Museum, Gu.225026

As early as the eighth century, the gourd was associated with wine ware, immortality, and fertility. Made of porcelain, ivory, or gold, double-gourd vases with two medallions representing "Great Fortune" or "Double Happiness" were set in the nuptial chambers in the palace.[1] The design for this specific vase with two auspicious medallions was created by the imperial workshop of the Qianlong period. Like the majority of commissioned religious and decorative objects in the Qing dynasty, this gold vase is among the most prestigious of the imperial products.

With both a sandalwood pedestal and a chain at its mouth, the vase could be displayed in a cabinet as decoration or suspended as a censer. The exterior is embellished with openwork, relief, and repoussé decorations in a network of octagons, alternating between the characters for ten thousand (*wan*), longevity (*shou*), and happiness (*xi*). The *ruyi* mushroom patterns encircling the top rim run parallel to the lotus petals around the base, adding to the motifs for well wishes and enhancing the vase's decorative splendor. HL

1. *GGBWY* 2006.

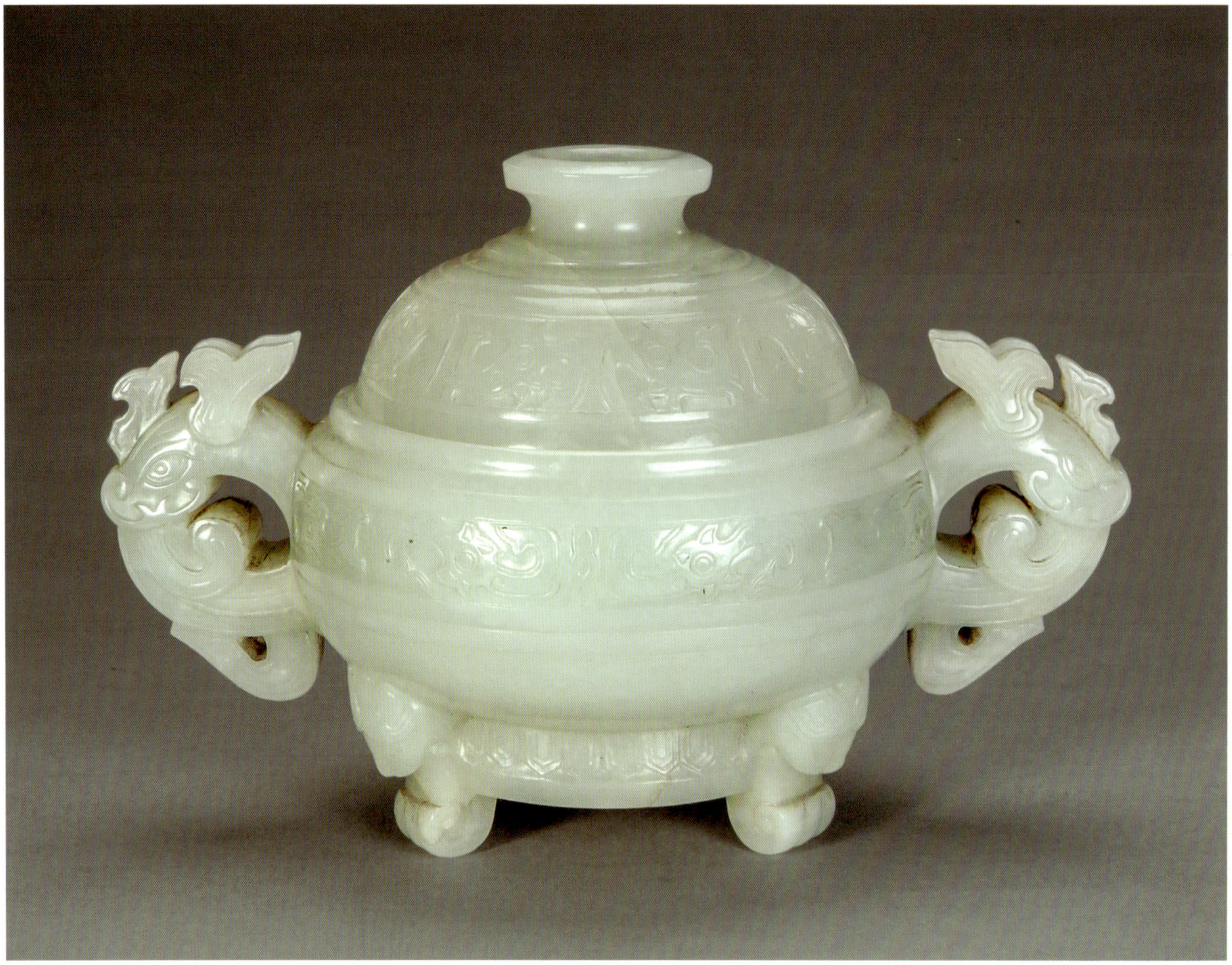

80.1 清 青白玉三式: 仿古銅獸耳蓋爐
Incense Burner in the Form of an Ancient Bronze Vessel
H. 10 cm (3.94 in.), W. 15.5 cm (6.1 in.), Mouth Dia. 8.8 cm (3.46 in.)

80.2 清 青白玉三式: 仿古銅雙耳饕餮紋壺
Vase in the Form of an Ancient Bronze Vessel
H. 12 cm (4.72 in.), W. 4.5 cm (1.77 in.)

80.3 清 青白玉三式: 福壽圓蓋盒
Container with the Character for Longevity, 19th century
Qing dynasty (1644–1911)
Nephrite
H. 3 cm (1.18 in.), W. 5.9 cm (2.32 in.)
Palace Museum, Gu.103865-1-3/3

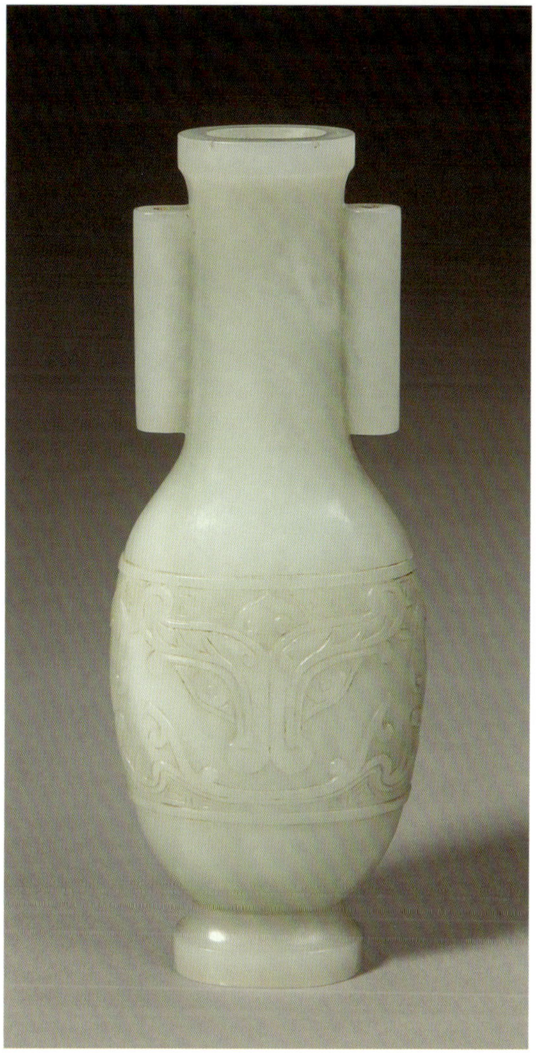

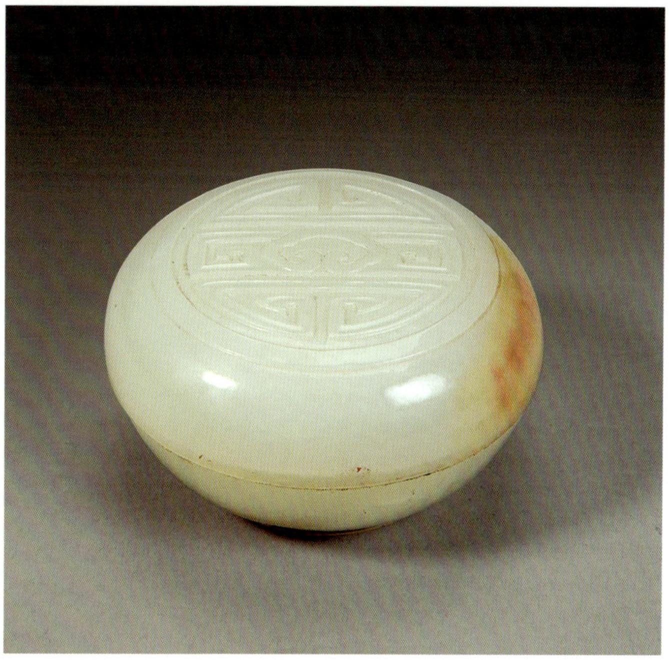

This set of three vessels reflects the revival of an ancient aesthetic movement that flourished in the Qing court along with a revival of jade works. Sets of vessels were commonly displayed on altars and reflect the importance of incense burning at ritual ceremonies; it was believed that burning incense allowed Daoist priests or devotees to communicate with the gods. Incense burning became widespread from the third century BC onward and is still practiced today in China.

All three objects here were made of fine quality Hedian (Hetian) white jade from the Xinjiang region in northwest China. The incense burner with handles was adapted from a type of ancient bronze vessel. Its exterior relief features four long-tailed phoenixes. The openwork dragon handles are of a classical style seen in bronze vessels.

The bottle with cylindrical ears was mirrored after the *hu*, another ritual bronze, in form and design. The animal-mask design represents the mythical *taotie*, whose fierce face had the magical power to ward off evil spirits. The container for holding incense is decorated with a roundel in shallow relief bearing the character for longevity (*shou*) and a stylized cloud with the head of the *ruyi* mushroom, a traditional combination in Daoism that symbolizes immortality. HL

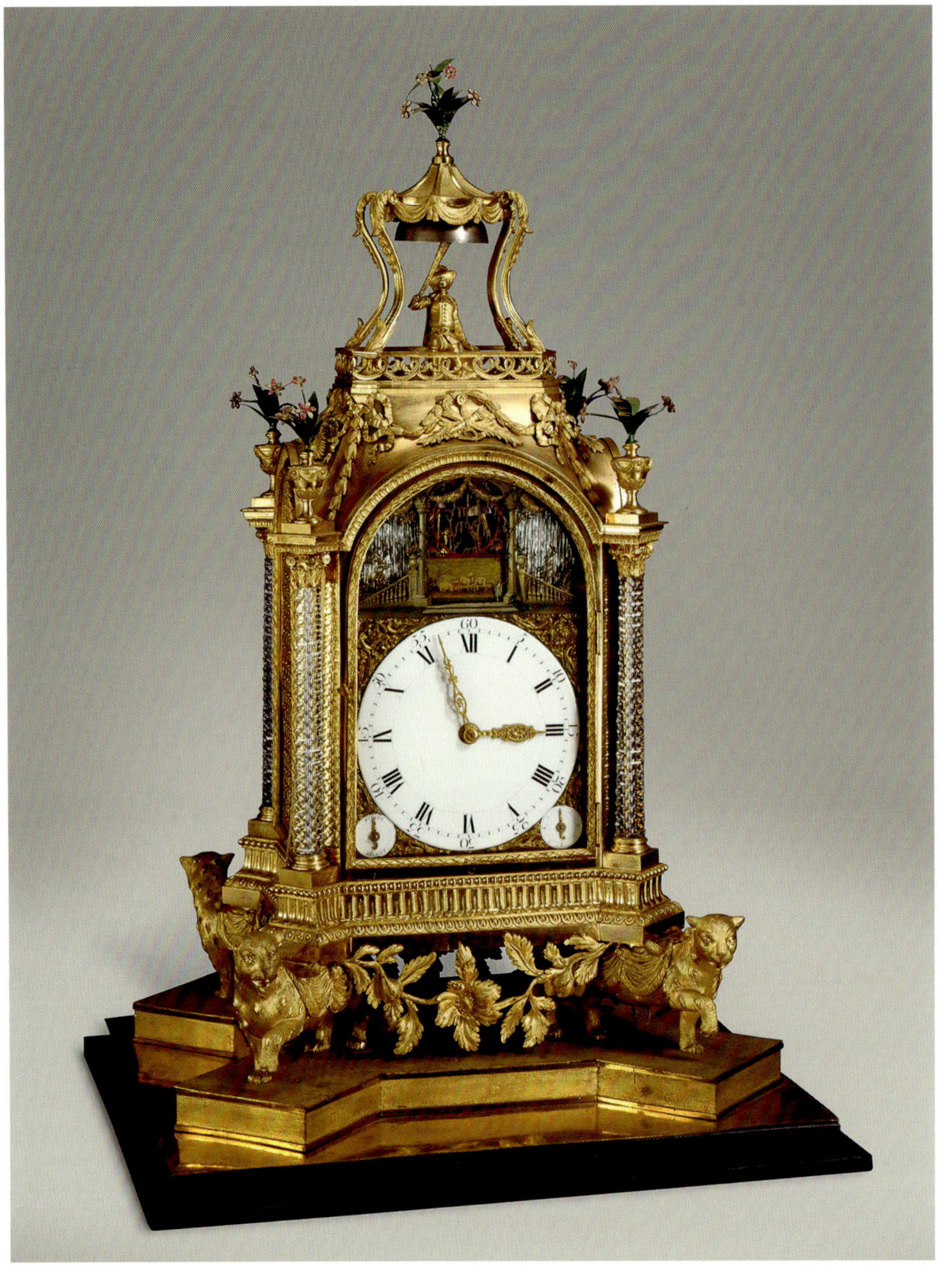

81 十八世紀 英國製銅鍍金四豹馱鐘

Clock Supported by Four Leopards, 18th century
Probably English
Gilt bronze, silver, glass, enamel
H. 105 cm (41 in.), W. 63 cm (24.75 in.), D. 56 cm (22 in.)
Palace Museum, Gu.182644

This English-made mantel clock's enamel dial and machinery are encased in an arch that represents Western architecture. Below the large dial, two smaller dials control the striking mechanisms of either strike/silence or musical modes. The walls are laid with pink textiles framing a miniature scene of grazing sheep. At the top of the tower, a figure in Western clothes lifts a baton as if to strike the bell that hangs from the roof. The clock, which features a mirrored back, rests on four leopards, each with a front paw lifted. Flowers, garlands, and woven patterns in relief, openwork, and appliqué embellish the structure.

Until European clocks arrived in China in the 1500s, the Chinese had used traditional timepieces for seventeen hundred years. In 1584, the first Chinese-made clock modeled after the European version was produced in Zhaoqing, Guangdong Province. European missionaries began to flood China, often landing in Guangdong Province, the neighboring Macau region, and other parts of the eastern coast. Those with special training in medicine, science, art, and astrology received appointments by the Qing court. When a famous cargo vessel, *L'Amphitrite,* brought European clocks and other goods to China, the Qing court established its own shop to make timepieces. HL

Inscription: "Coleman," engraved on the back of the metal clockwork

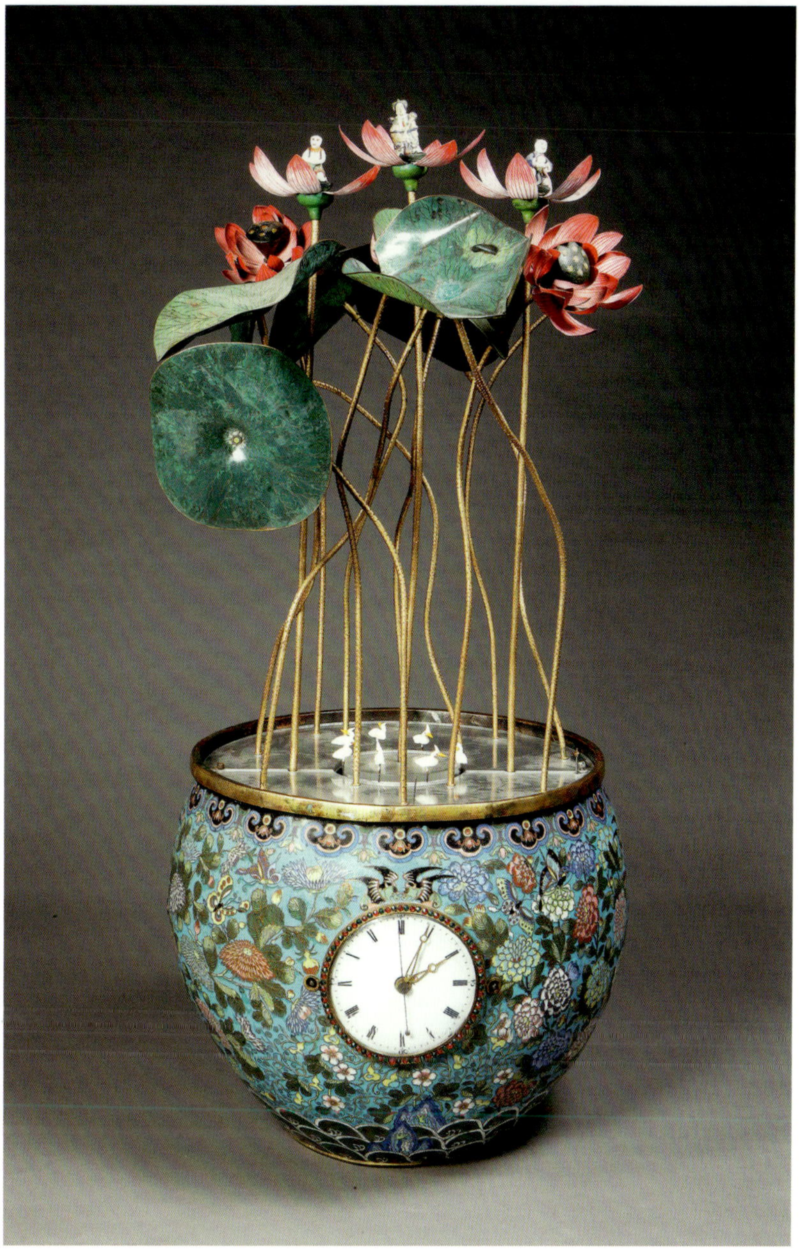

82 清乾隆 銅鍍金嵌琺琅西王母慶壽鷺鷥荷花缸旋轉鐘

Music Clock on a Planter with Lotus Pond and Daoist Immortals

Qing dynasty, Qianlong period (1736–95)

Gilt copper alloy with enamel inlay (cloisonné), gemstone, glass, enamel

Overall H. 122 cm (48.03 in.), Pot Dia. 49 cm (9 in.), Watch Dia. 17 cm (6.69 in.)
Palace Museum, Gu.183083

This piece is one of few surviving works produced by the imperial workshop for clock making, where court-appointed European engineers supervised Chinese artisans from Guangdong Province.[1]

The exquisite quality and sophisticated engineering of this timepiece raised the status of clocks from simply functional to highly creative. As a reference to the Daoist concept of immortality, a lotus pond in three-dimensional form surmounts the timepiece. White egrets frolic on water made of mirrored glass as golden lotus stems rise up to support pink flowers and green leaves. A striking contrast forms between the white enameled dial and the surrounding butterflies and flowers, traditional symbols of love and fertility.

The clockwork and the wiring for the movable pond scene rest inside the base. The two mechanisms can be operated separately or together: the clockwork spring sits behind the hole at the left of the dial; opposite is a spiral spring for the music and moving parts. When the clock is wound, the lotus petals open, revealing the human and animal figures within. Accompanied by music, the kneeling boy and monkey perform and offer peaches to the goddess, Queen Mother of the West, who sits and enjoys the music. HL

1. Feng (1932) 1995.

83 清乾隆戊子年 金漆紫檀乾隆御題韓幹唐明皇試馬圖掛屏

Screen with a Scene of Emperor Minghuang on Horseback, approx. 1768
Qing dynasty, Qianlong period (1736–95)
Sandalwood *zitan* frame, wood screen painted with gold and silver, metal fittings
H. 87 cm (34.25 in.), W. 55 cm (21.65 in.)
Palace Museum, Gu.210064

This wooden screen features Emperor Qianlong's depiction of the classic painting *Emperor Minghuang Riding the Horse,* attributed to the Tang-dynasty court painter Han Gan (act. 750–790). In a calligraphic critique, Qianlong scrutinizes past emperors for the purpose of his own political gain.[1]

Here, Emperor Qianlong's seven-line verse gives his interpretations of separate paintings of two Tang-dynasty emperors—one heroic, one weak. Emperor Taizong (599–649) made his empire the largest in Asia at the time. His military success is heavily attributed to his six warhorses, which have been immortalized by generations of artists. One such painting, *The Six Horses* by Zhao Lin (act. 1136–89), evoked Qianlong's praise for Taizong's heroism, which "won eternal respect."

The lower scene depicts a famous calamity known as the An Lushan mutiny, which forced Emperor Minghuang (685–762) to flee the capital for Shu (Sichuan Province) in 756. In Qianlong's words, the emperor "sat on a dilapidated saddle with atrophied hands and a drunken, flushed face, and even protected by two bodyguards, he trembled. . . . Ah, how powerful the founder was but how weakened the successor. . . . Banquets lessen one's ambition, and wine poisons one's mind; all this made one forget the heavenly mandate." HL

Inscriptions: 戊子新春月御題 (Inscribed by the emperor in early spring of the year *wuzi,* 1768) and 子子孫孫永保鑒之 (To be forever treasured for generations)

Seals, eighteen belonging to Qianlong, including: 乾隆御覽之寶, 乾隆鑑賞, 古稀天子, 三稀堂精鑑璽, 樂壽堂鑑藏寶, 宜子孫

1. National Palace Museum 1976, vol. 6, sec. 3, chap. 69, p. 26.

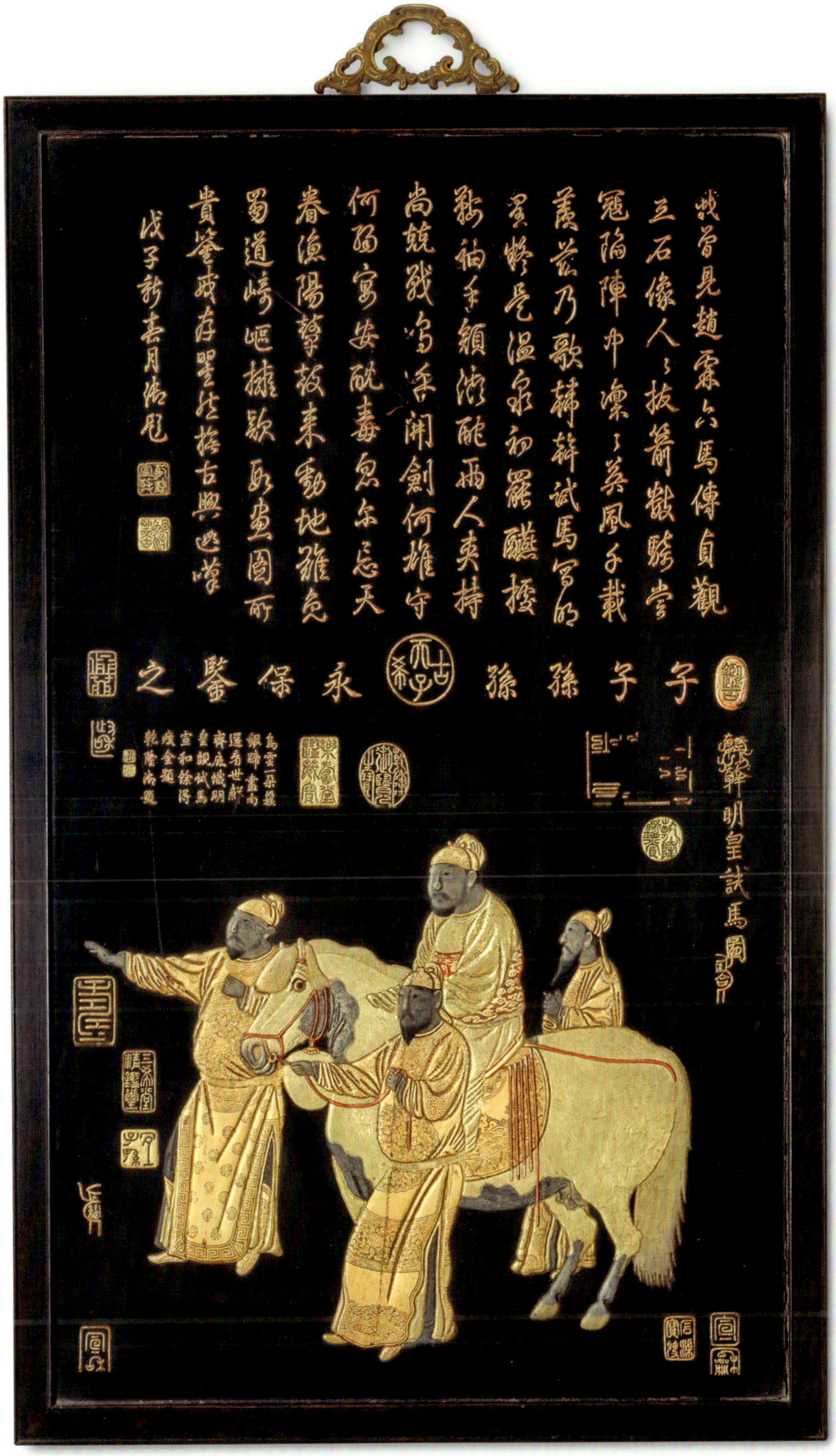

84 清 紫檀木邊座點翠松竹圖插屏

Floor Screen with Pine and Bamboo, 18th century
Qing dynasty (1644–1911)
Sandalwood *zitan,* kingfisher feather, metal with polychrome enamel, glass
H. 220 cm (86.6 in.), W. 116.5 cm (45.87 in.)
Palace Museum, Gu.209110

Workshops in Guangzhou (Canton), particularly in the eighteenth century, consistently introduced products with new forms and new types of decoration. Many hardwood items like this screen were either commissioned by the court or presented as tributes and decorated the imperial palaces.

Framed in sandalwood, the central panel of this screen features turquoise-colored bamboo with kingfisher feathers, expressing the literati spirit of toughness and tenacity. As part of their experimentation with various mediums, the Guangzhou workshops adopted the turquoise-and-black color scheme from polychrome porcelain *wucai* ware that was in fashion beginning in the early 1700s.

The solid frame is carved with stylized dragon designs and mounted with an openwork flange. The screen sits on a supporting panel and is stabilized by four gourd-shaped sandalwood stands that flank an apron in both the front and back. The lower supporting panel encases a metal plaque rendered with an extremely complicated enamel depiction of dragons amid flower scrolls. Incorporating acanthus leaves and sinuous designs, the wooden carved scrolls epitomize the high rococo design in European decorative arts. This work is an example of the recherché objects that the Guangzhou workshop produced on official imperial orders. HL

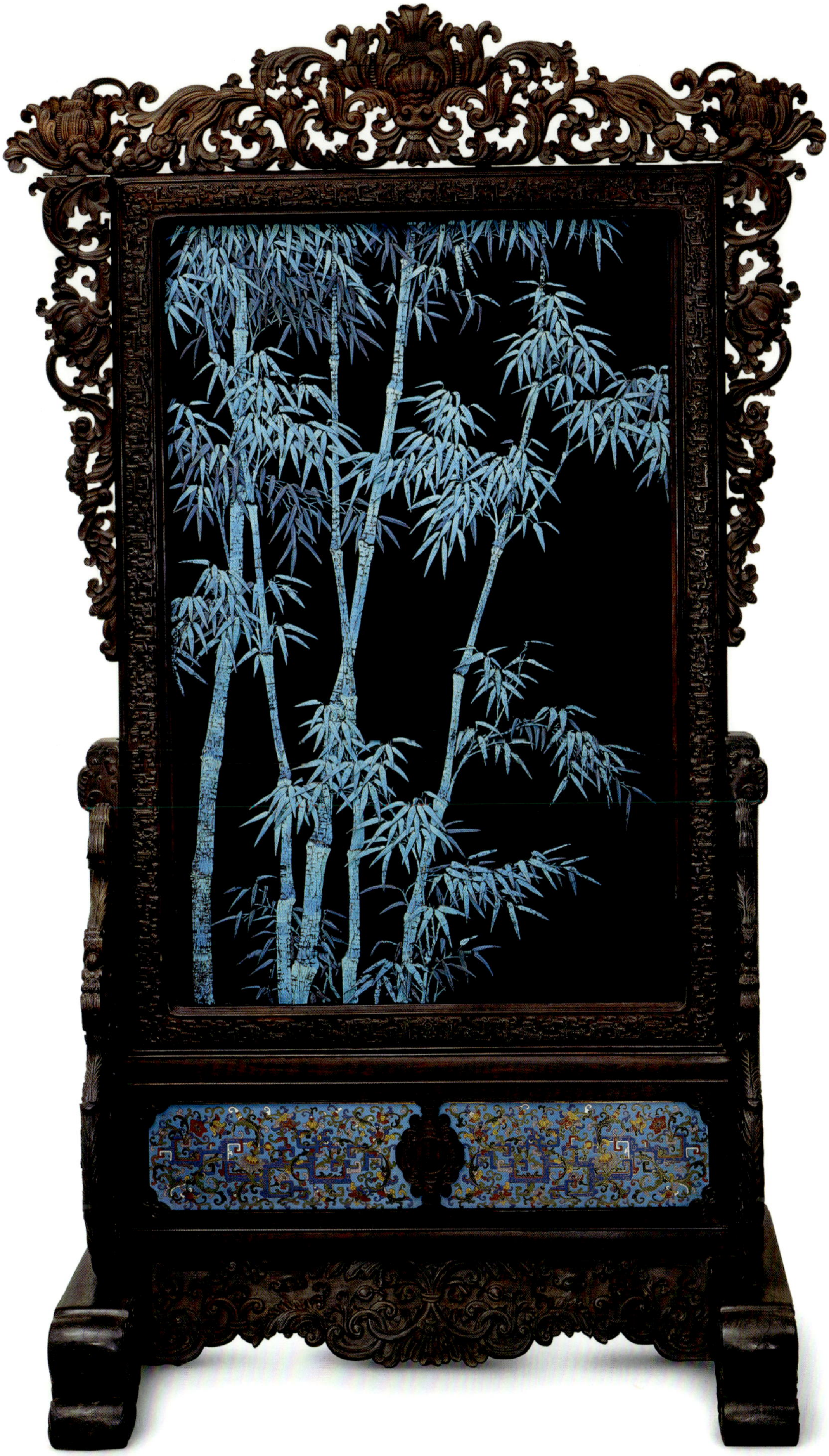

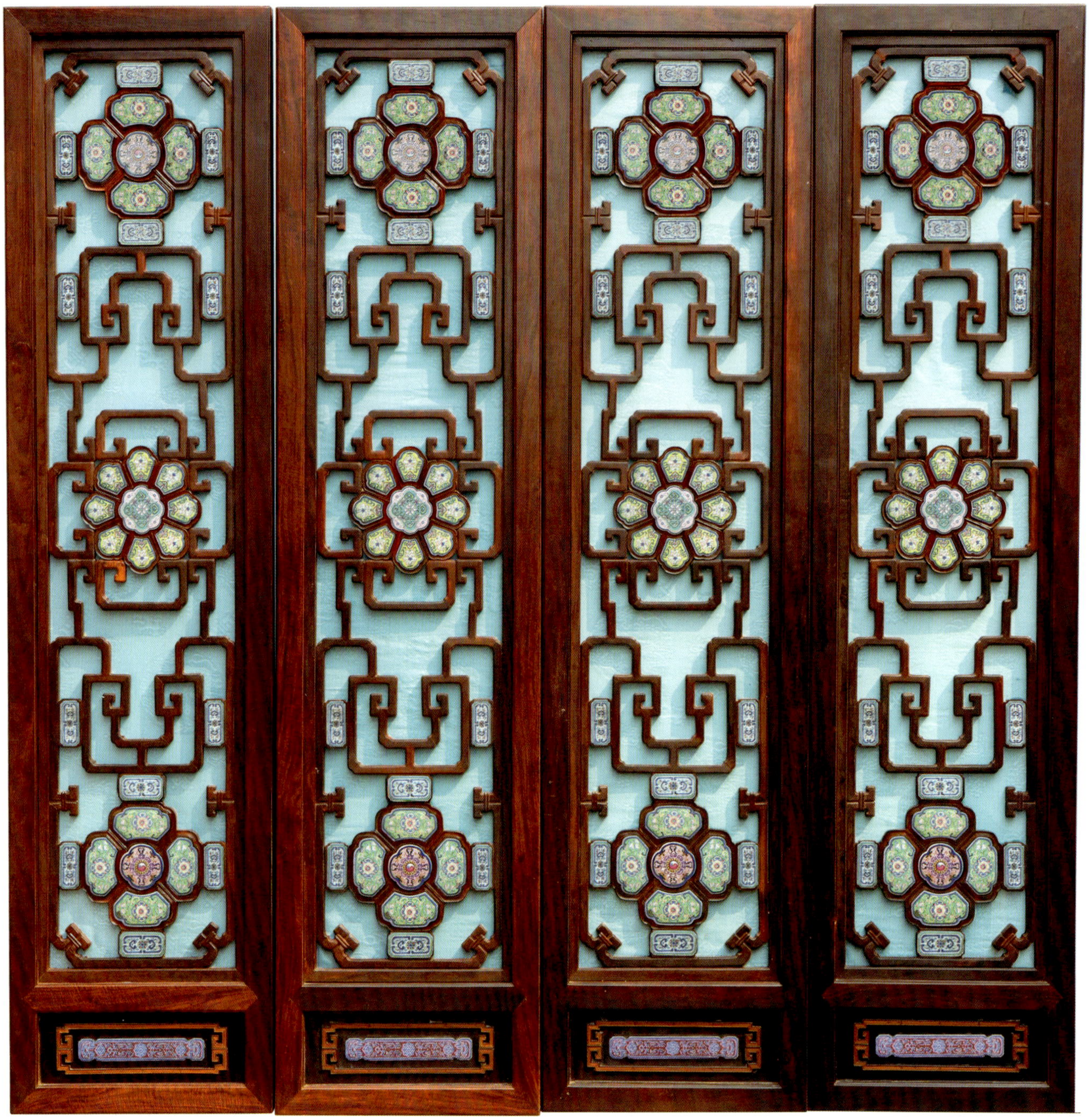

85 清乾隆 寧壽宮乾隆花園延趣樓嵌瓷片檻窗

Four Window Panels, approx. 1772–77
Qing dynasty, Qianlong period (1736–95)
Wood and porcelain

H. 168 cm (66.14 in.), W. 170 cm (66.93 in.), D. 8.5 cm (3.35 in.)
Palace Museum, Gujianlin.12

This screen was made for the windows in the Pavilion of Lasting Amusement (Yanqulou), a side building on the western hill in the third courtyard within Emperor Qianlong's private garden in the Palace of Tranquil Longevity (Ningshougong, rebuilt 1771–79).[1]

Emperor Qianlong had planned to retire in the sixtieth year of his reign, honoring his grandfather, Kangxi, who ruled for sixty-one years, the longest single reign in Chinese history. As emperor, Qianlong launched more than twenty ambitious architectural projects throughout the metropolis. In the Forbidden City's northeastern corner, the Ming-era's southern-style gardens were chosen as the location for the Palace of Tranquil Longevity, the emperor's retirement residence. The layout's hidden corridors, meandering hills, unusual rocks, and winding waters created an elaborate design.

The vast complex features extravagant and ingenious creations. Especially noteworthy are the frameworks for the interior doors, windows, and wall cabinets, which were made of hardwood, as well as the veneered surfaces with marquetry of ceramics, brocades, metals, bamboo weavings, and jade, reflecting the most contemporary trends. This screen, deeply traditional on the one hand, took inspiration from the popular phrase for four joys (*sixi*). On the other hand, its unfamiliar structure utilized wood and porcelain for an extraordinary visual freshness that was ultramodern. HL

1. GGBWY 1980, 3, 5.

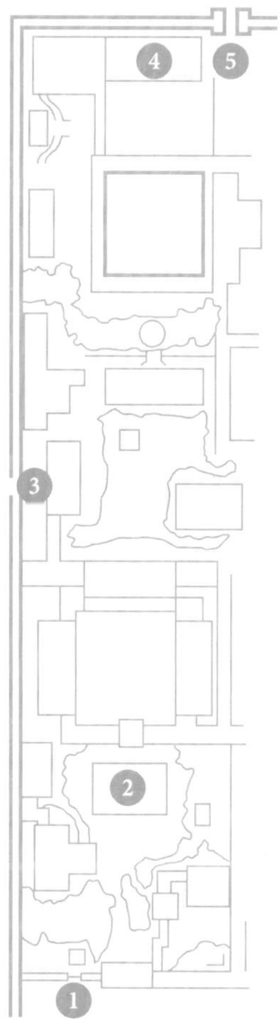

Fig. 1 Plan of Qianlong Garden

1. Gate of Radiating Auspiciousness
2. House of Ancient Splendor
3. Pavilion of Lasting Amusement
4. Studio for Retirement from Diligent Service
5. Gate of Staunch Obedience

Drawing after plan by Yu Zhouyun and Fu Lianxing. GGBWY 1980, 3, 5.

86 清乾隆 御製三星圖頌緙絲加繡軸

In Praise of the Three Stars, 1782–92

Qing dynasty, Qianlong period (1736–95)

Hanging scroll; cut-silk (*kesi*) tapestry with silk and metallic threads, embroidery, painted design

H. 220.66 cm (86.87 in.), W. 133.03 cm (52.37 in.)

Virginia Museum of Fine Arts, Gift of Mr. Christopher T. Chenery, 64.41

This remarkable silk tapestry depicts legendary Chinese deities known as the Three Stars. The man holding a child is the God of Happiness, or Jupiter. To his left and wearing a crown, the God of Prosperity (known as Wenchang), who is the sixth star in the Ursa Major constellation, looks on, as the God of Longevity, a symbol of the South Star, offers a peach. The children in the scene represent immortal boys. The picturesque scene includes floating clouds, mountains, peach-laden trees, and peonies and chrysanthemum in full bloom. The entire tapestry is woven in the cut-silk (*kesi*) technique. Gold and silver embroidery form the figures' costumes, and their facial features are painted in fine lines. The integration of cut-silk weaving, embroidery, and painting makes this scroll one of the most spectacular tapestries produced in the Suzhou imperial workshops during the eighteenth century.

Like other cut-silk tapestries, this scroll may be an imitation of an identical painting. Also in the Palace Museum collection, a small painting of the same Three Stars[1] may have served as a draft detail for VMFA's tapestry. This detail bears a colophon signed and dated to 1777 by Emperor Qianlong. The date may suggest the tapestry was created in the same year (1777) or shortly thereafter. Emperor Qianlong obviously favored the subject and wrote prose dedicated to it in 1782, as woven in the tapestry. His prose expressed the emperor's desire to build a society of harmony, happiness, wealth, and continuity, represented by the Three Stars.

There are nine Three-Star cut-silk scrolls registered in the second and third editions of the *Midian Zhulin*, the imperial collection catalogues, published in 1793[2] and 1816.[3] This VMFA work bears five woven seals of Emperor Qianlong. After comparing these seals to those recorded on the catalogued scrolls, it becomes evident that the VMFA work does not match any tapestry documented in the catalogues and that it is not included in the *Midian Zhulin* catalogues.

This scroll was remounted in 2011 with funds provided by the Ellen Bayard Weedon Foundation. LJ

Inscription, woven in the tapestry, a rhymed prose, signed and dated: 乾隆壬寅清和月御筆 (Written by Emperor Qianlong in the 4th month of the *renyin* year, 1782)

Seals: 古稀天子之宝, 犹日孜孜, 乾隆鉴赏, 乾隆御览之宝, 秘殿珠林

1. Fu 2005, 118, fig. 9.
2. Wang and Dong 1793, vol. 1.
3. Yinghe et al. 1816, vol. 1.

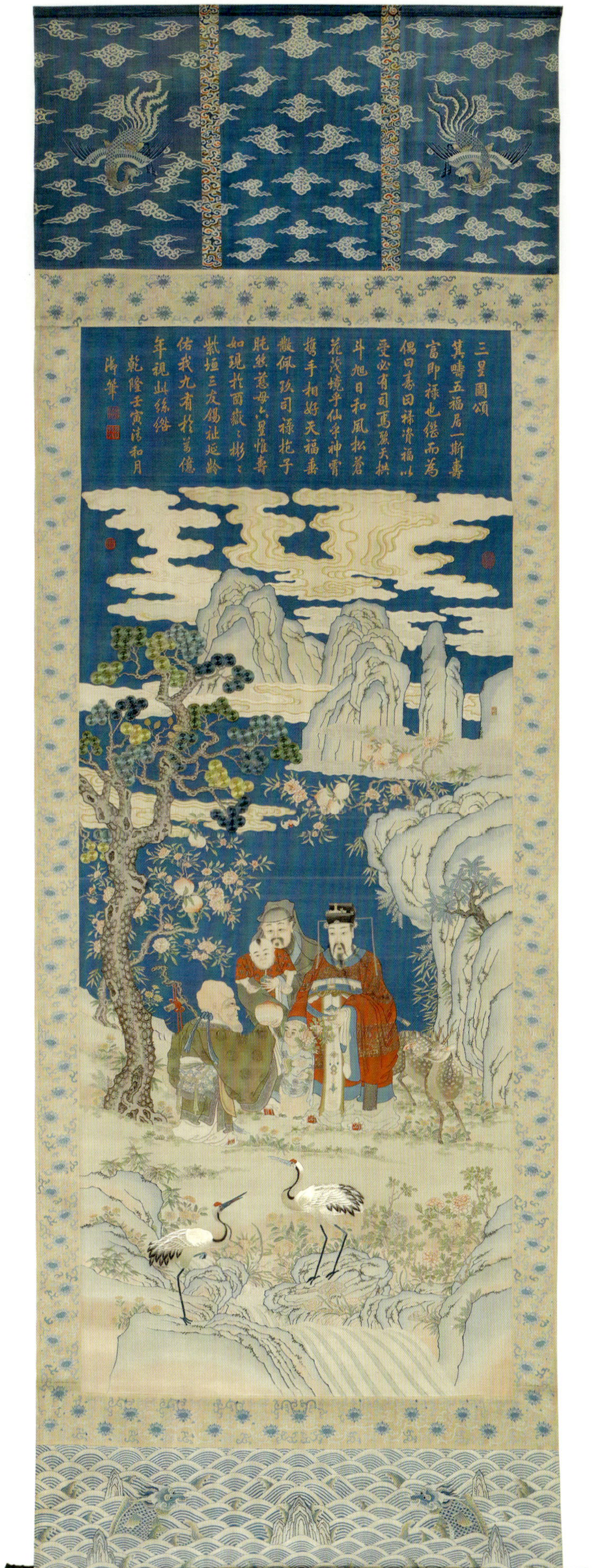
三星圖頌
箕疇五福居一斯壽
富即祿也繼而為
偶曰壽曰祿濟福以
受必有司篤蔭天拱
斗旭日和風松蒼
花茂境乎仙乎神霄
攜手相好天福垂
徽佩玖司祿抱子
眈然慈母六星惟壽
如現於西嶽〻彬〻
紫垣三友錫祉延齡
佑我九有於萬億
年視此絲綸
乾隆壬寅清和月
御筆

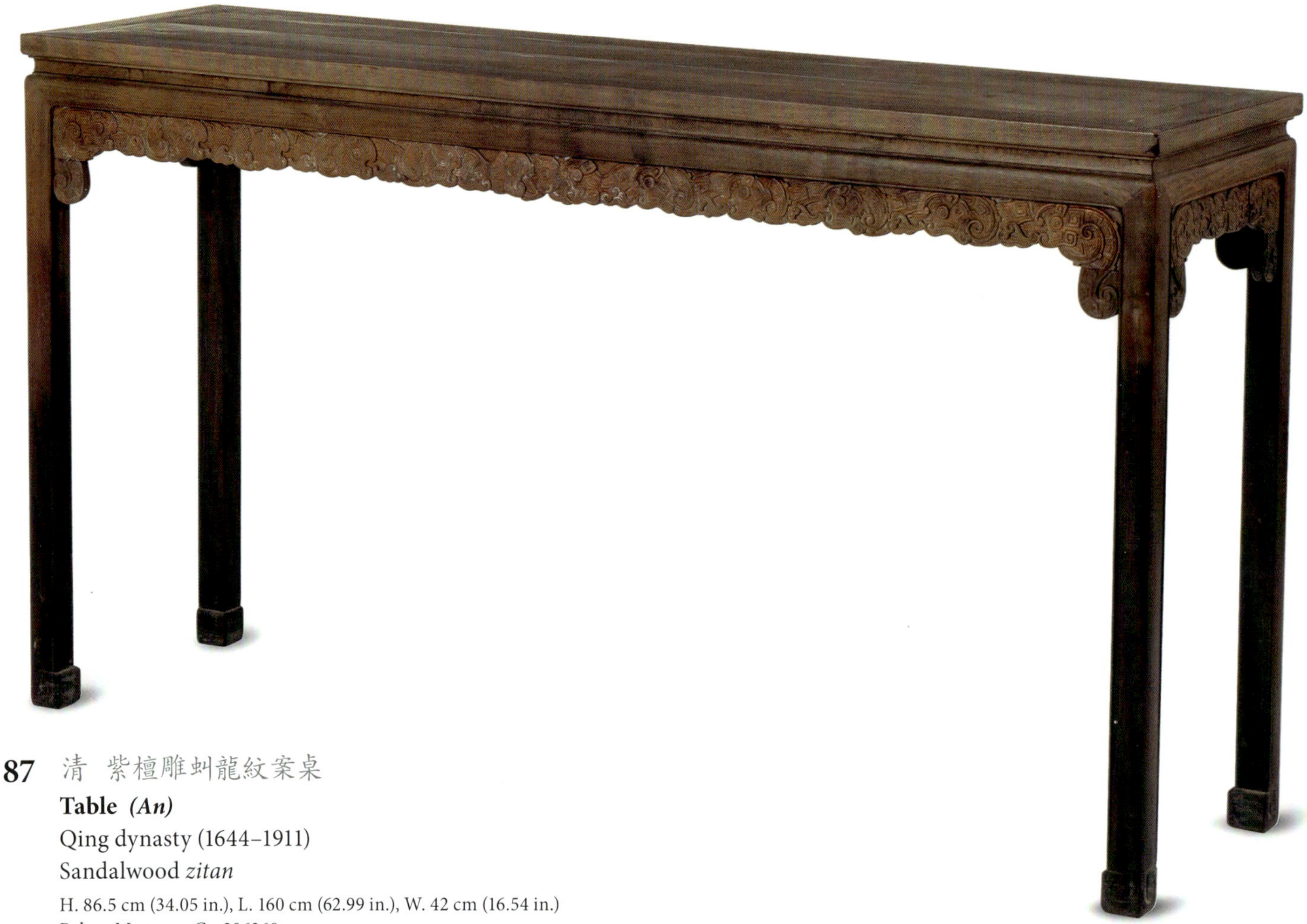

87 清 紫檀雕蚼龍紋案桌

Table ***(An)***

Qing dynasty (1644–1911)

Sandalwood *zitan*

H. 86.5 cm (34.05 in.), L. 160 cm (62.99 in.), W. 42 cm (16.54 in.)

Palace Museum, Gu.206260

Hundreds of wooden tables found in the Forbidden City fall under one of two categories. The tall rectangular tables, called *an,* were used to display ritual or decorative objects. The short tables, known as *ji* or *kangji,* were set on large resting platforms or beds called *kang.* Fine examples of each are presented here. Both tables possess a carefully rendered form and capture the spirit of Ming-dynasty woodwork's elegant simplicity conveyed in less elaborate cascading and congruous framework.

A traditional joint, known as mortise-and-tenon, holds the tabletop and its vertical legs together. The union of mortise (a rectangular hole of varying depths) and interlocking tenon adds strength and stability to the joint.

This rectangular *an* table has a standard frame-constructed top. A narrow waist is visible under the top frame. At the four sides, the curvilinear aprons, carved with stylized dragon patterns in high relief, are mortised, tenoned, and half-lapped onto the legs. The legs are straight, forming a rectangle, and end in hoof-shaped feet.
HL

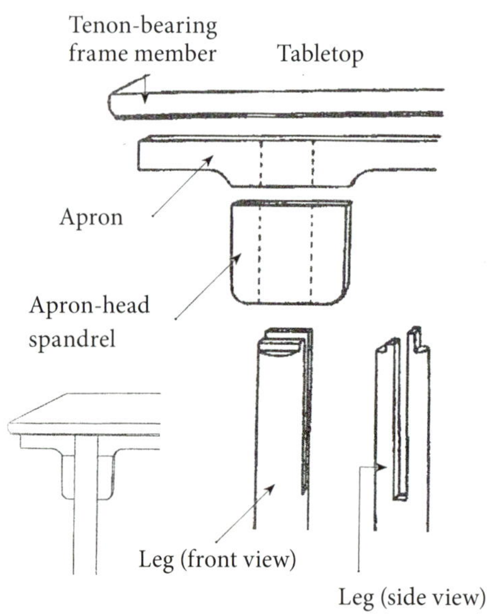

Fig. 2 Mortise-and-tenon construction
Drawing after Elongated Bridle Joint by Hu and Song, 2009, 23

88 清 紫檀木炕几

Table *(Kangji)*

Qing dynasty (1644–1911)

Sandalwood *zitan*

H. 32 cm (12.60 in.), L. 89 cm (35.04 in.)
W. 41 cm (16.14 in.)
Palace Museum, Gu.206976

The *ji,* or *kangji,* table was placed on a large resting platform. The top panel of this table is made of standard miter with a mortise-and-tenon frame construction. At the corner of each of the four sides, the aprons are half-lapped onto the legs. The four legs stretch downward, curving dramatically inward toward hoof-shaped feet, highlighting the table's balance and precision. HL

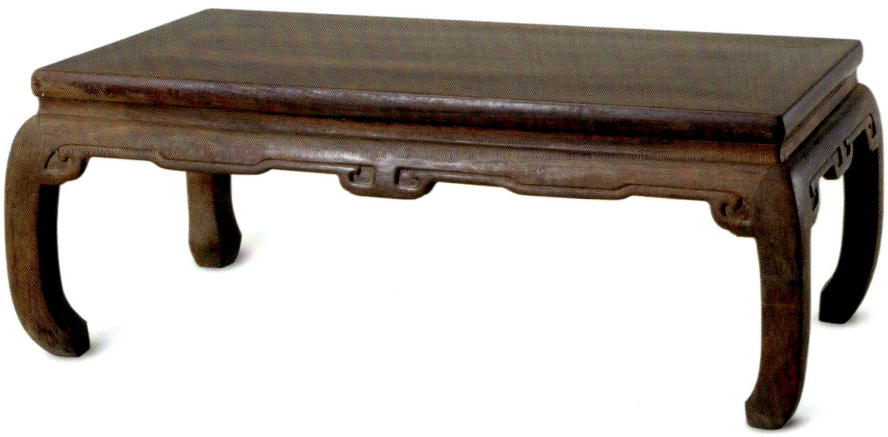

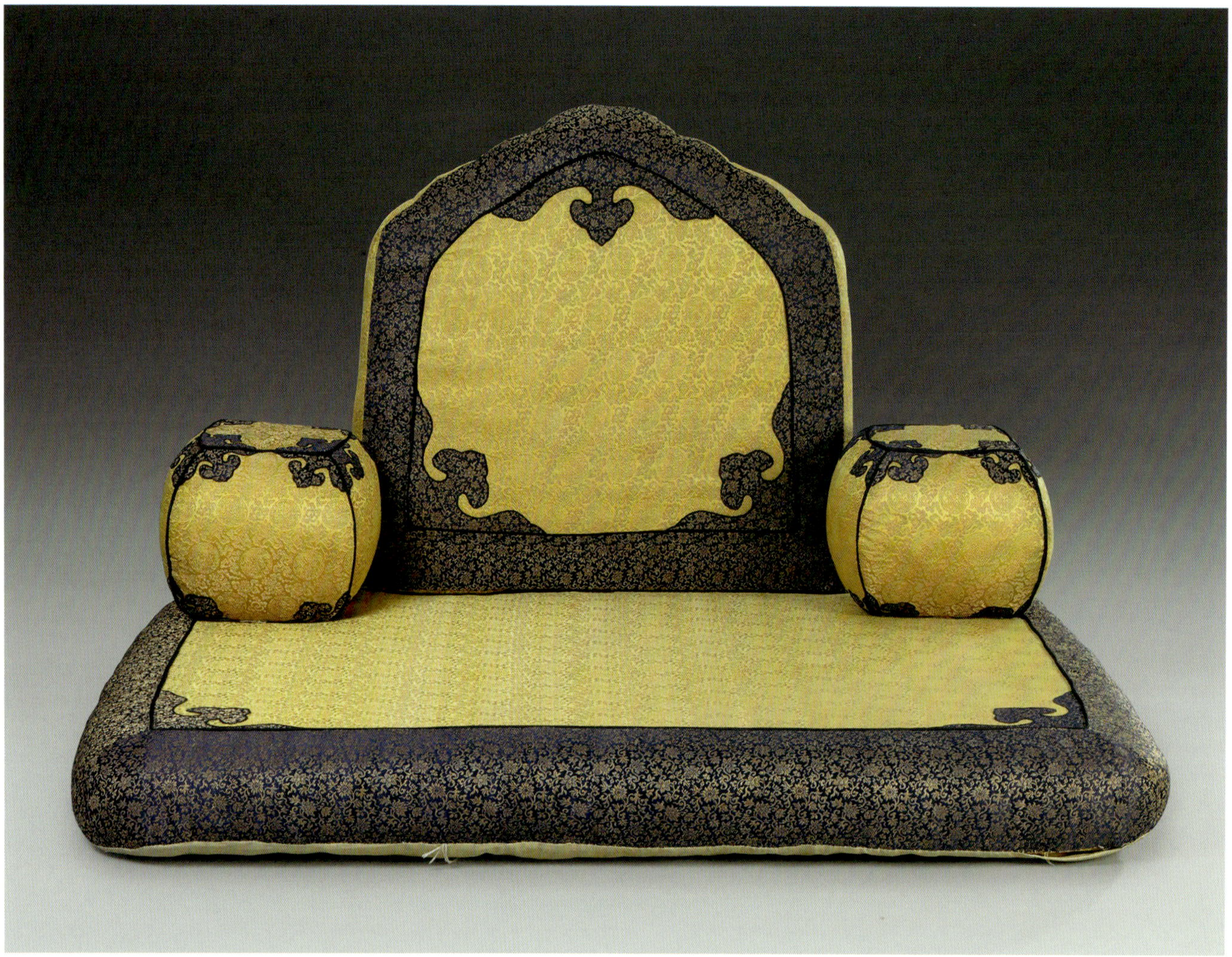

89 清 黄色江寧綢深藍金織勾蓮雲紋錦邊坐褥、靠墊、迎手一套

Cushion Seat

Qing dynasty (1644–1911)

Tabby (*jiangchou*) with woven design; brocaded trims with woven design

Seat cushion: L. 9 cm (3.54 in.), W. 112 cm (44.09 in.), D. 90 cm (35.43 in.)
Back cushion: H. 58 cm (22.83 in.), W. 62 cm (24.41), D. 9 cm (3.54 in.)
Arm rests: H. 20 cm (7.87 in.), W. 24 cm (9.45 in.)
Palace Museum, Gu.74682-1/4, Gu.74682-2/4, Gu.74682-3/4, and Gu.74682-4.4

In a style introduced by Qing-dynasty furniture makers, this cushion seat was designed to accommodate the Manchu custom of writing while sitting on a large couch or resting platform. In chambers in the Forbidden City, such a seat can be found in various arrangements on large couches in an office or study. An emperor often sat on a cushion with his legs crossed and leaned back, often propping another cushion against the wall.

A dull yellow woven fabric with patterns of stylized lotus scrolls covers this cushion. Widely used in the Qing palaces, silk woven of predyed yellow threads was routinely produced and managed by the Jiangning (Nanjing) Weaving Service, under the supervision of Imperial Weaving (Zhizao), a branch of the Imperial Household Department. The fabric was recorded in the imperial inventory under the abbreviated name, Jiang silk (*jiangchou*).[1] Appliquéd brocade in gold-threaded floral designs form borders with intersections and corners that feature shapes of *ruyi* mushrooms. The cushions were stuffed with cotton wadding. HL

1. CCTP 2005, 28, 124; Kuhn 2012, 434.

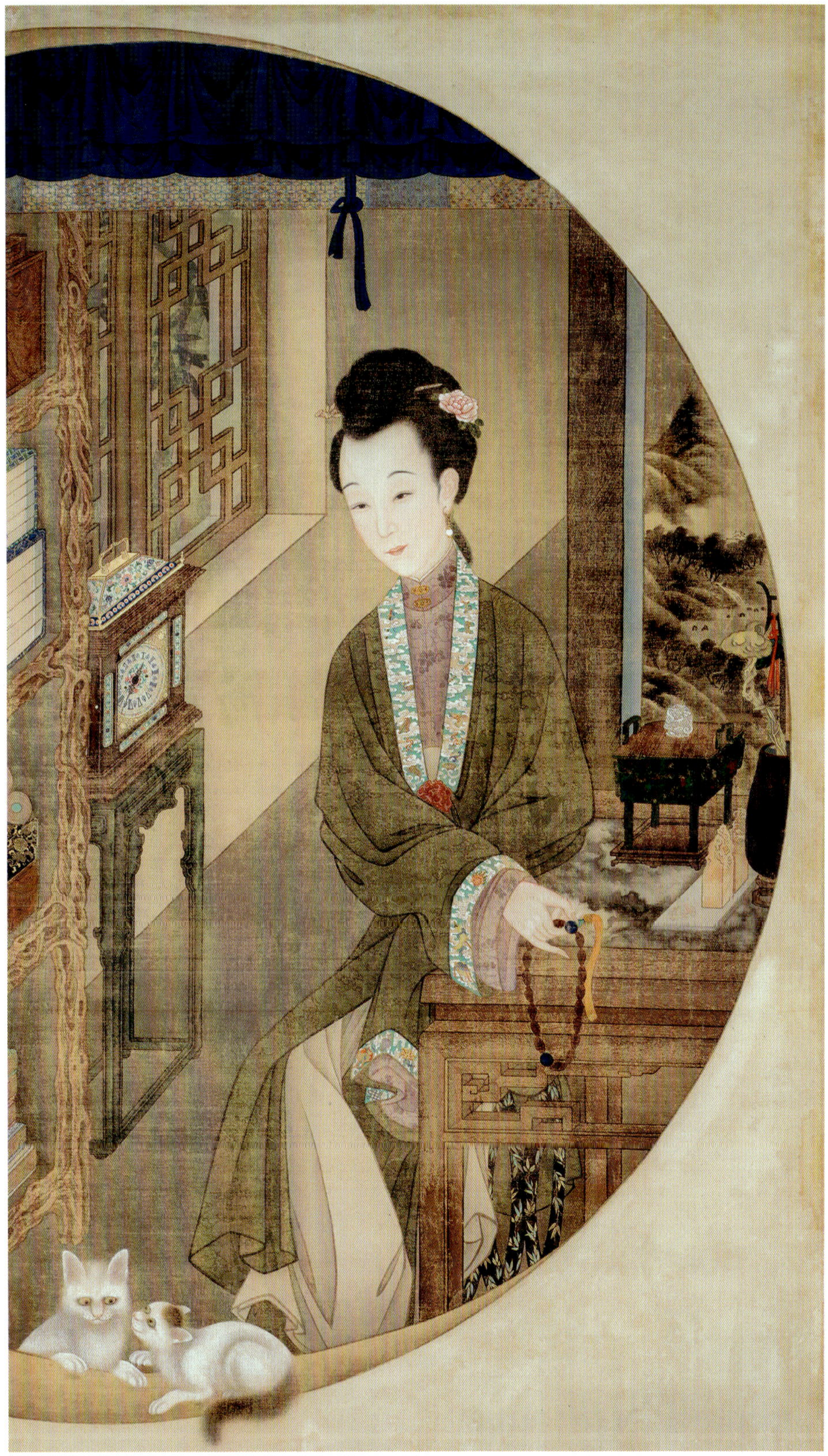

90.1 清康熙 胤禛親王(雍正)妃行樂圖 捻珠觀貓 絹本設色

Looking at the Cats from the series **Yinzhen's Consorts Partaking in Pleasurable Activities,** approx. 1709–23

Qing dynasty, Kangxi period (1662–1722)

Hanging scroll; ink and color on silk

H. 184 cm (72.44 in.), W. 98 cm (38.58 in.)

Palace Museum, Gu.6458-9/12

These paintings are from a series that portrays the daily activities of court women in the imperial residence. The setting and models are equally important, conveying an intimacy and establishing a juxtaposition between feminine figures and masculine objects. Of the twelve paintings, only five bear calligraphic inscriptions, four of which express loneliness, anxiety, despair, melancholy, or hopelessness. The metaphorical meanings of these depictions have been debated for decades.

The painting on the previous page (cat. no. 90.1) imparts a sullen tone as well. Dressed in a sage-green cloth, a female subject counts beads, a practice for reciting Buddhist scripture. One by one, she counts the beads as if counting days. Like the figure in the painting to the right, she is surrounded by masculine objects: the hardwood table with stone seals and the black jar with a dagger-axe. The landscape hanging at a distance from the bookshelf expresses a disconnect between the female and the room's masculine objects. Two cats in the foreground add warmth to the scene.

The woman in a Ming-era Han-style robe over a grayish garment (cat. no. 90.2) sits on a tree-root couch and looks into a bronze mirror. Her right hand rests on a Ming-style warmer. The screen behind her separates the couch from the bookshelf on the wall. The screen's calligraphy conveys a handwritten poem by Yinzhen (future Emperor Yongzheng), who laments the loneliness and the transience of female youth. The calligraphy's inscription references a nickname for Yinzhen, used only when he was still Prince Yong: 破尘居士 (Lay Buddhist Beyond Worldly Affairs).

The room's scholarly air was characteristic of Chinese studios belonging to educated men and the court elite, represented here by the setting's antiques and contemporary works: the twelfth-century purple narcissus planter by the window, the fifteenth-century red-glazed plate containing the fruit known as Buddha's hand citron, the seventeenth-century bamboo stool that holds a teacup, and a contemporary water boiler.

The subject of these paintings and the figures' identities have been in dispute since 1983. Some scholars speculate that the subject may have been inspired by the genre of "beauty" paintings in China, and therefore the women are generalized "beauties" and not particular individuals.[1]

However, a recent discovery sheds light on the paintings' contents. According to an imperial inventory in 1863, for safety reasons these paintings were moved from the Hall of Buddha to the Hall of Imperial Longevity (Shouhuangdian) in the Palace of Harmony and Peace (Yonghegong), Yinzhen's residence when he still held the title of Prince Yong. The registration numbers of this set match the series titled *Twelve Majesties,* which indicates the figures are Prince Yong's consorts.[2]

A comparative analysis of female members of Yongzheng's family found that several bear similar physical characteristics, making it plausible that either some or all of the figures in the series of twelve were modeled after the then-consort Wula Nala (d. 1731), who was crowned empress in 1723.[3]

Nevertheless, the paintings have an air of stoicism and internal tension, conveyed by the figures, interior decor, and calligraphy on four of the pieces. Yinzhen's years as a prince were marked by unrest, as he competed with his brothers for their father's favor and for the throne. Ultimately, Yinzhen succeeded by feigning disinterest and a lack of ambition. HL

1. Zhu 2013.
2. Lin 2013.
3. Yang 2013.

90.2 清康熙 胤禛親王(雍正)妃行樂圖 裘裝對鏡 絹本設色

Looking into a Mirror from the series **Yinzhen's Consorts Partaking in Pleasurable Activities,** approx. 1709–23
Qing dynasty, Kangxi period (1662–1722)
Hanging scroll; ink and color on silk
H. 184 cm (72.44 in.), W. 98 cm (38.58 in.)
Palace Museum, Gu.6458-1/12

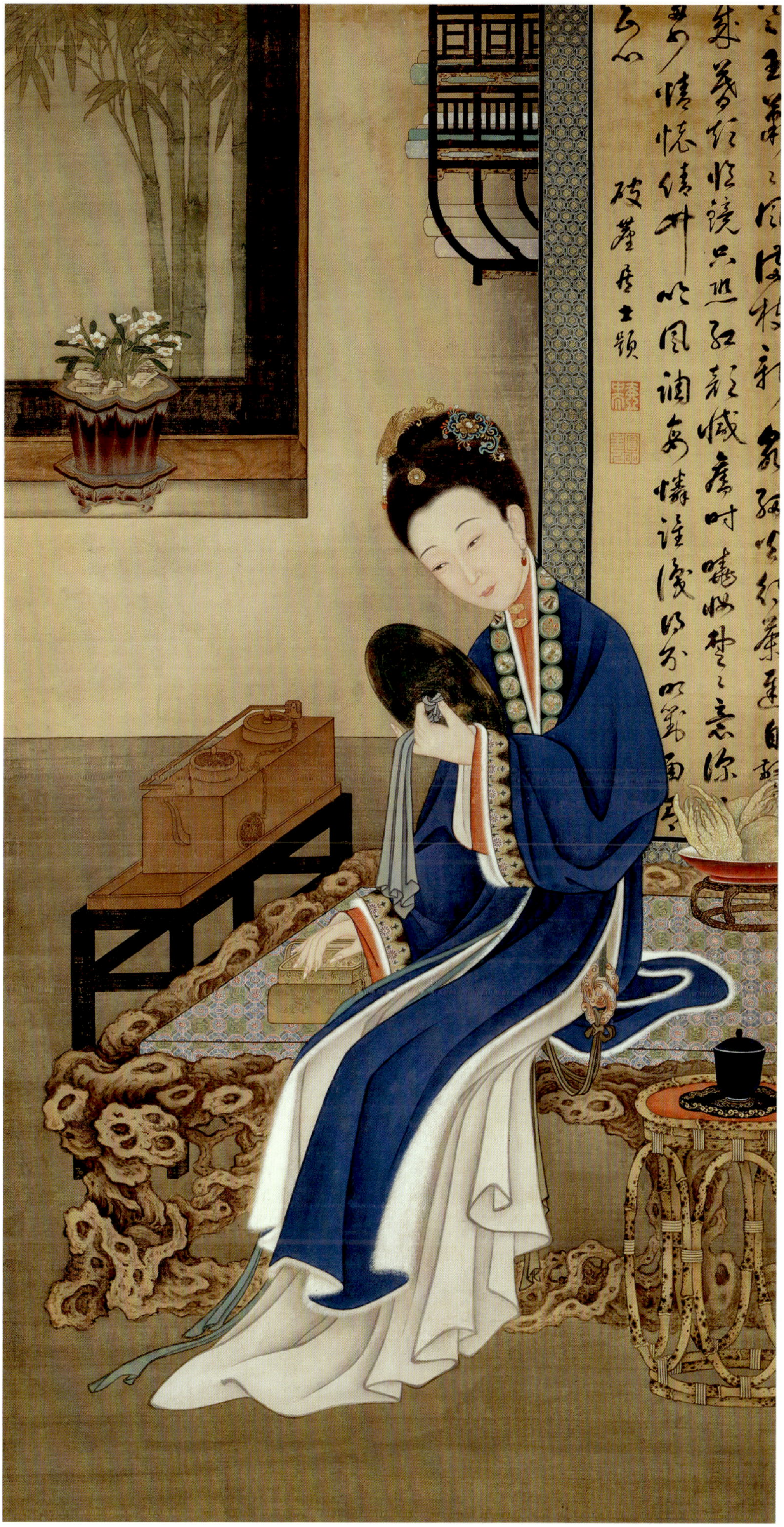

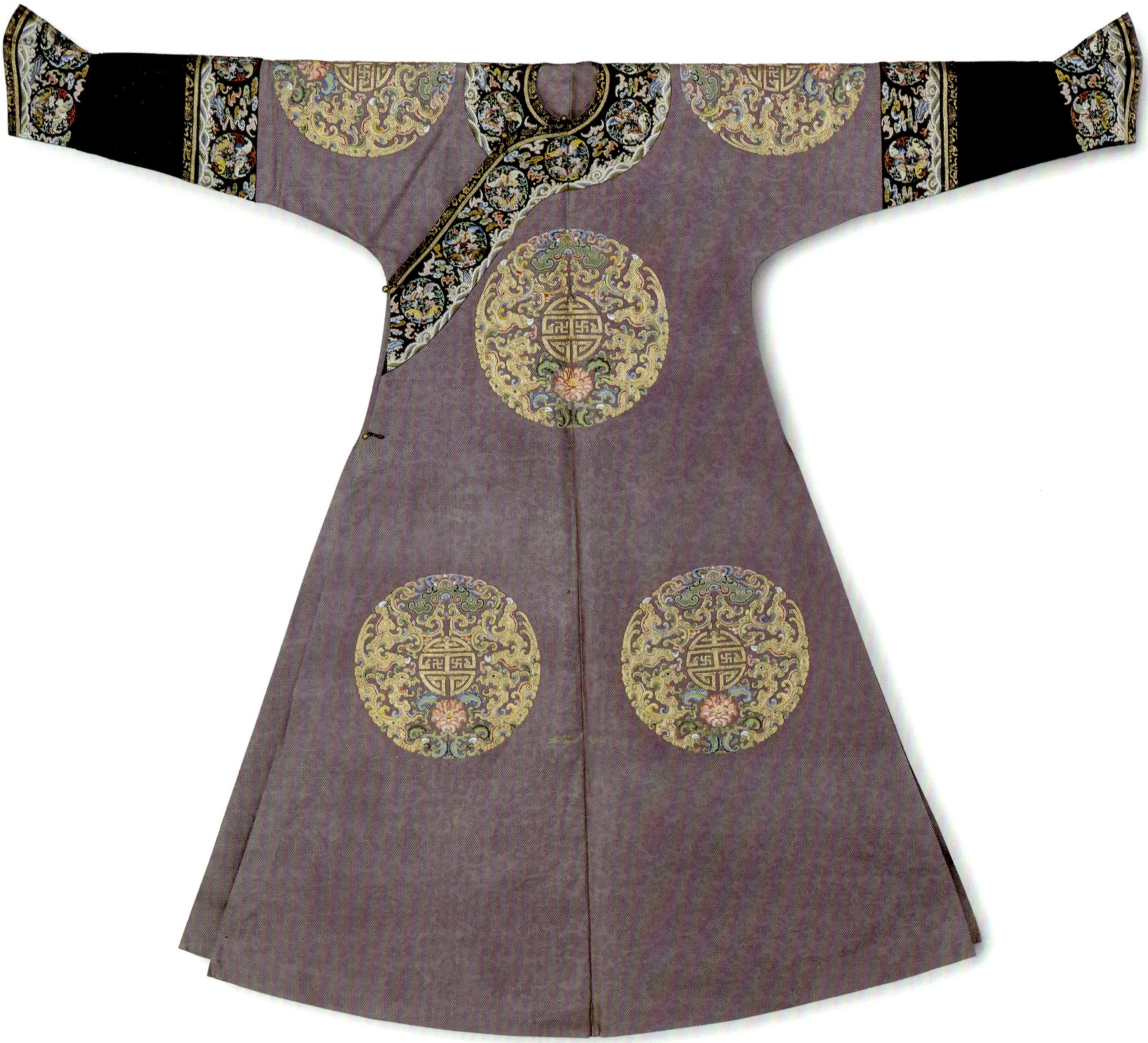

91 清乾隆 藕荷色紗綴繡八團金夔龍慶壽紋女單龍袍

Woman's Robe with Dragonet Medallions, 1778

Qing dynasty, Qianlong period (1736–95)

Tabby (*sha*) with embroidery and appliqués; brass buttons

Body: L. 147 cm (57.87 in.); Overall sleeves: L. 150 cm (59.06 in.); Hem W. 122.5 cm (48.23 in.)
Palace Museum, Gu.42157

Noblewomen wore this Manchu-style full-length robe in summer. Its design features an oval neckline, sleeves formed by two joined sections, and cuffs shaped like horse hooves. On the right side, an opening extends all the way down to match the slit on the lower left side. The principal motif of dragonets, instead of five-clawed dragons, indicates its semiformal function as auspicious attire, or *jifu,* worn for celebrations. Although the medallion design was considered dignified Manchu attire, dragonets and butterflies were designated for middle-level members such as wives of princes, according to Qing regulations on wardrobe and attire.

The outer fabric was made of a lovely mauve-colored tabby, a kind of thin woven gauze, and was rendered with intricate embroidery depicting stylized dragonets flanking a central medallion of swastikas and the longevity character (*shou*).[1] Appliquéd trims were hand embroidered with an array of small medallions presenting pairs of fluttering butterflies among clouds and flying bats over ocean waves. Together, the motifs in this one fabulous robe celebrate longevity, nobility, good fortune, and happy matrimony.

The meticulous rendering of details underscores the significance of these traditional techniques. Handmade stitches of overlapping, knitting, locks, loops, and knobs in multiple colors were carefully organized into a cohesive arrangement with a rich texture. HL

Inscription, handwritten in ink on a yellow silk tag that was originally attached to the robe: Lavender gauze with appliqués of eight medallions. Received on the 28th day of the 11th month in the 43rd year of the Qianlong reign, 1778.

1. CCTP 2006, 161.

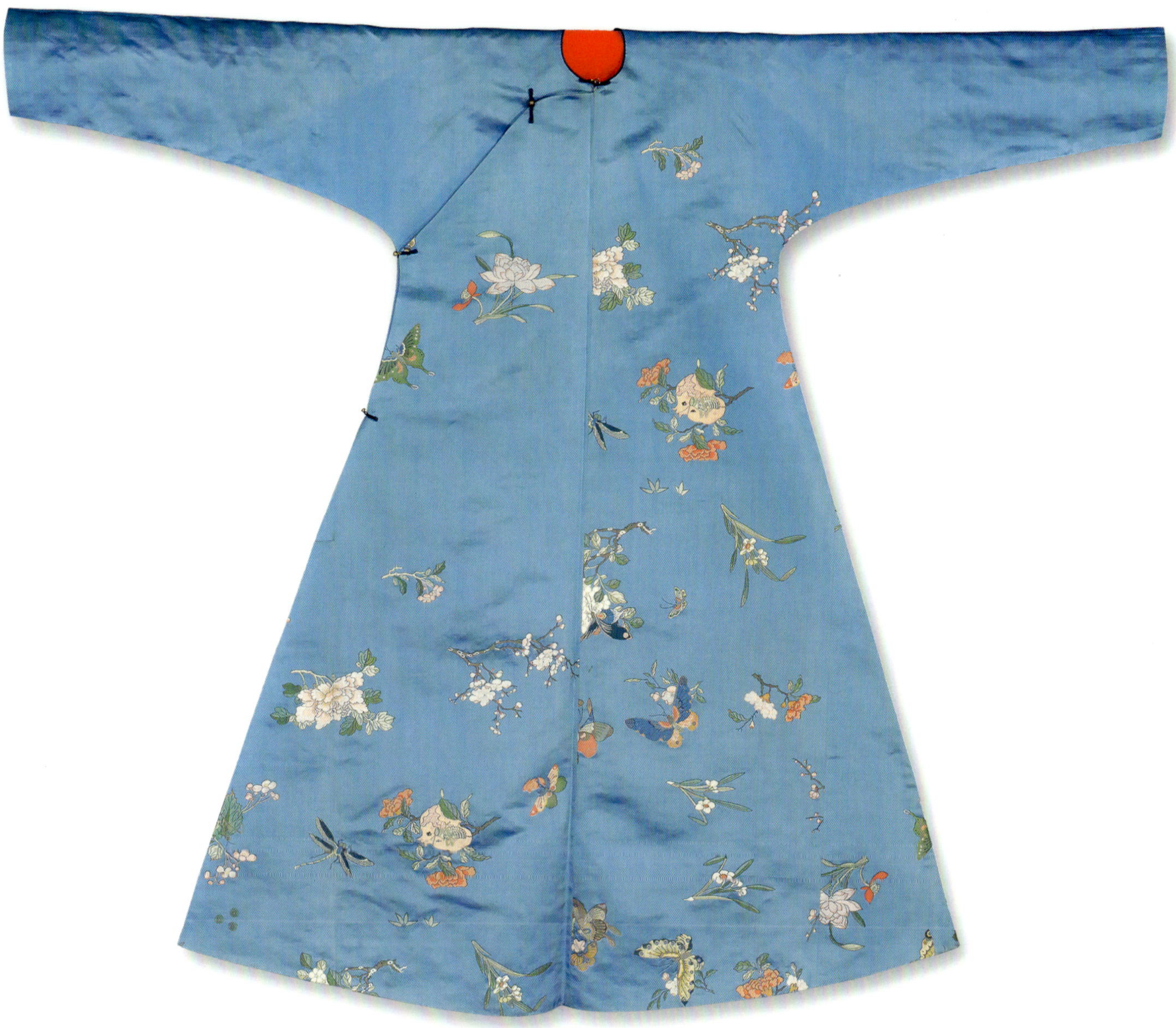

92 清乾隆 月白緞織彩圖紋百花飛蝶草蟲袷襯衣

Woman's Robe with Butterflies and Insects amid Flowers, 1778

Qing dynasty, Qianlong period (1736–95)

Satin with woven polychrome design; damask lining with woven design

Body: H. 142 cm (55.91 in.); Overal sleeves: L. 172 cm (67.72 in.); Hem W. 120 cm (47.24 in.)
Palace Museum, Gu.42137

This lined robe, which was made for a consort of Emperor Qianlong, is one of the few surviving articles of clothing from the Qing imperial storage. Slightly different from the semiformal robe to the left, this garment—with its sealed lower-left side and sleeves that are connected across the shoulders—was designed for everyday wear.[1]

Professional weaving techniques incorporated different types of stitching and high-quality silk threads to create colorful motifs on the silk ground.[2] On the yellow damask lining, single-colored patterns reflect innovations in other disciplines of the time, including embroidery, ceramics, lacquer, painting, and wood carving.

The unusually complicated woven motif depicts more than a dozen flowers and various species of insects, far surpassing the complexity of most contemporary textile designs. Scattered among flower blossoms are butterflies, mantises, grasshoppers, and dragonflies, which symbolize nobility, longevity, good fortune, prosperity, and well wishes for many sons. The color scheme is splendid with bright colors that brilliantly decorate the blue silk. Such fine-quality court attire was attributed to the factories in either Suzhou or Jiangning (today's Nanjing) and their silk weavers, who were supervised by the imperial workshop for weaving.[3] HL

Inscription, handwritten in ink on a yellow silk tag that was originally attached to the robe: Hundred-flower-satin robe with moon-white lining. Received on the 28th day of the eleventh month in the 43rd year of the Qianlong reign, 1778

1. CCTP 2006, 199.
2. Kuhn 2012, 439.
3. Ibid., 434–35.

93 清嘉慶 明黃色團龍紋暗花江綢貂皮鑲銀鼠皮喜字馬褂

Man's Reversible Jacket with Characters for Happiness

Qing dynasty, Jiaqing period (1796–1820)

Damask, sable, ermine

Body: H. 70 cm (27.5 in.); Overall sleeves: L. 144 cm (56.7 in.); Hem W. 72 cm (28.35 in.)
Palace Museum, Gu.44967

This particular jacket epitomizes the extravagant attire worn at royal celebrations such as weddings or birthdays. In general, its style—featuring five gilt engraved brass buttons down the front, drop-shoulder sleeves, and side slits—had become fashionable casual wear for men during the Qing dynasty. While the name, "horse jacket," implies ease of movement, especially for horseback riding or martial arts, its lavish, reversible design indicates more formal use.

One side is made entirely of imperial yellow damask with woven dragon medallions; both the color and the emblem were the sole privilege of the imperial family. The reverse side was assembled from pieces of brownish marten fur, over which the character for double happiness had been cut out forty-six times, and the openwork strokes were then filled in with matching pieces of ermine.[1] The controlled tone of the golden-yellow dye and the perfect weaving of the complicated patterns gave the jacket a noble air. The cut-out and sewn-on characters reveal superb leather-making skill and expertise. HL

1. CCTP 2006, 218.

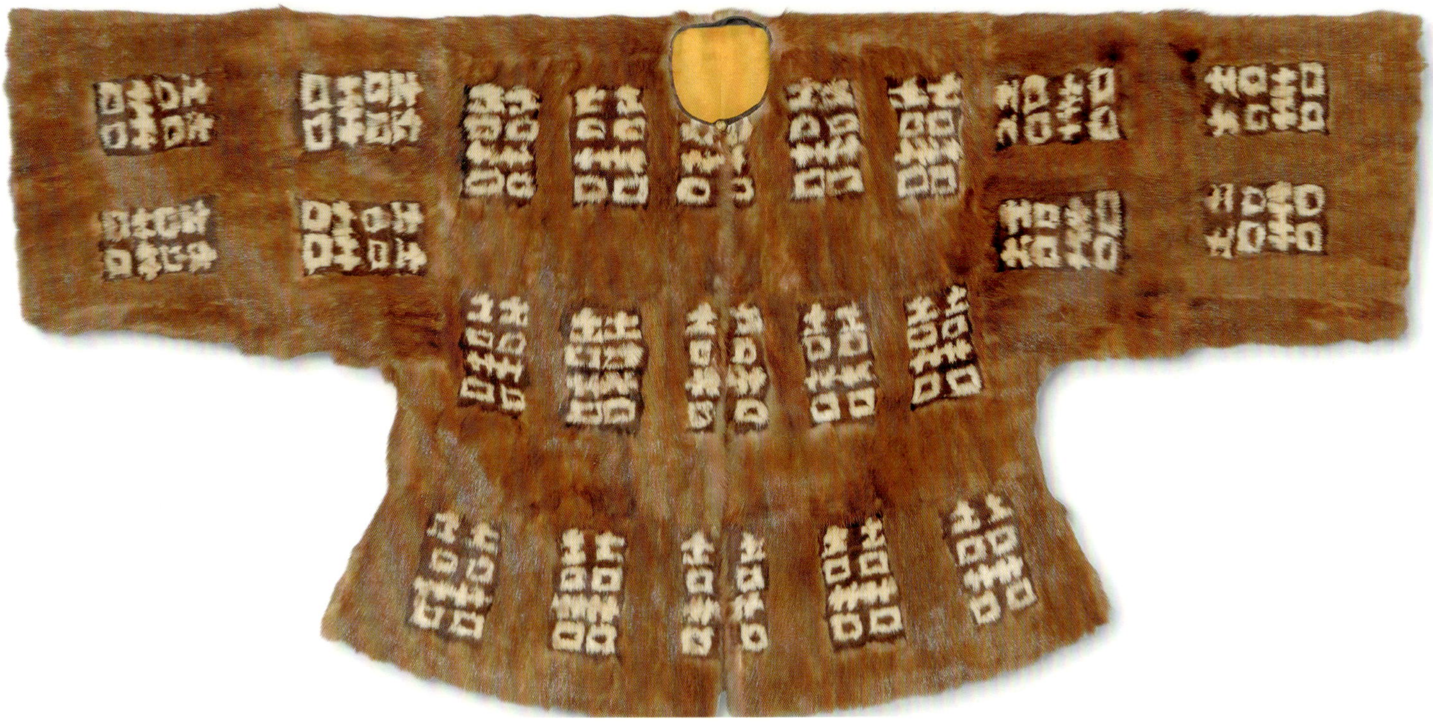

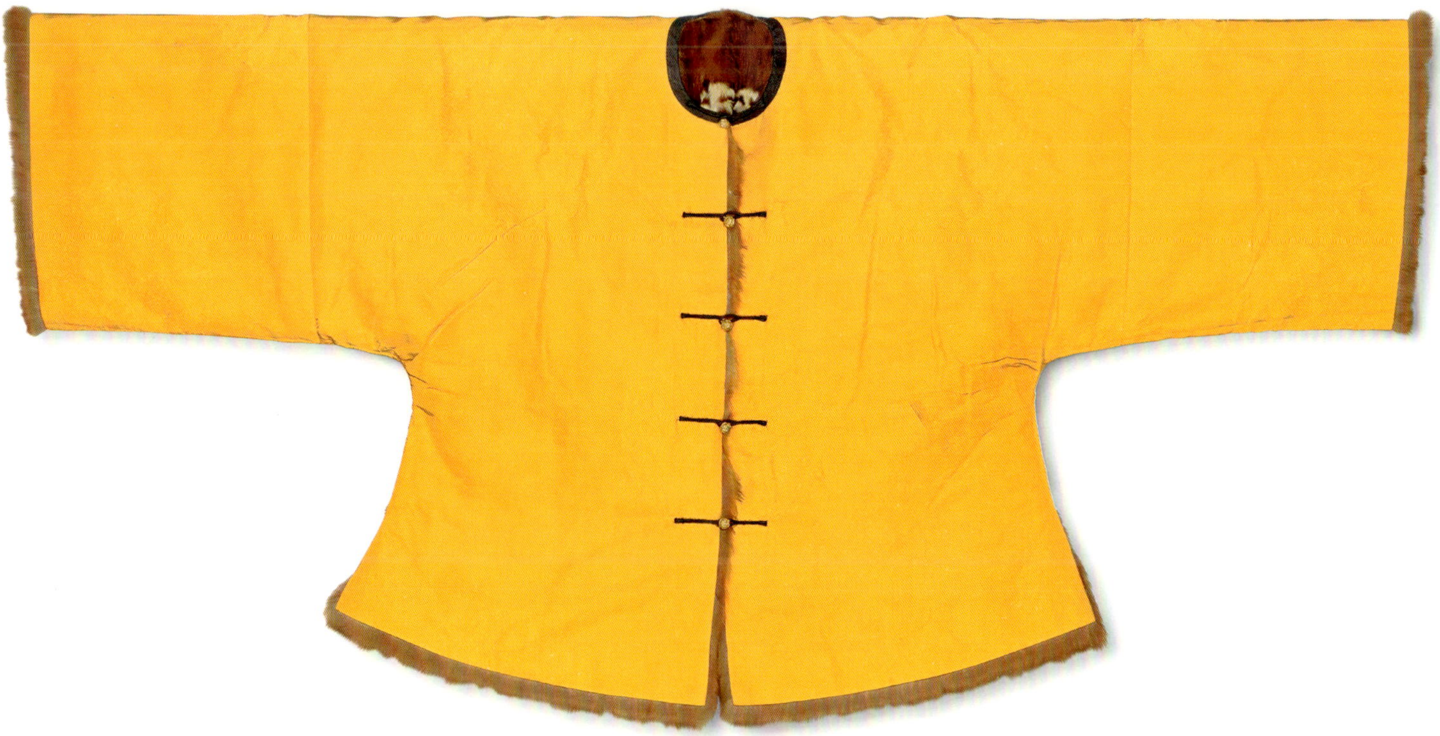

94 清光緒 月白色緞平金繡六合一統小帽

"Unity of the Six" Cap for a Man

Qing dynasty, Guangxu period (1875–1908)
Satin with embroidery and floss tassels
H. 15 cm (5.91 in.), Rim Dia. 17 cm (6.69 in.)
Palace Museum, Gu.59729

Originally a style worn by Han working peasants, this type of round cap became fashionable for men during the Qing dynasty. For emperors, the caps were adorned with special emblems to reflect their regal lifestyle. Because this cap's red knit knob with long floss tassels resembles a *lingzhi* mushroom head with a long stem, the form traditionally known as *ruyi,* the cap was given the name "wish-granting ruyi hat." The six panels that were sewn together to form the dome shape represent an old cosmic saying: *liuhe yitong,* which means "unity of the six directions of heaven, earth, and the four cardinal directions." Wearing the cap reminded the emperor of his mission to bring unity to the world. This particular cap was made of cobalt blue satin with multicolored embroidery. The band and the six sections, which are held together by golden floral brocaded trims, feature the auspicious symbols of bats flying over ocean waves coupled with the longevity character (*shou*) in various forms and repeated patterns.[1] HL

1. CCTP 2006, 258.

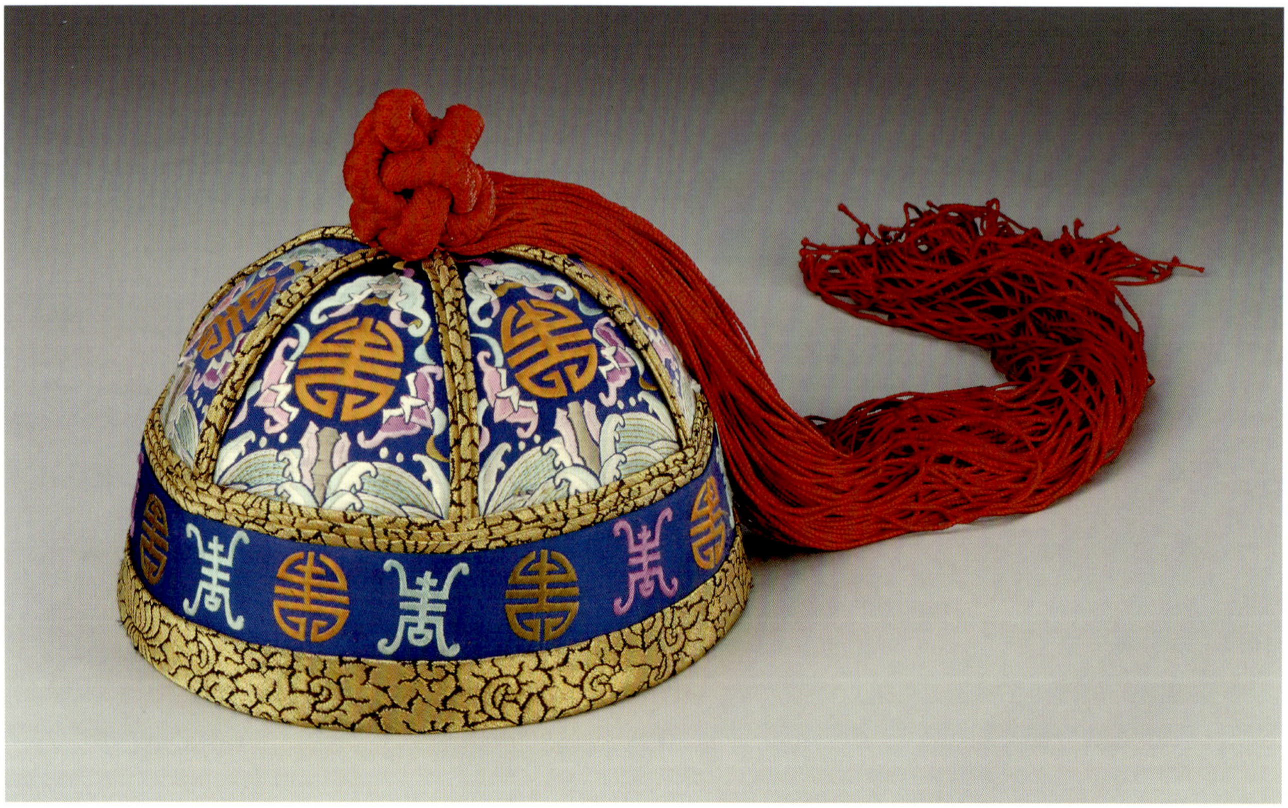

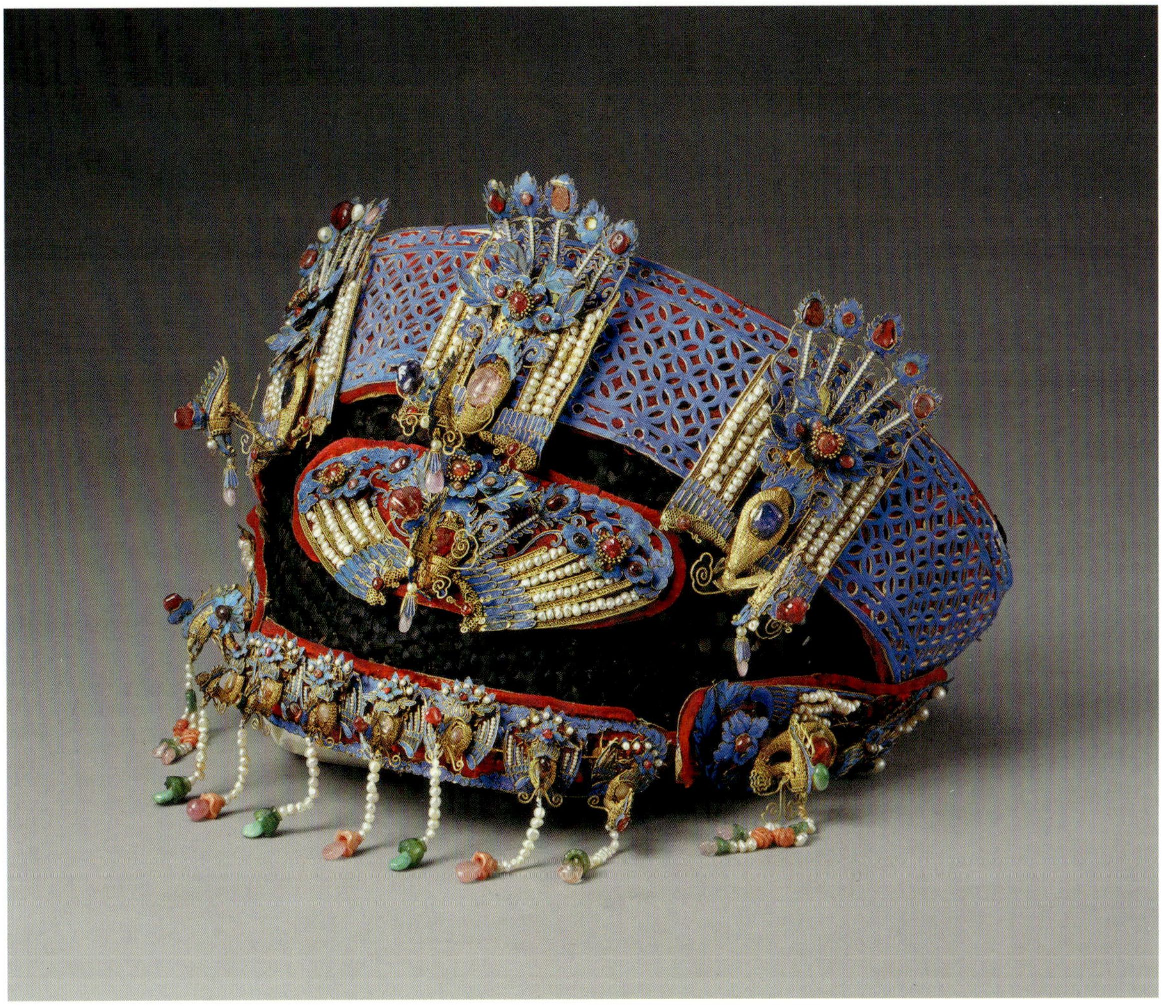

95 清光緒 銅鍍金累絲點翠嵌珠石鳳鈿子

Woman's Headdress with Phoenix Procession

Qing dynasty, Guangxu period (1875–1908)

Metal wire, silk cords, cardboard, velvet, gilt-copper, kingfisher feather, pearls, garnet, coral, nephrite, jadeite, turquoise, quartz, lapis lazuli, ruby, tourmaline

H. 19 cm (7.48 in.), W. 30 cm (11.81 in.), Rim Dia. 17 cm (6.69 in.)
Palace Museum, Gu.59708

This type of headdress, known as *dianzi* (meaning "filigree"), was commonly worn by court women at important ceremonies that required semiformal attire. Headdresses that were fully decorated and adorned with phoenixes were considered superior. The dazzling procession of phoenixes symbolizes heavenly forces and female virtue. Using traditional rattan, bamboo, metal, and textile, the hats were outstanding for their colorful gemstones and meticulous execution.

This hat was constructed in a three-layer process, starting with the structural skeleton and stuffing and finishing with the decoration. The frame was knitted with metal wires, which were wrapped in dark silk cords or floss. Pieces of turquoise cardboard over red velvet were placed around the top and the upper and lower bands. Lastly, high-relief accessories were affixed to the turquoise cardboard. Pearls, flowers made of kingfisher feathers, and gemstones decorate the wings and tails of the large flying phoenixes. Smaller birds carry pearls and a flower bud of emerald jadeite and pink quartz. Adding a lustrous effect, strings of white pearls hang from the lower edge with vivid gems that form auspicious symbols of a bat, musical chime, double happiness, fish, double fish, and eternity knots.1 HL

1. CCTP 2004, 72.

96 清 花蝶點翠鈿子飾片

Hat Ornament with Flowers and Butterflies

Qing dynasty (1644–1911)

Kingfisher feather, silk and gold-wrapped thread, glass, thick paper

Box: H. 18 cm (7.09 in.), W. 33 cm (12.99 in.)
Palace Museum, Gu.71466-7/8

Court women embraced the new style of headdress, richly adorned turquoise-colored hats known as *dianzi* (cat. no. 95). In time, bright kingfisher feathers became the new trend in headdress ornaments. The tributes of kingfisher feathers received from Siam (Thailand) increased by as many as six hundred pieces yearly by the 1790s.[1] Even turquoise enamels or similarly colored materials were used to create an effect reminiscent of these blue feathers. This design concept extended to a variety of hair ornaments, combining gemstones such as emeralds with pearls to express botanic themes, as seen in the arrangement on this background sheet for the dianzi headdress. If sewn on the hat, the openwork design provides spaces for alternating gemstone rosettes or pearl beads.

This turquoise foundation sheet, made of hard, thick paper, is comprised of openwork mesh forming hexagonal stars alternating with nine clusters of flower blossoms. From the central petals, tiny flowers protrude, highlighting golden threads with glass drops for the stamens. Four butterflies with antennae knitted of gold-wrapped threads flit toward the center.

The cardboard box, mirroring the shape of its contents, was custom made. The motifs on the outer lid consist of rows of flying red birds amid white and blue clouds, forming a contrast in colors. HL

1. Zhang (compiled 1941) 1990, 196.

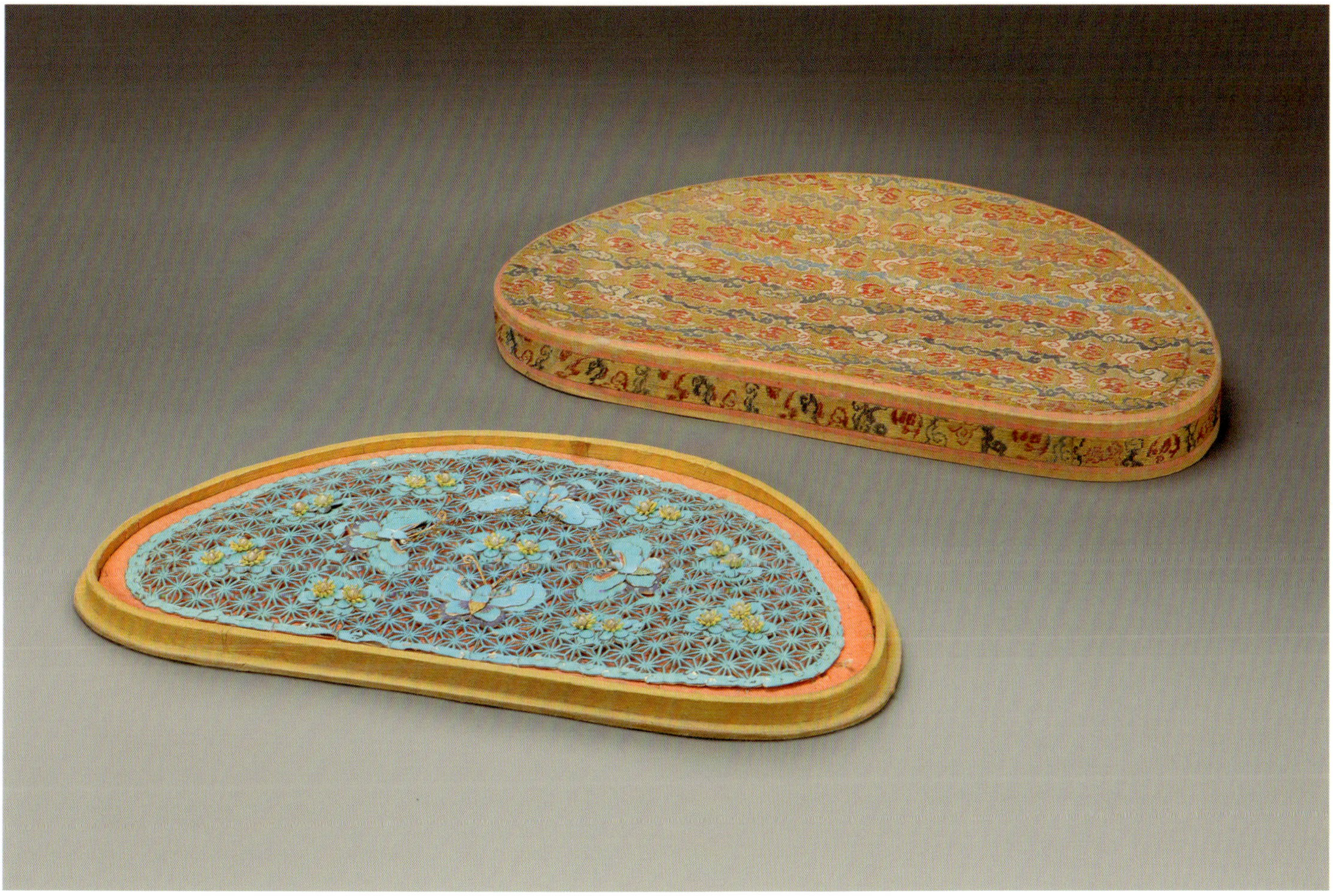

97 清 鑲寶石碧璽牡丹花蝶髮簪

Hairpin with Peony and Butterfly

Qing dynasty (1644–1911)

Gilt silver, tourmaline, jadeite, pearl

L. 25 cm (9.8 in.), W. 11 cm (4.33 in.)

Palace Museum, Gu.9960

Manchu men, who shaved their heads in the front and wore a long braid down the back, abandoned the Han custom of wearing hair ornaments. However, such adornment became increasingly important for women. Hairpins were decorated for women with an assortment of flowers and insect symbols, gilded networks of wires and mounts, and gemstones that sway and sparkle.

This hairpin contains symbols for nobility and happy matrimony: a gilded silver stalk splitting into branches with a peony blossom, flower buds, and a butterfly. A popular image in China, the peony is set here with gemstones in the form of yellow-green petals, white pearls, green leaves, and pink buds. As the wearer of the hairpin moved about, the butterfly, a symbol of love, would flap its jadeite wings.

For thousands of years, head ornaments were designed using a single medium. In the fourth century, a few hair ornaments emerged with multiple mediums, such as gold with gemstone inlays.[1] By the Ming dynasty (1368–1644), single items were adorned with five or more precious materials such as ruby, pearl, turquoise, malachite, and topaz.[2] By the eighteenth century, jewelry makers began to use materials that added movement, including bouquets of flowers mounted in gold and silver. HL

1. *Wenwu* 1993, 11, 3, color pl. 1.
2. He and Knight 2008, 36.

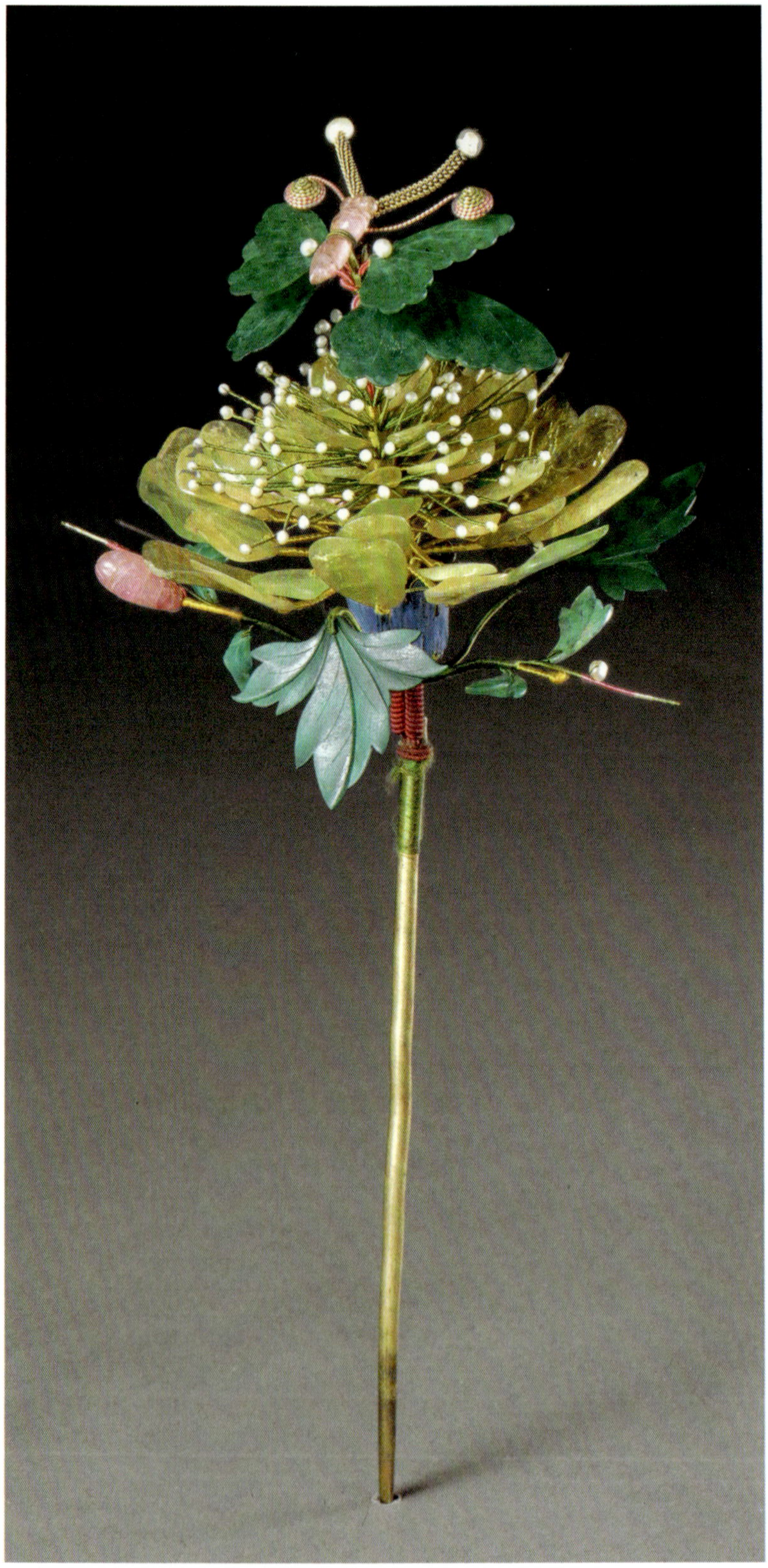

98 清翠扁方

Headdress Bar
Qing dynasty (1644–1911)
Jadeite
L. 34.8 cm (13.70 in.), W. 3.3 cm (1.3 in.)
Palace Museum, Gu.9962

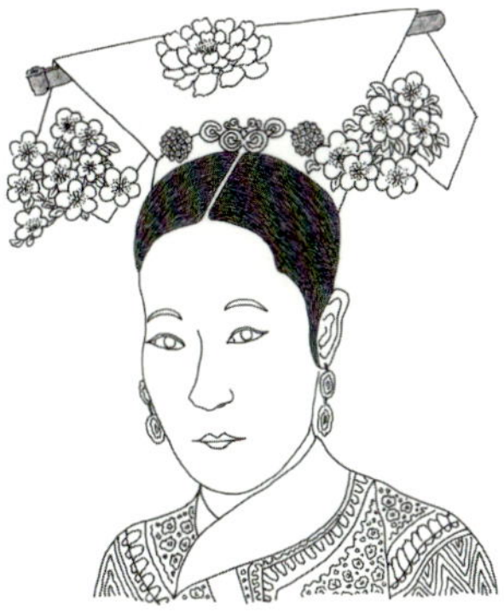

Fig. 3 Headdress

The hairstyle known as "large expanding wings" was stabilized with a long jadeite bar (*bianfang*). Drawing by Andrew Siu (b. 1949)

During the nineteenth century, women used precious materials and bright colors to increase the height and grandeur of their headdresses. Unlike traditional coiled hairstyles, the new style, which required a T-shaped cloth, produced a sculpture-like result given the name "large expanding wings." Fresh or silk peony blossoms were set in combination with the cloth. This style replaced most other headdresses worn by Manchu women.

To create "large expanding wings," the hair was pulled back, then formed into two bundles and flattened with viscous vegetable oil so that it could be folded upward to the left and right; it was then covered with a T-shaped headdress made of black silk, velvet, or gauze, all molded by a hard interior frame. Inside its folded top edge, it was horizontally stabilized with a long rectangular bar, known as *bianfang,* made of either gold, silver, ivory, jade, or the shell of the hawksbill turtle. As in this example, a single block of emerald jadeite has a five-petal plum flower (right end), a prevalent botanical image in Chinese art and a symbol of the virtues of faithfulness and tenacity. HL

1. Yang 2006, 322.

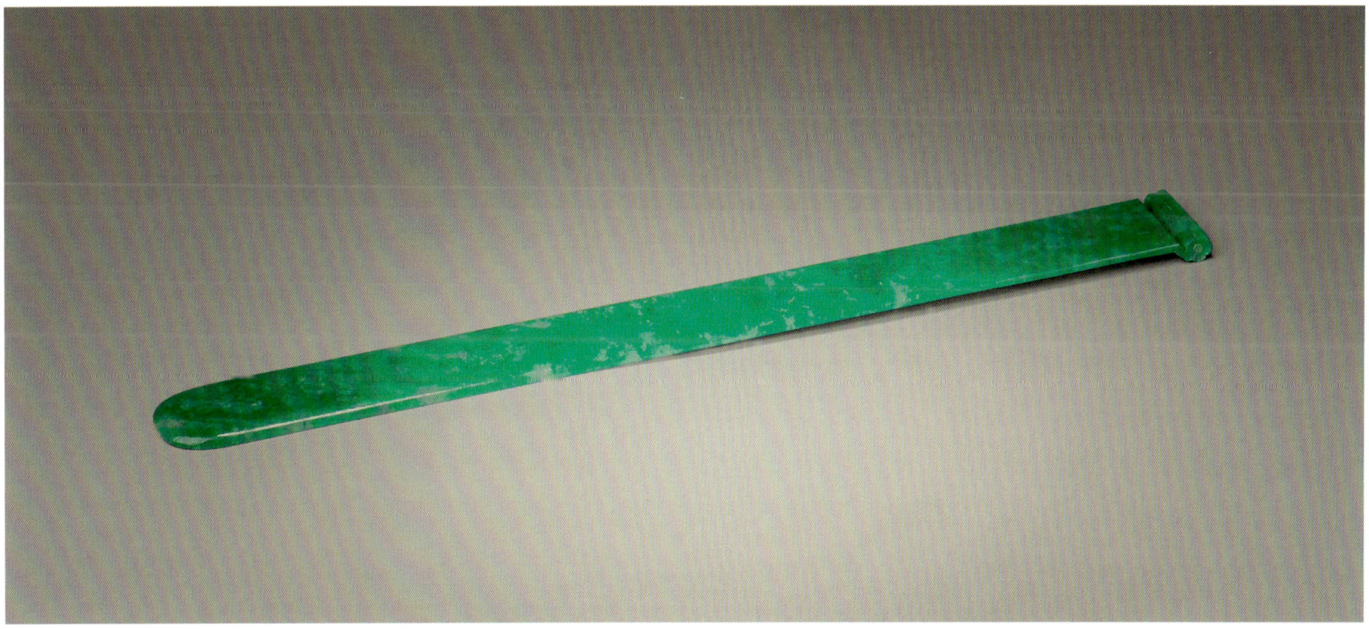

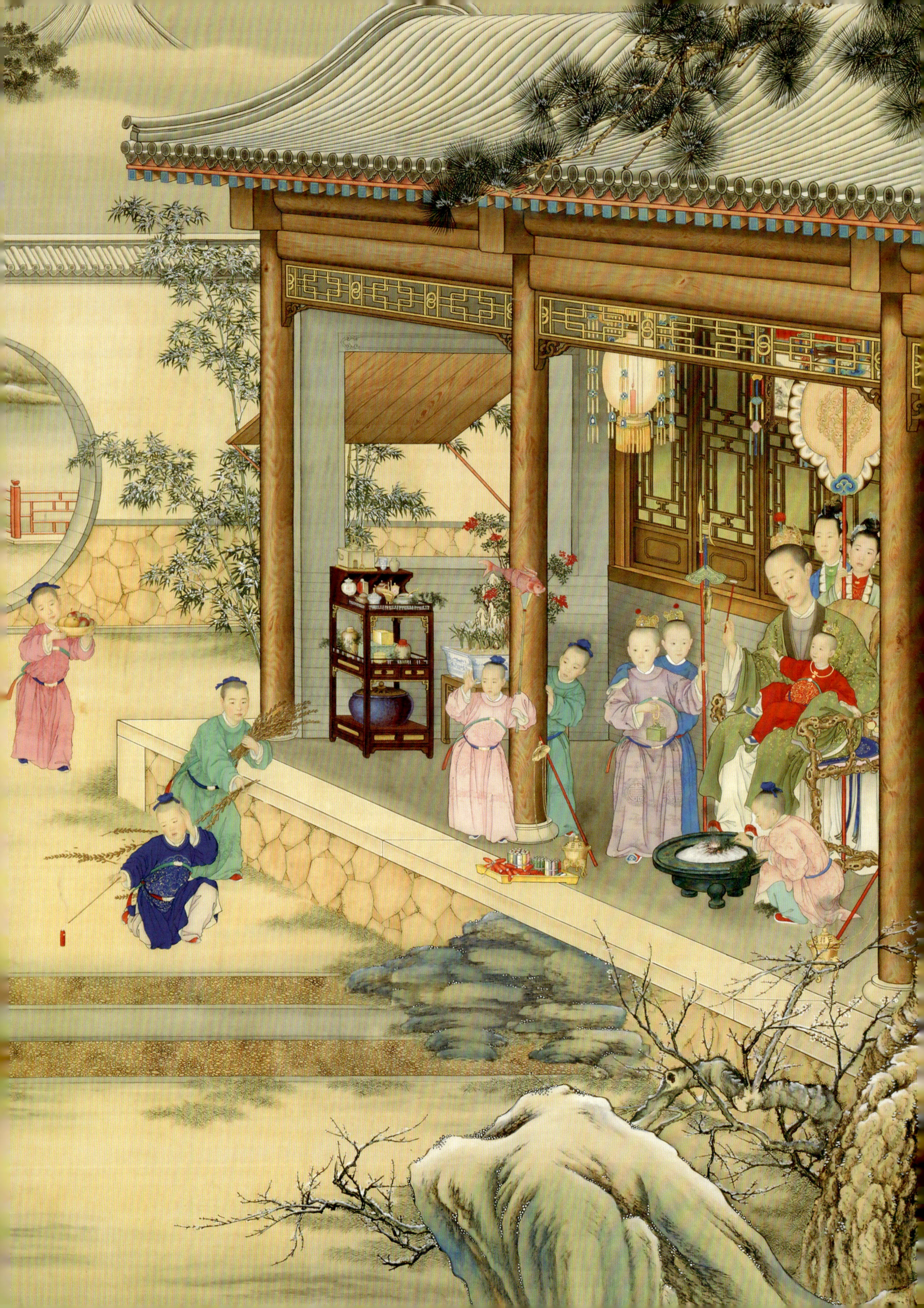

筆沾恩雨

Court Paintings of the Qing Dynasty

Brushes Dipped in the Benevolent Imperial Rain[1]

Hou-mei Sung

When the Manchu rulers first conquered Ming China and established the Qing dynasty in 1644, they faced the daunting challenge of effectively ruling a predominantly Han population while creating a political-religious system that maintained tribal order in the frontier regions. Qing rulers started with a Ming-based bureaucratic framework, yet they also made adjustments to ensure Manchu supremacy. Thus, the government sought to balance two competing principles: to continue longstanding Chinese traditions and to exert absolute control. This dichotomy also characterized the world of Qing court painters.

To win the support of the literati, Qing rulers presented themselves as preservers and restorers of Chinese culture and art.[2] From the Kangxi emperor (r. 1662–1722) to the Qianlong emperor (r. 1736–95), numerous court painters, including Western missionary artists, were recruited in the Ming tradition. While Qing court painters served in the Zaobanchu imperial workshop of the Imperial Household Department (Neiwufu), the existence of a Qing Painting Academy (Huayuan) remains an area of continued controversy.[3] The issue may be resolved through a better understanding of the little-explored history of the Ming Painting Academy, on which the Qing Painting Academy was modeled. The research presented herein sheds new light on how major institutional changes in the early Ming dynasty transformed the Ming Painting Academy. Pivotal changes occurred in 1414, when Emperor Yongle (r. 1403–24) made the decision to place all his senior court painters in the Directorate of Imperial Accoutrements (Yuyongjian). By grouping the court painters together with the other artisans serving in the eunuch-supervised imperial agency, the emperor not only lowered the court painters' official and social status but also forever altered the function of their art. In other words, they became the personal employees of the ruler.[4]

From the very beginning of their rule, Qing leaders adopted the political system and all-important institutions of the Ming dynasty, including the court painters' organization and operating systems. The Imperial Household Department, which supervised the Qing court painters, was in fact a greatly expanded and further-centralized version of the Ming eunuch-controlled institutions in charge of inner court operations, including the Silijian (the most powerful of such eunuch-controlled institutions). Also inherited from Ming rule was the court painters' workshop. The Zaobanchu workshop for Qing court paintings (later named Ruyiguan), located near White Tiger Hall (Baihudian), was the old site of the Ming dynasty Hall of Benevolence and Wisdom (Renzhidian), where Ming court painters served.[5]

Following Ming practice, Qing court painters were recruited mainly through the recommendations of court or local officials. Eunuch officials then presented candidates' works to the emperor for approval. Qing court painters, like their Ming predecessors, were assigned to different palaces and halls and stratified by varying levels of skill and salary.[6] As another carryover from Ming rule, talented sons or brothers of leading senior Qing court painters could inherit positions offered with imperial approval.

The Ming Painting Academy flourished from 1426 to 1505. Although Qing rulers used the Ming model to reestablish court painting, they focused on that dynasty's later years, the period after the Chenghua era (r. 1465–87) when the Ming Painting Academy's decline had commenced. In 1505, after waves of protests against the strong imperial patronage of court painters, Emperor Zhengde (r. 1506–21) was pressured to carry out a series of drastic measures concerning the court painters, which eventually led to the disintegration of the Painting Academy in the late Ming. Emperor Zhengde's actions included a critical reduction in the number of court painters and the abolishment of the Jinyiwei ranking system of the academy. Stripped of their official Jinyiwei titles and privileges, those remaining continued to serve in the inner court under the eunuch-supervised Directorate of Imperial Accoutrements (Yuyongjian).[7] This late-Ming court painters' organization and operating system then became the model for the Qing court, which explains why the Qing did not have a fully organized painting academy.

The Qing emperors, especially Kangxi, Yongzheng, and Qianlong, skillfully used Chinese art as an imperial instrument to assert their legitimacy as Confucian-style rulers. To accomplish this, Qing emperors worked closely with their court painters but controlled and scrutinized their works much more than Ming rulers did. Qing court painters were often assigned themes and designs, and their drafts or sketches were subject to imperial approval before they were permitted to complete the works.[8] Major categories of Qing court painting include imperial portraits (cat. nos. 3, 8, 46, 48); historical depictions of imperial activities such as official ceremonies for major events and festivals, campaigns, receptions for foreign delegations and the offering of tributes, rituals of imperial hunting, and expeditions to southern China (cat. no. 20); portraits of imperial horses (cat. nos. 34, 35); and auspicious or seasonal decorations (cat. nos. 111, 112, 113, 114). While most of these paintings were designed to glorify the emperor and can be traced to the Ming court, the Qing rulers also created new themes to convey specific messages of their own. For example, in his imperial portrait, Emperor Kangxi (cat. no. 46) positioned himself in front of tall stacks of Chinese books that, along with the open volume in front of him, serve as reminders of his remarkable accomplishment and major contribution to the Chinese literary world: the compilation of the monumental *Dictionary of Chinese Characters (Kangxi Zidian),* later known as the Kangxi dictionary. Following Kangxi's example, the Qianlong emperor had numerous portraits created of himself. They were similar and equally innovative. One Qianlong portrait shows him as a traditional Chinese scholar-official working at his desk, and another playful rendition depicts the emperor as an ancient Chinese scholar sitting in front of his own portrait (cat. no. 49).

Another unique aspect of Qing court painting is the participation of a large group of Western missionary painters, including Lang Shining (Guiseppe Castiglione, Italian, 1688–1766) (cat. no. 34), Wang Zhicheng (Jean Denis Attiret, French, 1702–1738), Ai Qimeng (Ignatius Sickeltart, Bohemian, 1708–1780) (cat. no. 35), He Qingtai (Louis Antoine de Poirot, French, 1735–1813), An Deyi (Joannes Damascenus Salusti, Italian, d. 1781), and Pan Tingzhang (Giuseppe Panzi, Italian, 1734–before 1812). These artists developed a blend of Chinese and European styles to accommodate imperial tastes. This hybrid nature of styles is evidenced in the carefully controlled shading and reduced contrast between light and shadow in depicting both the facial features in the imperial portraits as well as the subtleties of form in the horse paintings. In the meantime, Western approaches to create the illusion of three-dimensional forms through light and perspective also influenced many leading Qing court painters, including Jiao Bingzhen (1689–1726), Leng Mei (approx. 1670–1742), Ding Guanpeng (act. 1708–71), and Jin Tingbiao (d. 1767; cat. no. 109).

Qing court painting represents the last great chapter in China's dynastic painting history. The Qing rulers, being true heirs to the Ming legacy, successfully met the challenges of their time not only by reinstituting court painters to remain in keeping with Chinese traditions but also by adapting to changes arising from contemporaneous needs. While demonstrating their wide intellectual interests in Chinese arts and culture, the Manchu rulers exercised great control in shaping court painting. If the formation of Qing court painting is too complex to be analyzed here, it can at least be summarized by the script of a seal Emperor Qianlong bestowed to his leading court painters: "Brushes Dipped in the Benevolent Imperial Rain." Although clearly inspired by the Ming imperial seal of "Daily Approaching the Pure Radiance" (Rijin qingguang), which was awarded to leading masters in the painting academy during the Chenghua era (1465–87), the script of the Qing seal suggests a slightly more controlled and constrained imperial patronage.

NOTES

1. The phrase 筆沾恩雨, "brushes dipped in the benevolent imperial rain" is the script of an imperial seal of the Qianlong emperor. It typically appeared on paintings by his leading court painters, including Ai Qimeng, Jiang Pu, and Zhao Bingchong.
2. Ye 2002; Ho 1967, 189–95.
3. Yang 1994, 156–75; Chou and Brown 1985; Yang 1985, 54–68; Yang 1991, 3–11; Zhu 2001, 1–6; Wang 1996, 161–67; and Chi 2006, 127–52.
4. Sung 2006; Sung 1992; Sung 1991b, 30.
5. Yang 1994, 158.
6. See note 4.
7. Ibid.
8. See Yang 1985, 1988,1991, 1994; Zhao 2011.

99 明宣德 繆輔繪 魚藻圖軸 絹本設色

Fish and Water Plants

Miao Fu (act. 1426–35)

Ming dynasty, Xuande period (1426–35)

Hanging scroll; ink and colors on silk

H. 171.3 cm (67.44 in.), W. 99.1 cm (39.02 in.)

Palace Museum, Xin.97993

Miao Fu is unlisted as a Ming court painter, and nothing is known about his biography. In fact, the only information about him comes from his signature on this single extant work. Judging from the formal signature indicating his ranks and the imperial seal, this painting was an official work created for imperial use.

Fish painting became increasingly popular among Ming court painters after the Xuande era (1425–35). This painting depicts a large carp in a pond surrounded by aquatic plants and smaller fish.[1] The carp was considered a superior fish and a popular subject of Chinese painting after the Song dynasty (960–1279), when it became a symbol of a highly accomplished scholar. The choice was based on the Chinese belief that dragons and fish, especially carp, are related species. According to an ancient Chinese fable, every spring numerous fish would gather at the Dragon Gate between two steep mountain cliffs and try to jump over the gate to transform into dragons. Carp were the only candidates qualified to do so. Thus, the dragon-transforming carp (*hualongli*) became the symbol of an outstanding scholar about to join the dragon, a symbol of the emperor. In the Ming dynasty, carp continued to symbolize outstanding scholars and leading officials, but Ming court painters created numerous new themes and designs to convey specific political and social messages of their time.[2] Here, the carp, with its dragon-like whiskers and curled tail, most likely refers to a Ming hualongli. HMS

Inscription: 武英殿直錦衣衛鎮撫蘇郡繆輔寫 (Miao Fu from Sujun serving as Judge of the Embroidered Uniform Guard Unit in the Wuying palace)[3]

Seals: 良佐 *Liang Zuo* and 日近清光 *rijin qingguang* (Daily Approaching the Pure Radiance)

1. The painting is published in ZGHHQJ 1997, pl. 169, p. 40; Mu 1985, pl. 8; and He and Knight 2008, 210, cat. no. 117.
2. See: Sung 1995, a, b; Sung 2009.
3. After the Xuande era, the Ming court adopted the military ranking system to rate court painters and to differentiate their salaries. For a detailed discussion of the Ming court painters' ranking system, see Sung 2006.

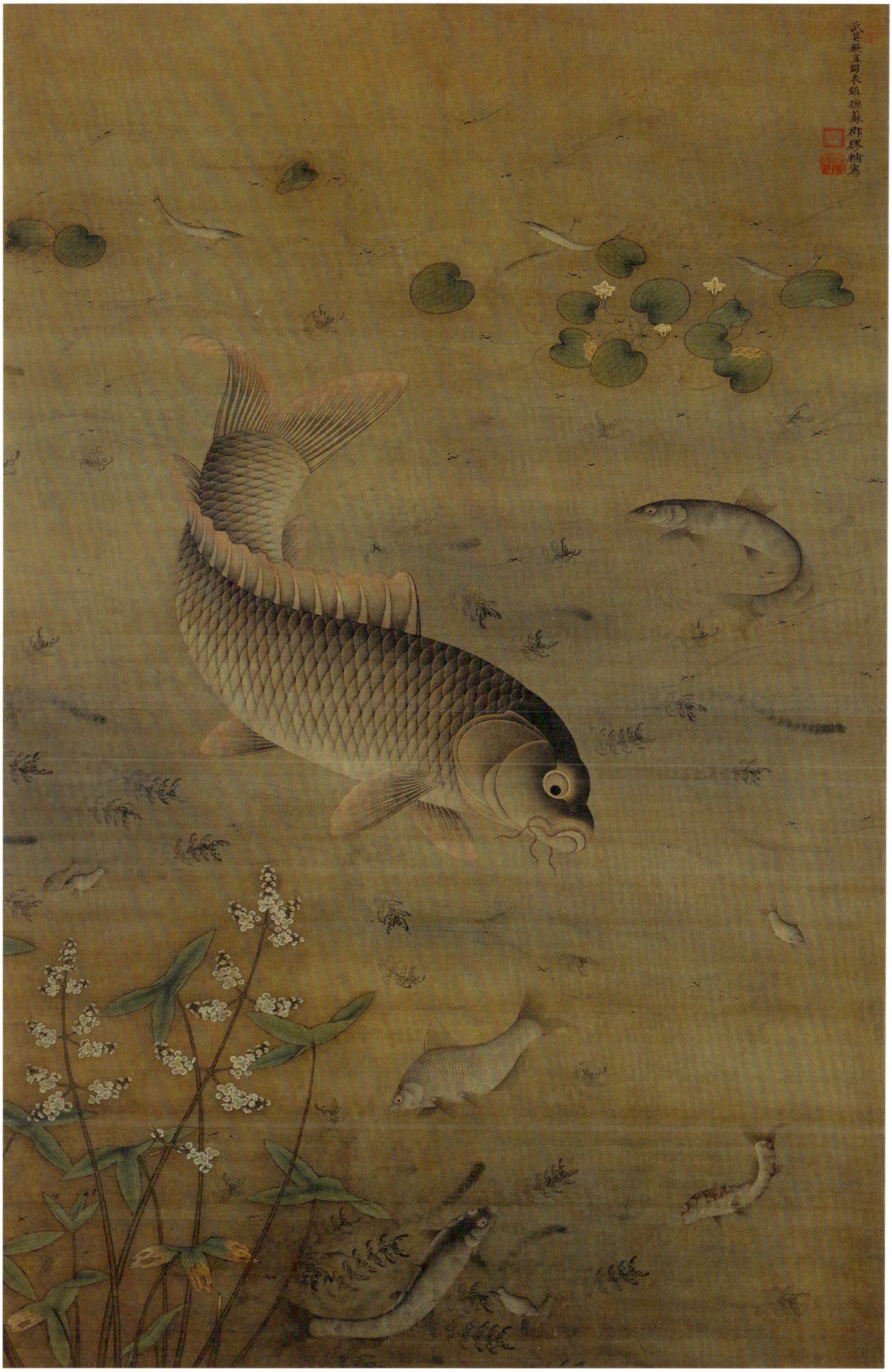
武英殿直錦衣鎮撫蘇郡繆輔精寫

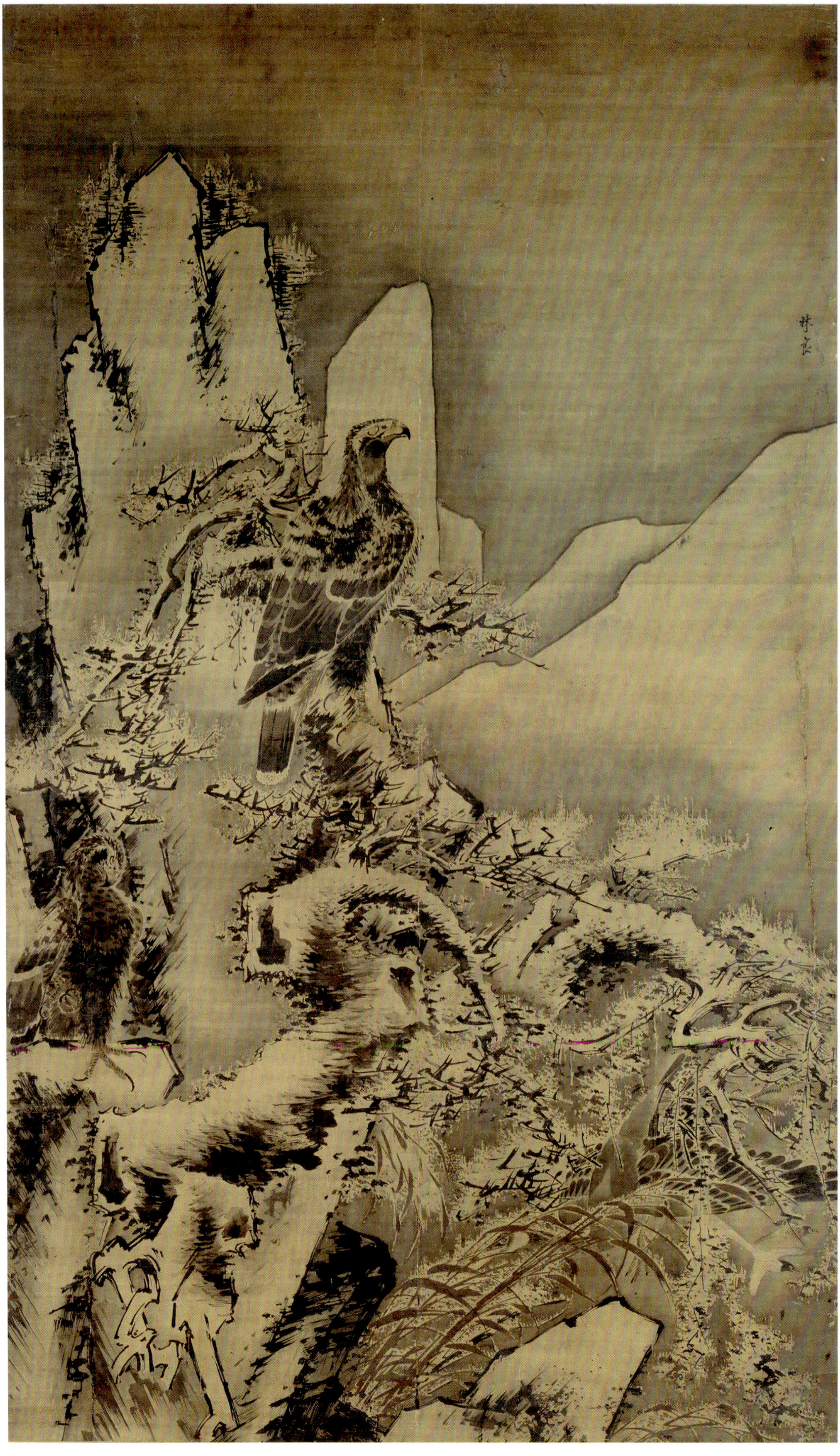

100 明 林良繪 雪景鷹雁圖軸 絹本水墨

Eagles and Wild Goose

Lin Liang (Chinese, approx. 1424–1500)
Ming dynasty (1368–1644)
Hanging scroll; ink on silk
H. 299 cm (117.72), W. 180.5 cm (70.06 in.)
Palace Museum, Xin.151411

Lin Liang, a court painter during the middle of the Ming dynasty, specialized in flower-and-bird subjects. His unique style is characterized by his preference for monochrome ink and a cursive and dynamic brushwork, which often transform the conventional themes and styles into a fresh personal expression.[1]

Here, in this large hanging scroll, Lin creates a bold design of two large eagles perched on a snowy cliff. The scene's drama contrasts the eagles' tranquility to the turbulent atmosphere of a stormy sky, drifting snow, and swirling leaves. Graded ink washes create one of the most innovative depictions of such a theme. The eagles' fallen victim, a goose, lies hidden amid wild, tangled brush. Typical of this traditional theme, Lin downplays the connection between the eagles and their victim and transforms a bird of prey into a symbol of courage and strength. Indeed, the eagle at the top, calm and dignified, evokes the image of a strong and courageous leader. The surrounding green pines that persevere in the snowstorm further enhance this symbolism. HMS

Inscription: 林良 Lin Liang

Seal: 以善圖書 *Yishan tushu*

1. For Lin Liang's biography and eagle painting, see Sung 1991a.
2. Sung 2009.

101 明 摹周朗 佛朗國獻馬圖卷

Copy after Zhou Lang's Heavenly Horse from the Fulang Kingdom

Ming dynasty (1368–1644)

Handscroll; ink on paper

H. 30.3 cm (11.9 in.), W. 134 cm (52.8 in.)
Palace Museum, Xin.146486

This painting is based on an original work by Zhou Lang (act. 1340s), who served in the Directorate of Imperial Workshops (Shangfang) under Yuan emperor Shundi (r. 1333–68).[1] Little known today, Zhou enjoyed great fame during his lifetime for his horse-and-figure paintings. One of his best-known masterpieces was *Heavenly Horse from the Fulang Kingdom*. The painting portrayed Emperor Shundi receiving a horse as a gift from Pope Benedict XII (d. 1342). The horse arrived as a gift in 1342 with a Franciscan delegation led by Giovanni de' Marignolli (fl. 1338–53).[2] This historical event was interpreted by Shundi as an auspicious sign. The "celestial horse" was celebrated in court with numerous essays, poems, and paintings. Unfortunately, of these depictions, the only surviving painting is this copy made by a Ming-dynasty court painter.

As a faithful copy, this handscroll provides important clues to the design and style of the historical painting by Zhou. Zhou divided the handscroll into two halves. On the right half was the seated emperor, prominently positioned in the center and framed by two officials, three female attendants, and a eunuch. To the left of the emperor was the horse, accompanied by the foreign envoy. This painting also serves as a valuable source for reconstruction of the little-known horse-painting style of the late fourteenth century.[3] HMS

Inscription: 臣周朗奉敕畫 (Respectfully painted in imperial order by your servant Zhou Lang)

Seals: 周朗 *Zhou Lang*; 金门待詔 *Jinmen daizhao*

1. For Zhou Lang's biography, see Yu 1996, 487.
2. Arnold 1999, fig. 7–6, pp. 101–7.
3. Sung 2009, chap. 19, pp. 171–206.

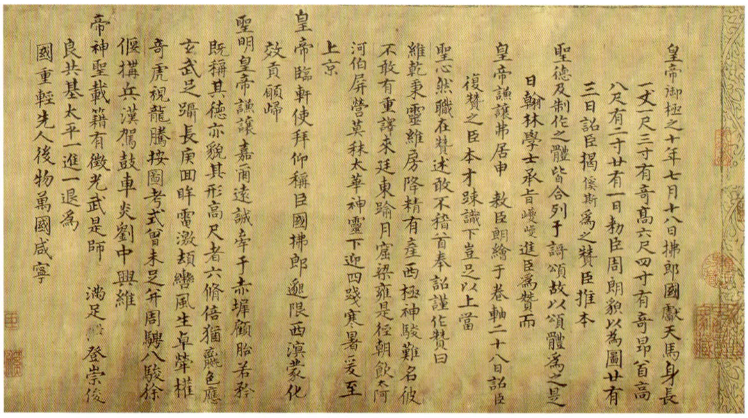

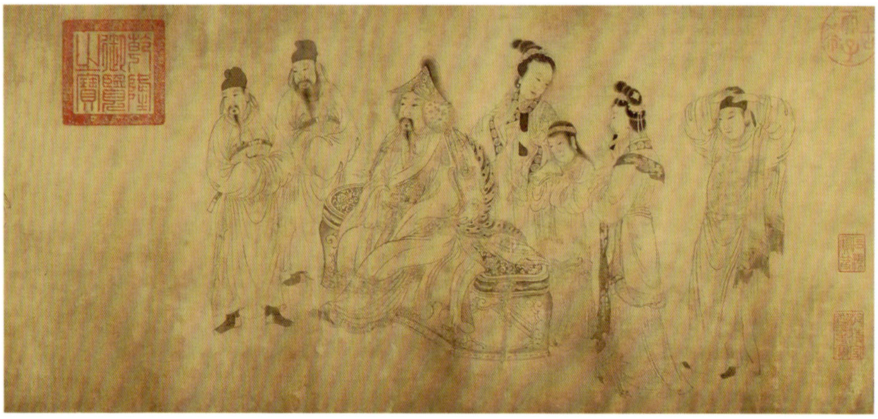

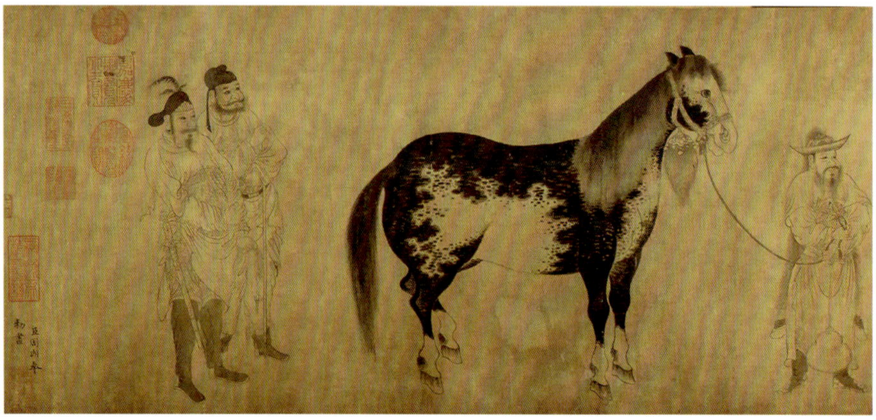

102 明 朱端繪 弘農渡虎圖軸 絹本設色

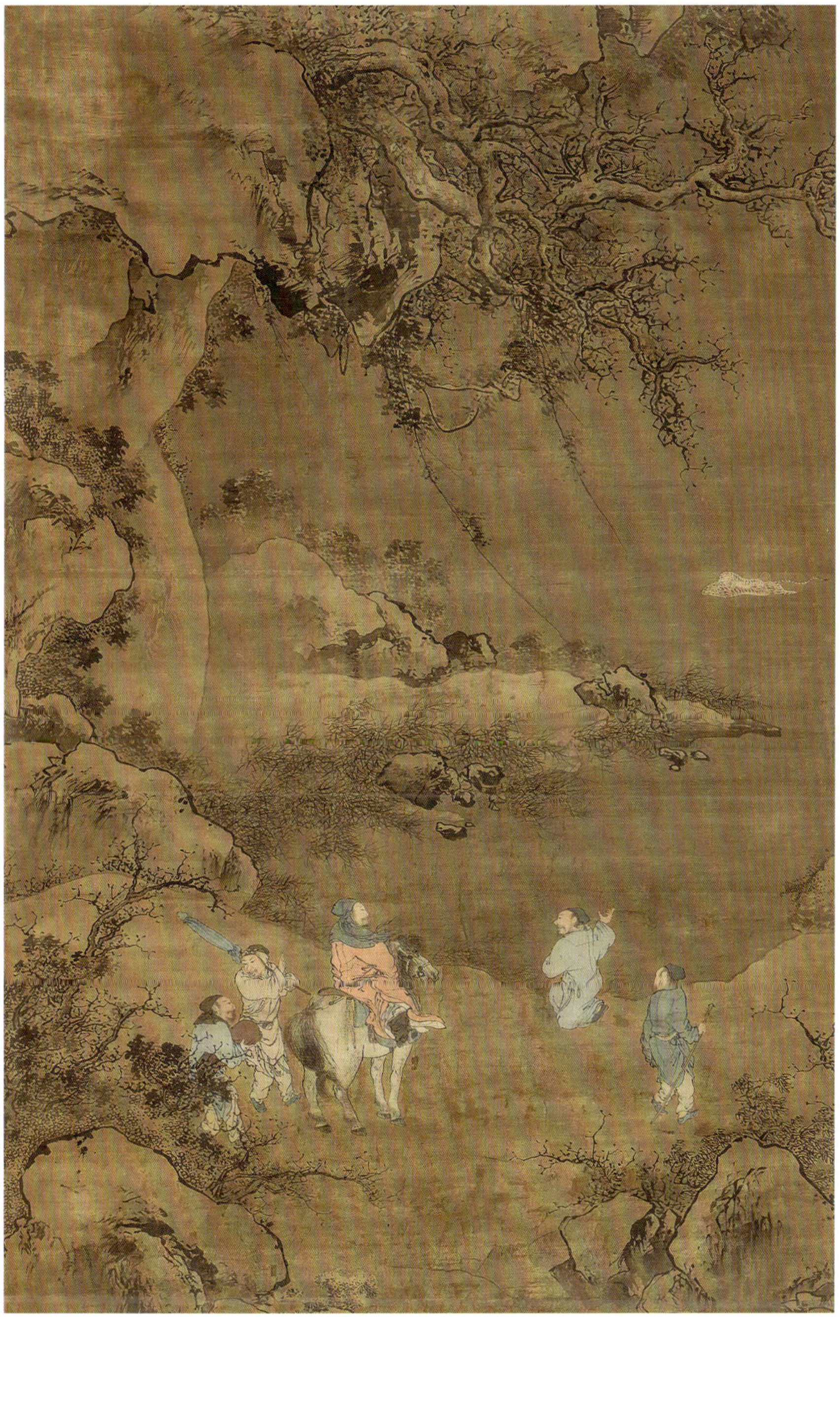

Tigers Crossing the River

Zhu Duan (act. 1501–20)
Ming dynasty (1368–1644)
Hanging scroll; ink and color on silk
H. 174 cm (68.50 in.), W. 113 cm (44.49 in.)
Palace Museum, Xin.54648

This painting's title refers to the legend known as Tigers Crossing the River at Hongnong and to the benevolent rule of Liu Kun, the governor of Hongnong during the Han dynasty (206 BC–AD 220). Surviving records claim that with Liu's appointment, a large population of tigers roamed the major roadways, leaving inhabitants of the district paralyzed with fear. However, the region prospered during the first three years of Liu's administration, and many tigers were seen crossing the river and leaving the district altogether. Later, when Liu became an official at court, the emperor asked how he achieved such amazing results. When Liu attributed his success to coincidence, everyone laughed at his innocent reply. Liu's modesty impressed the emperor, who said, "These are the words of a true leader." The emperor then ordered Liu's distinguished term as governor to be recorded. Since then, "tigers crossing the river" became a complimentary metaphor for meritorious governors.[1]

Although this legend dates back to the Han dynasty, the earliest known recorded example is *Three Tigers Crossing the River* by Li Yu of the Jin dynasty (1115–1234).[2] Li Yu's colorful painting depicts a family of three tigers crossing a river. Referencing the legend of Liu Kun, the painting conveys the didactic message that dangers—even tigers—depart when a benevolent ruler presides over a region. The only extant example of this theme is this work by Zhu Duan (act. 1501–20), the Ming court painter from Haiyan, Zhejiang Province. Zhu entered the court in 1501 during the late Hongzhi era (1488–1506). In the Zhengde era (1506–21), he was honored with the salary of a commander of the Imperial Guard in Embroidered Uniform (Jinyi zhihui).[3] HMS

Seal: 钦賜一樵圖書 *Qinci Yijiao tushu*

1. See Sung 2009, chap. 8.
2. See Li n.d., 5.
3. See Sung 2006, 57.

103 明 三教圖軸 絹本設色

The Three Religions: Laozi, Confucius, and Buddha

Ming dynasty (1368–1644)

Hanging scroll; ink and color on silk

H. 138.8 cm (54.65 in.), W. 73.5 cm (28.94 in.)

Palace Museum, Xin.196027

Most scholars agree that the spurious inscription on the upper right attributing this painting to Liu Guandao and dating it to 1280 was a much later addition and that it is more likely a work of the Ming dynasty. No further study, however, has been done about the subject or the significance of this work. The painting's current title, *The Three Religions,* refers to Confucianism, Buddhism, and Daoism. During the Song dynasty, these three major Chinese religions blended to form a fully established philosophical system called "unification of the Three Religions," which rose to prominence in the Yuan and Ming eras. In paintings, the new theme, known as *sanjiaotu,* depicted the founders of the three religions.[1]

However, this painting of nine figures does not represent a sanjiaotu. Rather than being the main focus, the founders of the three religions—Laozi, Confucius, and Buddha—are pushed to the painting's left fringe, where they stand together between two pine trees. Far more prominent are the remaining six figures, each a distinctive character. Until now, no attempt had been made to identify the group, known only as ancient immortals. However, their appearances, expressions, attire, and activities, as well as the objects they carry identify them as the six key ancestors of Chinese civilization. The three in Daoist garb—all with loose hair, wearing no headdresses or footwear—are most likely three mythical characters, known as the Three Sovereigns (*sanhuang*). From front to back, they are Shennong, Nuwa, and Fuxi. Wearing a leaf cape and animal skirt, Shennong is best known for tasting numerous herbs and writing the classical text on agriculture and medicinal plants (*Shennong Bencao*). Thus, he is identified by holding a tall wooden stick and a bunch of rooted herbs. Nuwa, a creator deity known for mending the collapsed four columns of the universe with the feet of a great turtle, is seen holding a turtle. Standing behind them all, at the top right, the half-revealed figure who holds a blue-green rock is likely Fuxi. Supporting this identification is a depiction of Fuxi, made by Ma Lin (approx. 1180–after 1256), in the National Palace Museum, Taipei.[2]

The third group of three figures, dressed in official attire, are most likely the Three Sage Kings (Yao, Shun, and Yu). Being the first three model rulers of historical China, the three would complete the painting's design to represent each of the three realms *(sanjie)*: the three religious founders representing the celestial realm; the Three Sovereigns, the earth realm; and the Three Sage Kings, the human realm. Thus, the scene represents the three realms: the founders of the three religious, representing the celestial realm; the Three Sovereigns, the earthly realm; and the Three Sage Kings, the human realm. While a painting of this subject is rare, its emergence in the Ming is not unexpected. The popularity of embracing all three religions and the increasing trend to characterize ancient sages, demigods, and immortals in Ming dramas and novels must have paved the way for this painting's depiction. HMS

Inscription: 三教圖。至元十七春三月之朔御衣局使劉貫道敬繪 (The Three Religions, Liu Guandao, the Commissioner of the Imperial Wardrobe Service, respectfully painted this on the first day of the third month in the early spring of the *zhiyuan* 17th year, 1357)

1. The "Three Religions" refer to Confucianism, Buddhism, and Daoism. Although the blending and borrowing of each other's concepts and terms for the three religions started in the Six Dynasties. The "unification of the Three Religions" (*sanjiao heyi*) did not form a fully established philosophical system until the Song dynasty and rose to prominence in the Yuan and Ming eras. Representing this development was the emergence of the painting theme, the Three Religions (*sanjiaotu*), the founders of the three religions, Confucius, Shakyamuni, and Laozi.
2. The best-known masterpiece by Liu Guandao, dated the same year (1280), is *The Imperial Hunting Trip of the Yuan Emperor Shizu,* in the National Palace Museum, Taipei.

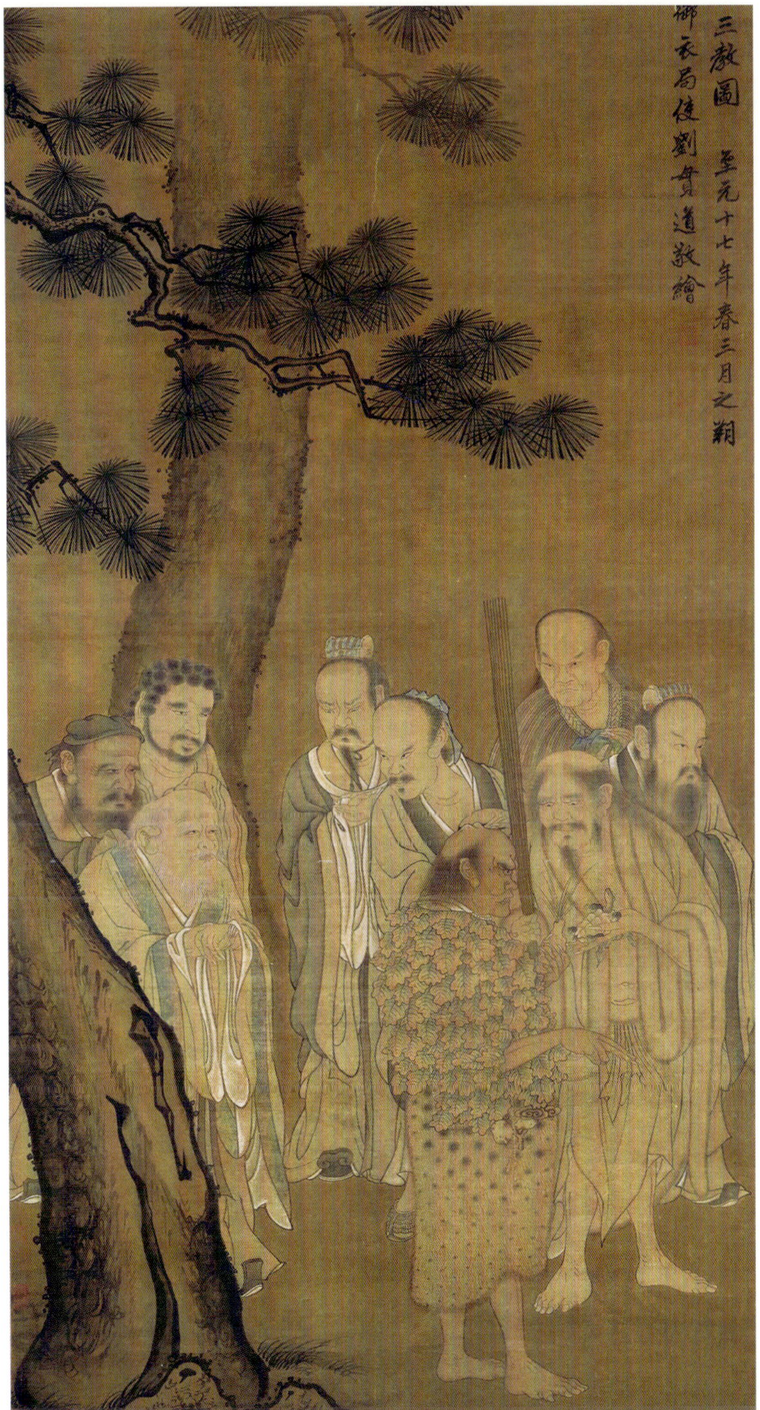
三教圖 至元十七年春三月之翔
御衣局使劉貫道敬繪

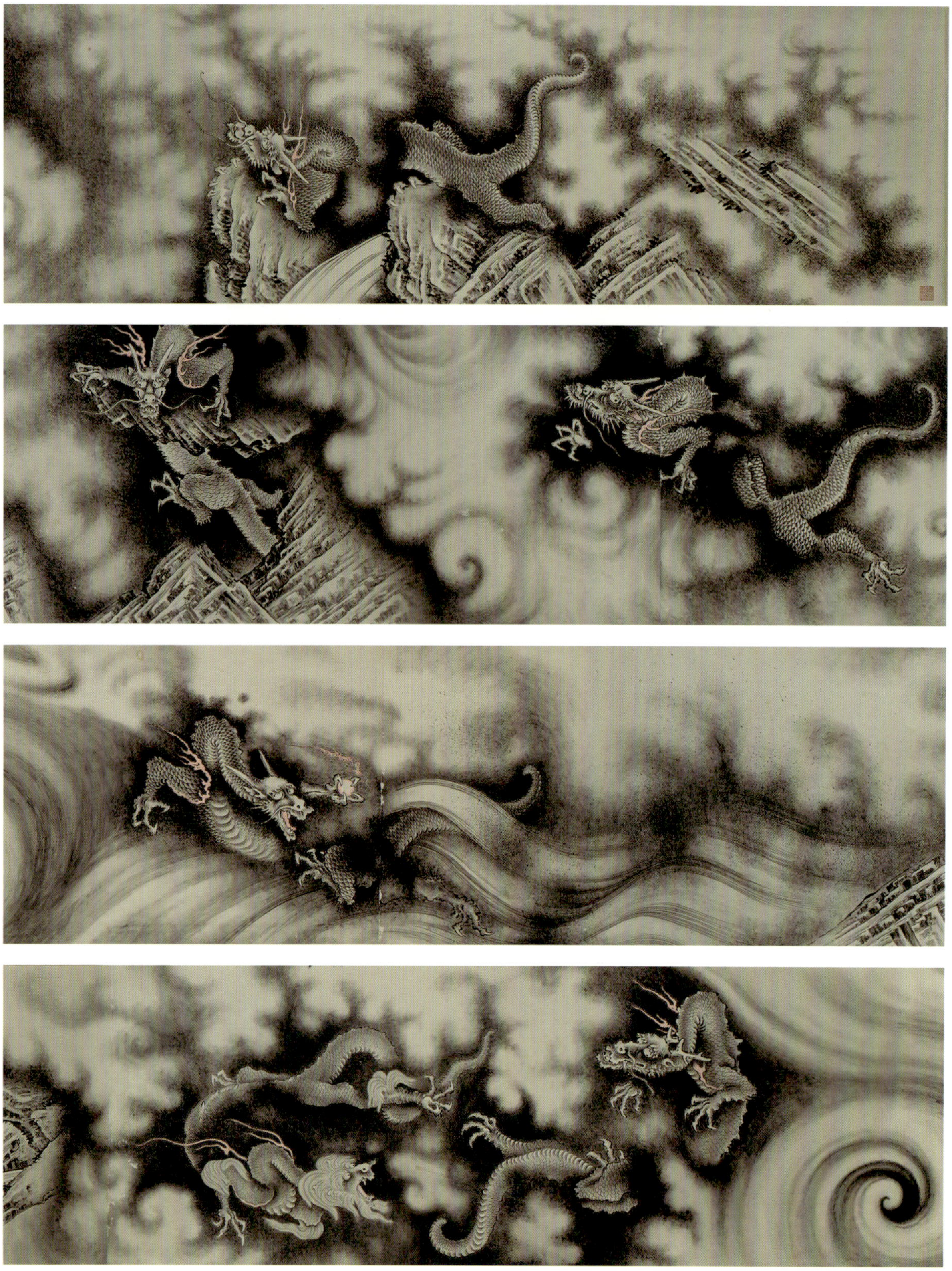

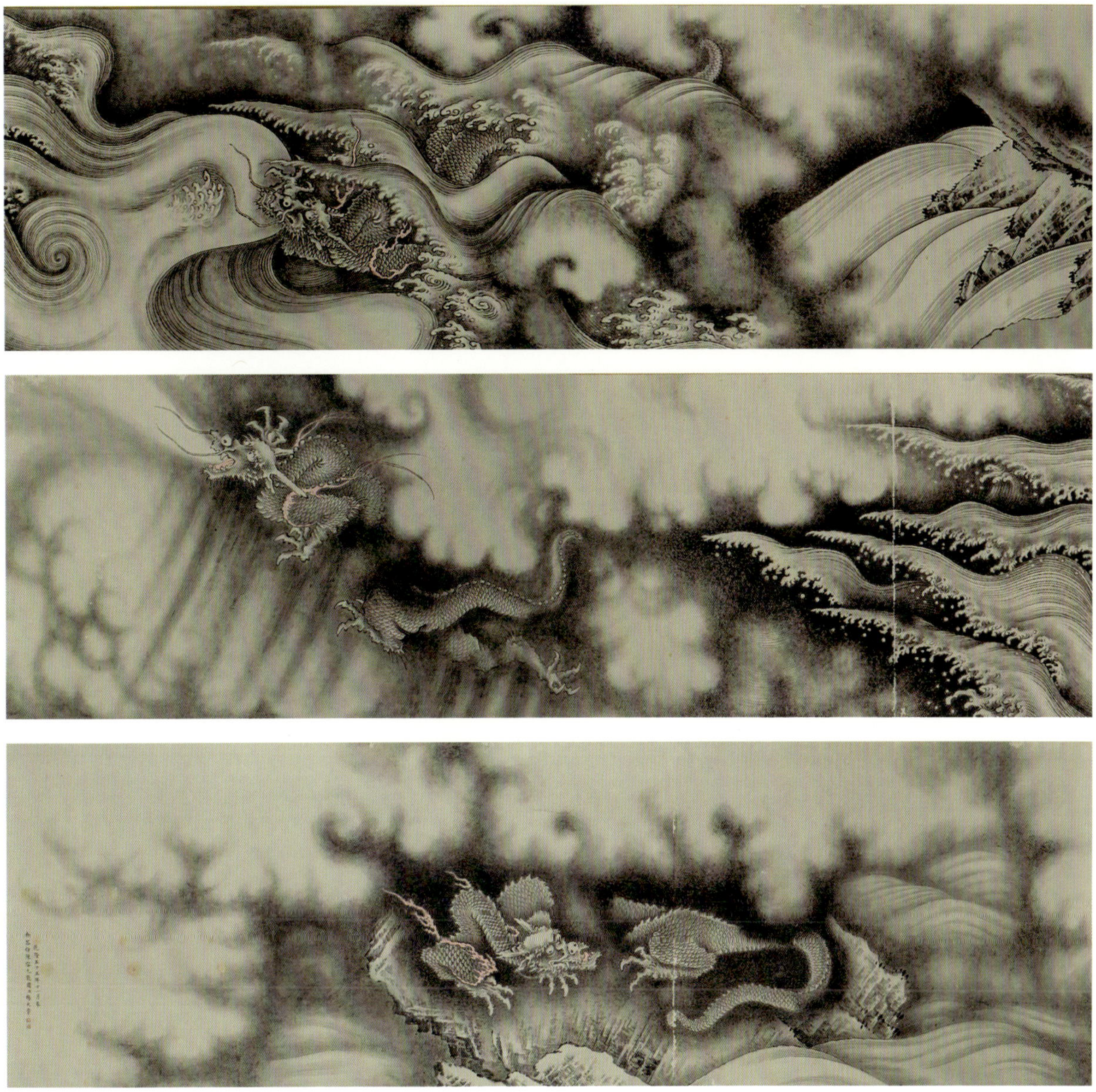

104 清乾隆 楊大章繪 仿陳容九龍圖卷 紙本設色

Nine Dragons, 1790
Yang Dazhang (act. late 18th century)
Qing dynasty, Qianlong period (1736–95)
Handscroll; ink and light color on paper
H. 46 cm (18.11 in.), W. 1045.5 cm (411.61 in.)
Palace Museum, Gu.5660

The dragon is the oldest and most powerful animal in Chinese mythology. This handscroll by Yang Dazhang depicts nine dragons and is a faithful copy of an original design by the Song master Chen Rong (approx. 1200–1260).[1] Chen's *Nine Dragons* incorporated the creatures' interactions with the natural elements in all three realms (the celestial realm, the earthly realm, and the water realm of the underworld) based on the mythical animal's symbolic association with Song philosophical and cosmological concepts. Here, in a sensitive and precise rendition of Chen Rong's *Nine Dragons,* Yang demonstrates his mastery of the Song dragon-painting tradition. The constantly changing background and the dragons' carefully coordinated positions, movements, and expressions successfully capture the creatures' constant transformation and elusive movement through clouds and in and out of caves and waves.[2]

Yang Dazhang was a court painter of the Qianlong reign. Although little biographical information is available today, judging from the dates of his surviving works, Yang was active in court from the 1770s to the 1790s. In addition to dragons, he was known for many other subjects, including flower-and-bird scenes, landscapes, and figures. HMS

Inscription: 乾隆五十五年十一月奉敕恭仿陳容九龍圖臣楊大章 (Respectfully copied after Chen Rong's Nine Dragons in imperial order by your servant Yang Dazhang in the 11th month of Qianlong 55th year, 1790)

Seals: 大 *Da*; 章 *Zhang*

1. The best-known example of Chen Rong's *Nine Dragons* is in the collection of Museum of Fine Arts, Boston. For a detailed discussion of this painting, see Tung 1997, 197–200, and Tseng 1957, 17–39.
2. For a more detailed discussion of Chen Rong's dragon-painting tradition and its influences on subsequent dynasties, see Sung 2009, 119–36.

105 明 夏景貨郎圖軸 絹本設色

Peddler in the Summer Garden, 16th century
Ming dynasty (1368–1644)
Hanging scroll; ink and color on silk
H. 186.4 cm (73.39 in.), W. 104.2 cm (41.02 in.)
Palace Museum, Gu.6187

Peddler scenes or *huolangtu* emerged as a popular painting subject during the Song dynasty (960–1279). These lively scenes typically depict a peddler tending to a portable bamboo stand packed with colorful merchandise and surrounded by village women and children. In a unique art form called *shuochang*, peddlers on the streets or in the markets recited their long list of goods in rhymed chants often accompanied by the beat of a small drum—a form of entertainment that was soon incorporated into folk drama. In both drama and painting, peddler scenes suggest a time of peace and prosperity.

During the Ming dynasty (1368–1644), the subject continued to be a favorite one for court painters. However, instead of the realistic depiction of a street peddler roaming the countryside as seen in Song examples, Ming peddler scenes, such as this example, often depict a staged event inside the imperial palace. All figures in this painting, including the sophisticated, elegantly attired peddler, are apparently not from the country village. Instead, the figures indicate an imperial setting, made complete by the garden and the peddler's luxurious goods. A long white tablet advertises "special fruits and snacks from the imperial park and ice-cold water from a jade pot." Above the tablet, two small silk hangings from the canopy advertise famous sweets from Fujian, Fu honey and Jian candy, both considered tribute offerings to the court since the Ming dynasty. All these details suggest that the peddler was someone designated to entertain the ladies and children in the court. The painting's seasonal touch is also typical of Ming-dynasty peddler paintings. HMS

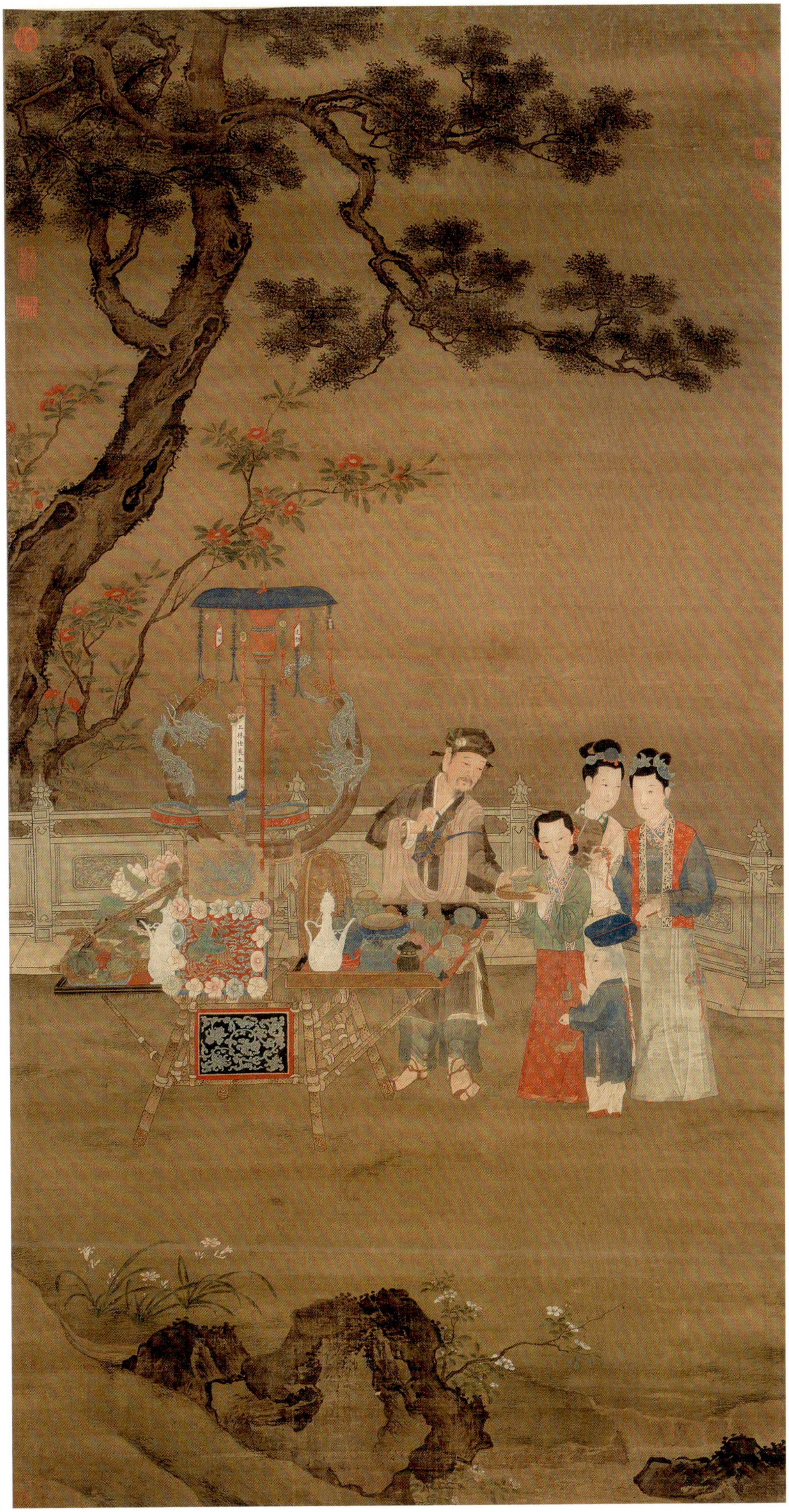

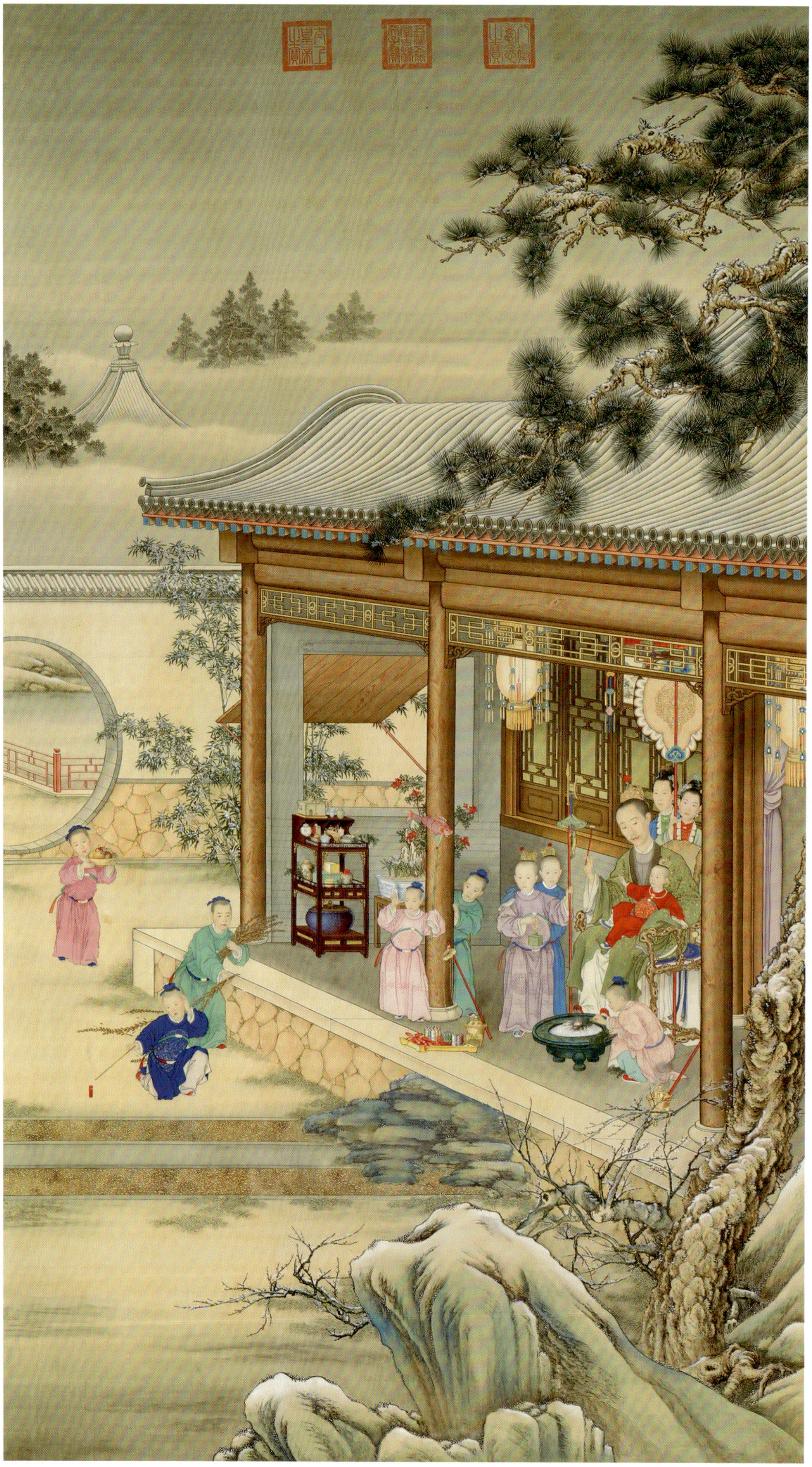

106 清乾隆 郎士寧繪 弘曆歲朝行樂圖軸 絹本設色

Emperor Qianlong Celebrating the New Year, 1736–38
Lang Shining (Giuseppe Castiglione, Italian, 1688–1766)
Qing dynasty, Qianlong period (1736–95)
Hanging scroll; ink and color on silk
H. 384 cm (151.18 in.), W. 160.2 cm (63.07 in.)
Palace Museum, Gu.6506

This painting portrays Emperor Qianlong's celebration of the New Year's Festival inside the palace. Intimate imperial portraits of this kind, typically called *xingletu*, became increasingly popular in the Ming dynasty (1368–1644), as evidenced by the numerous xingletu of emperors Xuanzong (r. 1426–35) and Xianzong (r. 1465–87). In the Qing dynasty (1644–1911), xingletu were regularly produced by court painters to record major events and activities of imperial life, both official and domestic. This painting, though not signed, was likely created collaboratively by three leading masters in the early Qianlong court: Lang Shining, Chen Mei, and Tang Dai.[1]

Here, the Qianlong emperor, dressed in casual clothing, appears as a young father enjoying the New Year's celebration with his children in the inner court of the imperial palace. Sitting inside a garden pavilion, the emperor holds a baby in his arms and watches his older children as they play with fire crackers. The baby and the two young boys standing to the emperor's immediate right are all wearing small gold crowns that are styled after their father's, identifying them as imperial sons.[2] The celebration is further enhanced by the emperor hitting a stone musical instrument or *jiqing*, a term that also means auspicious festivity. HMS

1. Chen 2010a.
2. Ibid. 2010b.

107 清乾隆 弘曆觀月圖軸 絹本設色

Emperor Qianlong Enjoying the Moon

Qing dynasty, Qianlong period (1736–95)

Hanging scroll; ink and color on silk

H. 139 cm (54.72 in.), W. 70 cm (27.56 in.)
Palace Museum, Gu.6517

This painting is one of numerous informal portraits presenting Emperor Qianlong as a cultured Han scholar-official. Here, under an osmanthus tree, the Manchu ruler, dressed officially in a beautiful purple robe, sits on a chair made of tree root and holds a *ruyi* scepter also made of tree root. The full moon and the blooming osmanthus indicate it is mid-autumn and time for the Moon Festival. Except for the first six years of his reign, the Qianlong emperor spent forty-eight Moon Festivals outside Beijing in Chengde at his Summer Mountain Villa (Bishu Shanzhuang), where the elevated pavilion known as Cloudy Mountain Landmark (Yunshanshengdi) was his favorite site from which to view the moon.

Here, the young emperor watches the moon with a wistful expression that suggests feelings of nostalgia and homesickness. A handsome boy stands behind him and holds a tall, imperial shielding fan decorated with twin dragons. Judging from the luxurious gold-decorated green silk robe and headdress, the boy is likely a favorite son of the emperor. To the emperor's left, an attendant offers a cup of tea on a small red lacquer tray. A three-tiered table holds all the necessities for the occasion.

Although unsigned, this scroll was most likely painted by a leading court painter familiar with Western techniques, which are evidenced by the soft shading on the faces and the architectural elements that establish perspective. A painting with very similar design is attributed to Leng Mei (d. 1742) in the National Palace Museum, Taipei.[1] HMS

1. See National Palace Museum 1994, 219.

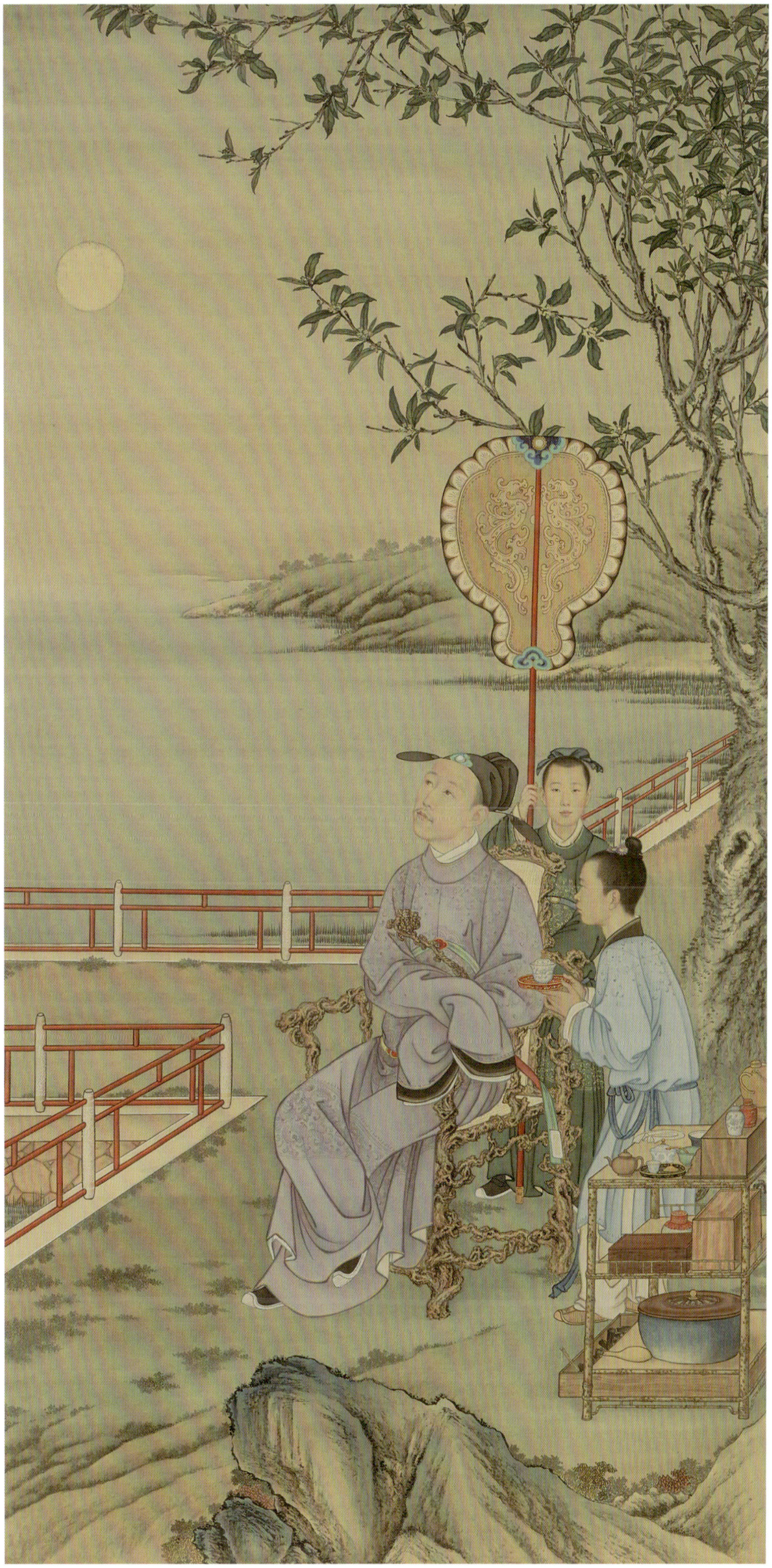

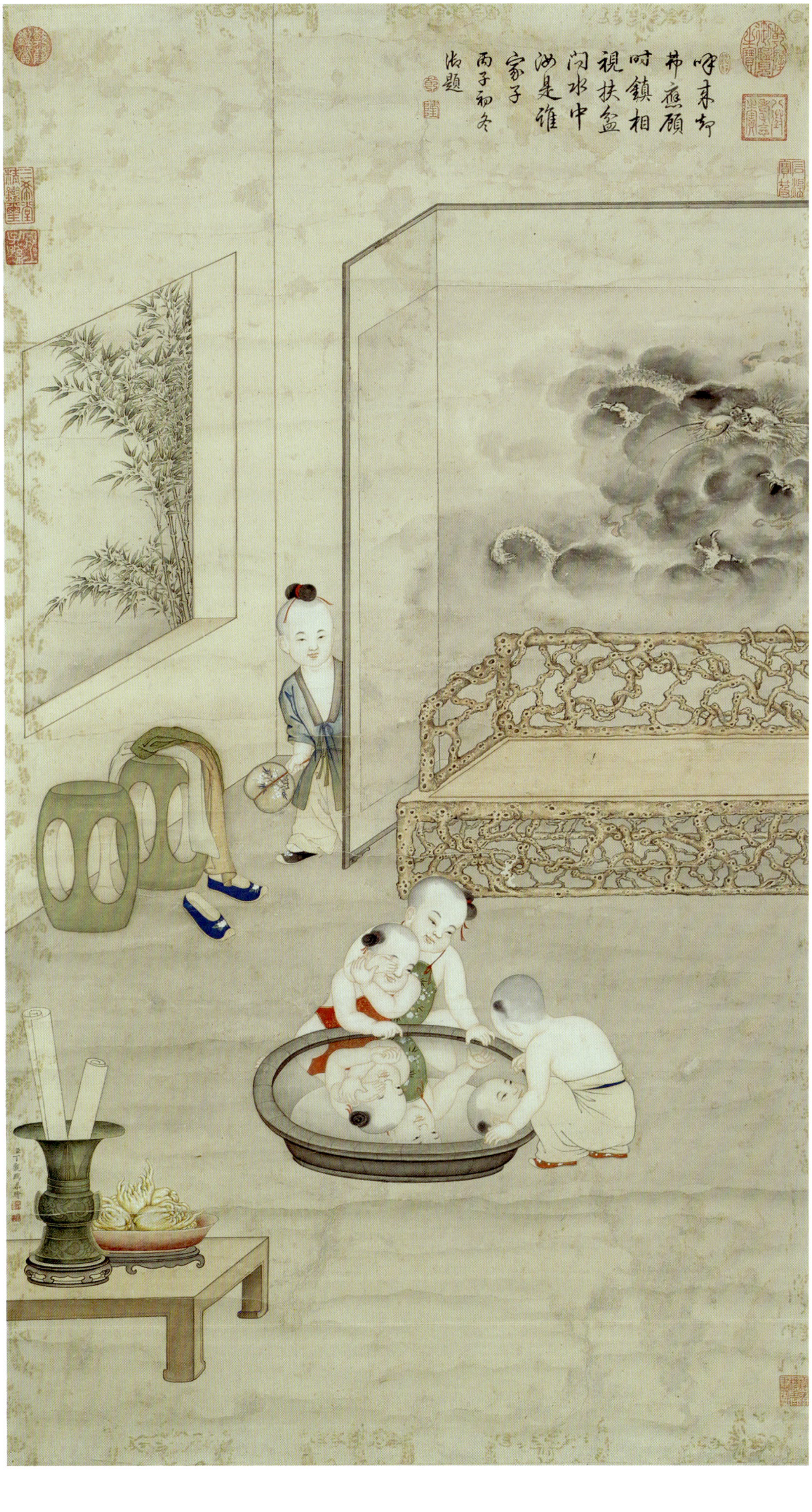

108 清乾隆 丁觀鵬繪 照盆嬰戲圖軸 紙本設色

Children Looking into a Basin

Ding Guanpeng (d. 1771)
Qing dynasty, Qianlong period (1736–95)
Hanging scroll; ink and color on paper
H. 102.5 cm (40.35 in.), W. 58.8 cm (23.15 in.)
Palace Museum, Gu.4791

Ding Guanpeng was a Qing court painter who specialized in figure painting. Little is known of his early life. He entered the court in 1726 (the fourth year of the Yongzheng reign, 1722–35). Ding must have impressed the emperor, because he was offered the highest rank for court painters as soon as he entered the court.[1] In addition to traditional Chinese figure painting, including Buddhist, Daoist, and secular figures, Ding also studied Western painting techniques with Lang Shining (Giuseppe Castiglione, Italian, 1688–1766) and Wang Zhicheng (Jean Denis Attiret, French, 1702–1768) and produced many oil paintings.

Here, Ding depicts four young boys playing in a room where a basin of water sits. Three boys, in the center of the foreground, observe their reflections in the water. The boy on the right points at his reflection, while another boy holds the youngest and playfully covers his eye. A fourth boy enters from behind a screen that is decorated with a dragon emerging from clouds. In front of the screen is a beautiful couch bed made from tree roots. The tender bamboo outside the window and the children's clothing suggest it is summer.

The depiction of children looking into a basin was a Song dynasty painting theme made popular by Liu Zongdao. Although no Song examples survive today, Liu's painting was described as depicting "a child pointing at his reflection pointing at him."[2] Ding apparently created his design based on this record. As an official work painted for the emperor, this painting conveys the wish that the emperor will have numerous male descendants. HMS

Inscription: 臣丁觀鵬恭繪 (Respectfully painted by your servant Ding Guanpeng)

Seals: 臣觀鵬 *chen Guanpeng*; 恭畫 *gonghua*

1. Nie 2011a.
2. Deng 1974, chap. 6, p. 46.

109 清乾隆 金廷標繪 群嬰鬥草圖軸 紙本設色

Children Playing in the Garden

Jin Tingbiao (d. 1767)

Qing dynasty, Qianlong period (1736–95)

Hanging scroll; ink and color on paper

H. 105.3 cm (41.46 in.), W. 79.5 cm (31.3 in.)

Palace Museum, Gu.5267

Jin Tingbiao (d. 1767) came from a family of painters in Wuxi, Zhejiang Province. His father, Jin Hong, specialized in both portraiture and landscape. Jin Tingbiao entered the court in 1757 after presenting Emperor Qianlong an album of his Luohan painting in the linear (*baimiao*) style during the imperial tour of the South.[1] As a highly skilled court painter, Jin won great imperial favor and produced numerous works upon imperial command, including some collaborative works with the leading Western painter Lang Shining (Giuseppe Castiglione, Italian, 1688–1766).[2]

In this painting, Jin depicts a group of young boys picking flowers and herbs and playing games in a garden. Paintings of children at play (*yingxitu*) have been a popular court painting subject since the Song dynasty (960–1279). Here, Jin combined two subjects: children at play and the seasonal activities of the Duanyang festival. The festival occurs on the fifth day of the fifth month of the lunar calendar, when it is midsummer and the sun feels the most intense. One of the oldest activities for the festival is picking medicinal herbs and hanging them at doors to ward off evil and toxins. Jin, like other Qing court painters, frequently produced paintings for the imperial celebration of various festivities and occasions. The ten healthy-looking boys featured here also convey the wish that the emperor will have numerous male descendants. HMS

Inscription: 臣金廷标恭繪 (Respectfully painted by your servant Jin Tingbiao) and a poem by Emperor Qianlong, dating to the *jiashen* year, 1764

Seal: 廷标 *Tingbiao*

1. Nie 2011b.
2. Yang 2010, vol. 14.

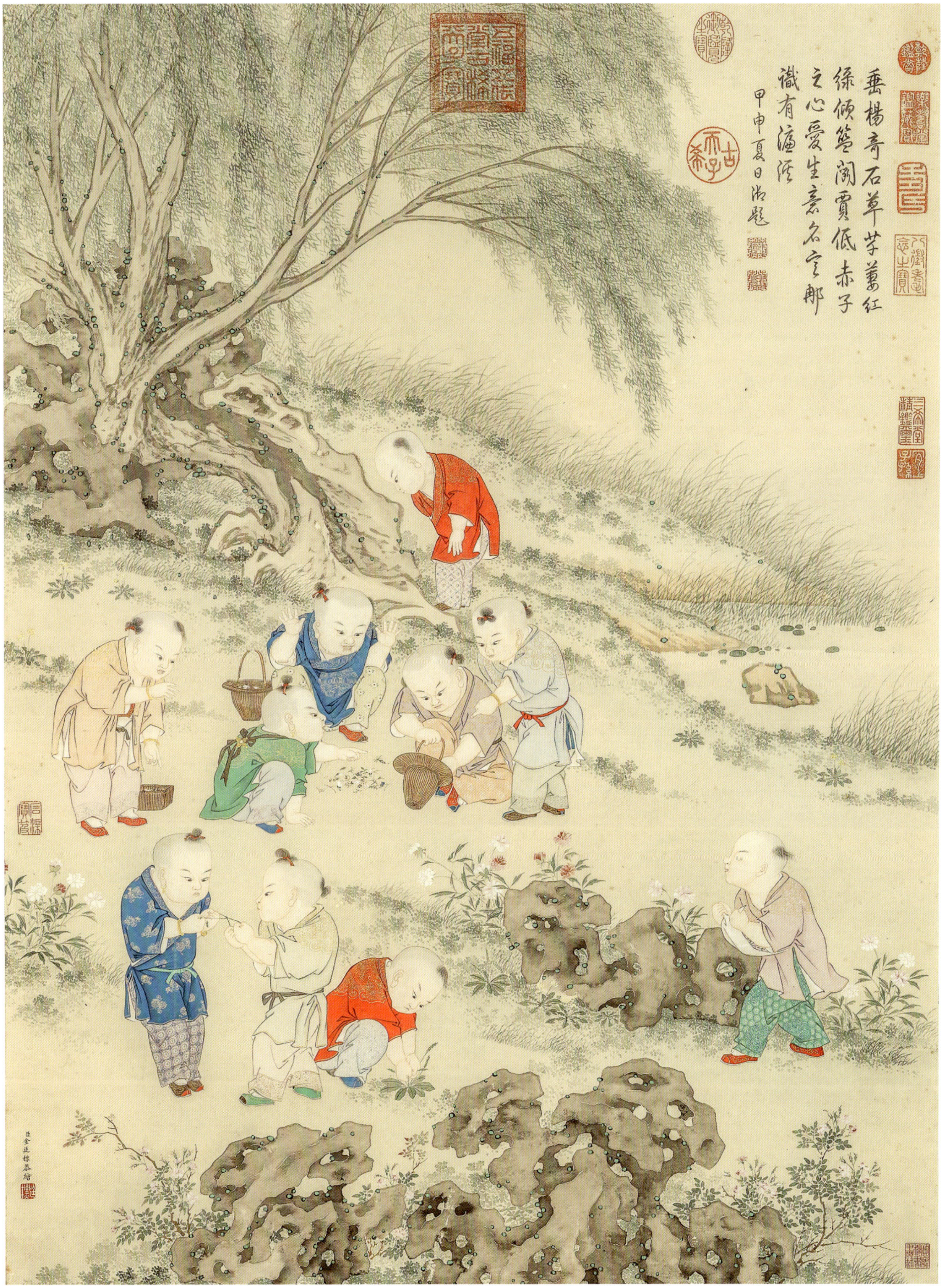

110 清乾隆 鄒一桂繪 杏花春燕圖軸
絹本設色

Apricot Flowers and Spring Birds
Zou Yigui (1686–1772)
Qing dynasty, Qianlong period
(1736–96)
Hanging scroll; ink and color on silk
H. 152.1 cm (59.88 in.), W. 50 cm (19.69 in.)
Palace Museum, Gu.5821

Zou Yigui was both a scholar and a painter in the Qianlong court. He came from a prominent family in Wuxi, Jiangsu Province. His father and uncles were all renowned poets and amateur painters. Zou had an illustrious career in court. He became a Metropolitan Graduate of the Imperial Examination (*jinshi*) in 1727 and eventually reached the high rank of vice minister in the Ministry of Rites. As a painter, Zou was best known for his flower-and-bird works, which mainly followed the style of Yun Shouping (1633–1690).

This painting, titled *Apricot Flowers and Spring Birds,* is based on a traditional Chinese flower-and-bird theme that can be traced to the Song dynasty (960–1279). However, Zou transformed and refreshed an old theme by adding the "blue-and-green" styled garden rocks and flowing river at the bottom, which not only enhances the vibrant colors of spring but also hints at an auspicious message. Since the Ming dynasty, the depiction of a running stream beneath a flowering tree, from which blossoms fall and float upon the water, is frequently referred to as *liufang*—a literary expression that means "lasting fragrance" and serves as a metaphor for leaving behind a fine reputation. The narcissus, which blooms in early spring, also serves as a welcome greeting for the Chinese New Year. HMS

Inscription: 臣鄒一桂恭畫 (Respectfully painted by your servant Zou Yigui)

Seals: 臣一桂印 *chen Yigui yin*;
小山 *Xiaoshan*

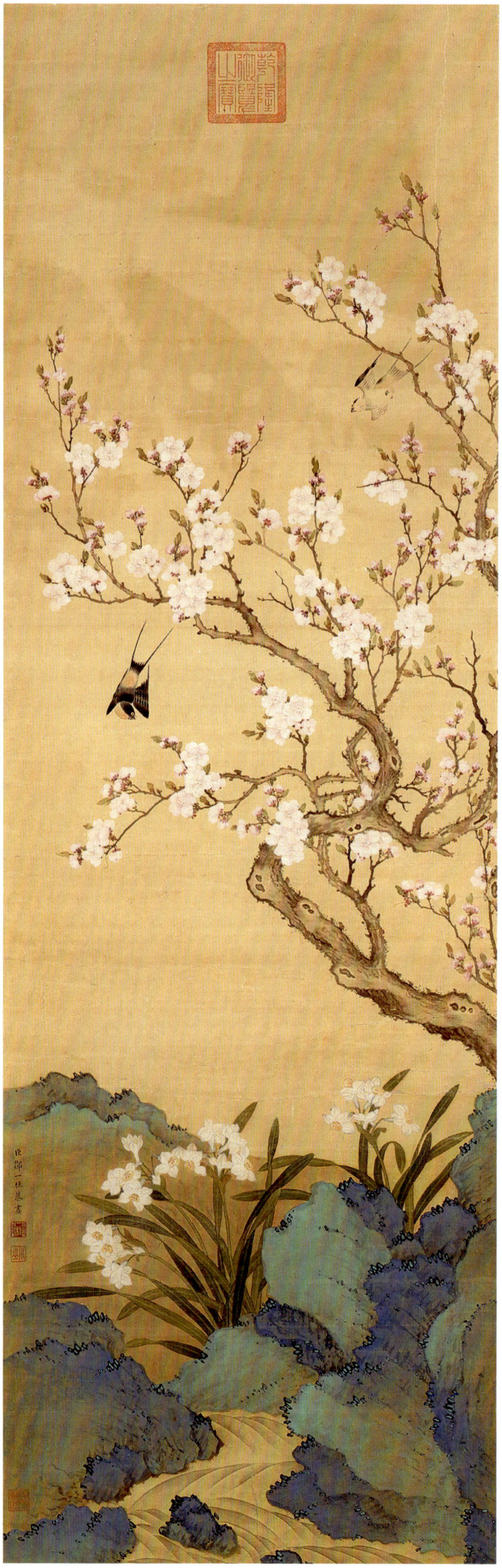

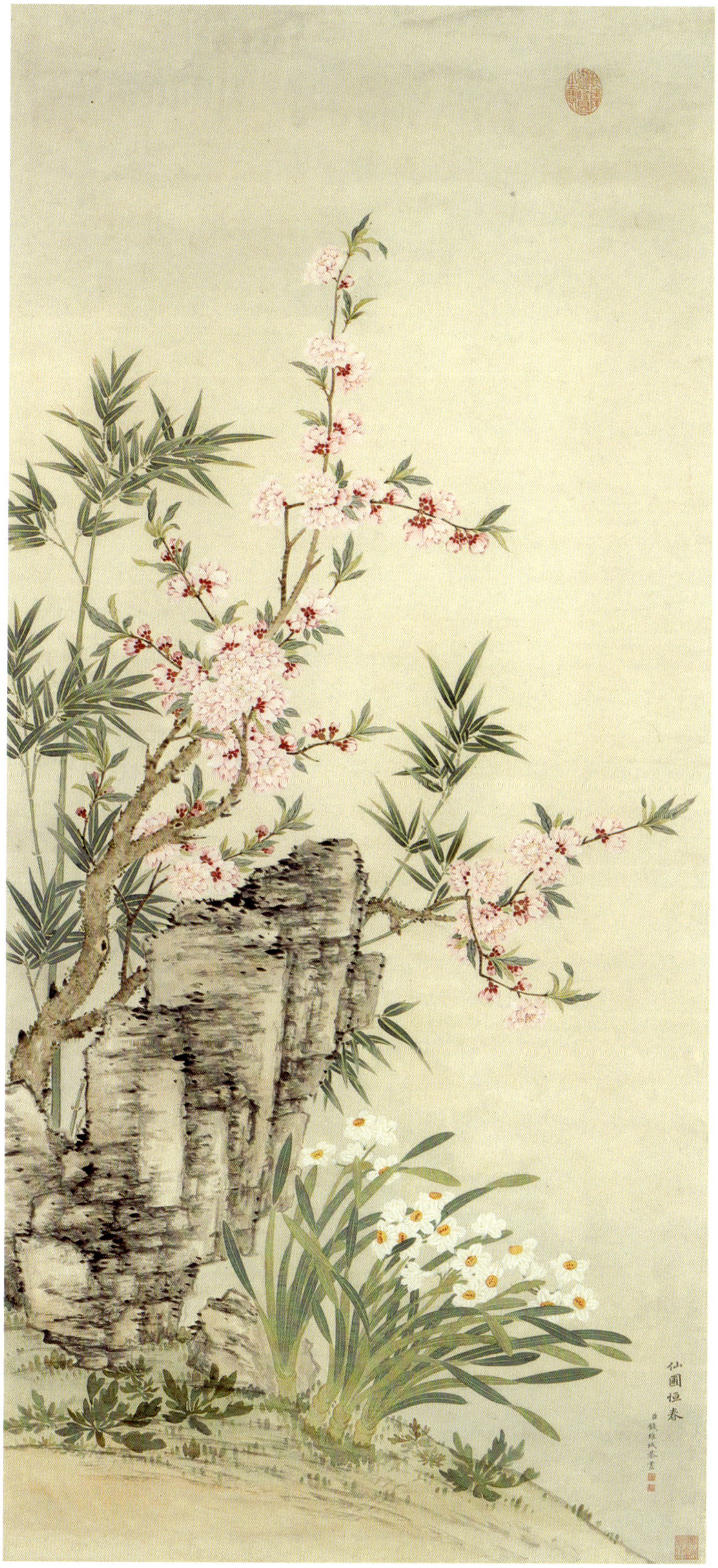

111 清乾隆 錢維城繪 仙圃恆春圖軸 紙本設色

Forever Spring in the Immortals' Garden

Qian Weicheng (1720–1772)

Qing dynasty, Qianlong period (1736–95)

Hanging scroll; ink and color on paper

H. 138 cm (54.33 in.), W. 63.5 cm (25 in.)

Palace Museum, Gu.5959

Qian Weicheng was a distinguished scholar, official, and painter in the Qianlong court. He won first place in the civil-service exams of 1745. A native of Changzhou, Jiangsu Province, Qian first learned painting from his grandmother, Chen Shu (1660–1736), a highly accomplished artist of both flower-and-bird and landscape subjects. He also studied the flower-and-bird painting style of Yun Shouping (1633–1690).

This painting depicts a blooming peach tree, narcissus, and stalks of young bamboo next to a garden rock. While all three plants thrive in the spring, specific associations with immortality are presented in the peach, a well-established symbol of Daoist immortality, and the narcissus, known as the "water immortal" or "the immortal who roams above the waves."[1]

Here, Qian used color washes without outlines (a technique called *mogu*) to create the richly colored flowers, revealing strong influences of Yun Shouping. Qian also displayed his skill in rendering landscapes in the structured and beautifully textured garden rock. The painting, formally titled, signed, and sealed, is likely an official work designated for celebrating the New Year or the spring festival in court. HMS

Inscription: 臣钱维城恭畫 (Respectfully painted by your servant Qian Weicheng)

Seals: 臣錢維城 *chen Qian Weicheng*; 敬事 *jingshi*

1. The fragrant blossoms are associated with a fairy described in the famous poem by Cao Zhi (192–232). Written in AD 222, the poem tells the romantic tale of Cao Zhi's meeting with the Nymph of the Luo River, a daughter of the mythical ruler Fuxi.

112 清乾隆 余省繪 花卉蟲蝶軸 紙本設色

Flowers, Grass, and Butterflies

Yu Sheng (1692–after 1767)
Qing dynasty, Qianlong period (1736–95)
Hanging scroll; ink and color on paper
H. 87.9 cm (34.61 in.), W. 41.9 cm (16.5 in.)
Palace Museum, Gu.5225

Yu Sheng, a native of Yushan, Jiangsu Province, came from a family of painters. His father, Yu Xun, his uncle Yu Huang, and his brother Yu Zhi (act. 1735–65) were all painters. Yu Sheng and his brother Yu Zhi both studied painting with Jiang Tingxi (1669–1732), a master of flower-and-bird scenes. Jiang, also a native of Yushan, later entered the court as an official painter and became a prominent official in the Kangxi (r. 1662–1722) and Yongzheng (r. 1723–35) reigns.

The two Yu brothers were also close associates of Hai Wang (d. 1755), the powerful minister of the Imperial Household Department (Neiwufu), who supervised all court painters serving in the Zaobanchu imperial workshop. In 1737, during the Qianlong reign, the brothers entered the court through the recommendations of Hai. Yu Sheng excelled among the court painters. In 1741, after only four years, he was promoted to the highest rank. Yu Sheng served for over thirty years as a court painter and won numerous awards from the emperor.

The inscription on the upper left was written by Liang Shizheng (1697–1763), who frequently served as a calligrapher for Emperor Qianlong. Both poems, written by Emperor Qianlong, describe the distinctive moods associated with the sights and sounds of autumn—the beautiful and fragrant but lesser-known late blooms, the fluttering butterflies, and the chirping insects. Judging from the similar motifs portrayed in this painting, the imperial poems might have served as the inspiration for Yu Sheng's work. HMS

Inscription: 臣余省恭畫 (Respectfully painted by your servant Yu Sheng) and Emperor Qianlong's poem transcribed by Liang Shizheng

Seals: 余 *Yu*; 省 *Sheng*

1. Nie 2011c.

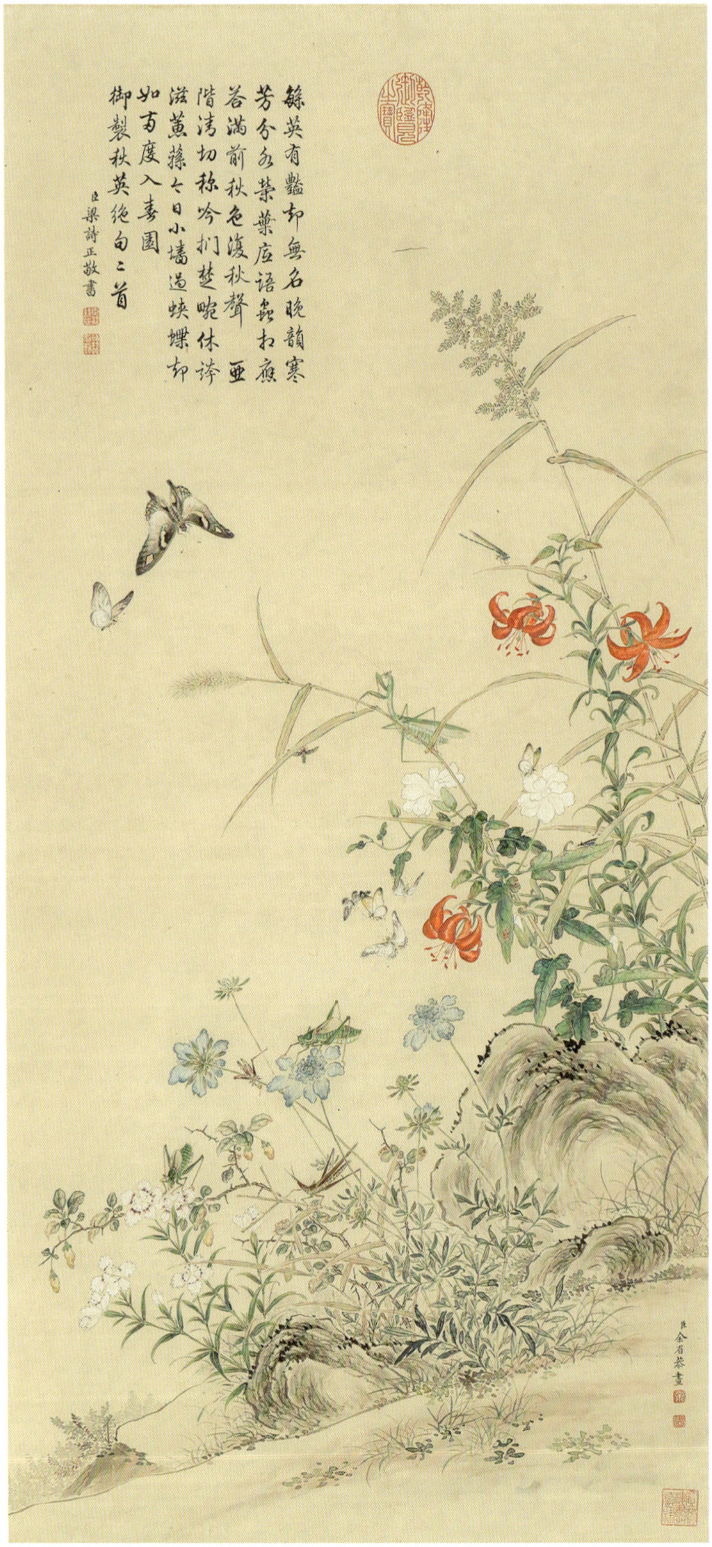

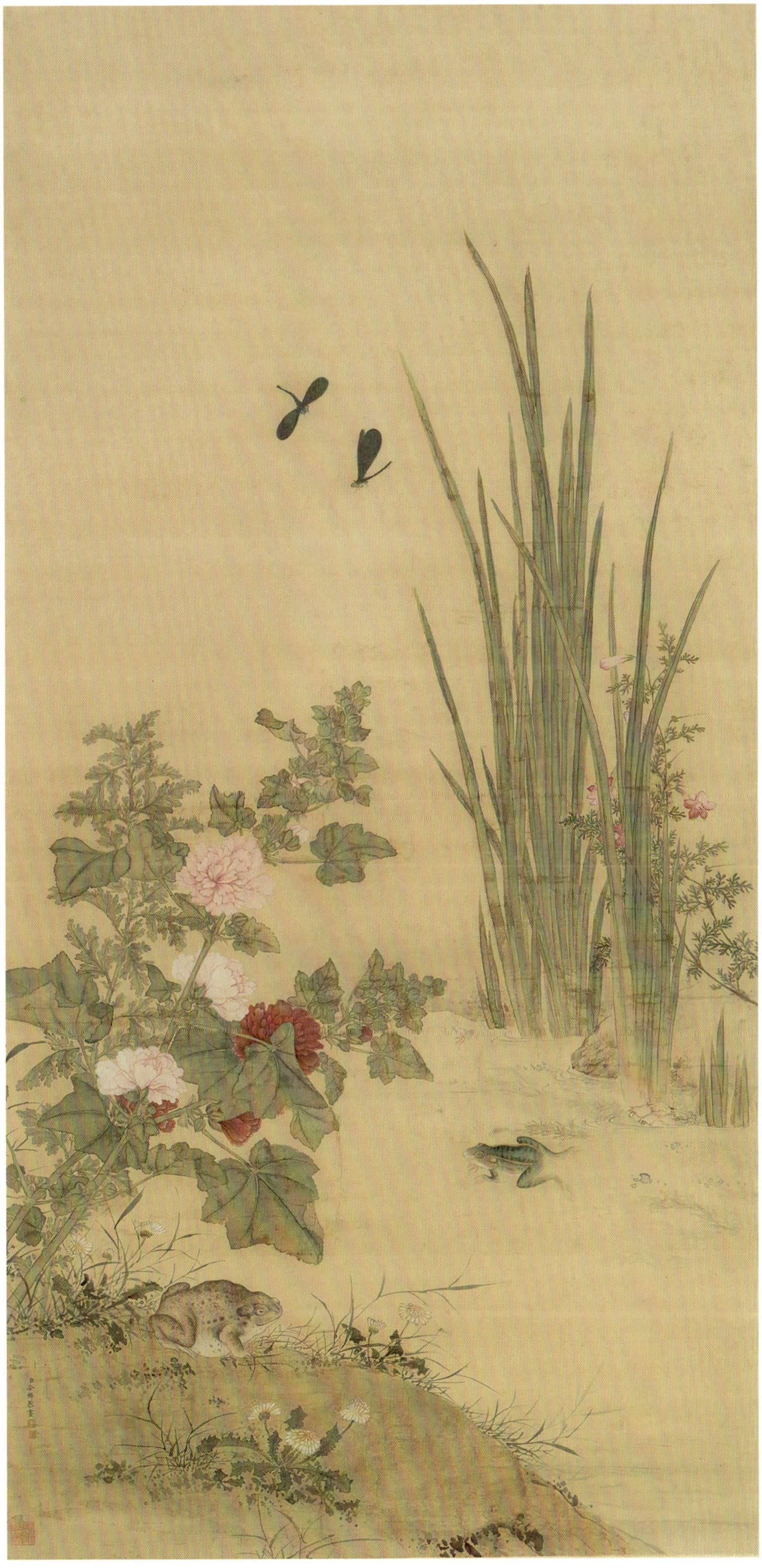

113 清乾隆 余穉繪 端陽景圖軸
絹本設色

Flowers and Plants
Yu Zhi (act. 1735–65)
Qing dynasty, Qianlong period (1736–95)
Hanging scroll; ink and color on silk
H. 137.3 cm (54.06 in.), W. 68.8 cm (27.09 in.)
Palace Museum, Gu.5230

Yu Zhi was the younger brother of Yu Sheng. Both brothers studied flower-and-bird painting with Jiang Tingxi (1669–1732), who later became a prominent court official. In 1737, during the Qianlong reign, Yu Zhi and his brother entered the court through the recommendations of Hai Wang (d. 1755), the minister of the Imperial Household Department (Neiwufu). In 1741, Yu Zhi was awarded the second rank for Qing court painters. It is recorded that, due to his illness, Yu Zhi left the court before his brother.[1]

Here, a landscape by Yu Zhi features the flora and fauna associated with the Duanyang festival (May 5 on the lunar calendar). The beautifully positioned peony, hollyhocks (*shukui*), wild chrysanthemum, wormwood (*aicao*), and calamus (*changpu*) are all Chinese medicinal herbs gathered during the festival to ward off evil and toxins. The toad here also refers to the Duanyang festival during which toads are collected and their venom used for treating illnesses associated with summer.

Yu Zhi's outstanding skill and talent is demonstrated in this simple, elegant design. The highly disciplined brushwork and the sophisticated shading and application of colors reveal the influences of his teacher, Jiang Tingxi, and the Song academic traditions Yu followed. Although restricted by Emperor Qianlong's imperial taste and the painting's specific function in court, Yu's innovative combination of summer plants and animal motifs and his sensitive depiction totally transformed a conventional subject into a unique lyrical expression of his own. HMS

Inscription: 臣余穉恭畫 (Respectfully painted by your servant Yu Zhi)

Seals: 余 *Yu*; 穉 *Zhi*

1. Nie 2011c.

114 清光緒 那拉氏繪 富貴延年圖軸 紙本設色

Flowers in Praise of Wealth and Longevity, 1904

Empress Dowager Cixi (1835–1908)

Qing dynasty, Guangxu period (1875–1908)

Hanging scroll; ink and color on paper

H. 101.8 cm (40.08 in.), W. 51.8 cm (20.39 in.)
Palace Museum, Gu.257057

Empress Dowager Cixi of the Manchu Yehenara clan was a resourceful woman who unofficially ruled the Qing dynasty from 1861 to 1908. In her later years, she developed an interest in painting and calligraphy and frequently awarded officials with her artwork. Cixi soon realized, however, that she was lacking in both talent and discipline. This realization led her to engage the female painter Miao Suyun (1841–1918). Miao, who was a widow, lived inside the palace and served Cixi for ten years. She not only tutored Cixi but also produced many paintings in Cixi's name.

Most of Cixi's paintings are simple sketches of flowers and birds of an auspicious nature, as exemplified by this depiction of a branch of blooming pink peonies. Peonies, known as the king of flowers in China, symbolize prosperity. According to Cixi's inscription on the upper right, she painted this in early October of 1904. However, judging from the fluent and well-disciplined brushwork and skillfully applied color washes, it is most likely a work painted by Miao in Cixi's name. HMS

Inscription: 光緒甲辰小陽上浣御筆 (Painted by her Majesty in the tenth month of the early *jiachen* year, 1904, of the Guangxu reign)

Seals: 含和履中 *Hanhe luzhong*; 日報平安 *Ribao pingan*

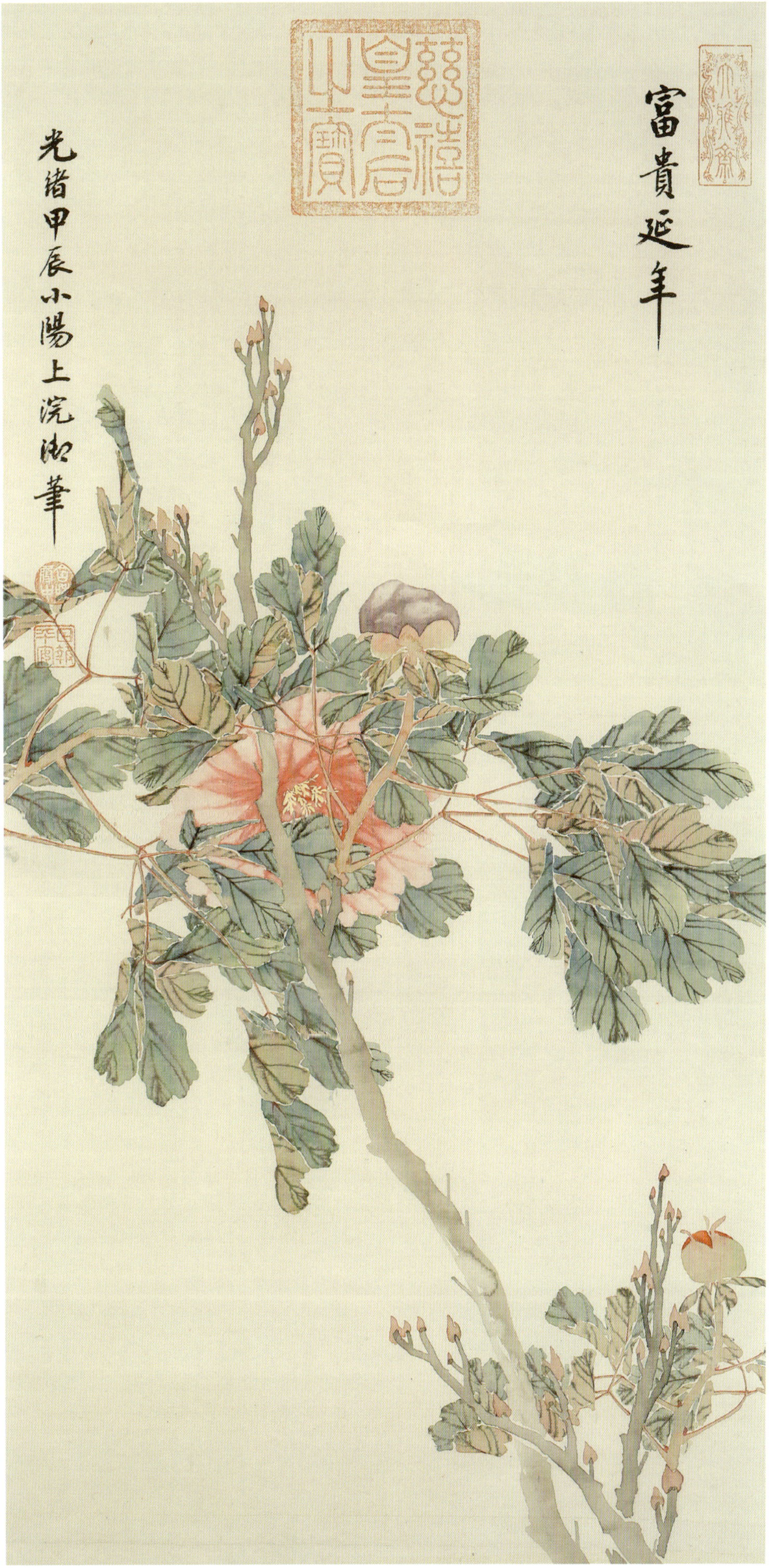
富貴延年

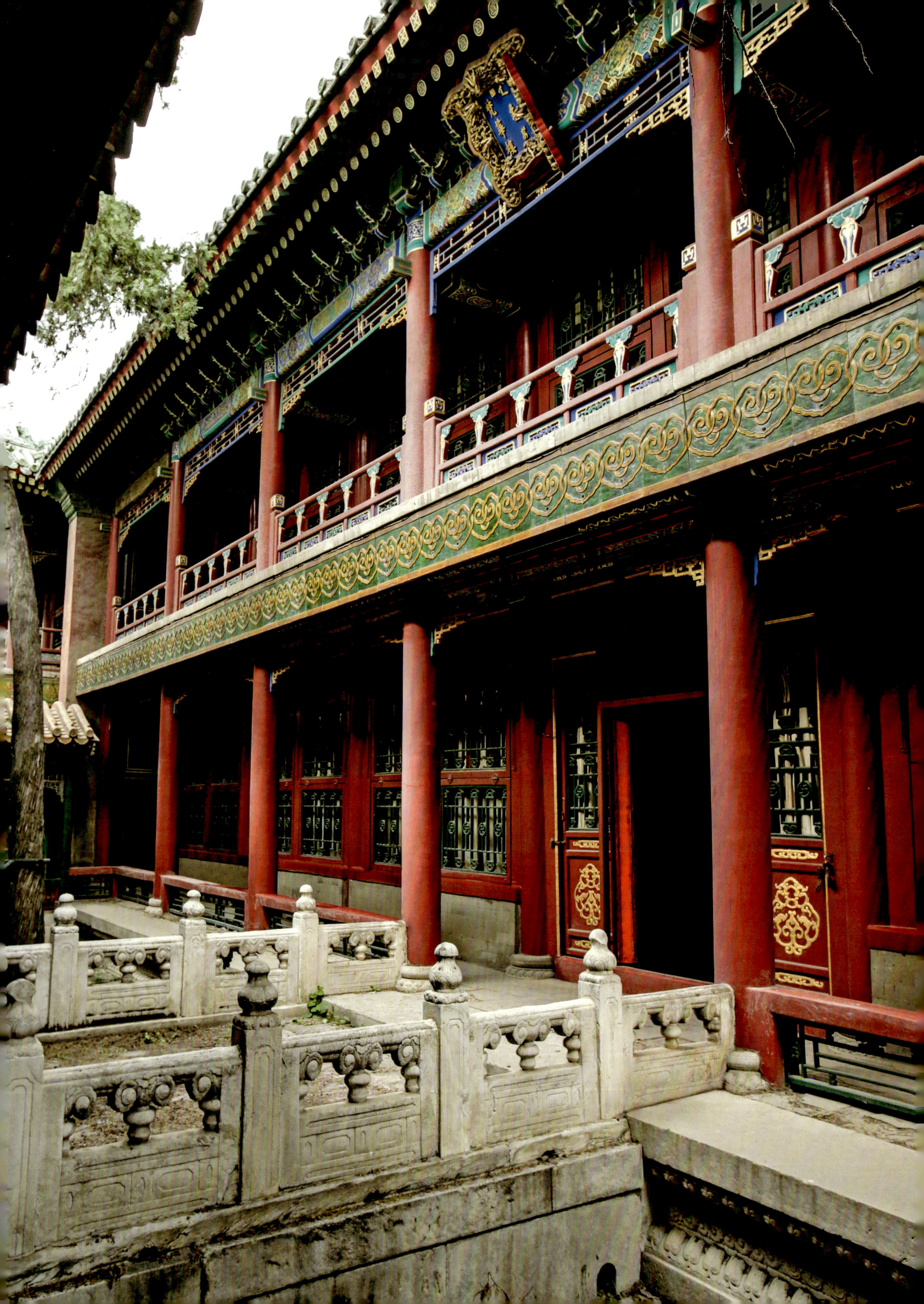

心清妙香

Religious Life in the Palace: Pavilion of Buddhist Glory in the Qianlong Garden

Ma Shengnan

Some Ming emperors and most Qing emperors and their families were pious adherents of Tibetan Buddhism, and Emperor Qianlong (r. 1736–95) was the religion's most faithful follower. During his reign, Qianlong's personal beliefs greatly influenced his decisions on every aspect of court life, from diplomatic policy to the decorations inside Yuling, his own mausoleum.[1] Today, the Palace Museum's collection boasts more than forty-eight thousand religious works, ninety percent of which are Tibetan Buddhist. The works include statues, printed and manuscript sutras, pagodas, offering objects, and sites of religious activities.

Occupying the 180 acres of what was once the Forbidden City, the Palace Museum contains approximately fifteen Tibetan Buddhist temples and chapels, some of which display original interior furnishings dating back to the Qing dynasty. The Pavilion of Buddhist Glory (Fanhualou) stands as an excellent example of such a temple. Located in the northeast corner of the palace, Fanhualou sits in Emperor Qianlong's retirement garden and is a structure known as a Six-Section Buddhist Hall (Liupinfolou) in Qing court archives. The Liupinfolou was created by Emperor Qianlong under the guidance of his spiritual teacher (guru), Third Changkya Rolpe Dorje (1717–1786) (cat. no. 123).[2] This kind of building served as the pantheon of the Geluk School (Gelukpa) of Tibetan Buddhism. Each floor of the structure's two-story hall has seven rooms, comprising a central room flanked by six rooms, three on each side, that symbolize the founder of Buddhism and the six steps in Gelukpa tantra exercises. In the center of each room stands a large stupa made of cloisonné, surrounded by *thangkas* and statues depicting deities related to each step of the exercise. Every statue was identified and cast with its name and the mark: Made in the Qianlong reign of the Great Qing dynasty. In every room, the emperor requested a displayed annotation to explain the step and its corresponding exercise. The annotations were written in Manchu, Mongolian, Chinese, and Tibetan in gold ink on a valuable dark cyan paper (*ciqingzhi*). These relics reveal the emperor's spiritual world and his understanding of Buddhist doctrine.[3]

Tibetan Buddhist art and artifacts in the Palace Museum's collection fall under two categories. The first category contains works given by high-ranking Tibetan and Mongolian lamas and political leaders who paid tribute to the Ming and Qing governments. The statues and thangkas in this category were created in Tibet, Nepal, India, and Swat (northern Pakistan). The second category includes works created by craftsmen from the Zaobanchu imperial workshop and the Hall of Rectitude (Zhongzhengdian), the two Forbidden City locations that produced the core of the Buddhist art collection. The art and artifacts from the Zaobanchu workshop and Zhongzhengdian reveal great stylistic differences from the tributes in the former category and are generally acknowledged as "court style."

The primary difference between the two categories can be seen in the deities represented. In works created in the Qing court, certain deities were repeatedly depicted to embody their special strengths. However, Tibetan tributes underscored the roles that deities played in tantric exercises. For example, a thangka depicts

Fig. 1 Pavilion of Buddhist Glory, 2005, © The Palace Museum

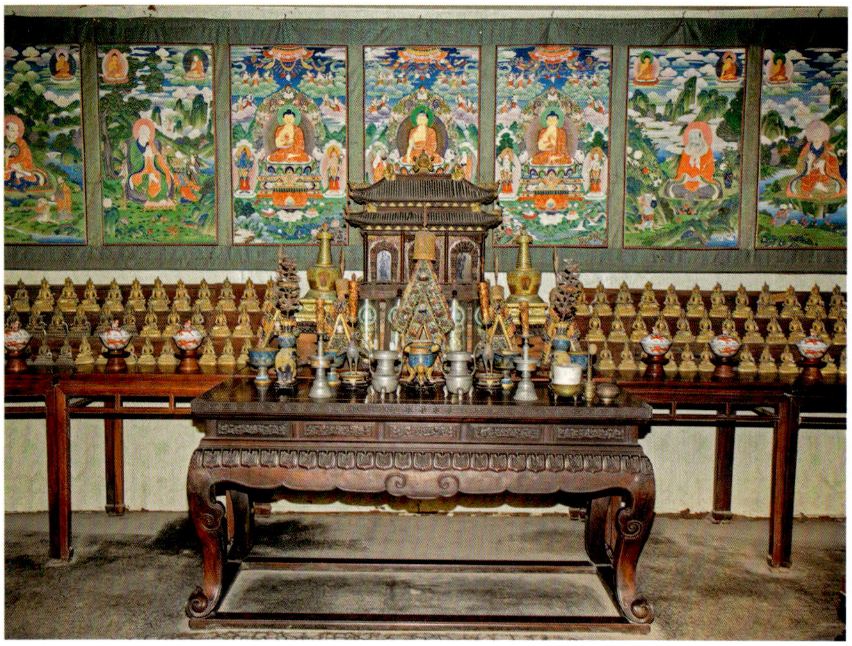

Fig. 2 Interior of Pavilion of Buddha's Sun, 2012, © The Palace Museum

Amitayus (cat. no. 121), the most highly worshipped deity, as the Buddha of Longevity, and the statue of Manjusri (cat. no. 120) portrays the deity of supreme wisdom and one that Qing emperors believed they incarnated. Avalokiteshvara, Arhat, Tara, Ushnisha Sita Tapatra, Maitreya, and Ushnishavijaya were also popular deities for depictions.

On the Tibetan Plateau, art styles varied depending on geographic areas. The artists in the Qing court studied and absorbed all existing styles and then created an extraordinary new style. In thangkas, the portraits of figures, clothes, and religious rituals are typically Tibetan, but the landscape elements in the background were often inspired by traditional literati paintings. In a number of portraits, the main figure's face is rendered in light and shadow, a style introduced to Chinese emperors by Western missionaries. Emperor Qianlong enthusiastically studied Tibetan Buddhist art iconography in both statues and pictorial designs. He decided the precise size and proportions based on Indian documents and identified multiple names and iconography for each deity. Emperor Qianlong ordered the Zaobanchu workshop to copy some masterpieces of the tributes. After comparing these works with originals, we can identify his personal aesthetic blend in the replicas.

Materials present another distinguishing characteristic of the two categories of religious works. Tibetan craftsmen used cotton and linen cloth to draw thangkas, but painters who worked inside the Forbidden City more often chose silk, making their thangkas thinner and smoother. Some embroidered scrolls and cut-silk (*kesi*) tapestries were made in Suzhou using the most genuine Chinese silk. Moreover, Emperor Qianlong was interested in learning about and improving copper alloy ingredients. Artisans invented a new kind of alloy (*zijin lima* or *dzhai ksim* in Tibetan), which contains a precious copper alloy and is a beautiful golden brown color. To make copper bells sound more sonorous, they conducted experiments for years until the high-tin formula was found.[4]

NOTES

1. Berger 2003.
2. Henss 2008.
3. Clark 1937.
4. Luo 2005.

115 明萬曆 吳彬繪 觀音大士像軸
絹本設色

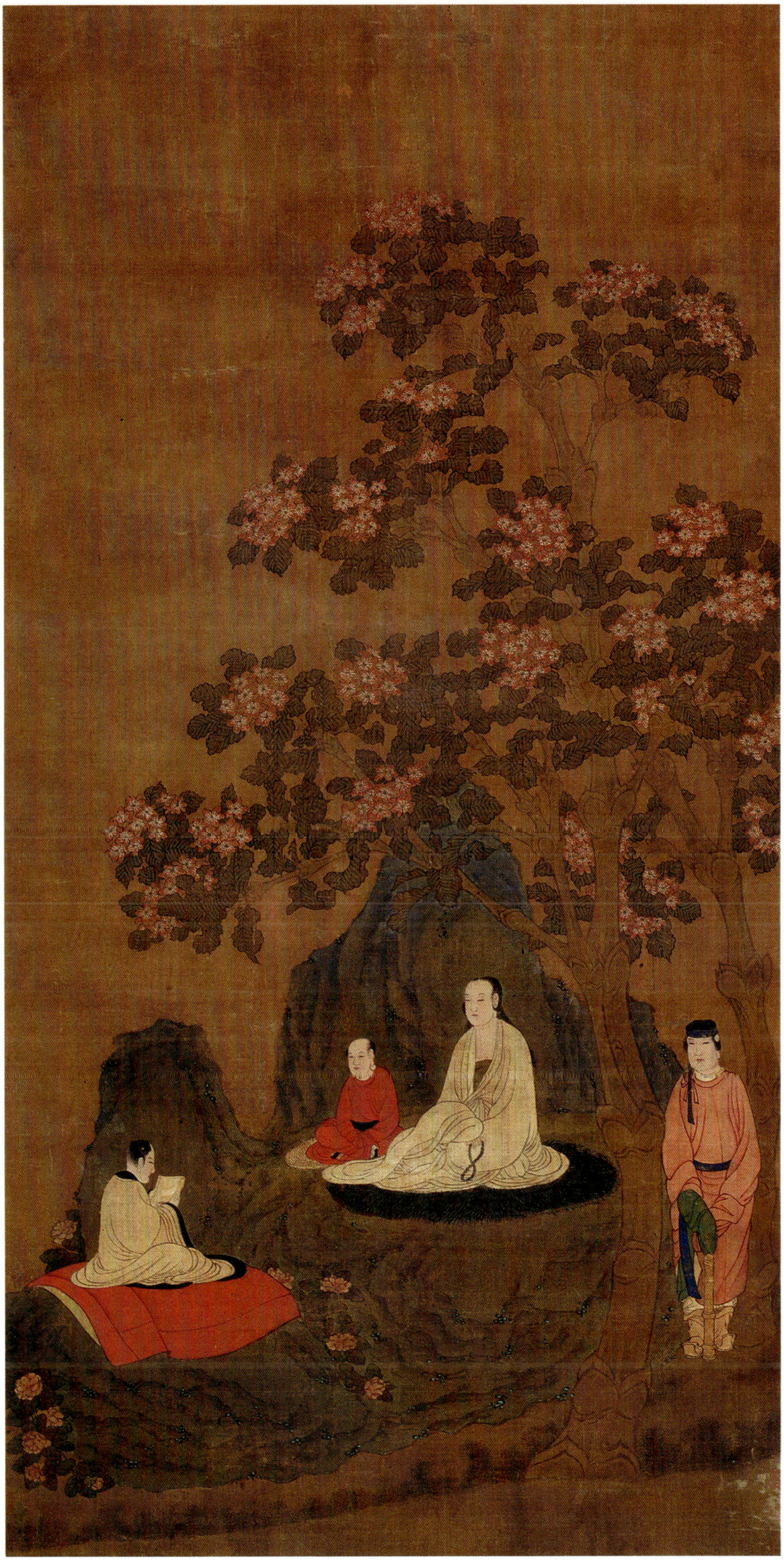

Bodhisattva Guanyin (Avalokiteshvara), approx. 1602
Wu Bin (act. 1568–1620)
Ming dynasty, Wanli period (1563–1620)
Hanging scroll; ink and color on silk
H. 145.9 cm (57.44 in.), W. 76.1 cm (29.96 in.)
Palace Museum, Xin.73981

This painting depicts bodhisattva Guanyin and his disciples sitting by the Bodhi trees in a rocky landscape. The white-robed Guanyin holds a rosary. His attendant, Longnü, sits to his right wearing a red robe. The figure seated across from them on a red mat may be Shancai, a young pilgrim who visited Guanyin in his quest for enlightenment as described in the *Avatamsaka Sutra*. The standing man looks like a servant, but his peculiar outfit and distracted look indicate he is a layman. The figures' static poses and various facial expressions convey a sense of divinity and secularity. This integration reflects the spiritual life of the Chan Buddhist masters, educated elites, and impious commoners at the turn of the seventeenth century.

The scene reveals the artist's own life as a Chan lay practitioner (*jushi*). A native of Putian, Fujian Province, Wu Bin relocated to Jiangning, today's Nanjing, in the 1590s. He lived the life of a recluse, reading, writing, and painting by the Xixiasi, a Chan monastery. Rendered in an innovative and eccentric style, Wu's works from this period show distinctive religious characters in landscape scenes[1] and interactions among Buddhist deities, jushi, and laymen. Wu's life took a dramatic turn in the early seventeenth century when he was employed as a court painter and later a court official at the Ministry of Works (Gongbu), where he served until 1625.

Although unsigned and undated, this scroll resembles another painting[2] dated to 1601–2, which also shares a similar Chan theme, a warm palette, fine lines, and eccentric landscape details. LJ

Seals, on the lower right: 吳彬之印 *Wu Bin zhiyin*; 文中 *Wenzhong*

1. Lu 2008, 95.
2. He and Knight 2008, cat. no. 140, pp. 249–50.

116 清乾隆 顧繡金剛經塔軸 絹本

Pagoda with the Diamond Sutra

Qing dynasty, Qianlong period (1736–95)

Hanging scroll; embroidery on satin, gold and silver threads

H. 212.7 cm (83.74 in.), W. 69.4 cm (27.32 in.)

Palace Museum, Xin.66904

Assembled on satin in eight sections, this embroidered scroll depicts a seven-story pagoda with multiple eaves. The first level shows Shakyamuni Buddha preaching to his disciple Subhuti, who is flanked by two heavenly guardians. In this scroll, a Buddha appears on all levels except the fourth where a pagoda reliquary, or symbol of Buddha, stands. Embroidery work conveys architectural details: inlaid base, balconies, doorjambs, brackets, beams, and bells hanging from the roof's corners.

A close examination reveals Chinese characters in the standard script (*kaishu*) embroidered in dark blue silk. In five thousand words, the *Diamond Sutra* recounts the dialogue between Shakyamuni and Subhuti and remains one of the most important Mahayana scriptures, favored especially by Chan devotees.

The time and effort invested in making this exquisite pagoda indicates the devotion of its followers. Made by the Gu family in Shanghai, this pagoda exemplifies their favorite Buddhist subject and distinctive needle techniques. Noted since the mid-Ming dynasty for their skills and craftsmanship, the Gu family flourished during the Chongzhen period (1628–44). Their work employs a variety of material, elegant colors, and innovative stitches.[1] Here, the embroidery includes flat gold stitches (*pingjinzhen*) for the pagoda; seed stitches (*dazi*) for the head of the Buddha; loop stitches (*taozhen*) for the Buddha's robe; and net stitches (*wangzhen*) for the costumes of the heavenly guardians.

Comparative works include a painted Yuan scroll of a *Diamond Sutra* pagoda,[2] from the National Palace Museum, Taipei, and a similar embroidered scroll of the *Diamond Sutra* pagoda auctioned at the China Guardians in Beijing in 2010. LJ

1. Chen 2005, 185.
2. GLGGBWY 1989, vol. 8, no. 4.

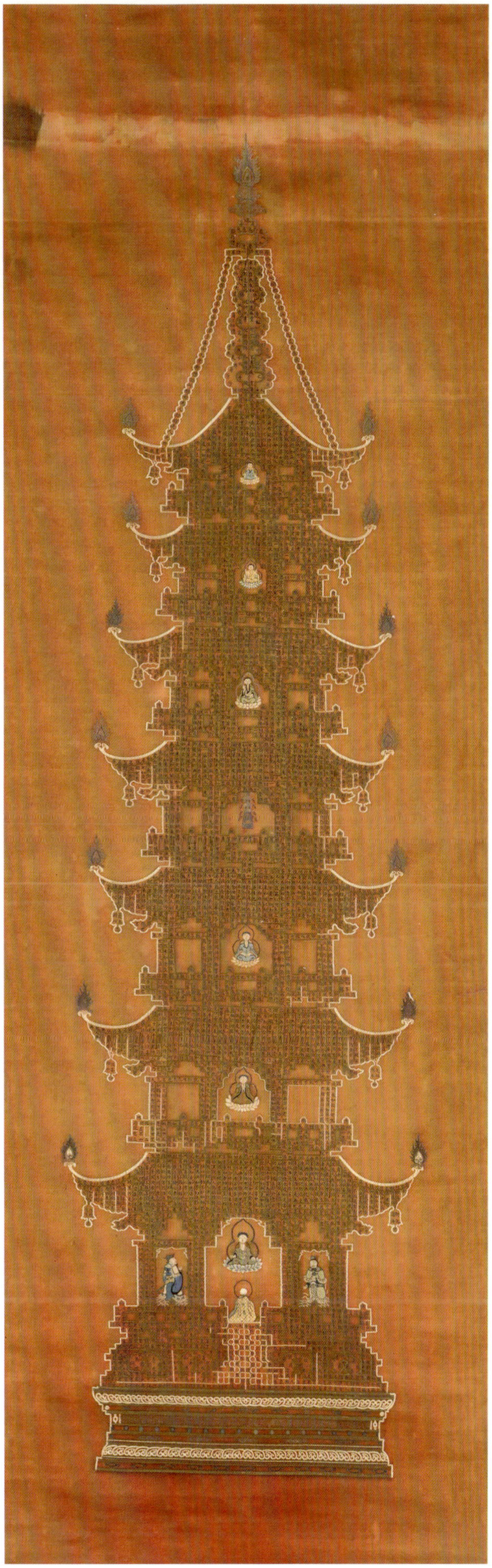

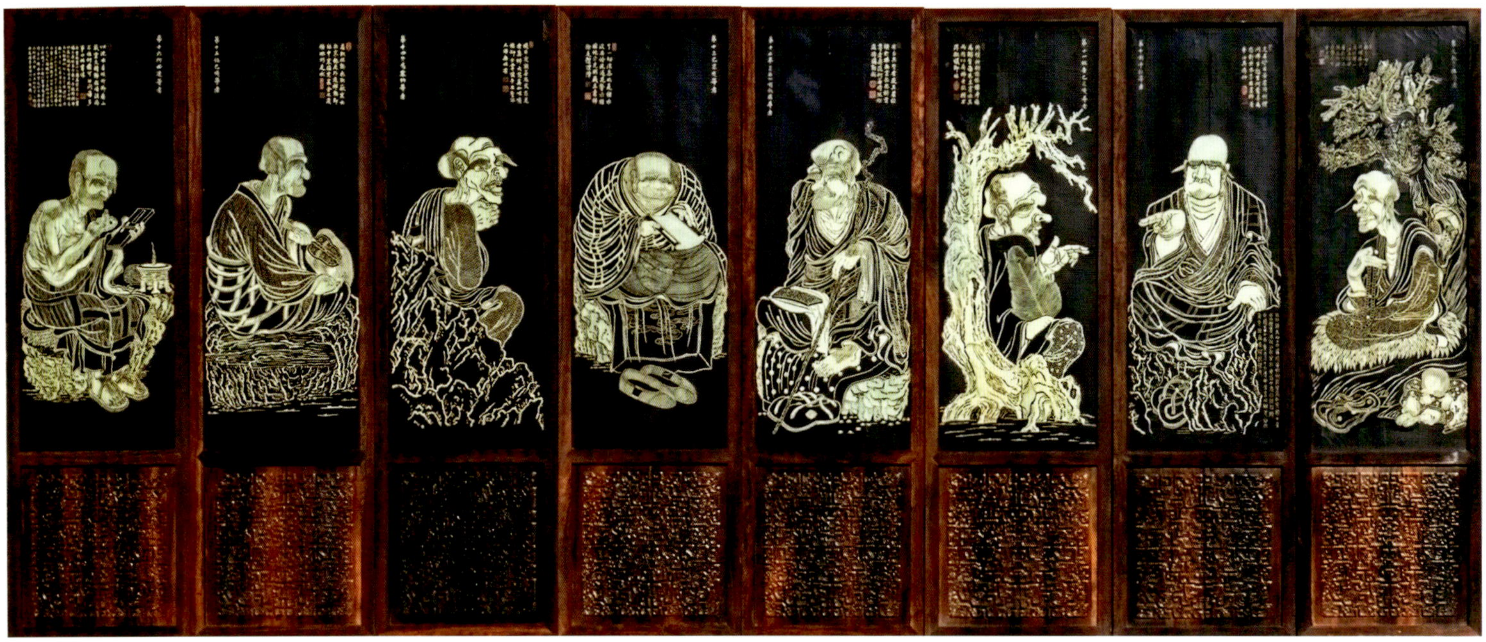

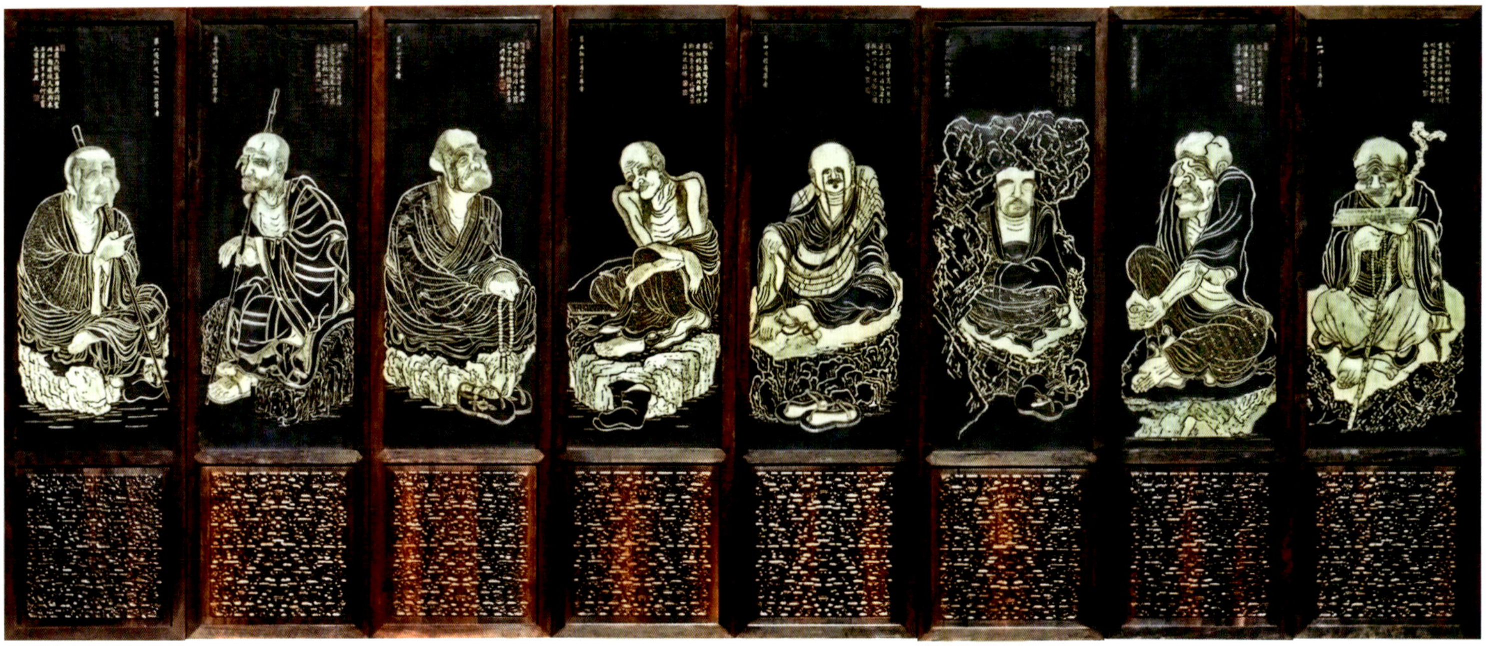

117 清乾隆 硬木嵌玉十六羅漢像屏

Sixteen Luohans (Arhats), approx. 1777
Qing dynasty, Qianlong period (1736–95)
Sixteen-panel folding screen; wood, jade inlay
Each panel: H. 218 cm (84 in.), L. 58.7 cm (28 in.), W. 6 cm (2.5 in.)
Palace Museum, Gu.198952

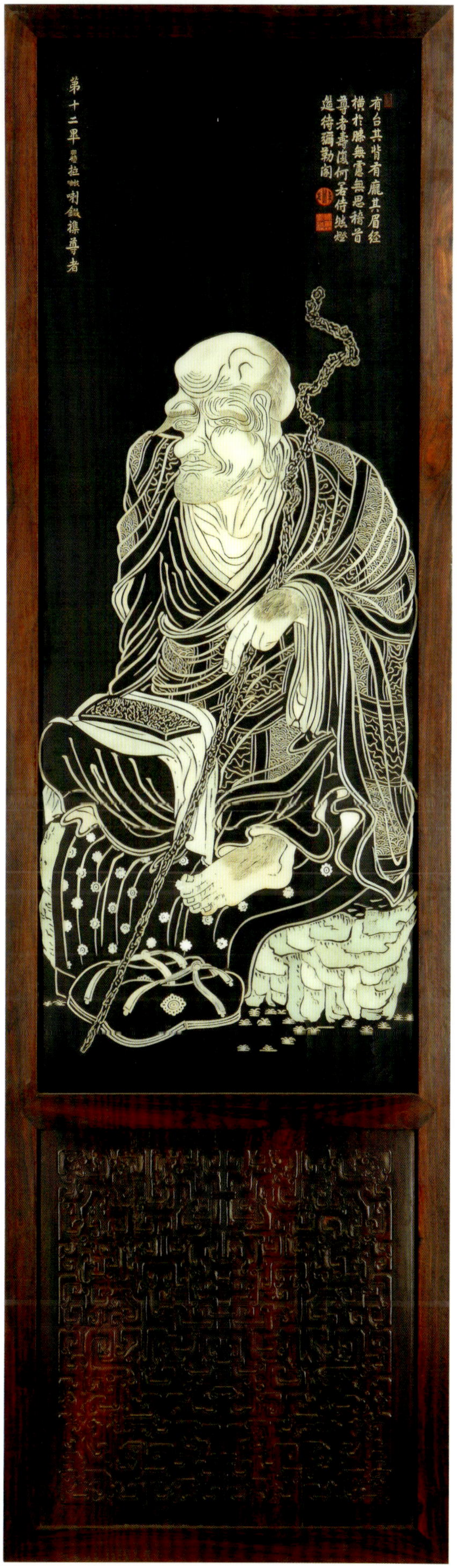

During his 1757 tour of the South, Emperor Qianlong visited the Sheng'en Temple in Hangzhou, where a monk master showed the emperor the temple's hidden treasure of sixteen enlightened beings, known as *luohans,* painted by Guanxiu (832–912), a monk painter. The emperor was fascinated with the images and added the luohans' names and an inscription to the painting. This screen, inlaid with jade imitating the painted image on a wooden frame, was offered to the emperor by a civil official named Guotai (d. 1782) during his service in Shandong Province in 1777–82. Emperor Qianlong installed this screen in his private chapel on the second level of the Pavilion of Illuminating Clouds (Yunguanglou) in the Qianlong Garden.

This screen depicts the sixteen luohans (*arhats* in Sanskrit), either seated on a rock or leaning against a tree, reading or meditating. Their bulging eyes, long eyebrows, and prominent noses reveal their divine and earthly natures. The attributes in their hands, such as sutras, rosaries, and shafts, illustrate their dedication to their faith. As an enlightened being, a luohan has achieved the highest level in Hinayana practice. With the rise of Mahayana Buddhism, an important role for the luohan was to remain in this world to guide others to salvation. Thus, the luohan became a symbol of longevity and dedication, especially significant to Emperor Qianlong in his retirement. Numbered from right to left, each panel bears the name of a deity, a poem by Emperor Qianlong, his signature, and two seals.

The reverse of the screen is painted in gold and light colors with seasonal flowers and plants, including bamboo, peony, vines, lotus, peach flower, rose, *osmanthus fragrans,* canna lily, camellia, narcissus, chrysanthemum, and okra.[1] In 1861, the original painting was destroyed during the Taiping Rebellion against the Qing court, making this surviving eighteenth-century edition more noteworthy. LJ

Seals:
乾隆寶宸 *Qianlong baochen;* 得來自在 *Delai zizai*

1. Berliner 2010, 168–70.

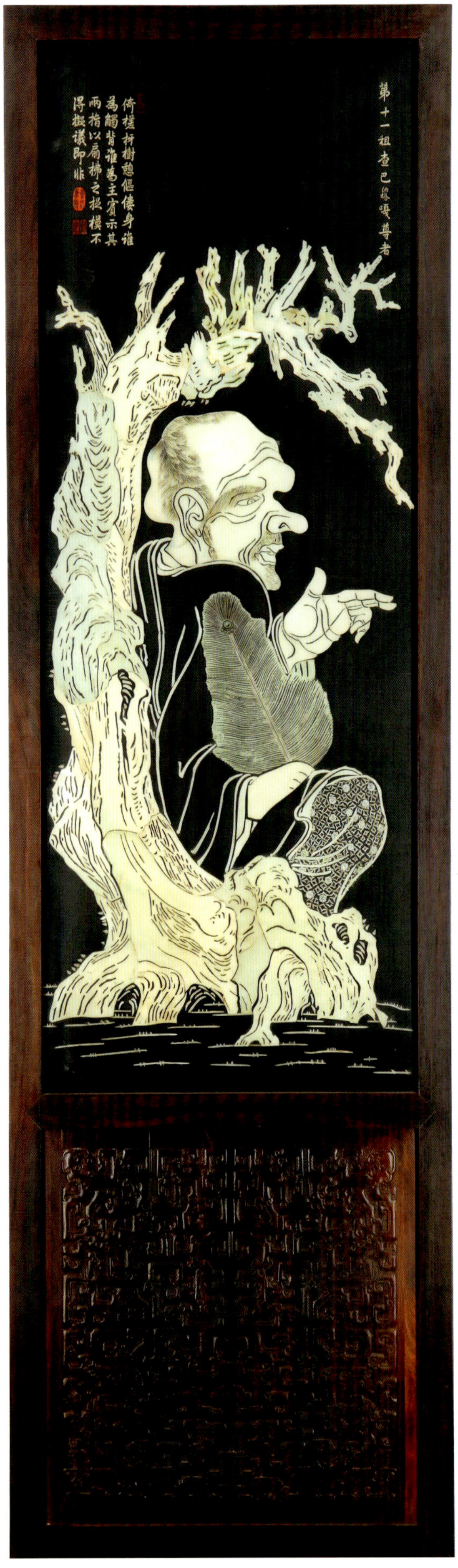

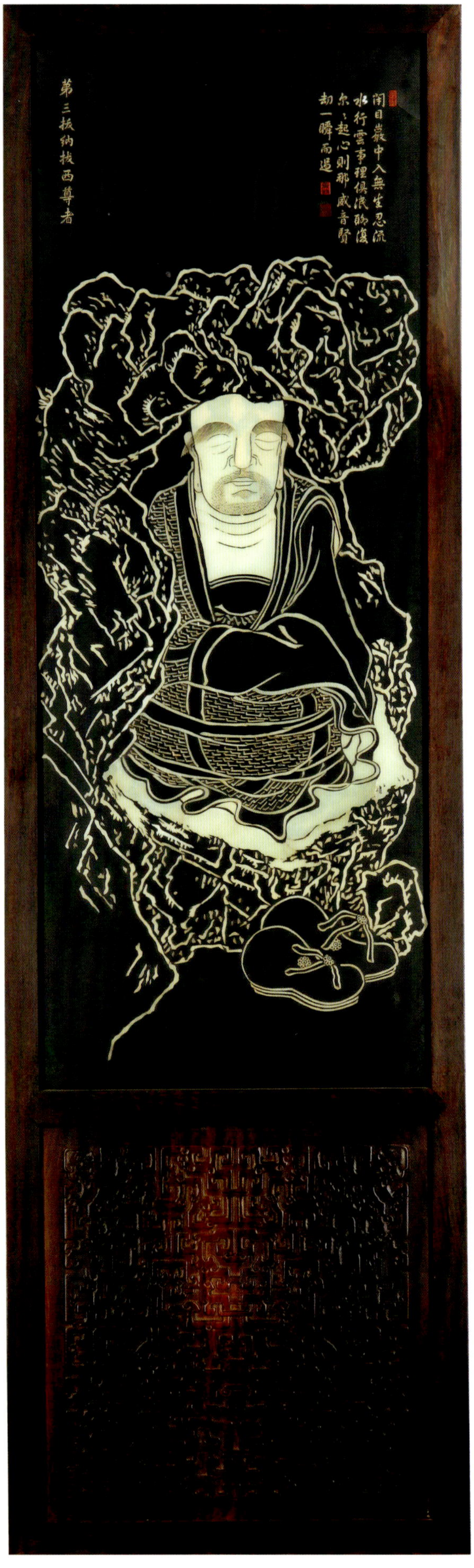
第三拔纳拔西尊者

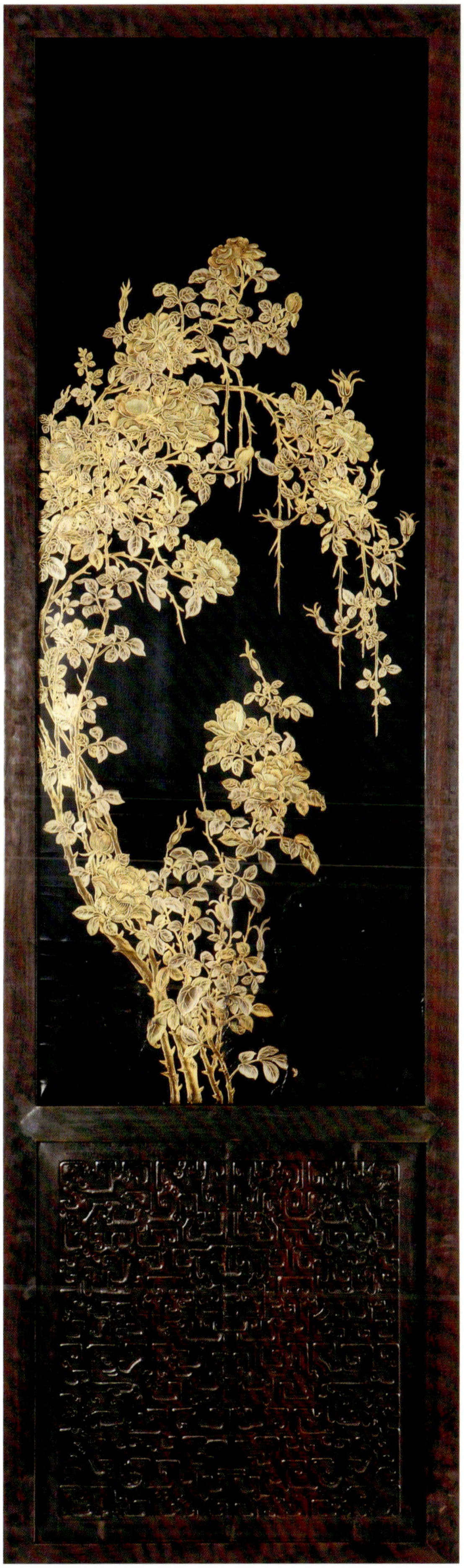

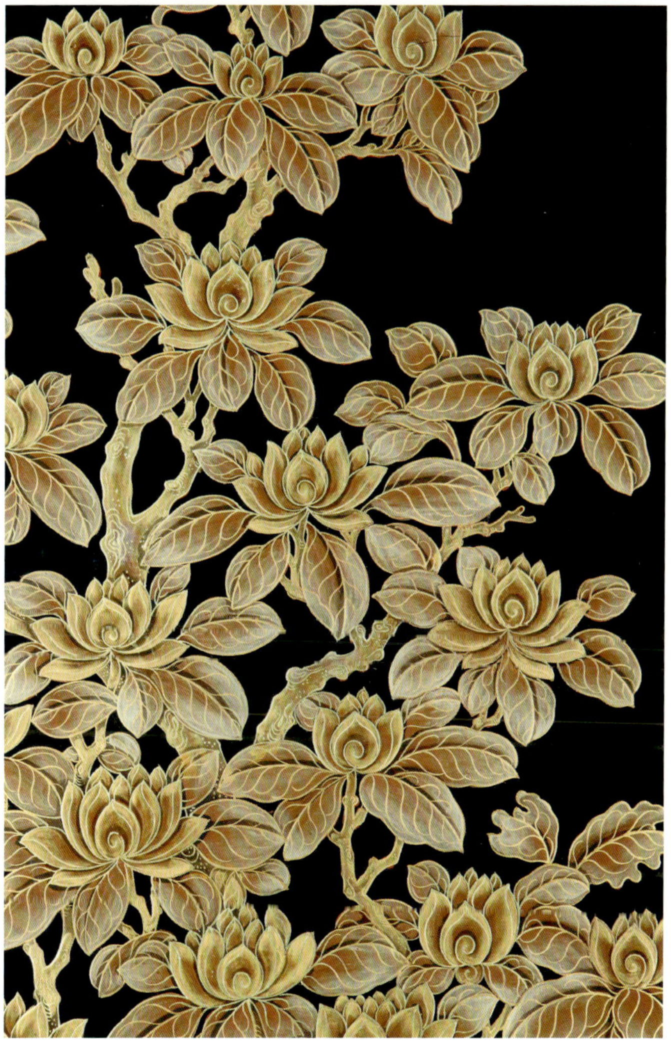

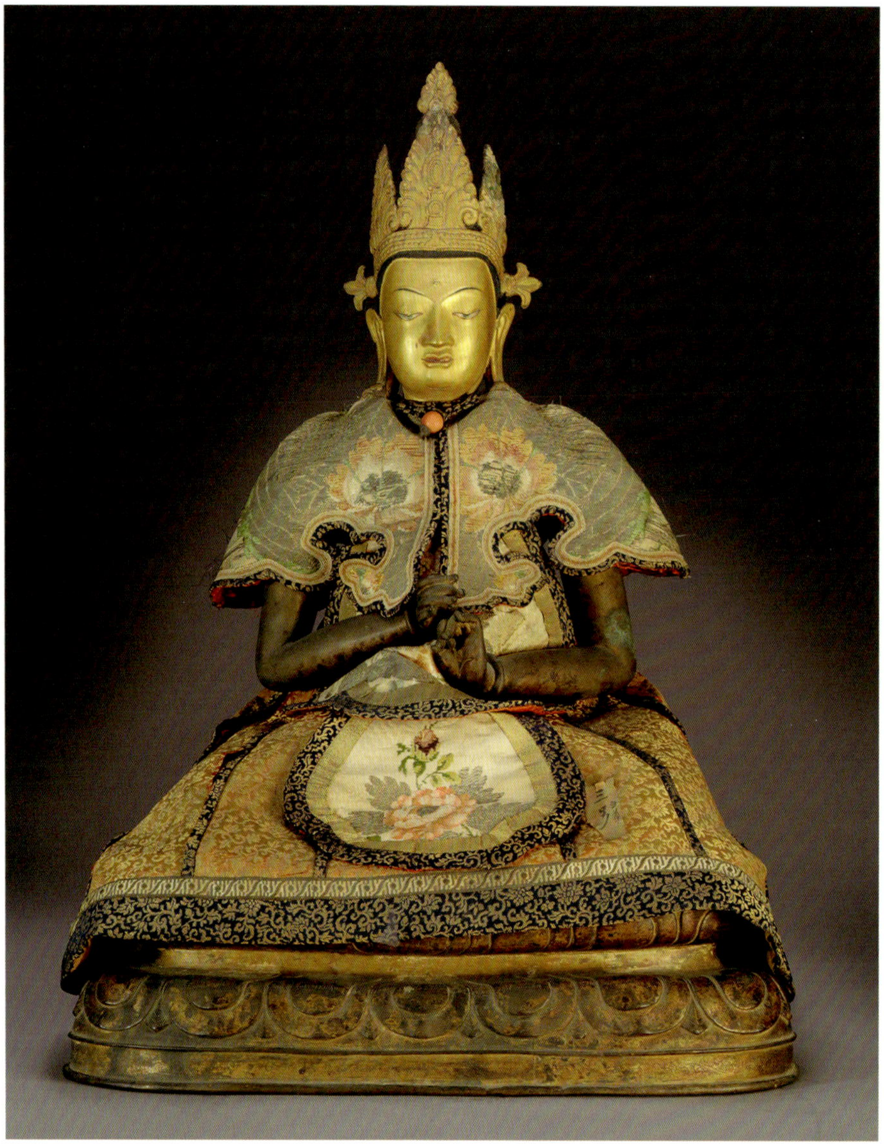

118 十七世紀 西藏 梵銅毘盧遮那佛

Virochana Buddha in Ritual Costume, 17th century
Tibetan
Copper alloy, gold dust, satin, cotton, coral
H. 54 cm (21.26 in.), W. 39.8 cm (15.67 in.)
Palace Museum, Gu.194129

This bronze statue depicts Virochana Buddha, the supreme deity in Tantric Buddhism and the Buddha of Infinite Light. Buddhism developed in Tibet in the seventh century when Songtsän Gampo (d. 649) expanded the territory and married Chinese princess Wen Cheng and Nepalese princess Bhrtuti. In the thirteenth century, when Mongols occupied Tibet and China, Kublai Khan (r. 1260–94) declared Tibetan Buddhism the state religion and appointed Drogon Chogyal Phagpa (1235–1280), the fifth leader of the Sakya school of Tibetan Buddhism, as the state preceptor.

This Virochana Buddha sits on a double-lotus platform in deep meditation. He wears a three-leaf crown and an elaborate silk robe that conceals his body. He makes his characteristic hand gesture for wisdom, while his facial expression conveys a sense of tranquility and grace. The crown, the broad face, and the wide lotus petals on the base reveal a distinctive classical Tibetan style of imagery that integrated the artistic elements of India, Nepal, and China.

In Tibetan Buddhist tradition, the process for making statues involved selecting materials, reviewing the design and model, assigning craftsmen, and performing rituals that prepared the statue for embodying a deity and possessing magical powers. Textiles were tailored to fit over a statue for worship and protection. The yellow satin robe worn by this Buddha features lotus blossoms embroidered with gold thread, cotton padding, and a red silk lining. His fashion mirrors that of high-ranking Tibetan masters and represents Emperor Qianlong's faith and devotion to Buddhist iconography. LJ

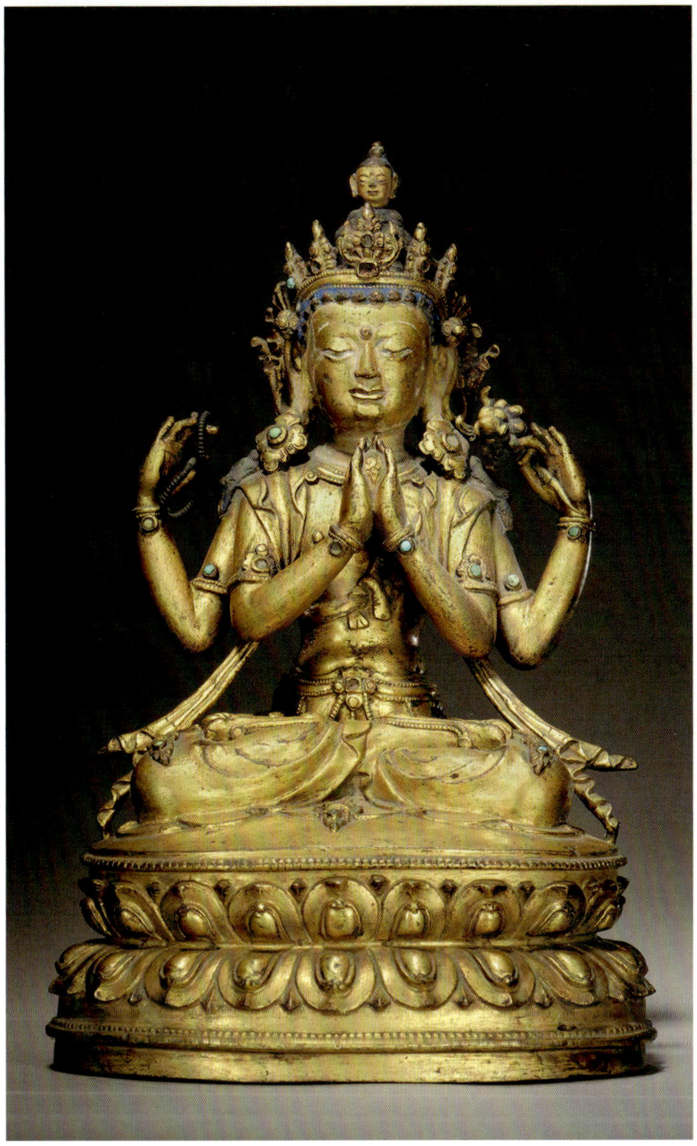

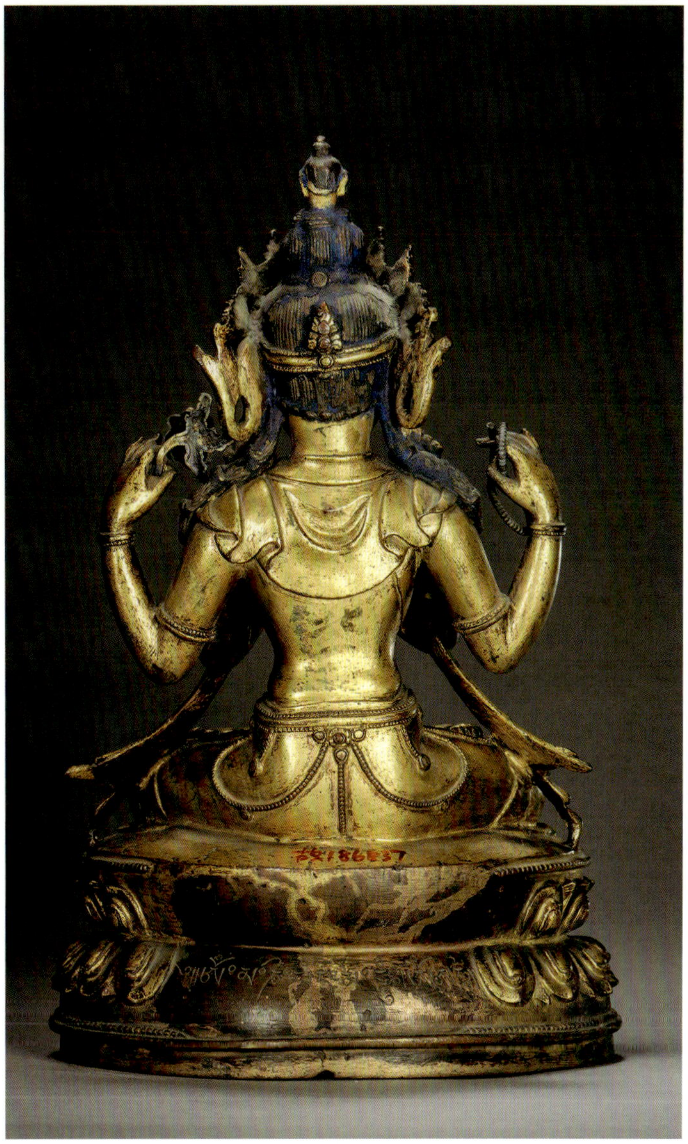

119 十五世紀 西藏 銅鎏金嵌松石四臂觀音菩薩

Four-Armed Bodhisattva Avalokiteshvara, 15th century

Tibetan

Gilt copper alloy, turquoise, pigment

H. 23.8 cm (9.37 in.), W. 15.3 cm (6.02 in.)

Palace Museum, Gu.186837

The four-armed Avalokiteshvara (named Shadkshari Lokeshvara in Sanskrit and Guanyin in Chinese) is the bodhisattva of compassion, a primary deity in Tibetan Buddhism and a visual focus during meditation. This bejeweled Avalokiteshvara wears a five-leaf crown surmounted with a Buddha's head and sits on a double-lotus pedestal. The antelope hide over his left shoulder symbolizes wisdom. His front two hands are holding a jewel, a symbol of enlightenment, in a gesture of adoration. His third hand holds a rosary and the fourth hand a lotus flower.

Turquoise stones are inlaid on his crown, earrings, armbands, bracelets, and sashes. The base of the statue is sealed and incised with a crossed *vajra,* which represents Tantric Buddhism. The iconographical detail and rich turquoise inlays resemble those on Tibetan Buddhist statues, known as *liuchonggan-lima* in the Qing court, made by Tibetan craftsmen in the Lhasa area in the mid-fifteenth century.

The six-syllable mantra ("om mani padme hum") and the body-speech-mind mantra ("om ah hum") are incised in Tibetan on the back of the lotus base.[1] Traditionally carved on stone or written on paper and chanted by practitioners of Tibetan Buddhism, the mystic mantra of six-syllables represents the Buddhist realms: gods, demigods, humans, animals, and ghosts, as well as hell. LJ

1. The Palace Museum provided the reading of the inscription.

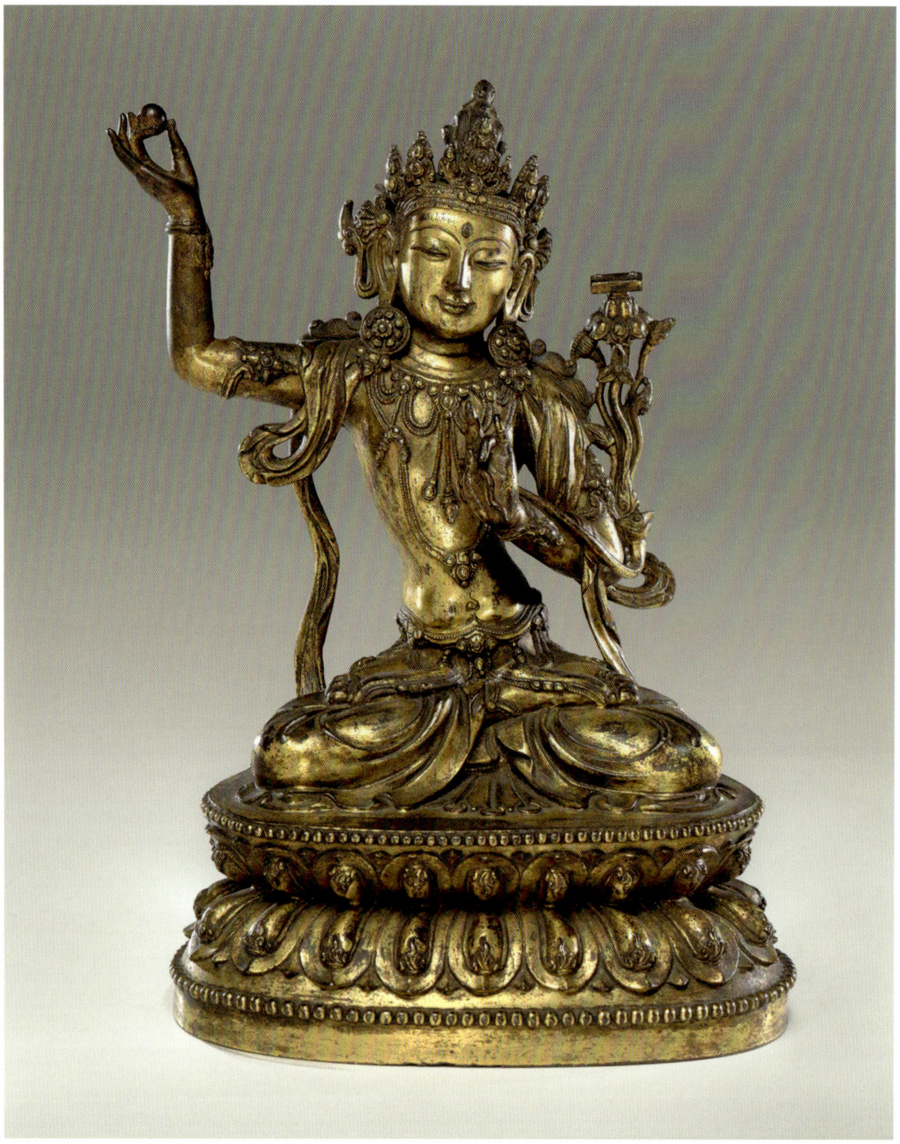

120 明永樂款 銅鎏金文殊菩薩坐像

Bodhisattva Manjusri

Ming dynasty, Yongle period (1403–24)

Gilded copper alloy, pigment

H. 26.04 cm (10 1/4 in.), W. 16.51 cm (6 1/2 in.), D. 10.16 cm (4 in.)

Virginia Museum of Fine Arts, Arthur and Margaret Glasgow Endowment, 73.77.1

Inspired by a Tibetan prototype, this statue depicts Manjusri, the bodhisattva of wisdom and a disciple of the Shakyamuni. Seated on a lotus pedestal, Manjusri holds a jewel in his right hand and a lotus flower in his left, surmounted by a sutra. He wears a five-leaf headdress, a symbol of the Five Wisdoms, a pleated robe, a sash, and lavishly ornamented armbands and bracelets.

Following Yuan Mongol rule, Ming emperors maintained a close relationship with Tibetan masters. Emperor Yongle (r. 1403–24) sent his mission envoys to Tibet to reaffirm the titles granted by Kublai Khan (r. 1260–94). At the invitation of Emperor Yongle, Fifth Karmapa Deshin Shegpa (1384–1415), who was a spiritual leader of the Kagyu sect, arrived at the Ming capital of Nanjing in 1406. He bestowed teachings and Tantric empowerments on the emperor in the palace. He also performed rites for the emperor's parents in Linggu Temple.[1]

Under Emperor Yongle's patronage, Tibetan Buddhist images like this were created by Chinese and Tibetan craftsmen in Beijing or Nanjing as visual aids for meditation, offerings to temples, and gifts to Tibetan and Mongolian leaders. LJ

Inscription, on the top of the front base: 大明永樂年施 (Bestowed in the Yongle year of the Great Ming)

1. Yang and Ma 1992, 115.

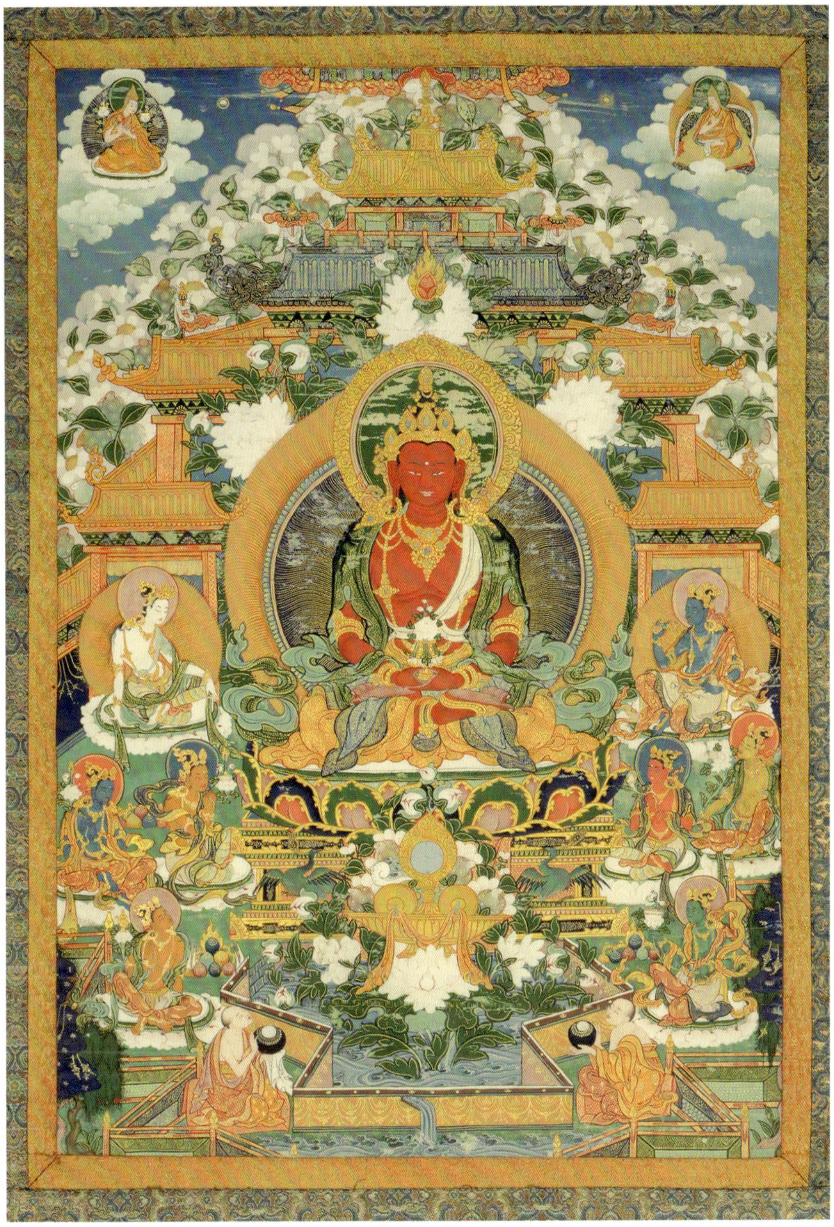

121 十八世紀 西藏 無量壽佛像軸 布本設色

Buddha of Infinite Life (Amitayus), 18th century
Eastern Tibetan
Pigments on cotton
H. 65 cm (25.6 in.), W. 45 cm (17.7 in.)
Palace Museum, Gu.6681-1/5

In keeping with a description in the *Sutra of Infinite Life,* this scene of the Western Paradise includes spectacular architecture, flowers falling from the sky, a lotus pond filled with offerings of the five senses, and trees blossoming with hanging jewels. The central figure is Amitayus, also known as Amitabha, the supreme deity of Pure Land Buddhism and the Buddha of Infinite Life. Sitting in meditation on a lotus throne, the red-bodied Amitayus wears a five-leaf jeweled crown and golden necklaces. Holding a longevity vase in his hands, Amitayus performs the meditation *mudra*—palms up with the right hand resting on the left. He is surrounded by eight bodhisattvas with Avalokiteshvara to his right and Vajrapani to his left. Above the Buddha are two spiritual leaders: Tsongkhapa (1357–1419), the founder of the Geluk school on the left; and the Seventh Dalai Lama, Kelzang Gyatso (1708–1757), on the right. The bottom scene illustrates two arhats in monastic robes, each holding an offering bowl. An image of the Buddha of Infinite Life was presented in the Qing court as a blessing for good fortune and longevity.

This work is one of more than one thousand *thangkas* from the Qing imperial collection, mostly assembled in the eighteenth century. These thangkas were gifts from religious leaders, imperial relatives, and court officers. The reciting lamas in the palace's Tibetan Buddhist complex (Zhongzhengdian) also created thangkas, following the standard of iconography and supervision of great masters such as Third Changkya Rolpe Dorje (cat. no. 123).[1] Although no inscription provides provenance or identifies the donor or maker, the work's orderly symmetric composition, its golden color scheme, and its combination of painterly and linear brushwork are characteristic of East Tibet, present-day provinces of Gansu and Qinghai. LJ

1. CCPT 2003, pp. 14, 110; cat. 100.

122 清乾隆 五方佛畫像軸 布本設色

Buddhas of Five Directions, 1772–75
Qing dynasty, Qianlong period (1736–95)
Pigment on cotton

Overall: L. 283 cm (53.94 in.), W. 179 cm (20.12 in.)
Each: L. 140 cm (55.1 in.), W. 25 cm (9.84 in.)
Palace Museum, Gu.200538

This set of five *thangkas* illustrates the Buddhas of the five directions in Vajrayana Buddhism. The five Buddhas, known as either the Five Dhyani Buddhas or the Buddhas of Five Wisdoms, include the white Virochana Buddha of the Center, who represents absolute truth; the blue Akshobya Buddha of the East, who represents timeless awareness; the red Amitabha Buddha of the West, who represents discernment; the green Amoghasiddhi Buddha of the North, who represents fulfillment; and the yellow Ratnasambhava Buddha of the South, who represents equality. The creatures these Buddhas used for travel—lions, elephants, peacocks, horses, or birds—are rendered on the bases of the thrones. Making hand gestures and holding attributes, thirty-five Confession Buddhas, seven in each thangka, sit around the five cardinal Buddhas. As described in the Mahayana sutra, confessing to the thirty-five Buddhas assists the believer in overcoming delusions and in achieving enlightenment.

These thangkas came from a chapel in Emperor Qianlong's retirement compound. According to the Zaobanchu imperial workshop archives, the thangkas of the five cardinal Buddhas were transferred on September 16, 1775, to the Forilou, a two-story temple hall constructed for Emperor Qianlong in 1772.[1] As a devoted Tibetan Buddhist, Emperor Qianlong ordered a number of Tibetan chapels built across the inner court and participated in every phase of design and installation. The thangkas were first painted by monks from the Zhongzhengdian complex and then mounted by craftsmen from the imperial workshop. According to the emperor's instruction, these thangkas were installed on the first level of the temple. LJ

1. Wang 2011a, 410–11.

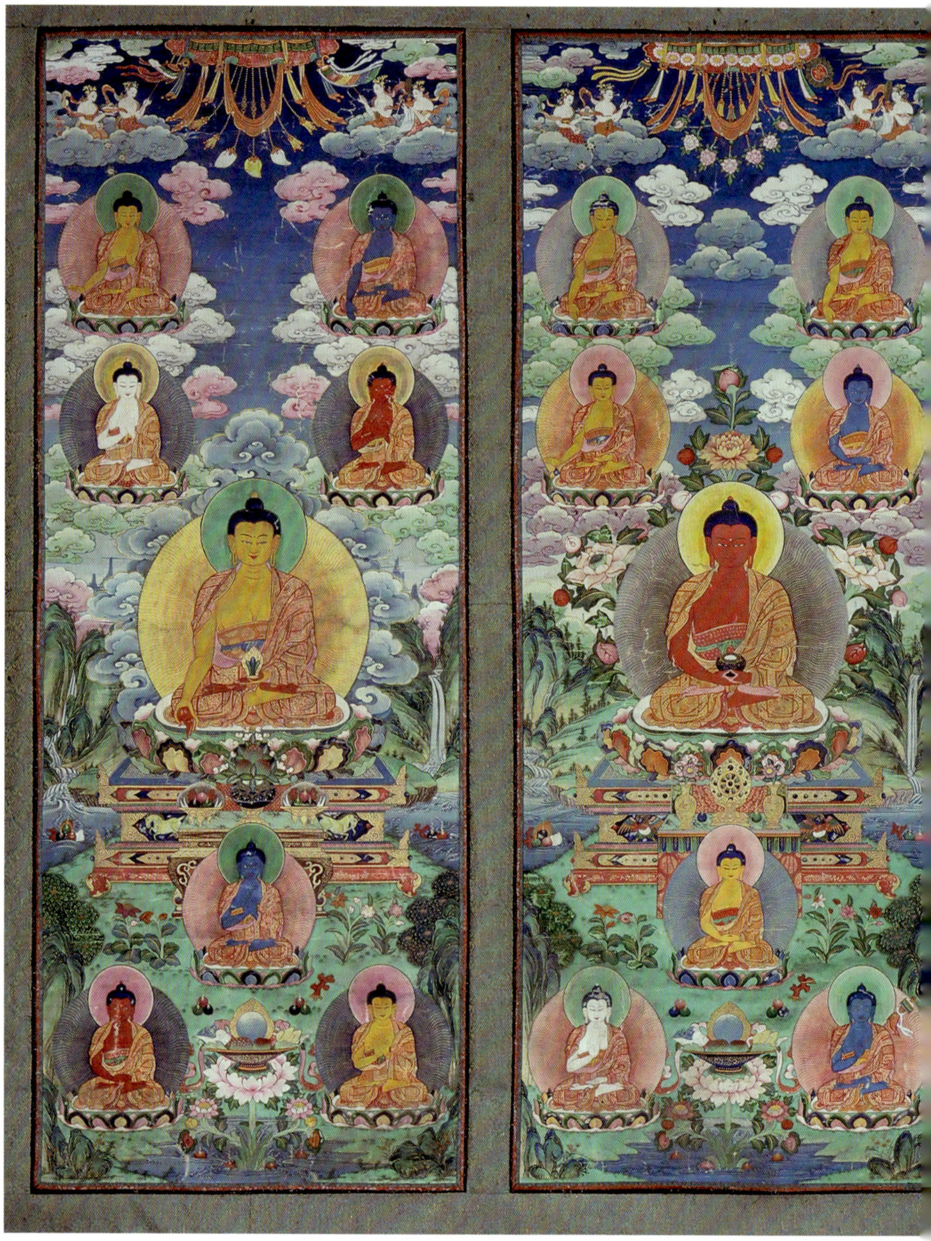

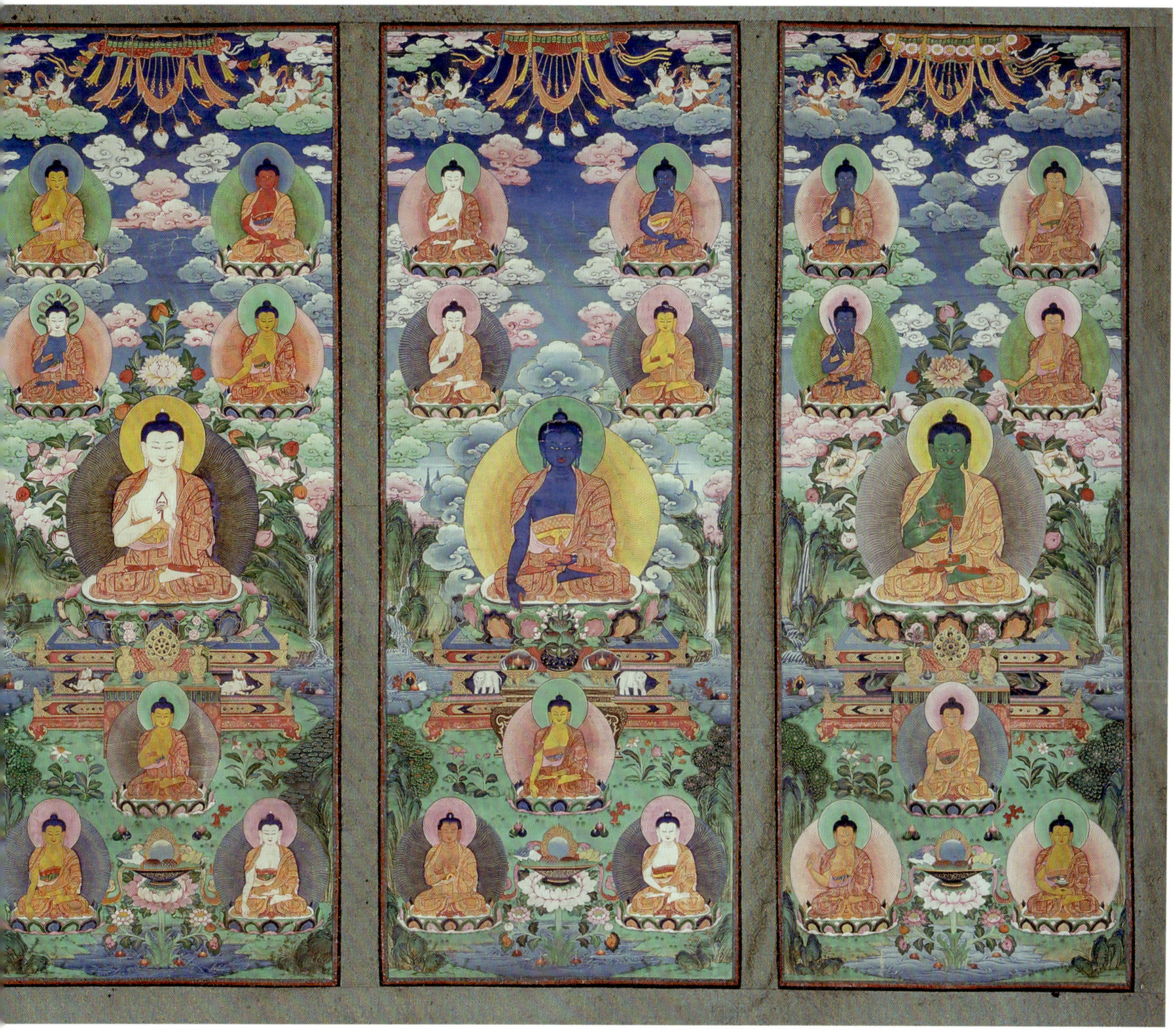

123 清乾隆 章嘉胡土克圖供養像軸 布本設色

Portrait of Third Changkya Rolpe Dorje, 1786

Qing dynasty, Qianlong period (1736–1795)

Pigment and gold on cotton

H. 117 cm (46 in.), W. 61 cm (24 in.)
Palace Museum, Gu.8899

In this portrait, Third Changkya Rolpe Dorje (1717–1786), a spiritual leader of the Geluk school of Tibetan Buddhism in Inner Mongolia, sits on a high throne surrounded by a landscape. Above him is Amitabha Buddha, flanked by Vajrabhairava on his right and Second Changkya Lobsang Choden (1642–1714) on his left. Three wrathful protective deities fill the lower register (from left to right: Yamantaka on a boar, six-armed Shadbhuja Mahakala, and Palden Lhamo on a mule). Displayed on the altar table are a *bumpa* vase with a peacock feather, bell, *vajra,* ritual mirror, drum, and skull cup. Ritual objects (an offering bowl, a whisk, and Buddist scriptures) rest on the throne.

In 1720, Third Changkya was identified as the reincarnation of the Second Changkya in Liangzhou, in today's Wuwei, Gansu Province, and took the monastic seat at the Guolong Temple (Youningsi) in today's Qinghai Province.[1] He arrived in Beijing in 1723 and studied Buddhist teachings with high-ranking monks. Changkya was honored as the state preceptor and managed Tibetan Buddhist affairs in Beijing, Inner Mongolia, Shanxi, and Chengde.[2] He traveled to Tibet twice and studied with the Fifth Dalai Lama. In the Qing court, he served as a consultant for identifying, making, and displaying Tibetan iconography. He died in 1786 during his annual summer retreat in Mount Wutai, where he was buried in the Zhenhai Temple. LJ

Inscription, on the reverse, written in Chinese, Manchu, Mongolian, and Tibetan: By order of Emperor Qianlong, the portrait was painted by court lamas from the Zhongzhengdian Buddhist compound in memory of Changkya; dated to the 26th day of the 12th month of Qianlong 51st year, 1786

1. Yang and Ma 1992, 297.
2. CCTP 2003, 23, cat. 31.

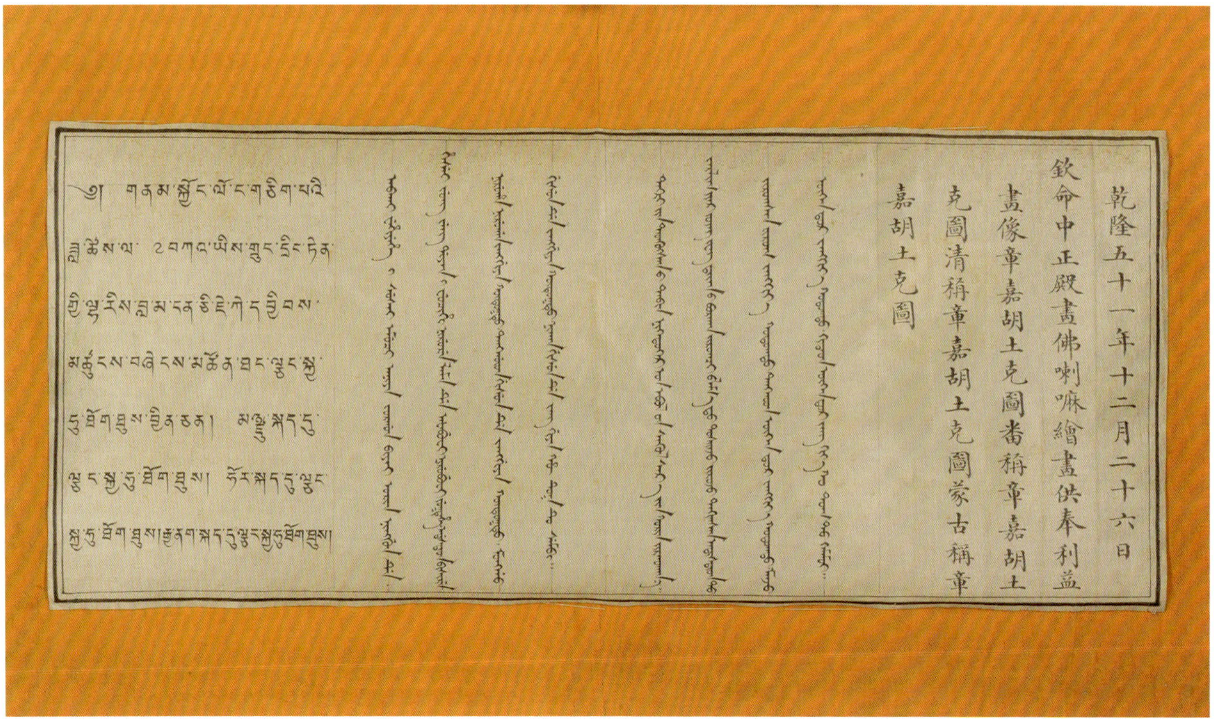

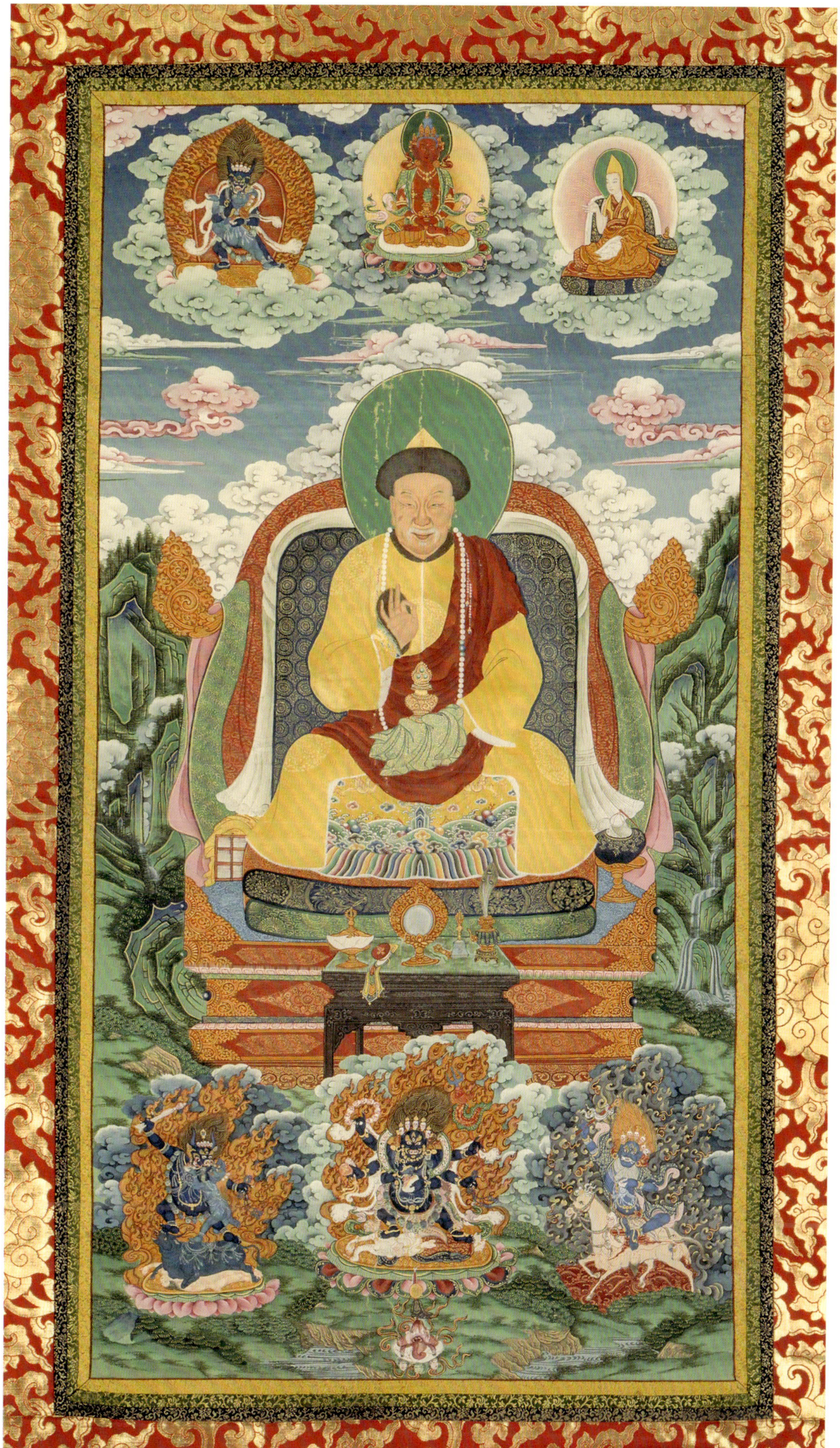

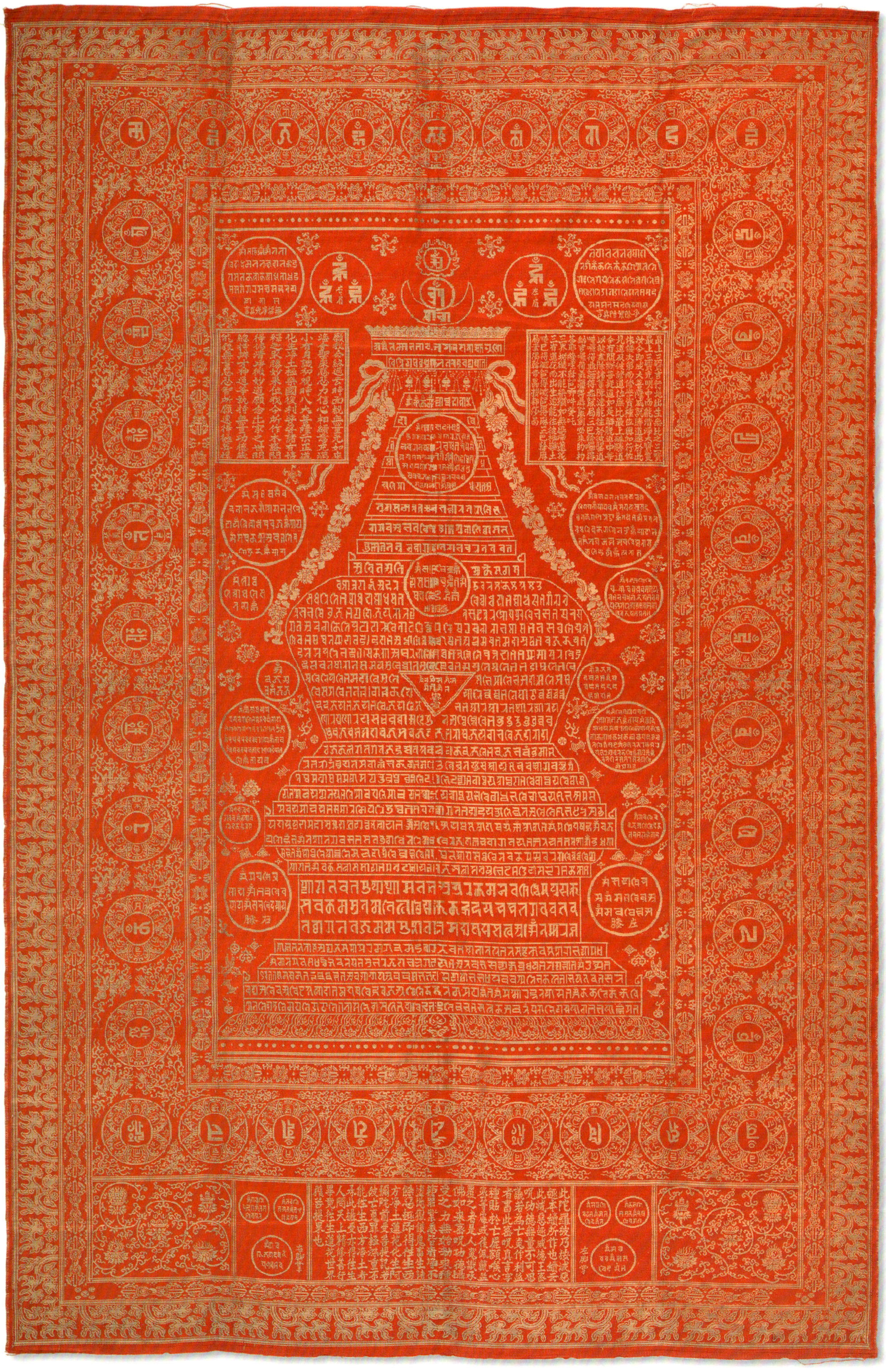

124 清光緒 織金紅色梵文陀羅尼經錦被

Dharani Sutra Coverlet

Qing dynasty, Guangxu period (1875–1908)
Brocade with silk and metallic threads

H. 191.8 cm (75.5 in.), W. 132 cm (51.97 in.)
Virginia Museum of Fine Arts, Gift of Brigadier General John S. Letcher, 81.42

In the geometric composition of a mandala, this single-layer coverlet is woven with the secret texts of Buddhas, bodhisattvas, and protective deities drawn from the *Dharani Sutra*. Translated into Chinese in the late seventh century, this sutra was believed to embody a magical power that guided the deceased to enlightenment in the afterlife. The coverlet was placed either on top of the deceased or underneath, where it was layered with other multicolored quilts.

The *Dharani Sutra* coverlet was brought to China in the early Qing dynasty with the development of Tibetan Buddhism. By the eighteenth century, sutra coverlets, which were made of cut-silk (*kesi*) weaving, satin, and brocade in Suzhou and Jiangning (Nanjing), were designated exclusively for the imperial family and later given as gifts to high-ranking officials. As recorded in the *Draft History of Qing Dynasty*, Dong Gao (1740–1818), a ritual official and the son of Dong Bangda (1699–1769), received a sutra coverlet from Emperor Qianlong when Dong Gao's mother died in 1797.[1]

The design of this quilt from the Virginia Museum of Fine Arts is similar to an example in the Palace Museum collection.[2] Here, the central design is a Tibetan-style stupa in the shape of an alms bowl with a nine-disc steeple, surmounted by a moon-and-sun finial. The stupa, surrounded by hanging garlands and auspicious symbols, is enclosed by borders of thirty-six lotus roundels, *vajras,* and leafy scrolls. The sutra texts and sacred mantras woven in Sanskrit are contained in the stupa and roundels. Marked in Chinese are the positions of the tomb owner's shoulders, navel, private parts, knees, and feet.

The inscription in the lower square, also in Chinese, reveals the coverlet's function, which was to expel evil spirits along the path to Western Paradise in the afterlife or to guide sinners toward rebirth in the present world. LJ

1. Zhao 1927, chap. 340.
2. Zhang and Yang 1992, 28.

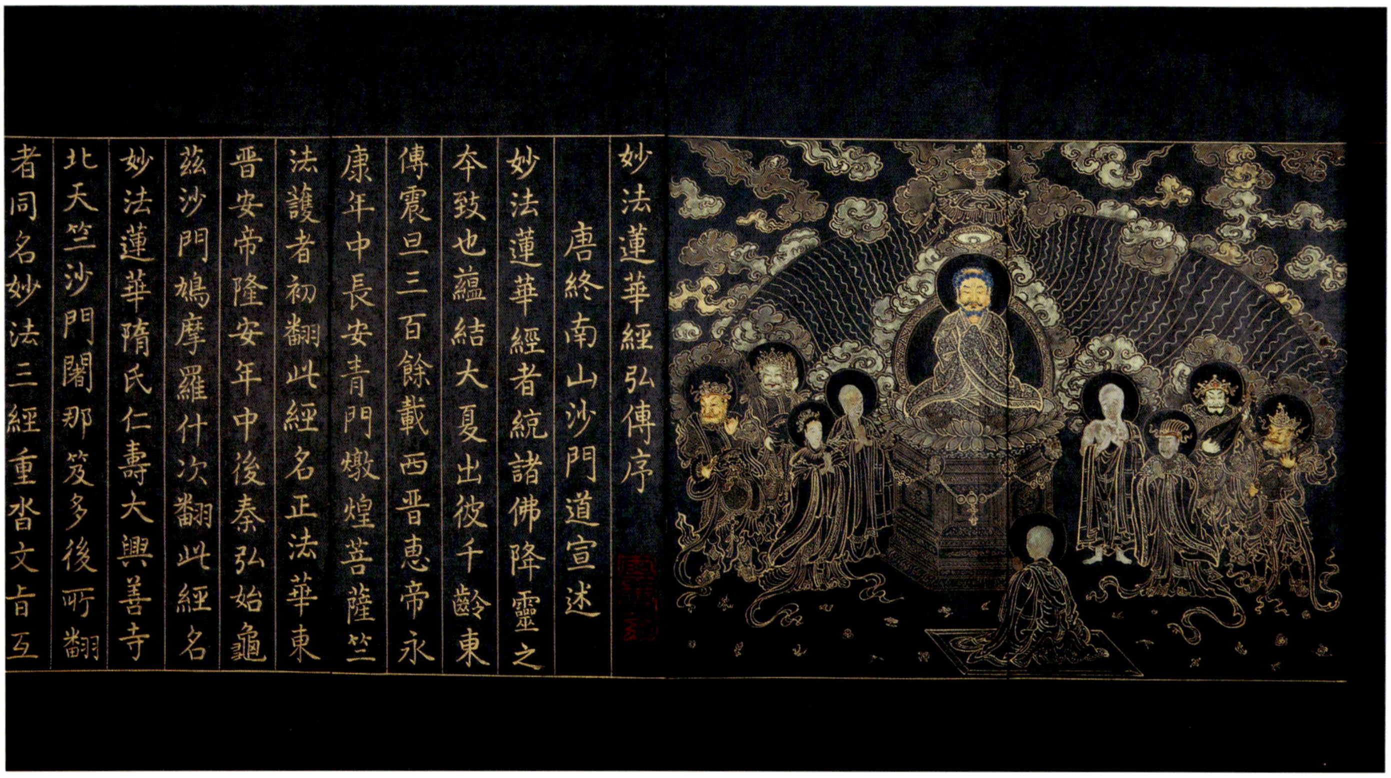

125 清乾隆十四年 御書《妙法蓮花經》泥金寫本

Lotus Sutra, dated 1749
Written by Emperor Qianlong (1711–1799)
Qing dynasty, Qianlong period (1736–95)
Three volumes of seven-volume series of folded manuscript; gold and silver dust on indigo paper
H. 21 cm (8.27 in.), W. 9.4 cm (3.7 in.)
Palace Museum, Shu.9484-1-1/7 and Shu.2125-2131

The Sutra of the Lotus Blossom of the Marvelous Dharma, commonly known as *Lotus Sutra,* is one of the earliest Mahayana scriptures, written around the first century BC. The *Lotus Sutra* recounts Shakyamuni Buddha's preaching to his followers toward the end of his life. Kumarajiva (Kuchean, 334–413), a great Buddhist scholar, translated the text from Sanskrit to Chinese around 402 AD. Once published, the sutra became one of the most popular and influential Buddhist scriptures in China and beyond, inspiring the formation of Chan Buddhism, the Zhenyan school, and the Tibetan mantra of six syllables.

The practice of copying sutras befits an act of devotion in Buddhism. Hongli, Emperor Qianlong (1736–95), a devoted Buddhist, copied a large amount of Buddhist sutras in his life, and *Lotus Sutra* was one of his favorites.

Handwritten by Emperor Qianlong, this series contains seven volumes and twenty-eight chapters, with a preface on the history of *Lotus Sutra.* Written in gold dust on indigo paper, the first volume of the sutra started on April 8, 1749, Buddha's birthday, and was completed on April 27. The last volume, also dated, was completed on August 25, 1749. Painted in gold and silver on the front and back of each book is a set of Buddhist symbols, known as the Eight Treasures, consisting of a parasol, fish, vase, lotus, conch, knot, banner, and wheel. A Song-styled brocade covers the sutra with designs of dragons and the longevity characters of *wan* and *shou.* LJ

Inscriptions, volume numbers inscribed on each cover with title script written in gold: 御書妙法蓮華經 *Yushu Miaofa lianhua jing* (Imperial Calligraphy of Lotus Sutra)

Seals: 忘機心宇曠 *Wangji xinyu kuang*; 筆花春雨 *Bihua chunyu* on Vol. 1; 雲霞思 *Yunxia si* on Preface

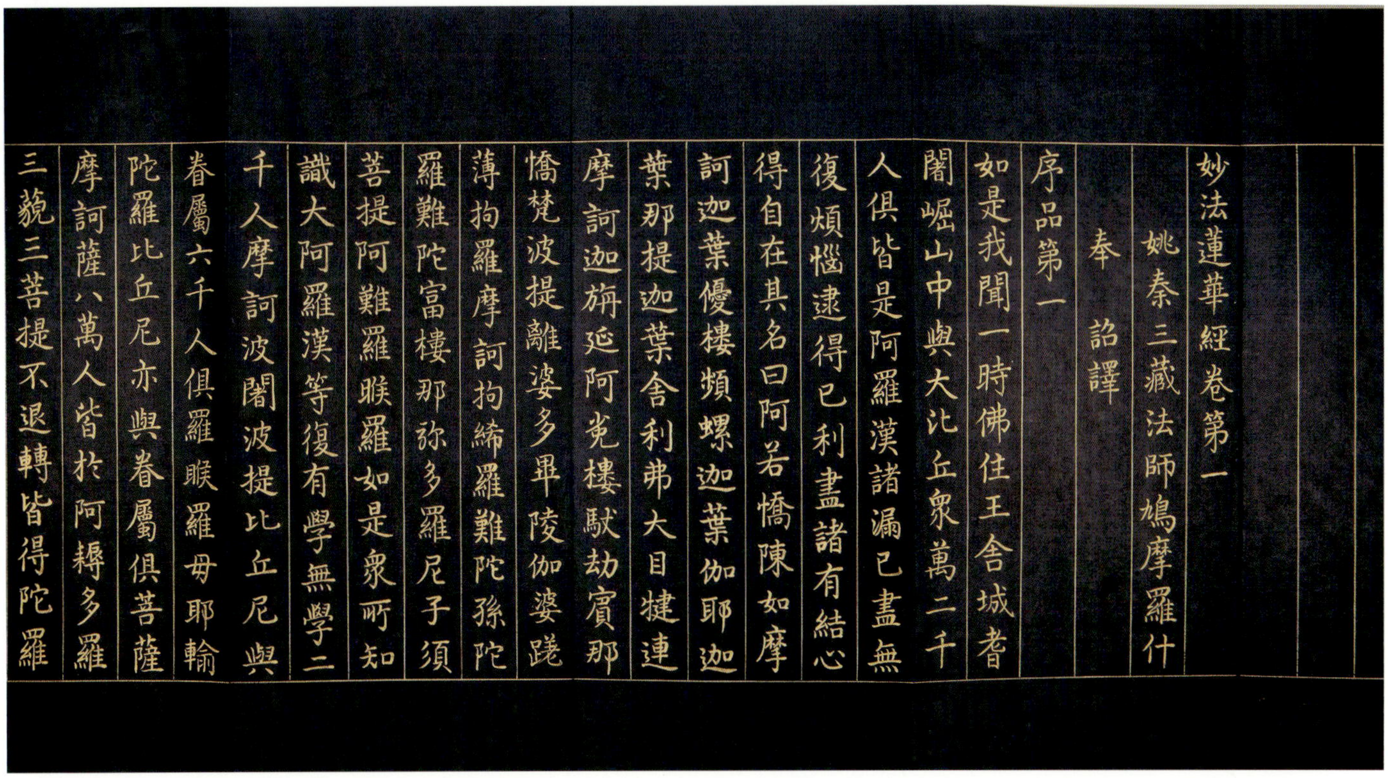
妙法蓮華經卷第一
姚秦三藏法師鳩摩羅什
奉 詔譯
序品第一
如是我聞一時佛住王舍城耆
闍崛山中與大比丘衆萬二千
人俱皆是阿羅漢諸漏已盡無
復煩惱逮得已利盡諸有結心
得自在其名曰阿若憍陳如摩
訶迦葉優樓頻螺迦葉伽耶迦
葉那提迦葉舍利弗大目揵連
摩訶迦旃延阿㝹樓馱劫賓那
憍梵波提離婆多畢陵伽婆蹉
薄拘羅摩訶拘絺羅難陀孫陀
羅難陀富樓那彌多羅尼子須
菩提阿難羅睺羅如是衆所知
識大阿羅漢等復有學無學二
千人摩訶波闍波提比丘尼與
眷屬六千人俱羅睺羅母耶輸
陀羅比丘尼亦與眷屬俱菩薩
摩訶薩八萬人皆於阿耨多羅
三藐三菩提不退轉皆得陀羅

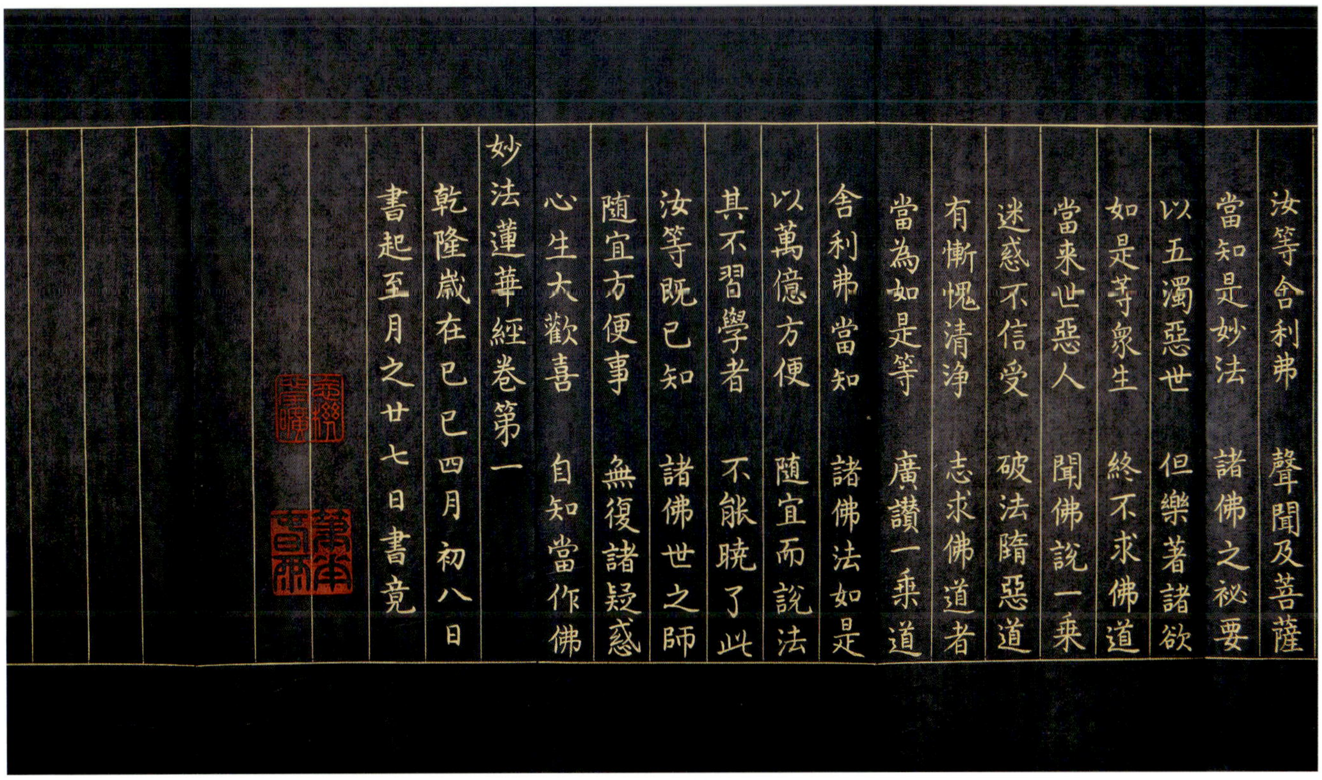
汝等舍利弗 聲聞及菩薩
當知是妙法 諸佛之祕要
以五濁惡世 但樂著諸欲
如是等衆生 終不求佛道
當來世惡人 聞佛說一乘
迷惑不信受 破法墮惡道
有慚愧清淨 志求佛道者
當為如是等 廣讚一乘道
舍利弗當知 諸佛法如是
以萬億方便 隨宜而說法
其不習學者 不能曉了此
汝等既已知 諸佛世之師
隨宜方便事 無復諸疑惑
心生大歡喜 自知當作佛
妙法蓮華經卷第一
乾隆歲在己巳四月初八日
書起至月之廿七日書竟

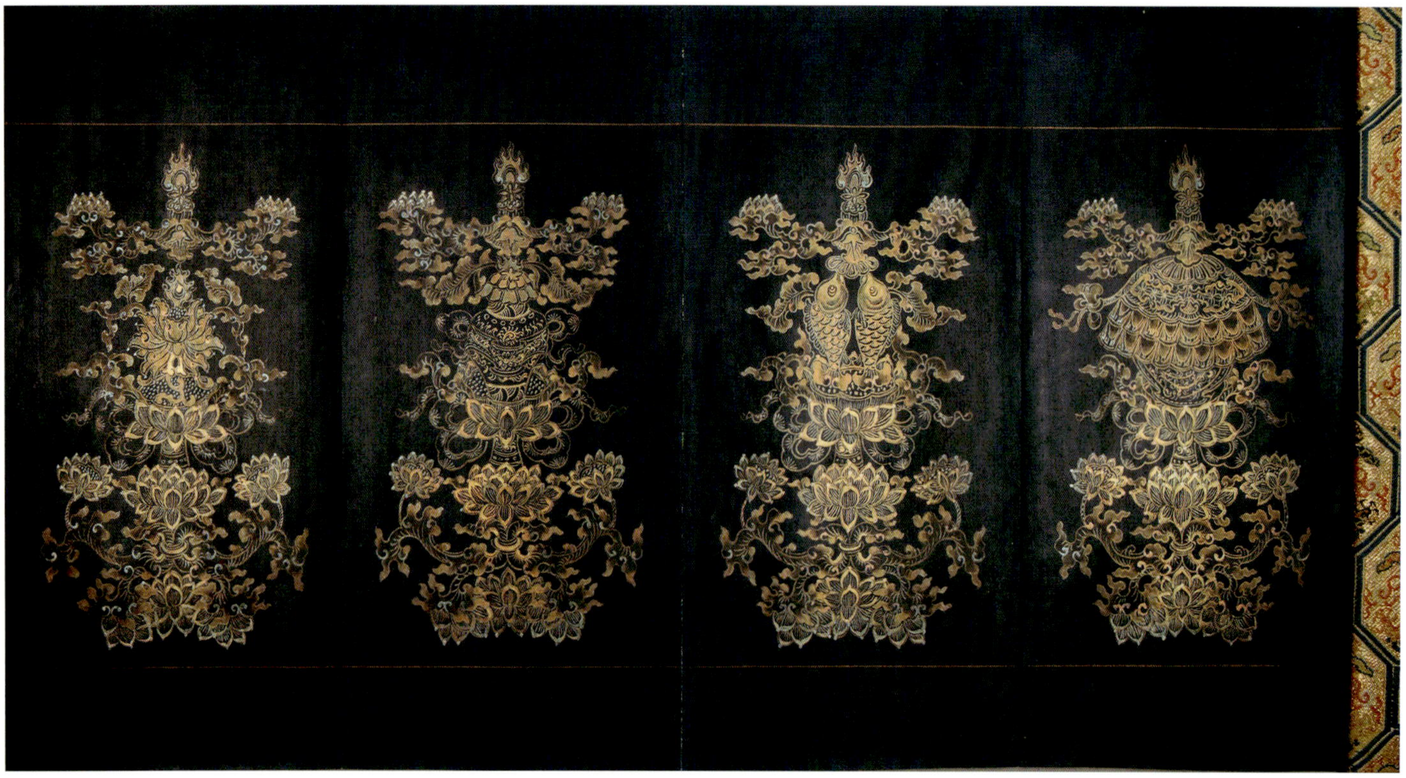

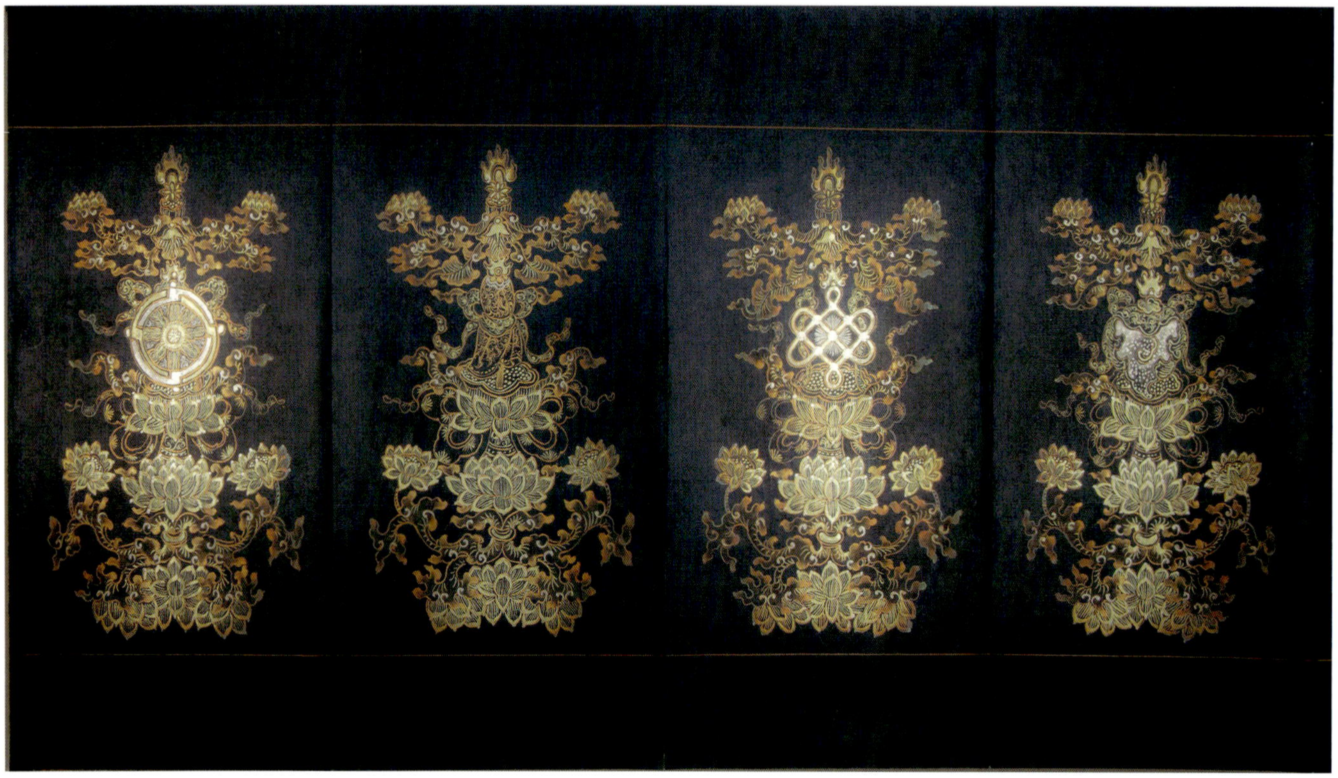

126 明宣德 藍色棋子地填花紋錦夾袱

Wrapper with Geometric and Floral Designs

Ming dynasty, Xuande period (1426–35)

Brocaded tabby, silk tabby lining

L. 40.5 cm (15.94 in.), W. 40.5 cm (16 in.)

Palace Museum, Gu.62549

Made of plain yellow silk tabby lining and brocaded satin, this wrapper may have been used to cover sutras or other religious objects for transferring and storing. The wrapper here exhibits a unique design with its golden colors, geometric shapes, and loose composition.

The fabric and design are derived from a type of silk brocade, known as Song brocade, created during the Song dynasty (960–1279) in Suzhou, one of the three ancient silk-production centers in China, along with the Yun brocade of Nanjing and the Shu brocade of Sichuan. The Ming court established the imperial weaving office in Suzhou to ensure quality and innovative brocades. When making fabric like this, craftsmen undertook more than twenty procedures, from silk reeling to dyeing and weaving. The brocaded patterns were woven in a structure of warps interspersed with wefts. Multiple shuttles were used to create the background pattern and the designs on the top. LJ

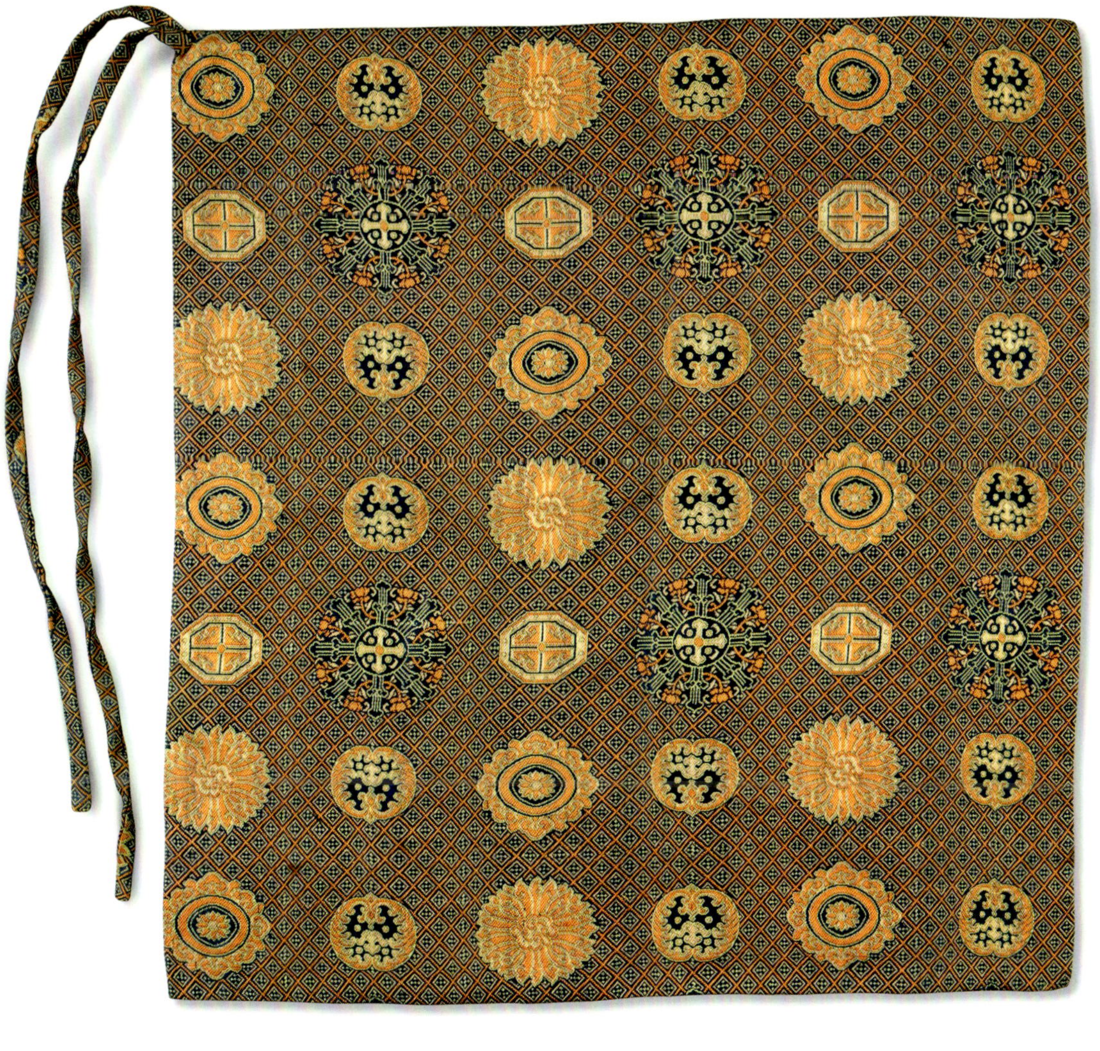

127 清乾隆 銅鍍金嵌料石鏤空塔

Stupa Model

Qing dynasty, Qianlong period (1736–95)
Gilt copper, nephrite, glass, lapis lazuli, quartz, precious stones, *zitan* wood

Pagoda: H. 43.8 cm (17.24 in.), W. and L. 17 cm (6.69 in.)
Stand: H. 5.6 cm (2.2 in.), W. 18.8 cm (7.4 in.)
Palace Museum, Gu.185385

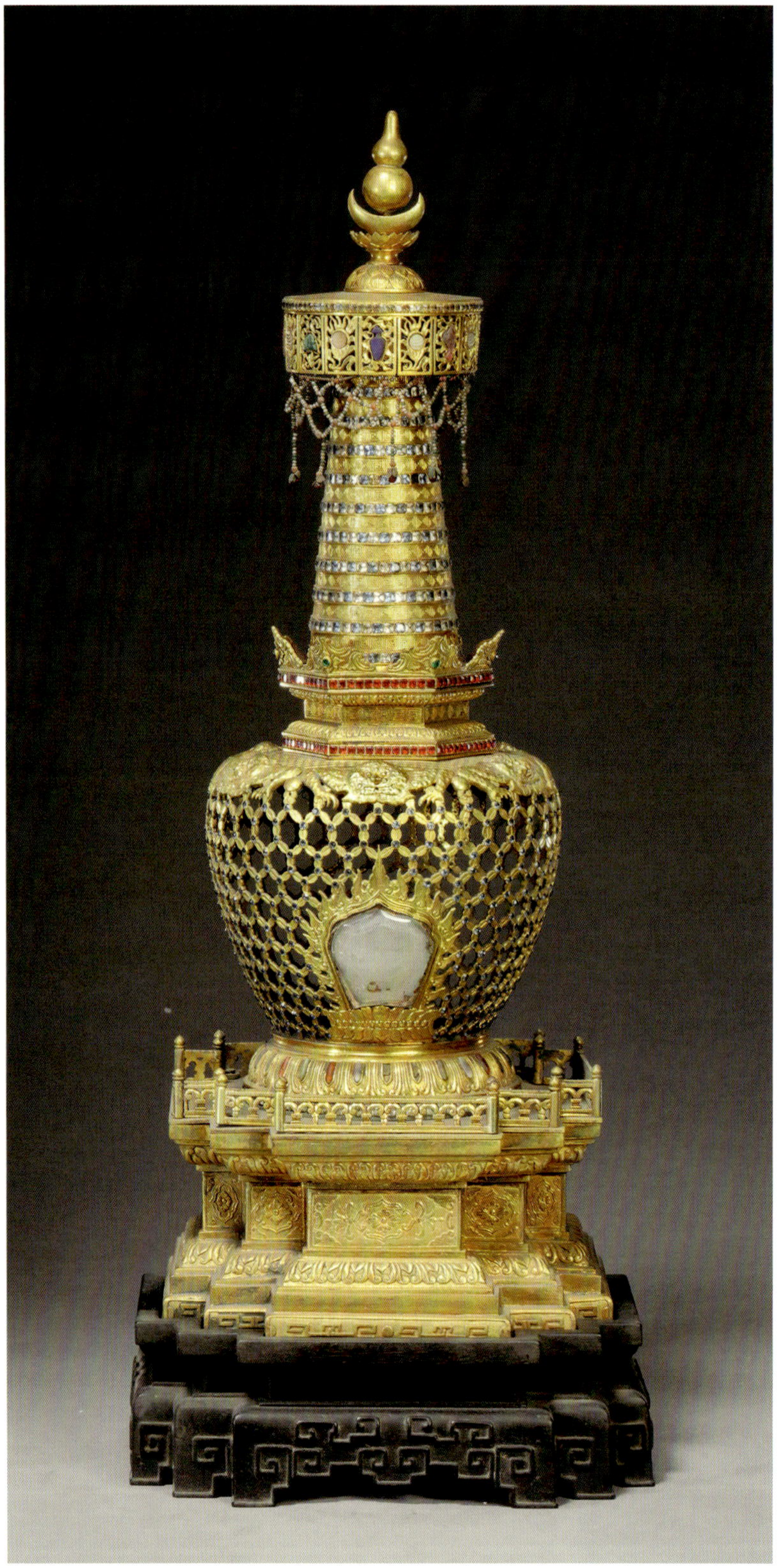

Originally a funeral mound in India, the stupa became a holy place for holding Shakyamuni Buddha's reliquary in the sixth–fifth centuries BC. With the spread of Buddhism, the stupa evolved as a sacred monument for housing Buddhist statues, paintings, sutras, and ritual objects, as well as the cremated remains of high-ranking monks. The Tibetan stupa was introduced to China in the thirteenth century when the Yuan rulers adopted Tibetan Buddhism as the state religion. Thereafter, miniature stupas were built as reliquaries and offerings.

This votive stupa consists of four sections: a squared pedestal base, an inverted-dome body, a tiered pinnacle, and a parasol surmounted by a moon-and-sun finial. The multicolor precious-stone inlay symbolizes the five elements and their relationships to enlightenment. The yellow base stands for earth, the blue dome for water, the red reliquary chamber for fire, the green parasol for air, and the plain moon-and-sun finial for space. The highlights of decorative details include the openwork overlay on the body, jade inlay over the front niche, and the beaded chains hanging from the parasol. The elaborate design represents the remarkable craftsmanship of the imperial workshop during the Qianlong period. LJ

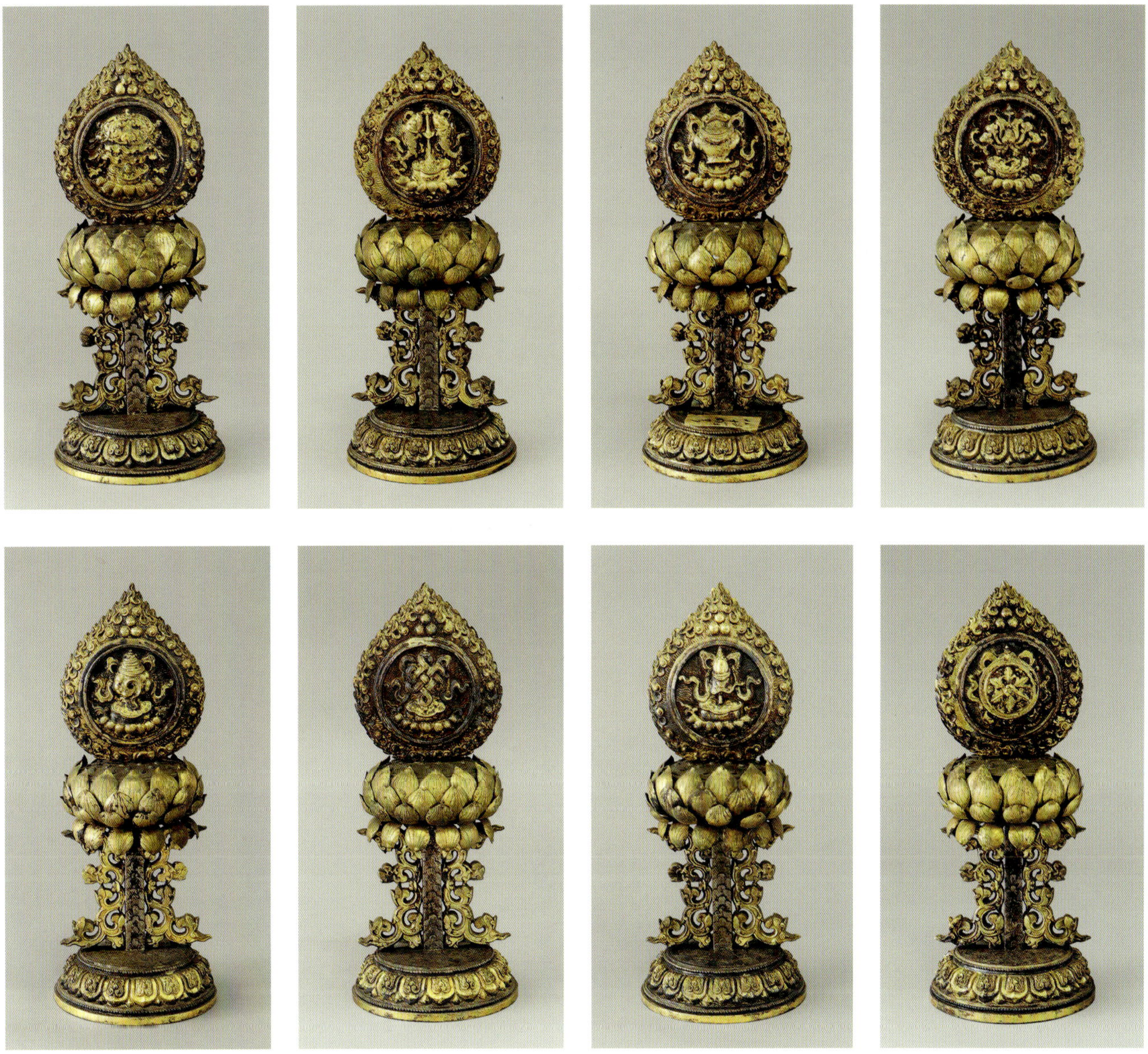

128 清乾隆 銅鍍金八寶供器

Eight Offering Treasures

Qing dynasty, Qianlong period (1736–95)

Gilt bronze

H. 25.5 cm (10 in.), Base Dia. 10.5 cm (4.13 in.)
Palace Museum, Gu.184599.1-8

According to legend, Shakyamuni Buddha received eight precious objects when he attained enlightenment under a Bodhi tree. These objects, also known as the Eight Treasures, later became Buddhist icons, teaching tools, and auspicious symbols. The Eight Treasures are placed on an altar table in front of paintings or sculptures of Buddhist deities.

Made for the Qing imperial court, each offering in this set of eight sits on a lotus stand. The offerings (from left to right) feature the following symbols: the parasol, which represents freedom; the fish, a symbol of vitality; the vase, a sign of wisdom; the lotus, as purity in the mortal world; the conch, a symbol of Buddha's sacred speech; the knot, which represents eternity; the canopy, a symbol of protection; and the wheel, which represents everlasting Buddhist law. LJ

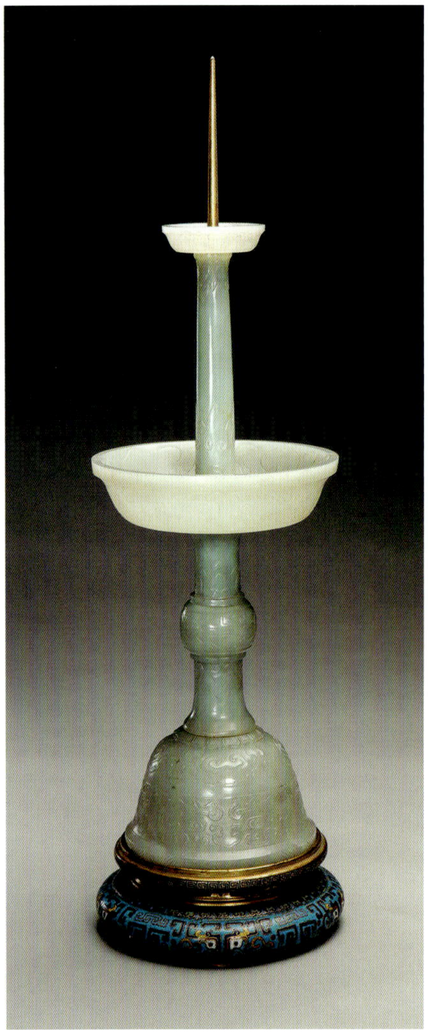
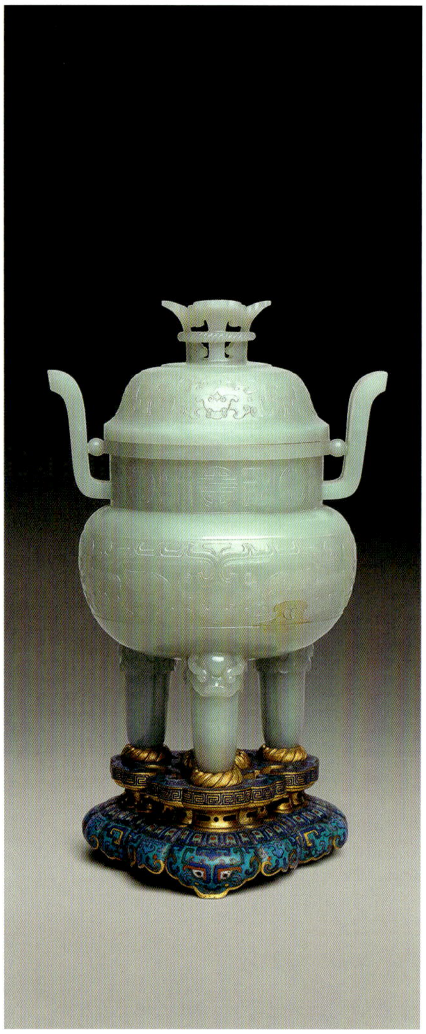
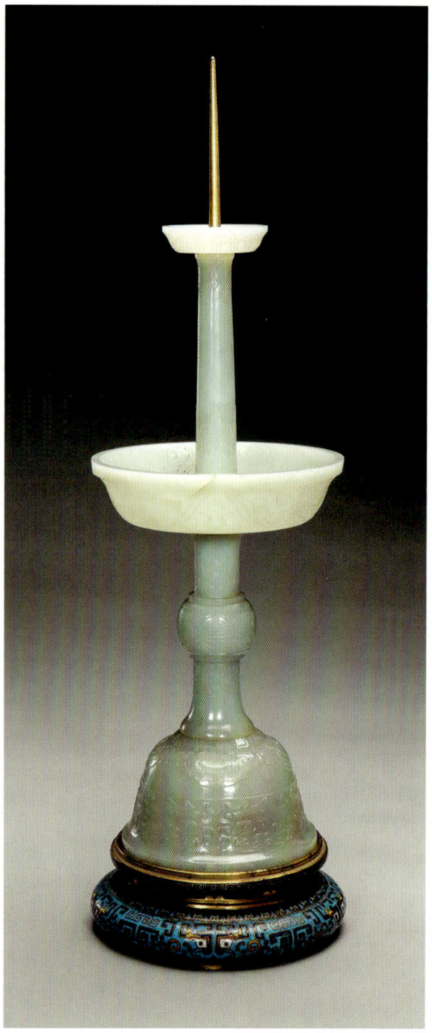

129 清乾隆 慈寧宮青玉雙耳獸面紋三足蓋爐 壽字勾雲紋燭台

Three Altarpieces: Incense Burner and Two Candle Stands

Qing dynasty, Qianlong period (1736–95)

Nephrite, cloisonné, copper sticks

Candlestands: H. 54 cm (21.26 in.), Dia. 16.2 cm (6.38 in.)
Burner: H. 25.3 cm (9.96 in.), Belly Dia. 19.5 cm (6.1 in.); Overall: H. 31 cm (12.2 in.)
Palace Museum, Gu.93897-1/5, Gu.93897-2/6, and Gu.93897-3/7

As part of a set of five offerings, this burner and pair of candle stands were originally from the Cining Palace, a residential area built for widowed empresses in the Ming and Qing dynasties (cat. no. 23). These altarpieces, which are from a palace chapel, probably belonged to Empress Dowager Chongqing (1693–1777), Qianlong's mother. The longevity character (*shou*) incised on the vessels suggests that the set might have been a birthday gift.

In the shape of a tripod, the burner is carved with mythological beasts, and the swastika and shou symbols appear on the neck. Made of two-color Hetian jade, each candle stand has six parts: a base, two plates, two stems, and a metal candle stick. The low-relief designs include lotus petals, clouds shaped like *ruyi* mushrooms, and the longevity character. The lid features stylized bats on the surface, and the knob has an openwork design of cloud motifs. The burner's legs are carved with animal heads in high relief. All three objects are supported by cloisonné stands. The consistency of the altarpieces and their bases indicates that the entire design came from the same craftsman. The translucent jade, its soft color, and the contrast between the jade and enamels represent eighteenth-century imperial craftsmanship at its best. LJ

130 明萬曆款 掐絲琺瑯八寶紋長方熏爐

Incense Burner with Symbols of Eight Treasures

Ming dynasty, Wanli period (1573–1620)

Copper alloy with gilding and polychrome enamel inlays

Cloisonné; enamels on copper

H. 8.1 cm (3.22 in.), L. 26.8 cm (10.6 in.), W. 14.4 cm (5.7 in.)

Palace Museum, Gu.116826

This excellent example of sixteenth-century cloisonné was made under the supervision of the Directorate of Imperial Accoutrements (Yuyongjian) in the Ming court. Its imperial cloisonné products are distinctive for their unique shapes, light colors, and religious functions. Here, the symbols of the Eight Treasures (*babao*) are intertwined with lotus sprays against a white background. Pierced swastika (*wan*) motifs, a symbol of Buddha's virtues and eternal blessings, cover the lid.

A devoted Daoist, Emperor Wanli promoted religious activities. He ordered the imperial publisher to print and distribute Buddhist and Daoist scriptures to temples across the country in the late sixteenth century. He and his mother, Empress Dowager Xiaoding (d. 1614), were dedicated temple patrons in Beijing. When Wanli died in 1620, his coffin was covered with a Daoist robe, and in the coffin he held a rosary, a ritual object used during meditation. LJ

Mark, located on underside, written in red enamel: 大明萬曆年造 (Made in the Wanli reign of the Great Ming dynasty)

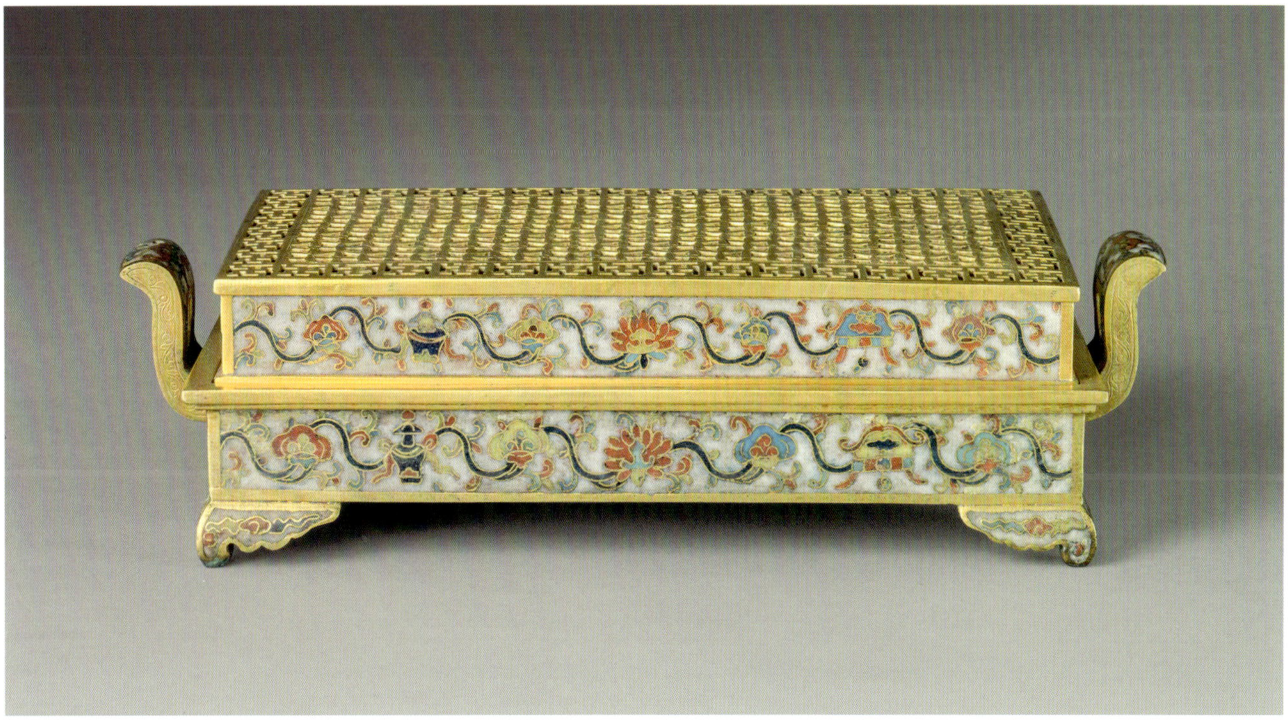

131 清 銅鎏金侍神像 雷霆行令使者張天君
Heavenly Lord Zhang, Thunder Deity
Qing dynasty, Kangxi period (1662–1722)
Gilt bronze, pigment
Overall H. 59 cm (23.25 in.), Base L. 29 cm (11.4 in.), W. 20 cm (7.9 in.)
Palace Museum, Gu.204793

132 清 銅鎏金九天尊像
Supreme Heavenly Lord, Thunder Deity
Qing dynasty, Kangxi period (1662–1722)
Gilt bronze, pigment
H. 64 cm (25.25 in.)
Palace Museum, Gu.204792

133 清 銅鎏金雷神侍神像 上清神烈陽雷苟元帥
Marshal Gou, Thunder Deity
Qing dynasty, Kangxi period (1662–1722)
Gilt bronze, pigment
Overall H. 56 cm (22 in.), Base L. 29 cm (11.4 in.), W. 20 cm (7.9 in.)
Palace Museum, Gu.204794

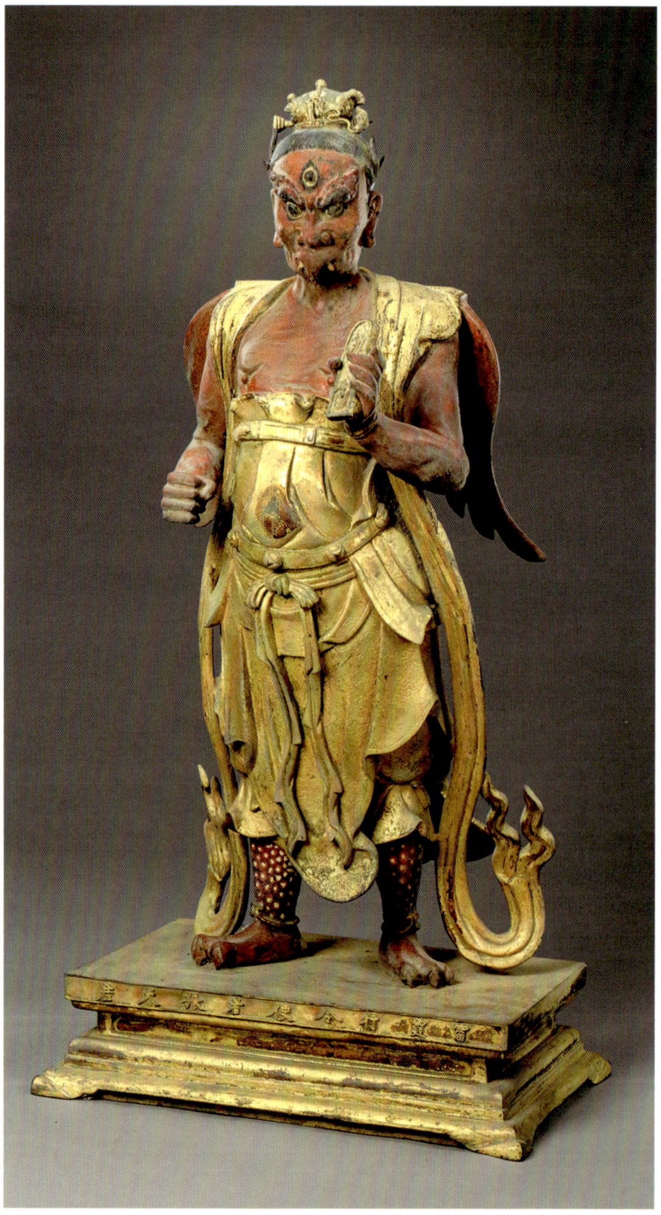

In Daoist legend, the gods of thunder possess a great force that could strike in the darkness, bring forth rain, and convert chaos into order. These three thunder deities were on display along with five others in the Hall of Thunder Deities in the Eastern Side Hall of a Daoist temple in the palace.[1] The central figure, the Supreme Heavenly Lord (cat. no. 132) and commander of the thunder division, is dressed in elaborate golden armor with a monster-mask buckle. His identity is revealed by his white face, three eyes, and bare feet. He is holding a sword in his right hand and gesturing with the other. The Supreme Heavenly Lord is flanked by two deities under his command. Heavenly Lord Zhang (cat. no. 131) resembles a birdlike creature with a beak, two wings, and talon-like feet, holding a tablet in his left hand and an ax, now lost, in the other. Marshal Gou (cat. no. 133) is dressed in armor, holding a chisel in his left hand and a hammer, now lost, in the right. Each gaurdian deity stands on a wooden base with his name and title carved in the front.

The Daoist temple known as the Hall of Heavenly Sky (Tianqiongbaodian) is located in the northeastern side of the palace. It is unclear when it was built. The court archives did not record any activities in the temple until 1728.[2] The condition of the statues suggests they might have been installed in the Kangxi period (1662–1722). Moreover, the features of the deities and the design of the stands resemble seventeenth-century stylistic expressions. LJ

1. Wang 2011a, 443–44.
2. Ibid., 436.

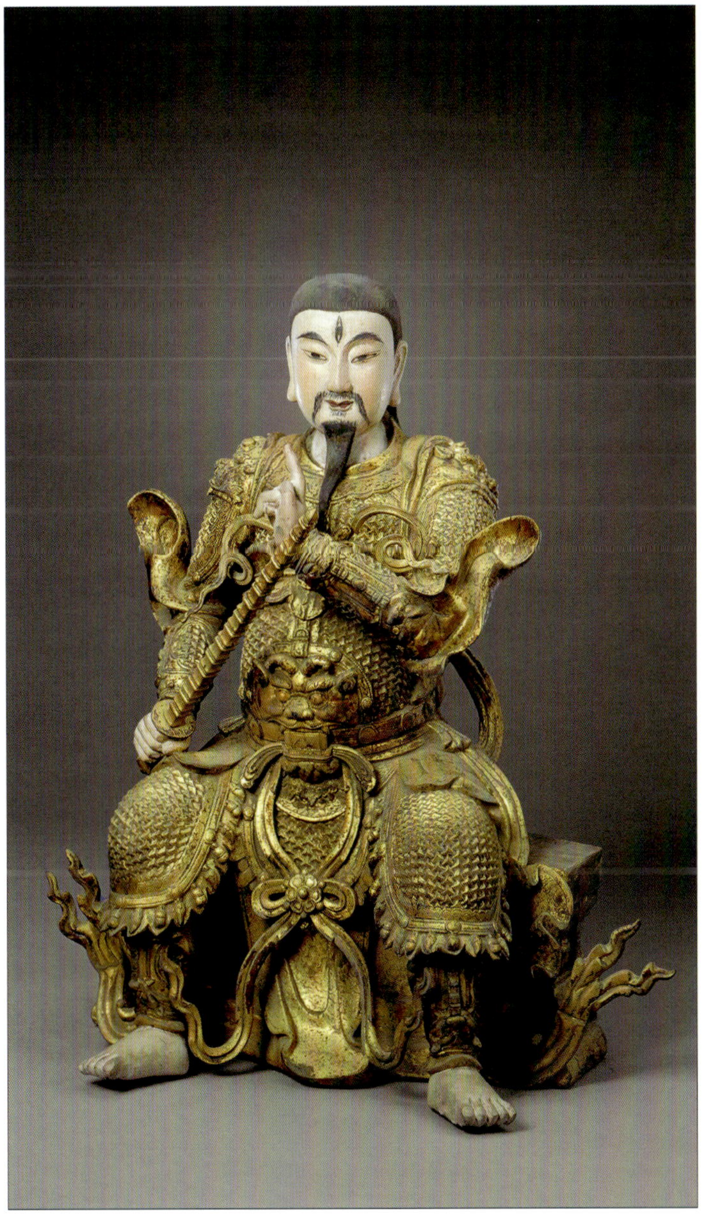

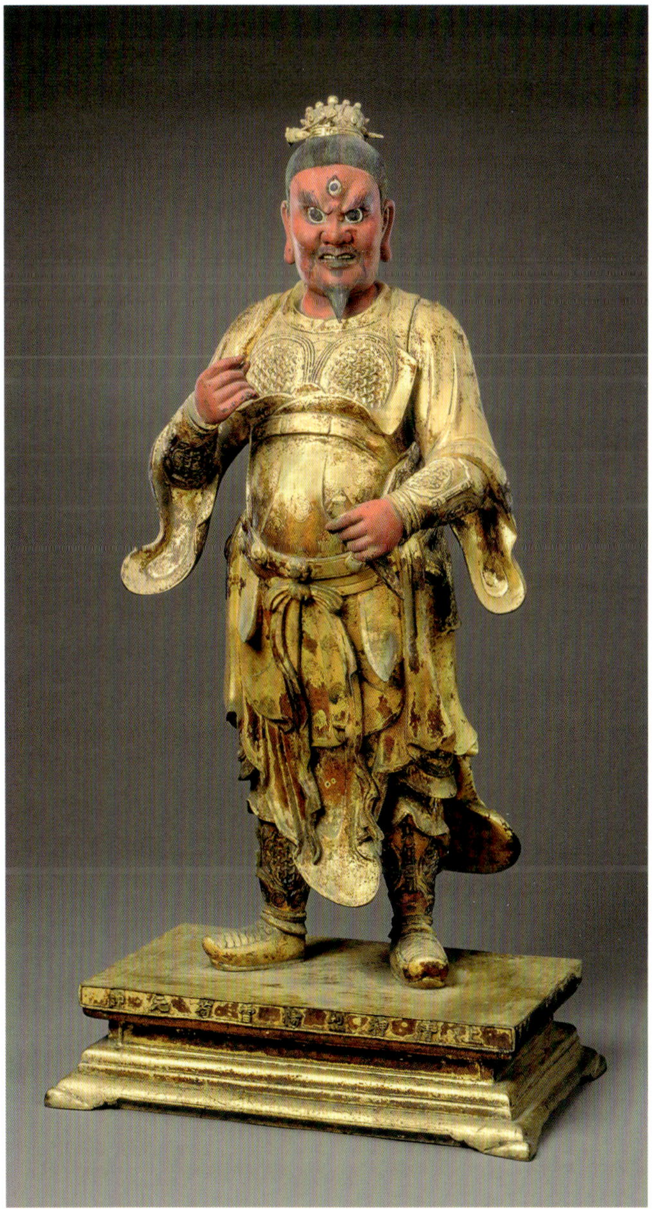

134 清道光 欽安殿陳設檔 道光二十年內務府抄本 紙本

Display Inventory of the Hall of Imperial Peace (Qin'andian), dated 1840

Qing dynasty, Daoguang period (1821–50)

One volume of bound manuscript; ink on paper

L. 36 cm (14.13 in.), W. 23.5 cm (9.25 in.)

Palace Museum, Shu.10493

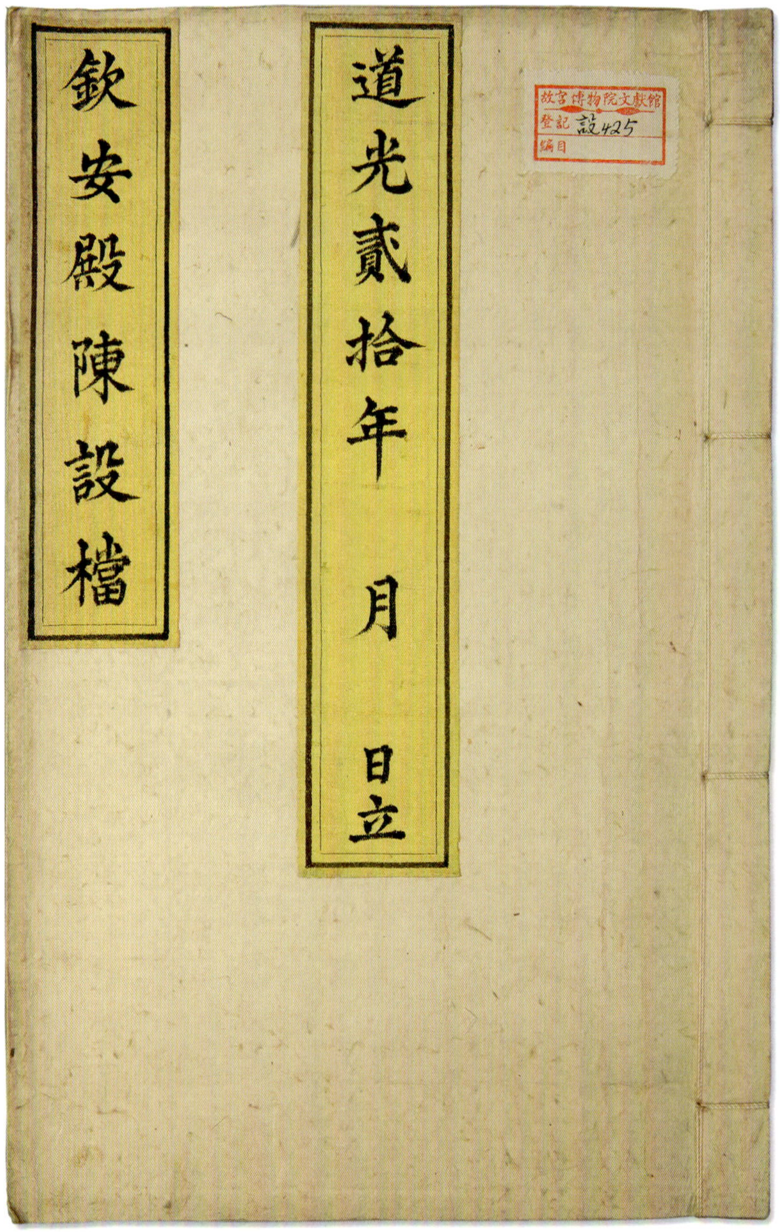

Beginning during the Kangxi period (1662–1722), the Qing court documented the inventories of imperial property. This bound manuscript is one of seven inventories taken of the Qin'andian, the most important Daoist shrine in the Forbidden City. The inventory was conducted by the Imperial Household Department (Neiwufu) in 1840. In three chapters totaling twenty-one pages, the book registers objects by name, quantity, and location in the temple. As a primary source, the inventory aids in the study of Daoist activities in the palace and the arrangement of objects in a manner true to their original display.

Located on the central axis of the Forbidden City, the Hall of Imperial Peace (Qin'andian) was built in 1415 by Emperor Yongle (r. 1403–24), who considered himself the reincarnation of Zhenwu, the principal Daoist deity and a protector of the palace from fire. According to this inventory, a gilt-bronze statue of Zhenwu sits on a brocaded cushion in the gold-foil wooden niche on the altar platform; he wears an embroidered dragon robe and a white-jade belt, holding a sword. Other works recorded in the inventory include Daoist statues (26), tablets of deities (3), bronze altarpieces (11 sets, 55 items in total), banners (16), altar tables (8), cloisonné elephants (1 pair), incense stands (14), flower vases (13), offering bowls (118), ritual objects (10), and sutras (26 sets). The platform outside the shrine displays a tablet in a bronze pavilion. An incense table, a tablecloth, Daoist scriptures, and a kneeling cushion appear at the temple entrance. LJ

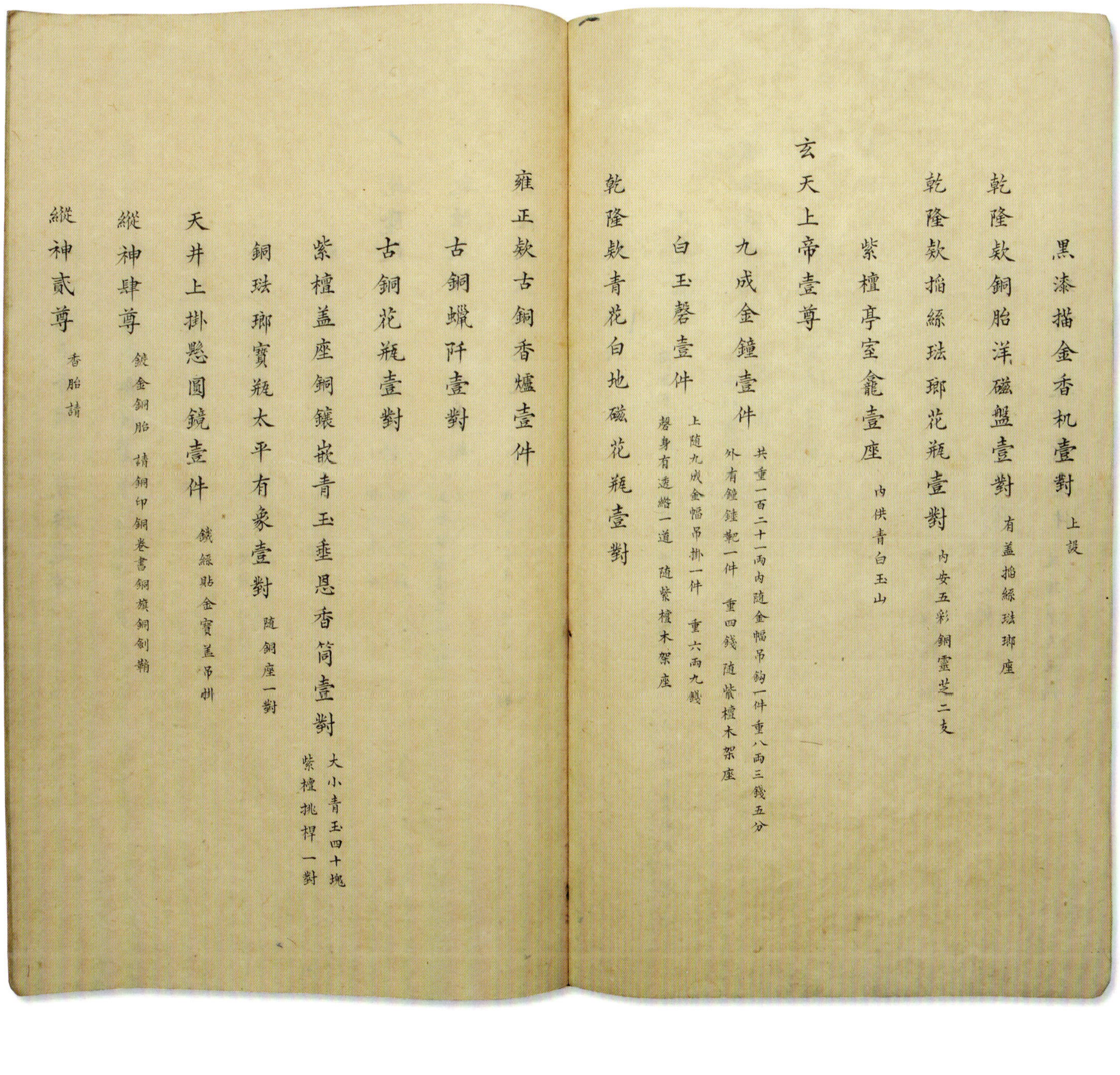

黑漆描金香机壹對 上設

乾隆款銅胎洋磁盤壹對 有盖掐絲琺瑯座

乾隆款掐絲琺瑯花瓶壹對 內安五彩銅靈芝二支

紫檀亭室龕壹座 內供青白玉山

玄天上帝壹尊

九成金鐘壹件 共重一百二十一兩內隨金幡吊鉤一件重八兩三錢五分 外有鐘錘靶一件 重四錢 隨紫檀木架座

白玉磬壹件 上隨九成金幡吊掛一件 重六兩九錢 磬身有透縚一道 隨紫檀木架座

乾隆款青花白地磁花瓶壹對

雍正款古銅香爐壹件

古銅蠟阡壹對

古銅花瓶壹對

紫檀盖座銅鑲嵌青玉垂恩香筒壹對 大小青玉四十塊 紫檀挑桿一對

銅琺瑯寶瓶太平有象壹對 隨銅座一對

天井上掛懸圓鏡壹件 鐵絲貼金寶盖吊掛

縱神肆尊 鍍金銅胎 請銅印銅卷書銅旗銅劍鞘

縱神貳尊 香胎請

Artists

Name		cat. no.
Ai Qimeng (Ignatius Sickeltart)	艾啓蒙	35
Cixi	慈禧	114
Ding Guanpeng	丁觀鵬	108
Ding Yunpeng	丁雲鵬	61
Hongli (Emperor Qianlong)	弘曆	125
Jia Quan	賈全	24
Jin Tingbiao	金廷標	109
Lang Shining (Giuseppe Castiglione)	郎士寧	8, 33, 34, 106
Leng Mei	冷枚	20
Lin Liang	林良	100
Miao Fu	繆辅	99
Qian Weicheng	錢維城	111
Qingkuan	慶寛	25
Wang Hui	王翬	20
Wang Shunchen	王舜臣	59
Wu Bin	吳彬	115
Xie Sui	謝遂	24
Yang Dazhang	楊大章	104
Yang Jin	楊晉	20
Yao Wenhan	姚文瀚	24
Yu Sheng	余省	112
Yu Zhi	余穉	113
Zhang Kai	張愷	60
Zhu Duan	朱端	102
Zou Yigui	鄒一桂	110

Emperors of the Ming and Qing Dynasties

Ming Dynasty

Birth Name	Life Dates	Reign Name	Reign Dates	Posthumous Name	Temple Name
Zhu Yuanzhang 朱元璋	1328–1398	Hongwu 洪武	1368–1398	Gao Di 高帝	Taizu 太祖
Zhu Yun Wen 朱允炆	1377–1402	Jianwen 建文	1399–1402	Hui Di 惠帝	None
Zhu Di 朱棣	1360–1424	Yongle 永樂	1403–1424	Wen Di 文帝	Taizong 太宗 Chengzu 成祖
Zhu Gaozhi 朱高熾	1378–1425	Hongxi 洪熙	1425	Zhao Di 昭帝	Renzong 仁宗
Zhu Zhanji 朱瞻基	1398–1435	Xuande 宣德	1426–1435	Zhang Di 章帝	Xuanzong 宣宗
Zhu Qizhen 朱祁鎮	1427–1464	Zhengtong 正統 Tianshun 天順	1436–1449 1457–1464	Rui Di 睿帝	Yingzong 英宗
Zhu Qiyu 朱祁鈺	1428–1457	Jingtai 景泰	1450–1456	Jing Di 景帝	Daizong 代宗
Zhu Jianshen 朱見深	1447–1487	Chenghua 成化	1465–1487	Chun Di 純帝	Xianzong 憲宗
Zhu Youtang 朱祐樘	1470–1505	Hongzhi 弘治	1488–1505	Jing Di 敬帝	Xiaozong 孝宗
Zhu Houzhao 朱厚照	1491–1521	Zhengde 正德	1506–1521	Yi Di 毅帝	Wuzong 武宗
Zhu Houcong 朱厚熜	1507–1566	Jiajing 嘉靖	1522–1566	Su Di 肅帝	Shizong 世宗
Zhu Zaihou 朱載垕	1537–1572	Longqing 隆慶	1567–1572	Zhuang Di 莊帝	Muzong 穆宗
Zhu Yizhun 朱翊鈞	1563–1620	Wanli 萬曆	1573–1620	Xian Di 顯帝	Shenzong 神宗
Zhu Changle 朱常洛	1582–1620	Taichang 泰昌	1620	Zhen Di 貞帝	Guangzong 光宗
Zhu Youjiao 朱由校	1605–1627	Tianqi 天啟	1621–1627	Zhe Di 悊帝	Xizong 熹宗
Zhu Youjian 朱由檢	1611–1644	Chongzhen 崇禎	1628–1644	Zhuang Lie Min Di 莊烈愍帝	Sizong 思宗

Qing Dynasty

Birth Name	Life Dates	Reign Name	Reign Dates	Posthumous Name	Temple Name
Nurhaci 努爾哈赤	1559–1626	Tianming 天命	1616–1626	Gao Di 高帝	Taizu 太祖
Huangtaiji 皇太極	1592–1643	Tiancong 天聰 Chongde 崇德	1627–1636 1636–1643	Wen Di 文帝	Taizong 太宗
Fulin 福臨	1638–1661	Shunzhi 順治	1644–1661	Zhang Di 章帝	Shizu 世祖
Xuanye 玄燁	1654–1722	Kangxi 康熙	1662–1722	Ren Di 仁帝	Shengzu 聖祖
Yinzhen 胤禛	1678–1735	Yongzheng 雍正	1723–1735	Xian Di 憲帝	Shizong 世宗
Hongli 弘曆	1711–1799	Qianlong 乾隆	1736–1795	Chun Di 純帝	Gaozong 高宗
Yongyan 顒琰	1760–1820	Jiaqing 嘉慶	1796–1820	Rui Di 睿帝	Renzong 仁宗
Minning 旻寧	1782–1850	Daoguang 道光	1821–1850	Cheng Di 成帝	Xuanzong 宣宗
Yichu 奕詝	1831–1861	Xianfeng 咸豐	1851–1861	Xian Di 顯帝	Wenzong 文宗
Zaichun 載淳	1856–1874	Tongzhi 同治	1862–1874	Yi Di 毅帝	Muzong 穆宗
Zaitian 載湉	1871–1908	Guangxu 光緒	1875–1908	Jing Di 景帝	Dezong 德宗
Puyi 溥儀	1906–1967	Xuantong 宣統	1909–1911	None	None

Bibliography

Frequently cited periodicals:

Zijincheng [Forbidden City], published by the Palace Museum, Beijing 紫禁城: 北京故宫博物院.

GGBWYYK, Gugong bowuyuan yuankan [Palace Museum Journal], published by the Palace Museum, Beijing 故宫博物院院刊: 北京故宫博物院.

Arnold 1999
Arnold, Lauren. *Princely Gifts and Papal Treasures: The Franciscan Mission to China and Its Influence on the Art of the West*, 1250–1350. San Francisco: Desiderata Press, 1999.

Berger 2003
Berger, Patricia Ann. *Empire of Emptiness: Buddhist Art and Political Authority in Qing China*. Honolulu: University of Hawaii Press, 2003.

Berliner 2010
Berliner, Nancy. *The Emperor's Private Paradise: Treasures from the Forbidden City*. New Haven, CT: Yale University Press, 2010.

Brown and Chou 1985
Brown, Claudia, and Chou Ju-hsi. *Transcending Turmoil: Painting at the Close of China's Empire, 1796–1911*. Phoenix, AZ: Phoenix Art Museum, 1985.

CCTP: The Complete Collection of the Treasures of the Palace Museum. 60 volumes. Hong Kong: Shangwu yinshu guan; Shanghai: Kexue jishu chubanshe. 故宫博物院文物珍藏品大系,香港商務印書館、上海科學技術出版社.

____1996. Vol. 14, *Paintings by the Court Artists of the Qing Court*, edited by Nie Chongzheng. 清代宮廷繪畫.

____2002. Vol. 47, *Snuff Bottles*, edited by Li Jiufang. 鼻煙壺.

____2003. Vol. 59, *Thangkas—Buddhist Paintings of Tibet*, edited by Wang Jiapeng. 藏傳佛教唐卡.

____2004. Vol. 57, *Treasures of Imperial Court*, edited by Xu Qixian. 宮廷珍寶.

____2005. *Textiles and Embroideries of the Ming and Qing Dynasties*, edited by Zong Zengying. 明清織繡.

____2006. Vol.30, *Costumes and Accessories of the Qing Court*, edited by Zhang Qiong. 清代宮廷服飾.

____2009. *Miscellaneous Enamelled Porcelains and Plain Tricoloured Porcelain*, edited by Li Jiufang. 雜釉彩素三彩.

Chang et al. 2008
Chang, Willow Weilan Hai, Yang Renkai, and David Ake Sensabaugh. *The Last Emperor's Collection: Masterpieces of Painting and Calligraphy from the Liaoning Provincial Museum*. Edited by J. May Lee Barrett. New York: China Institute Gallery, 2008.

Chen 1992
Chen Zongmao. *Zhongguo Chajing* [Classical works on Chinese tea]. Shanghai: Wenhua chubanshe, 1992. 陳宗懋: 中國茶經. 上海文化出版社1992.

Chen 2005
Chen Juanjuan. *Zhongguo zhijiu fushi lunji* [Essays on Chinese textiles and costumes]. Beijing: Zijinzheng chubanshe, 2005. 陳娟娟: 中國織綉服飾論集, 北京紫禁城出版社.

Chen 2006
Chen Pao-chen. "Xinxie zhiping: Qianlong dihou binfei tujuan he xiangguan de tantao" [An analytical reading of portraits of Emperor Qianlong and his consorts]. *Taida Journal of Art History* 21 (2006): 89-134. 陳葆真: 心寫治平—乾隆帝后妃嬪圖卷和相關議題的探討, 國立臺灣大學美術史研究集刊.

Chen 2010a
Chen Pao-chen. "Cong sifu 'sui chao tu' de biaoxian wenti tandao Qianlong huangdi de qinzi guanxi" [From four versions of New Year's depiction of the Qianlong Emperor's relationship with his sons]. *Guoli Taiwan daxue meishu shi yanjiu jikan* [Taida journal of art history], no. 28 (2010): 123–84. 陳葆真: 從四幅「歲朝圖」的表現問題談到乾隆皇帝的親子關係, 國立臺灣大學美術史研究集刊.

Chen 2010b
ChenPao-chen. "Yongzheng yu Qianlong er di han zhuang xingle tu de xushi yu yi han" [The reality and significance of the Xingletu imperial portrait paintings of Yongzheng and Qianlong emperors]. *Gugong xueshu jikan* [National Palace Museum research quarterly] 27, no. 3 (2010): 49-102. 陳葆真: 雍正與乾隆二帝漢裝行樂圖的虛實與意涵, 故宮學術季刊.

Chi 2006
Chi Jo-hsin. "Qianlong shiqide Ruyiguan" [The Hall of Self-Fulfillment in the Ch'ien-lung court]. *Gugong xueshu jikan* [National Palace Museum research quarterly] 23, no. 3 (2006): 127–52. 嵇若昕: 乾隆時期的如意館, 故宮學術季刊.

Clark 1937
Clark, Walter Eugene, and A. Staël-Holstein. *Two Lamaistic Pantheons*. Cambridge, MA: Harvard University Press, 1937.

Collani 2005
Collani, Claudia von. "Journal des voyages." *Variétés Sinologiques*, n.s., 95. Taipei: Ricci Institute, 2005.

Daqing Huidian (1886) 1963
Daqing Huidian [Laws and regulations of the Great Qing Dynasty]. 1816. Photo-offset copy, Taiwan: Yiwen yinshu guan, 1963. 大清會典. 光緒12年編, 臺北1963影印本.

Daqing Shilu 1964
Daqing Shilu (Gaozong) [The veritable records of the Qing dynasty] Chap. 570. Taipei: Taiwan Huawen shuju, 1964. 清高宗實錄. 卷五七零, 臺灣華文書局.

Daqing Tongli (1756) 1782
Daqing Tongli (Qin Ding) [Collected rituals of the Qing dynasty by imperial order]. Edited by Lai Bao et al. 1756. In *Siku Quanshu* [Complete library in four sections], 1782. 來保等編纂: 大清通禮. 四庫全書.

Deng 1974
Deng Chun. "Huaji." In *Huashi Congshu*, edited by Zhongguo shuhua yanjiu ziliaoshe [Resource Office for the Study of Chinese Calligraphy and Painting]. Taipei: Wenshizhe chubanshe, 1974. 鄧椿: 畫繼; 編者中國書畫研究資料社: 畫史叢書, 文史哲出版社.

Evarts 2010
Evarts, Curtis. "Mythical *Nanmu* and Chinese Classical *Nanmu* Furniture." Special edition, *Zijincheng* (2010): 32–45.

Feng (1932) 1995
Feng Chengjun, trans. *Notices biographiques et bibliographiques sur les Jésuites de l'ancienne mission de Chine (1552–1773)*. By Louis Pfister. Shanghai: Imprimerie de la Mission Catholique, 1932. Reprint, Beijing: Zhonghua shuju, 1995. 馮承鈞譯, 費賴之著: 在華耶穌會士列傳. 北京中華書局.

Feng 1996
Feng Nai'en. *Gu boli jianshang yu shoucang* [Ancient glass connoisseurship and collecting]. Changchun: Jilin kexue jishu chubanshe, 1996. 馮乃恩: 古玻璃鑑賞與收藏, 吉林科學技術出版社.

Fu 2005
Fu Dongguang. "Qianlong neifu shuhua zhuanghuang chutan" [A preliminary examination of the art of mounting at the Imperial Household Department in the Qianlong reign]. *GGBWYYK* 118, no. 2 (2005): 111–40. 傅東光: 乾隆内府書畫裝潢初探, 故宮博物院院刊.

Gao (ca. 1688) 1958
Gao Zhao. "Duanxi yanshi kao" [A study of inkstones from Duan River], ca. 1688. In *Meishu congshu* [Series of books on arts]. Photo-offset copy, Taiwan: Yiwen yinshu guan, 1958. 高兆 (1688): 端溪硯石考. 收入黃賓虹、鄧實編: 美術丛書. 藝文印書館影印本1958.

Gao (1591) 1968
Gao Lian. "Yanqing shangjian" [Notes from pure connoisseurship]. Edited by Yang Jialuo. In *Guanshang jilu* [A collection of connoisseurship], 1:242–47. Taipei: Shijie shuju, 1968. 高濂 (1591)：燕清賞箋. 楊家駱編: 觀賞集錄. 上冊, 242–247頁. 臺北世界書局.

GGBWY 1980
GGBWY: Gugong bowuyan [The Palace Museum, Beijing]. *GGBWYYK*. Beijing: Wenwu chubanshe, 1980. 故宮博物院院刊. 北京文物出版社.

GGBWY 2000
GGBWY: Gugong bowuyuan [The Palace Museum, Beijing]. *Qing Renzong yuzhi shi* [The poetry by Renzong Emperor]. 7 vols. Haikou: Hainan chubanshe, 2000. 清仁宗御製詩 七冊. 海口海南出版社.

Harrist and Fong 1999
Harrist, Robert E. Jr., and Wen Fong. *The Embodied Image: Chinese Calligraphy from the John B. Elliot Collection*. Princeton, NJ: Art Museum, Princeton University, in association with Abrams, 1999.

He and Knight 2008
He Li and Michael Knight. *Power and Glory: Court Arts of China's Ming Dynasty*. San Francisco: Asian Art Museum, 2008.

Henss 2008
Henss, Michael. "The Changkya Huthugtu Rölpai Dorje: Grand Lama of China (1717–1786)." *Han-Zang fojiao meishu yanjiu* [Studies of Sino-Tibetan Buddhist art]. Shanghai: Shanghai guji chubanshe, 2008. 漢藏佛教美術研究, 上海古籍出版社.

Hevia 2002
Hevia, James L. *Cherishing Men from Afar: Qing Guest Ritual and the Macartney Embassy of 1793*. Durham, NC: Duke University Press, 2002.

Ho 1967
Ho Ping-ti. "The Significance of the Ch'ing Period in Chinese History." *Journal of Asian Studies* 26, no. 2 (1967): 189–95.

Ho and Bronson 2004
Chuimei Ho and Bennet Bronson. *Splendors of China's Forbidden City: The Glorious Reign of Emperor Qianlong*. Chicago: Field Museum of Natural History, 2004.

Hu and Song 2009
Hu Desheng and Song Yonggi. *Chinese Classical Furniture: The Complete Illustrated Guide for Collectors*. Pleasantville, NY: Reader's Digest, 2009.

IOA 1990
Institute of Archaeology. *Dingling: The Imperial Tomb of the Ming Dynasty*. 2 vols. Beijing: Wenwu chubanshe, 1990. 科學院考古研究所、定陵博物館: 定陵. 北京文物出版社.

Kuhn 2012
Kuhn, Dieter, ed. *Chinese Silks*. New Haven, CT: Yale University Press; Beijing: Foreign Language Press, 2012.

Li n.d.
Li, Yu. "Sanhu duhetu" [Three tigers crossing the river]. Chap. 7 of *Huishi beikao*, edited by Wang Yuxian. *Siku Quanshu* [Complete library in four sections]. 李適: 三虎渡河圖, 王毓賢: 繪事備考, 7卷 四庫全書.

Lin 2009
Lin Lina. "Yongzheng chao zhi xiangrui fuying" [Auspicious omens and signs considered during the Yongzheng period]. Edited by Feng Mingzhu. *Yongzheng: Great Exhibition of Qing Shizong*. Taipei: National Palace Museum, 2009. 林莉娜: 雍正朝之祥瑞符應. 馮明珠主編, 臺北國立故宮博物院: 雍正: 清世宗文物大展.

Lin 2013
Lin Shu. "Meiren yu houfei hu? Shi'er meiren tu wei Yong Qinwangfei xiangkao" [Beauties? Consorts? Research on the twelve beauties who were the consorts of Prince Yong]. *Zijincheng* 220, no. 5 (2013): 124–47. 林姝: "美人歟? 后妃乎? 十二美人圖為雍親王妃像考."紫禁城 220, 2013.

Little and Eichman 2000
Little, Stephen, and Shawn Eichman. *Taoism and the Arts of China*. Chicago: Art Institute of Chicago in association with University of California Press, 2000.

Liu 1963
Liu Fenghan. *Yuanming yuan xingwangshi* [A history of the rise and fall of the Garden of Perfect Brightness]. Taipei: Wenxing shuju, 1963. 劉鳳翰: 圓明園興亡史. 臺北: 文星書局 1963 年.

Liu 1988
Liu, Pinsan. "Huama he langshiningde bajuntu" [Horse painting and Lang Shining's Eight Steeds]. *GGBWYYK*, no. 2 (1988):88–96. 劉品三: 畫馬和郎世寧的八駿圖, 故宮博物院院刊.

Lü 1981
Lü Jian. "Kangxi huafalang suoyi" [A discussion of painted enamels in the Kangxi Era]. *GGBWYYK*, no. 3 (1981): 93–94. 呂堅: 康熙畫琺瑯瑣議. 故宮博物院院刊.

Lu 2008
Lu Xiao. "Wu Bin Mi Wanzhong 'shaoyuantu' chutan" [Primary discussion about the "peony garden painting" by Wu Bin and Mi Wanzhong]. *Zijincheng* 166, no. 11 (2008): 95. 吕曉, 吳彬米万鍾"勺園圖"初探, 紫禁城.

Luo 2005
Luo Wenhua. *Longpao yu jiasha: Qinggong zangchuan fojiao wenhua kaocha* [Dragons and robes: Study of Tibetan Buddhist culture in the Qing palace]. Beijing: Zijincheng chubanshe, 2005. 罗文华:龙袍与袈裟-清宫藏传佛教文化考察, 北京紫禁城出版社.

Mei and Tao 2004
Mei Ninghua and Tao Xincheng, eds. "Jinyinqi" [Gold and sliver wares]. In *Beijing wenwu jingcui daxi* [Gems of Beijing cultural relics series]. Beijing: Beijing chubanshe, 2004. 梅寧華, 陶信成主編: 北京文物精粹大系. 金銀器卷. 北京出版社 2004.

Mingshi (ca. 1739) 1969
Mingshi [A history of the Ming dynasty]. Compiled ca. 1739. In *Ershiwu shi* [The histories of the twenty-five dynasties]. 9 vols. Republished in the photo-offset copy of the Kaiming edition, Taipei: Kaiming shudian, 1969. 明史(乾隆4年), 二十五史, 9冊. 臺北開明書店鑄版1969.

Mu 1985
Mu Yiqin, ed. *Mingdai yuanti zhepai shiliao* [Historical materials pertaining to court-style and Zhe school painting in the Ming dynasty]. Shanghai: Renmin meishu chubanshe, 1985. 穆益勤: 明代院體浙派史料, 上海人民美術出版社.

National Palace Museum 1969
National Palace Museum. *Qing caici* [Enameled ware of the Qing Dynasty]. Vol. 2 of *Gugong zangci* [Porcelain of the National Palace Museum]. Taipei, Hong Kong: Cafa, 1969. 故宮藏瓷: 清彩瓷.

National Palace Museum 1976
National Palace Museum. *Qing Gaozong yuzhi shiwen quanji* [The complete collection of poetry and compositions by Gaozong Emperor]. Photo-offset copy in 10 vols. Taipei: National Palace Museum, 1976. 清高宗御製詩文全集, 影印本十冊.

National Palace Museum 1981
National Palace Museum. *Qingdai danseyou ciqi tezhan* [Catalogue of a special exhibition of Qing-Dynasty monochrome porcelains]. Taipei: National Palace Museum, 1981. 清代單色釉瓷器特展，臺北: 國立故宮博物院.

National Palace Museum 1989
National Palace Museum. *Gugong shuhua lu* [Illustrated catalogue of the paintings of the National Palace Museum]. Taipei: National Palace Museum, 1989. 臺北國立故宮博物院: 故宮書畫圖錄. 臺北國立故宮博物院.

National Palace Museum 1994
National Palace Museum. *Gugong shuhua tulu* [Illustrated catalogue of Chinese painting in the National Palace Museum]. Vol. 13. Taipei: National Palace Museum, 1994. 国立故宫博物院: 故宫书画图录, 国立故宫博物院.

Nie 1984
Nie Chongzheng. "Qinggong waiguo huajia Aiqimeng" [Aiqimong, the foreign painter in the Qing Court]. *Zijincheng*, no. 2 (1984): 47–48. 聶崇正: 清宮外國畫家艾启蒙, 紫禁城.

Nie 1988
Nie Chongzheng. "Zhongxi wenhua jiaoliu zhongde langshining" [Lang Shining in the artistic exchanges of Chinese and Western arts]. *GGBWYYK*, no. 2 (1988): 72-79. 聶崇正: 中西藝術交流中的郎世寧, 故宮博物院院刊.

Nie 2001
Nie Chongzheng. "Qingdai gongting huihua he huajia" [Qing dynasty court paintings and painters]. *Qingdai gongting huihua* [Qing court paintings]. Beijing: Zijincheng chubanshe, 2001. 聶崇正: 清代宮廷繪畫和畫家, 清代宮廷繪畫, 北京故宮博物院, 紫禁城出版社 2001.

Nie 2008
Nie Chongzheng. *Qinggong huihua yu xihua dongjian* [The relationships between Qing paintings and Western influences]. Beijing: Zijincheng chubanshe, 2008. 聶崇正: 清宮繪畫與[西畫東漸], 北京紫禁城出版社.

Nie 2009
Nie Chongzheng. "Yongzheng 23 nian de lang Shining" [Giuseppe Castiglione in the 23rd year of the Yongzheng Reign]. In *Ch'ing Shizong wenwu da zhan.* [Harmony and integrity—The Yongzheng Emperor and his times]. Taipei: National Palace Museum, 2009. 聶崇正: 雍正二十三年的朗世寧. 臺北國立故宮博物院: 雍正, 清世宗文物大展.

Nie 2011a
Nie Chongzheng. "Gongting huajia Ding Guanpeingeng Ding Guanhe xiongdi" [The court painters, Ding Guanpeng and his brother Ding Guanhe]. *GGBWYYK*, no. 8 (2011): 84–93. 聶崇正: 宫廷画家丁观鹏、丁观鹤兄弟, 紫禁城.

Nie 2011b
Nie Chongzheng. "Gongting huajia Jintingbiao zunian jiqizuopin" [Dates and works of the court painter Jin Tingbiao]. *GGBWYYK*, no. 6 (2011): 72–77. 聶崇正: 宫廷画家金廷标卒年及其作品, 故宮博物院院刊.

Nie 2011c
Nie Chongzheng. "Qing gongting huajia yusheng yuzhi xiongdi" [The Qing Court painters, Yu Sheng and Yu Zhi]. *Zijincheng*, no. 10 (2011): 80–89. 聶崇正: 清宮廷畫家余省、余樨兄弟, 紫禁城.

Ouyang and Fong 2008
Zhongshi Ouyang and Wen Fong. *Chinese Calligraphy*. New Haven, CT: Yale University Press, 2008.

Qingshi (1913–27)1971
Qingshi [A history of the Qing dynasty]. 1913-27. Republished by Guofang yanjiu yuan [Academy of National Defense], Taiwan: Chengwen chubanshe, 1971. 清史 9冊. 國防研究院，台灣成文出版社.

Rawski 1998
Rawski, Evelyn S. *The Last Emperors: A Social History of Qing Imperial Institutions*. Berkeley: University of California Press, 1998.

Rawski and Rawson 2005
Rawski, Evelyn S., and Jessica Rawson, eds. *China: The Three Emperors, 1662–1795*. London: Royal Academy of Arts, 2005.

Suishu (ca. 651) 1969
Suishu [A book of the Sui dynasty]. Vol. 3 of *Ershiwu shi* [The histories of twenty-five dynasties]. Compiled ca. 651. Republished in the photo-offset copy of the Kaiming edition, Taipei: Kaiming shudian, 1969. 隋書, 二十五史,3冊. 台灣开明书店铸版本1969.

Sung 1991a
Sung Hou-mei. "Lin Liang and His Eagle Painting." *Archives of Asian Art* 44 (1991): 95–102.

Sung 1991b
Sung Hou-mei. "The Formation of the Ming Painting Academy." *Ming Studies* 29 (Spring 1991).

Sung 1992
Sung Hou-mei. "Chinese Painting of the Early Ming and Its Historical Background." *Proceedings of the International Symposium on Recent Studies of Chinese History*. Department of History, National Taiwan University, August 1992.

Sung 1995a
Sung Hou-mei. "Chinese Fish Painting of the Sung and Yuan Dynasties and Its Symbolic Meanings." *National Palace Museum Bulletin* 30, nos. 1 & 2 (May–June 1995): 1–40.

Sung 1995b
Sung Hou-mei. "Chinese Fish Painting of the Ming Dynasty and Its Symbolic Meanings." *National Palace Museum Bulletin* 30, nos. 3 & 4 (July–August, September–October 1995): 1–40.

Sung 2006
Sung Hou-mei. *The Unknown World of the Ming Court Painters: The Ming Painting Academy*. (日近清光) Taipei: Liberal Arts Press, 2006.

Sung 2009
Sung Hou-mei. *Decoded Messages: The Symbolic Language of Chinese Animal Painting*. New Haven, CT: Yale University Press, 2009.

Tang 1735
Tang Ying. "Taowu xulue beiji" [Epitaph of a summary of ceramics affairs]. Photo-offset copy of the Wenyuange edition of 1784, vol. 517, chap. 135, pp. 712–913. Taipei: Shangwu yinshu guan, 1983–86. 唐英：陶務敘略碑記(又稱:陶成紀事碑). 景印文淵閣四庫全書, 臺北商務印書館 1983–1986.

Tseng 1957
Tseng Hsien-chi. "A Study of the Nine Dragons Scroll." *Archives of the Chinese Art Society of America* 11 (1957): 17–39.

Tung 1997
Tung Wu. *Tales from the Land of Dragons: One Thousand Years of Chinese Painting*. Boston: Museum of Fine Arts, 1997.

Wang and Dong 1793
Wang Jie and Dong Gao. *Midian zhulin xubian* [Pearl forest of the secret hall], 2nd. ed. Beijing: Wuyingdian, 1793. 王傑, 董誥: 秘殿珠林續編, 北京武英殿, 乾隆五十八年.

Wang 1996
Wang Menglou. "Qingdai gongting huihua yishu dangyi." *GGBWYYK*, no. 10 (1996): 161–67. 王梦麐: 清代宫廷绘画艺术当以, 故宮博物院院刊.

Wang 2007
Wang Yaoting. *Shin-shih-jie—Lang Shining yu Ch'ing-gong hisyang-feng* [New visions at the Ch'ing Court: Giuseppe Castiglione and Western-style trends]. Taipei: National Palace Museum, Taipei, 2007. 王耀庭: 新視界 郎世寧與清宮西洋風, 國立故宮博物院.

Wang 2011a
Wang Zilin. *Ming Qing huanggong chenshe* [Installation of the Ming and Qing Palace]. Beijing: Zijincheng chubanshe, 2011. 王子林: 明清皇宮陳設, 北京紫禁城出版社.

Wang 2011b
Wang Zilin. *Zai Qianlong de xingkong xia: Qianlong huangdi de jingsheng shijie* [Under the sky of Qianlong: Emperor Qianlong's spiritual world]. Beijing: Zijincheng chubanshe, 2011. 王子林: 在乾隆的星空下: 乾隆皇帝的精神境界, 北京紫禁城出版社.

Wenwu 1980
Wenwu [Cultural Relics] 5 (1980): 48. 文物. 北京: 文物出版社.

Wenwu 1993
Wenwu [Cultural Relics] 11 (1993): 3, color pl. 1.

Wenwu 1995
Wenwu [Cultural Relics] 10 (1995): 25.

Xin Tangshu (ca.1060) 1969
Xin Tangshu [A new history of the Tang dynasty]. Vol. 5 of *Ershiwu shi* [The histories of twenty-five dynasties]. Republished in the photo-offset copy of the Kaiming edition, Taipei: Kaiming shudian, 1969. 新唐书(约1060年), 二十五史, 5冊. 臺北开明书店铸版本1969.

Yang 1985
Yang Boda. "Qingdai huayuanguan" [A review of the Painting Academy of the Qing dynasty]. *GGBWYYK* 3 (1985): 54–68. 杨伯达: 清代画院观, 故宫博物院院刊.

Yang 1988
Yang Boda. "Langshining zai qing neitingde chuanzuo huodong jiqi yishu chengjiu" [Lang Shining's creative activity and artistic achievements in the Inner Court of the Qing dynasty]. *GGBWYYK*, no. 2 (1988): 3–26. 楊伯達: 郎世寧在清內廷的創作活動及其藝術成就, 故宮博物院院刊.

Yang 1991
Yang Boda. "Qing Qianlongchao huayuan yange" [History of the Painting Academy of the Qianlong period of the Qing dynasty]. *GGBWYYK* 1 (1991): 3–11. 杨伯达: 清乾隆朝画院沿革, 故宫博物院院刊.

Yang 1993
Yang Boda. "Lang Shining zhai Qing neiting de chuangzhuo hedong ji yishu chengjiu" [Lang Shining's activities and art achievements in the Qing court]. *Qingdai yuanhua* [Qing dynasty court paintings]. Beijing, Zijincheng chubanshe, 1993. 楊伯達: 郎世寧在清內廷的創作活動及其藝術成就: 清代院畫, 北京紫禁城出版社.

Yang 1994
Yang Xin. "Qingdai Yongqian shiqi de gongting huihua." In *Yangxin meishu lunwenji* [Collection of essays on art by Yang Xin]. Hong Kong: Shangwu yinshu guan, 1994. 楊新: 楊新美術论文集, 商務印書館.

Yang 2006
Yang Boda. *Yang Boda lunyu* [Yang Boda's discussions on jade]. Beijing: Zijincheng chubanshe, 2006. 楊伯達: 楊伯達論玉. 北京: 紫禁城出版社.

Yang 2010
Yang Wanyu. "Qing Qianlong gongting huashi—Jin Tingbiao huihua yanjiu" [Research on paintings by Jin Tingbiao, the Qing court painter of the Qianlong Era]. *Yiyiwenzi* 14 (2010): 25–88. 楊婉瑜: 清乾隆宮廷畫師—金廷標繪畫研究, 議藝份子.

Yang 2013
Yang Xin. "Yinzhen weiping meiren tu tanmi" [An investigation into the mystery behind the screens of Twelve Beauties]. *Zijincheng* 220, no. 5 (2013): 94–119. 楊新: "胤禛圍屏美人圖探秘," 紫禁城.

Yang and Ma 1992
Yang Guiming and Ma Jixiang. *Zangchuan fojiao gaoseng chuanlue* [Biography of the eminent monks in Tibetan Buddhism]. Xining: Qinghai renmin chubanshe, 1992. 楊貴明, 馬吉祥: 藏傳佛教高僧傳略, 青海人民出版社.

Ye 2002
Ye Gaoshu. *Qingchao qianqi de wenhua zhengce* [Qing dynasty cultural policy]. Taipei: Daoxiang chubanshe, 2002. 葉高樹: 清朝前期的文化政策, 台北稻鄉出版社.

Yinghe et al. 1816
Yinghe et al., comp. *Midian zhulin sanbian* [Pearl forest of the secret hall], 3rd ed. Beijing: Wuyingdian, 1816. 英和等辑: 秘殿珠林三編, 北京武英殿, 嘉庆二十一年.

Yu 1992
Yu Zhouyun. "Zijincheng shijian jinglue yu mingdai jianzhu kao" [Brief discussion on the beginning of construction of the Forbidden City and the study of Ming architecture]. In *Zijincheng Shanji* [Records of the construction of the Forbidden City], edited by Zhu Chuanrong. Beijing: Zijincheng chubanshe, 1992. 于倬云, 紫禁城始建略與明代建築考 朱傳榮編輯, 禁城營繕記, 北京紫禁城出版社.

Yu 1996
Yu, Jianhua. *Zhongguo meishujia renming cidian* [Biographical Dictionary of Chinese Artists]. Shanghai: Shanghai renmin meishu chubanshe, 1996. 俞劍華: 中國美術家人名辭典, 上海人民美術出版社.

Yunlu et al. (1766) 2004
Yunlu et al., eds. *Huangchao liyi tushi* [Illustrated ritual regulations of the Imperial dynasty]. Beijing: Wuyingdian, 1766. Reprint, Yangzhou: Guangling chubanshe, 2004. 允祿等編撰: 皇朝禮器圖式, 北京武英殿, 重印本, 揚州廣陵書社.

ZGDYLSDAG 2005
Zhongguo diyi lishi dang'an guan [The first library of Chinese historical documents]. *Qinggong Neiwufu zaobanchu dang'an zonghui* [The complete documents from the Imperial Household of the Qing Dynasty]. 55 volumes. Beijing: Renmin chubanshe, 2005. 中國第一歷史檔案館、香港中文大學文物館合編：清宮內務府造辦處檔案總匯. 人民出版社.

Zhang 1983
Zhang Linsheng. "Shilun Qinggong huafalang gongyi fazhanshi" [The developmental history of painted-enamel craftsmanship in the Ch'ing Palace]. *GGXSJK* [National Palace Museum Quarterly] 17, no. 3 (Spring 1983): 25–38. 張臨生: 試論清宮畫琺瑯工藝發展史. 故宮學術季刊17卷 3期.

Zhang 1989
Zhang Rong: "Tihong Feilong yanhe" [Carved red lacquer "Flying Dragon" banquet box]. *Zijincheng*, no. 4 (1989): 16. 張榮: 剔紅飛龍宴盒. 紫禁城.

Zhang 1990
Zhang Naiwei, ed. *Qinggong shuwen* [The legacy of the Qing imperial palace]. Beijing: Zijincheng chubanshe, 1990. 張乃煒主編: 清宮述聞. 北京: 紫禁城出版社.

Zhang 2002
Zhang Hongxing. *The Qianlong Emperor: Treasures from the Forbidden City*. Edinburgh: National Museums of Scotland, 2002.

Zhang 2007
Zhang Deshan. *Jiantao guan Tang Ying* [Tang Ying—The supervisor of the imperial ceramics industry]. Beijing: Zhongguo shehui chubanshe, 2007. 張德山: 監陶官唐英. 北京: 中國社會出版社 .

Zhang and Yang 1992
Zhang Fengrong and Yang Huilan. "Minghuang zhijin tuoluoni jinbei" [Imperial yellow dharani sutra quilt]. *Zijincheng* 68, no. 1 (1992): 28–29. 張鳳榮, 楊惠蘭: 明黄織金陀罗尼經被, 紫禁城.

Zhao 2011
Zhao, Minzhu. "Qingdai gongting huihua yiji ditu zhizuo gongyoude zhidushi Beijing." *Nanjing yishu xueyuan xuebao meishu yu sheiji* [Journal of Nanjing Arts Institute, Fine Arts and Design], no. 3 (2011): 91–93. 趙敏住: 清代宮廷繪畫以及地圖制作共有的制度史背景, 南京藝術學院學報: 美術與設計.

Zhao et al. 1927
Zhao Erxun et al., eds. *Qingshi gao* [Draft history of the Qing dynasty]. Beijing: Qingshi guan, 1927. 趙爾巽等編撰: 清史稿.

Zheng 1991
Zheng Minzhong. "Dui liangzhang Jinqin de chubu yanjiu" [A tentative study of two zithers of the Jin period]. *GGBWYYK*, no. 4 (1991) 3–15. 鄭珉中: 對兩張晉琴的初步研究. 故宮博物院院刊.

ZGHHQJ 1997
Zhongguo huihua quanji [Complete selection of Chinese painting]. Vol. 10. Beijing: Wenwu chubanshe, 1997. 中國繪畫全集.

ZGQQQJ 1993
Zhongguo qiqi quanji [The complete works of Chinese lacquerware]. Vol. 6, Qing dynasty, edited by Zhu Jiajin and Xia Gengqi. Fujian: Meishu chubanshe, 1993. 中國漆器全集, 福建美術出版社1993, 6冊: 清. 朱家溍、夏更起主編.

ZGTCQJ 2000
Zhongguo taoci quanji [The complete works of Chinese ceramics]. Vol. 13, pt. 2. *Ming Dynasty*, edited by Wang Liying. Shanghai: Renmin meishu chubanshe, 2000. 中國陶瓷全集, 13冊下: 明代, 王莉英主編. 上海 人民美術出版社.

ZGYQQJ 1993
Zhongguo yuqi quanji [The complete works of Chinese jades]. Vol. 5, *Sui Tang Ming* [Sui, Tang through Ming dynasties], edited by Yang Boda. Shijiazhuang: Hebei meishu chubanshe, 1993. 中國玉器全集, 河北人民美術出版社 5冊: 隋-明. 楊伯達主編.

Zhu 1985
Zhu Jiajin. "Yongzheng nian de jiaju zhizao kao" [A study on furniture manufactory of the Yongzheng Era]. *GGBWYYK* A, no. 3 (1985): 105-21; B, no. 4 (1985): 79–87. 朱家溍: 雍正年的傢具製造考. 故宮博物院院刊.

Zhu 2001
Zhu, Jiaqian. "Qingdai yuanhua mantan." [Random commentary on Qing court painting]. *GGBWYYK*, no. 5 (2001): 1–6. 朱家溍: 清代院畫漫談, 故宮博物院院刊.

Zhu 2013
Zhu Yong. "Ruhua meijuan, sishui liunian, Yongzheng huangdi yu meiren tu" [Yongzheng Emperor and the depictions of the Twelve Beauties]. *Zijincheng* 220, no. 5 (2013): 16–40. 祝勇: 如花美眷, 似水流年, 雍正皇帝與美人圖. 紫禁城.

INDEX

Note: Some illustrations are denoted by italicized page references; illustrations that run with the commentary are not specifically listed here.